How to Count Animals, more or less

UEHIRO SERIES IN PRACTICAL ETHICS

General Editor: Julian Savulescu, University of Oxford

How to Count Animals,
more or less

Shelly Kagan

OXFORD
UNIVERSITY PRESS

OXFORD
UNIVERSITY PRESS

Great Clarendon Street, Oxford, OX2 6DP,
United Kingdom

Oxford University Press is a department of the University of Oxford.
It furthers the University's objective of excellence in research, scholarship,
and education by publishing worldwide. Oxford is a registered trade mark of
Oxford University Press in the UK and in certain other countries

First Edition published in 2019

Impression: 1

Published in the United States of America by Oxford University Press
198 Madison Avenue, New York, NY 10016, United States of America

British Library Cataloguing in Publication Data
Data available

Library of Congress Control Number: 2018956840

ISBN 978-0-19-882967-6

Printed and bound in Great Britain by
Clays Ltd, Elcograf S.p.A.

For Gina,
again, and always

Contents

Acknowledgments

This book is based on a series of lectures I gave at Oxford in November 2016. I am grateful to the Uehiro Foundation on Ethics and Education for their generous support of the lecture series, and to the Uehiro Centre for Practical Ethics for the warm welcome and the stimulating discussions, both at the lectures themselves and elsewhere at Oxford. Since I am quite certain I would never have written the book were it not for the invitation to give those lectures, I am especially grateful to Julian Savulescu, for extending the invitation, and to Jeff McMahan, for persuading me to accept it.

Why did I need persuading? Because the Uehiro Lectures in Practical Ethics are indeed supposed to be on *practical* ethics. I take this to mean that there should be at least some actual discussion of real choices that people may face, a genuine attempt at applying the otherwise rather unremittingly abstract ideas that moral philosophers frequently debate. As someone whose own work in moral philosophy lies very firmly on the abstract, theoretical side of the spectrum, I certainly admire the work of those who do applied or practical ethics; but I have never thought of myself as among them.

As it turns out, I was probably right about that. What follows is indeed a discussion of animal ethics, and by current conventions I suppose this does indeed count as a topic *within* practical ethics, but I fear that the discussion itself is about as abstract a treatment of the topic as one could offer. Those who hope for guidance on pressing questions like (for example) when, if ever, it is morally permissible to experiment on animals, whether it is permissible to keep animals as pets, or companions, or whether we are morally permitted to cull wild deer to prevent starvation in the larger herd, will find no explicit answers here; they won't even find any direct discussion of such questions. I do think that the ideas I put forward should be relevant for addressing genuinely practical concerns like these more directly, and I very much hope that this comes sufficiently close to being a contribution to practical ethics to fulfill the terms of the promise I made to the Uehiro Centre. But I am rather less confident of the latter than I am of the former.

A different sort of acknowledgment is in order as well. While developing my views about animal ethics my thinking was constantly stimulated by the writings of other moral philosophers, several of whom have already made major contributions to the subject. There are too many authors for me to try to list them all here, but I particularly enjoyed reading and thinking about works by Peter Singer, Tom Regan, David DeGrazia, and especially Jeff McMahan.

Nonetheless, in what follows I almost never directly engage with the ideas of these or other philosophers. My goal here is not to offer a careful critical assessment of the specific theses or arguments that other theorists have put forward, but rather to try to sketch an alternative approach to animal ethics, a view which, if not altogether original, nonetheless does seem to me to differ in significant ways from the views commonly put forward by others. To be sure, at times I find it helpful to mark out my own position by way of contrast with some alternative, and sometimes I go so far as to quote from someone else's writings. But even when I do this, I am not trying to reconstruct or to respond to any particular person's position. So when I quote it is only because the words or passage quoted strike me as suggestive or helpful for my own purposes. Accordingly, I deliberately avoid mentioning the names of the people I am quoting—or may otherwise have in mind—in the body of the text itself, for I am making no claims to exegesis. I have been inspired by the views of others, but I am not here trying to discuss the views of any particular person.

Introduction

One of the most striking developments in moral philosophy over the last half century has been the remarkable explosion in the discussion of animal ethics, that part of moral philosophy that deals with our moral obligations toward (nonhuman) animals. It would of course be an exaggeration, but only a mild one, to say that fifty years ago philosophical discussion of the treatment of animals was virtually nonexistent. The topic suffered from something close to complete neglect. On the rare occasion when a moral philosopher had something to say about animals, it was largely a matter of admitting—albeit only in passing—that it was wrong to be cruel to them, that the gratuitous infliction of pain was morally problematic. And then, for the most part, the matter was typically left at that.

Fifty years later the pendulum has swung the other way. Animal ethics is now a well entrenched subdiscipline within the field of moral philosophy as a whole. There is an ever growing cascade of books and articles devoted to the subject, a constant stream of journals and conferences. What's more, it seems to me that a particular philosophical position within animal ethics has emerged as well.

I hesitate to say that it is the *dominant* view. I doubt if there is enough consensus in the philosophical literature on animal ethics to have much of anything substantive lay claim to a title like that. But it does seem to me that many theorists are drawn to some version of the view I have in mind.

Here's the basic idea. According to this view, otherwise similar harms or benefits for people and animals count equally from the moral point of view. "Pain is pain," as the point is sometimes put.[1] In this sense, animals and people can be said to have the same moral status. To be sure, there are important differences between people and other animals, including differences in terms of which goods and which bads are likely to be at stake in any given case. These, in turn, can make it morally appropriate to treat people and animals differently. But that's not because animals somehow count *less* than people do, from the

---

[1] Singer, *Animal Liberation*, p. 20; DeGrazia, *Taking Animals Seriously*, p. 234.

moral point of view. On the contrary, *similar* goods (or similar bads) are to be treated the same, regardless of whose interests are at stake. That is to say, in and of itself it matters not at all whether we are talking about the interests of a person or the interests of an animal. Similar interests are to be given equal weight in our moral deliberation, regardless of whether we are dealing with a person or an animal. Strictly speaking, everyone has the *same* moral status.

For obvious reasons, it would be natural to call this position *egalitarianism*. It assigns the same weight to the interests of animals and of people. It gives the same moral status to both, considering neither group higher or lower than the other.

But for still other reasons, equally obvious, it would be potentially misleading to call the position in question egalitarianism, for the label is already in use as the name for views that hold that equality has moral significance in its own right (for example, that there is value in the equal distribution of welfare). Since I intend to eventually discuss egalitarian principles of this sort, using the term "egalitarianism" for the first sort of view as well would only invite needless confusion. So we'll need another name for the position I am trying to describe.

Accordingly, I propose to call the view in question *unitarianism*, since it holds that there is only one kind of moral status—a status shared by both people and animals. The name is far from ideal, I suppose, but I cannot think of a better one, and if nothing else it has the advantage that "unitarianism" is not already the name of any sort of prominent position in moral philosophy.

Unsurprisingly, unitarians differ from one another in all sorts of ways. For it is one thing to say that all of us—people and animals alike—have the same moral status. It is quite another thing to spell out what that status involves, just how it is that we are morally required to treat one another. Thus there can be, for example, unitarian *utilitarians*, instructing us to bring about the greatest balance of pleasure over pain. As unitarians, such utilitarians simply remind us to count the pleasures and pains of animals every bit as much as the pleasures and pains of people. And there can be unitarian *deontologists* as well, instructing us, say, to avoid harming the innocent (even if the results of harming them would be better overall). As unitarians, such deontologists remind us to avoid harming innocent *animals*, just as we are to avoid harming innocent people. In short, almost all of the sundry debates within normative ethics remain contentious and unresolved even if we embrace unitarianism. In and of itself, unitarianism doesn't tell us how to treat people or animals; it only tells us that the same fundamental rights extend to all.

As we will see, there is a lot to be said in favor of unitarianism. But one advantage should be apparent from the start. If we accept unitarianism then it is reasonably easy to see how to *extend* our moral theory so that it covers not only people but animals as well.

The truth, of course, is that in the past almost all of our moral theorizing has been limited to thinking about people. And while, as I have just observed, the debates in normative ethics are far from resolved, it does seem fair to say that for the most part what we have been working our way towards, by means of these debates, is a normative theory that would accurately tell us about the obligations that people have toward *people*. So even if you have such a normative theory worked out to your own satisfaction, strictly speaking you still face the question of how to extend or generalize that theory so that it covers animals as well. Unitarianism provides a simple and straightforward answer to that question: our interactions with animals are governed by the very same set of principles that govern our interactions with people (as spelled out by your favorite normative theory). Armed with a normative theory adequate for dealing with people, there is no further work to be done.

In contrast to the unitarian approach to animal ethics, it seems to me that common sense embraces, rather, a *hierarchical* approach, where animals count, but count in a lesser way.[2] On this alternative view, people have a higher moral status than animals do. There are still restrictions on how we are to treat animals, but these are not the very same restrictions that govern our treatment of people. People have rights that animals lack, or have stronger rights, or perhaps a person's interests count for more than (or count in different ways from) an animal's.

Admittedly, one should probably hesitate before making confident assertions about common sense in this area. Some people apparently believe that animals don't have any sort of moral standing at all; they are merely one more resource to be used as we see fit.

I suppose there is a sense in which a view like this—where animals lack moral standing altogether—could still be described as hierarchical, since people clearly have a higher status on this account than animals do. But similarly, there is a sense in which such a view could instead be called unitarian, since it holds that there is indeed only a *single* moral status (that had by people). But as I intend to use the terms, at any rate, *neither* label applies to those who simply deny the moral standing of animals. As I intend to use the terms, both unitarians and hierarchy theorists agree that animals do indeed count, morally speaking; animals have moral standing. Unitarians and hierarchy theorists differ only in

---

[2] Although closer to common sense, the hierarchical view has few explicit defenders in the philosophical literature. Kazez, *Animalkind*, is a notable exception (see, especially, chapters 5 and 6).

terms of whether animals have the very same moral status as people or a lower one. Accordingly, if enough people believe that animals don't count morally at all, then it would be a mistake to claim that common sense embraces a hierarchical approach.

I suspect that most people reject the extreme claim that only people count. What I take to be the common view, rather, is that animals do indeed count morally, but they simply do not count in the very same way that people do. Animals count for *less*.

Of course, here too, there remains tremendous room for disagreement. In addition to the familiar debates from normative ethics about the details of our obligations toward people, questions about the appropriate *extension* of our normative theory now become pressing and difficult. After all, it is one thing to say that animals count, but in a lesser way. It is quite another thing to spell out exactly how they count, what it really means to say they count in a lesser way. If the interests of animals are not to be counted in precisely the same fashion as the interests of people, how then *are* they to be counted? Although it does seem to me to be true that common sense accepts a hierarchical approach (or, at a minimum, it is true that a lot of people accept something *like* that idea), I don't think there is anything close to a clear understanding of what the lesser standing of animals entails.

In this book, I am going to argue for a hierarchical approach to animal ethics. Given what I have just said, then, at best I can only partially claim the mantle of common sense. I do think that many readers will find my central thesis—that the right approach to animal ethics is a hierarchical one—to be fairly obvious, hardly worth arguing for. But at the same time, if I am right that there is nothing like a consensus about what the lower status of animals comes to, then I imagine that the various specifics yet to come will remain controversial.

However, it is probably best to admit right from the start that I won't actually be developing a detailed hierarchical theory. At best, I am going to offer a sketch of what a theory like that might look like. In fact, truth be told, in many places—really, in most places—all I will be doing is trying to point out how desperately far we currently are from having an adequate moral theory when it comes to the treatment of animals. Unlike the unitarians, who think it a relatively trivial matter to extend moral theory to cover animals, I find myself thinking that we remain very much in the dark about how best to do that. I can only say how to count animals *more or less*.

I do however want to emphasize one point before we go any further. Although I will be defending a hierarchical approach to animal ethics, I do so with considerable misgivings, for I am afraid that some may come away thinking that my aim to is to defend an approach that would justify much or all of our current treatment of animals. After all, it seems reasonable to suggest that it is part of the commonly accepted view that our treatment of animals is, in the main (even if not in all specifics), morally acceptable; and I have already suggested that the common view is a hierarchical one. So in defending hierarchy, aren't I defending—in broad strokes, at least, if not with regard to every detail—our current treatment of animals?

But nothing like this is remotely the case. Our treatment of animals is a moral horror of unspeakable proportions, staggering the imagination. Absolutely nothing that I say here is intended to offer any sort of justification for the myriad appalling and utterly unacceptable ways in which we mistreat, abuse, and torture animals.

In this regard the unitarians have an easier time of it. No one would be tempted for even a moment to suggest that we already treat animals in anything like the way that morality requires us to treat people. So unitarians are very well positioned to condemn current practices for the moral monstrosities that they are.

But that doesn't make unitarianism the truth. On the contrary, it seems to me to be true both that animals count for *less* than people and yet, for all that, that they still count *sufficiently* that there is simply no justification whatsoever for anything close to current practices. It may be less straightforward to condemn our abuse of animals once one embraces a hierarchical view, but it is still important to do so.

Having said that, however, I should nonetheless warn the reader that the requisite arguments for the unjustifiability of our treatment of animals will not be found in what follows. To work out those arguments with care one first needs to articulate in detail the appropriate hierarchical normative theory; and as I have already suggested, it seems clear to me that we are very far indeed from having anything like that. This book is intended as a contribution to the attempt to produce the relevant hierarchical theory. But the truth is, it throws out far more questions than it answers.

1

Standing

1.1 Standing and Status

My central claim with regard to the morality governing our interactions with animals is that an appropriate theory here will be hierarchical, recognizing that people have a higher moral status than animals do.

Of course, this claim needs to be qualified and clarified in various ways. For example, the short statement just given might create the misimpression that I think we should recognize exactly two levels of moral status, one had by people, the other had by animals. In point of fact, however, it seems to me that an adequate theory will actually recognize multiple levels, since not all animals have the same status. For that matter, it seems to me likely that not all *humans* have the same status either. My claim is only that *people* have a higher status than animals; and the simple fact is that not all humans are people.

In making this last point, I am following the standard philosophical practice of distinguishing between being a human and being a person. Humans are members of our biological species, *Homo sapiens*. But when I speak of a person, I have in mind a creature—of whatever biological (or nonbiological!) sort— that has certain characteristic psychological capacities and thoughts, a creature that is rational and self-conscious, aware of itself as existing across time.[1] Almost all adult humans are persons in this sense of the term, but obviously enough no *newborn* humans are. And, tragically, not all adult humans are persons either. Some adult humans are sufficiently severely cognitively impaired that they fall short of possessing the sophisticated cognitive capacities that I mean to be picking out in calling someone a *person*.

On the other hand, and this point is worth emphasizing as well, there is no reason to assume that the class of persons is limited to some subset of humans. It could well turn out that some of the other animals with which we share the planet are in fact *people* (a term I will often use as the plural of "person"), despite our long-standing failure to recognize them as such. If so, they too will have a

---

[1] See Singer, *Practical Ethics*, pp. 73–5, for some further discussion of the contrast.

higher moral status than that had (or those had) by the relevant "lower" animals. However, having now acknowledged this important point, there is no need to be constantly repeating it explicitly. So unless context indicates otherwise, when I refer simply to "animals"—saying for example that animals have a lower moral status—it should be understood that I have in mind only nonhuman animals that fall short of being people.

There will be more about much of this in what follows. But let's start by trying to get clearer about the very idea of moral status. My claim is that people have a higher moral status than animals. But what, exactly, are we talking about when we talk about moral status?

In answering this question it may help to begin with an even more fundamental concept, that of *moral standing*. To say that something has standing is to say that it counts, morally speaking, in its own right. There are moral principles limiting how we may treat the object in question. But beyond that—and this is the crucial point—if we violate these principles, we *wrong* that being. That is to say, our duties with regard to the being are owed, at least in part, to the being itself. Ideally, we should act, at least in part, for the being's own sake.

As it happens, providing precise analyses of the various locutions that I've just helped myself to—wronging, owing a duty to, acting for the sake of something—turns out to be a surprisingly difficult matter.[2] I won't try to offer such analyses here. Happily, I suspect that most of us have a ready enough grasp on the relevant ideas; and in any event, a few examples are likely to be more helpful here than some contentious philosophical explications. Thus, to start with the most obvious case, we all believe that people have moral standing: it would be morally unacceptable to gratuitously rip someone's arm off, and if we were to do that we would not only be acting immorally, we would be wronging the person we were harming. In contrast, most of us comfortably believe that there is nothing wrong with ripping off a petal from a flower. We are not wronging anyone or anything when we do this, and in particular we are not wronging the plant.

Of course, in some cases it *is* morally wrong to rip a petal off of a flower. If the plant is your prize orchid, then it may well be morally wrong for me to harm it. But even in this case I do not wrong the *flower*. Rather, I wrong you. I may have a duty to not harm the orchid, but this is not a duty I owe to the plant itself, I only owe it to you. So even here, the plant does not have moral standing.

---

[2] Obviously, these terms don't all mean the same thing. But since I am only using this series of locutions to help to locate the intuitive concept of moral standing, focusing on any single one of them would invite needless controversy.

That's why the crucial point is not whether there are moral limits to how we may treat any given object. With sufficient ingenuity we can always come up with a scenario in which moral limits of some sort will exist. The question, rather, is whether the object counts in its own right, for its own sake. And what most of us believe, obviously enough, is that this is not the case when it comes to plants. People have moral standing, but plants, it seems, lack it.

Admittedly, some dissent from this judgment, arguing that plants do have moral standing, despite the common belief to the contrary. But right now the question is not the validity of the common judgment that plants lack standing. The point is only to understand what that claim comes to.

What about animals? Here too this is a point where we find some differences of opinion. As I noted in the introduction, there are some individuals who think that animals don't count at all, simply lacking any kind of moral standing. But most of us, at any rate, think otherwise. If someone were to gratuitously rip off the leg of a *mouse*, for example, I take it that almost all of us would think this morally unacceptable, and—the crucial point—most of us believe that to do so would be to wrong the mouse itself, regardless of whether anyone else was wronged as well. Intuitively, then, the mouse counts *in its own right*. Which is just to say, most of us recognize that the mouse has moral standing.

This use of the term "moral standing" is fairly minimal. To say that something has standing is to say that it counts, but it is not yet to say just what the relevant limitations are with regard to how we treat it. It is here that the notion of *status* comes into play. We can use the idea of status to refer to the sets of normative features governing how we are to treat those things that have moral standing.

Thus, for example, if we are morally required to count the interests of some individual a given way, then that is part of its moral status. If we must refrain from hurting it, say, or lying to it, then that too is part of its status. If we must aid it, or rescue it in times of need, or defend it against threats, that is part of its status as well. If it is inviolable, say, never to be harmed no matter what the circumstances, that is part of its status; and if, instead, it may be harmed, or its interests permissibly sacrificed under specified circumstance, then that too is part of its (rather different) moral status. We can think of each creature as having a normative profile, consisting in the set of features that govern how it is to be treated. Talk of a given being's moral status is a way of referring to the contents of that profile.

In principle, at least, it would seem that the moral status of one being could differ from that of another. Two creatures could be similar in that both had moral standing of some sort, and yet for all that, one of them could have a more encompassing, or more demanding, or more extensive normative profile than the other. In this sense, the first creature would have what we would naturally think of as a higher or greater moral status. If, for example, it was wrong to impose a given sacrifice upon a person (despite the good results that this would bring about), and yet it was morally permissible to impose a comparable sacrifice upon a cow (for the same results), then this might warrant our saying that people have a higher moral status than cows.

I say that this *might* warrant ascribing a higher moral status to people, because the particular normative feature I have just described would only be one of the many features governing our interactions with people or with cows. To be sure, this feature is such that—if it obtained—it would be natural to think of people as having a stronger or more significant moral claim in this regard than cows. But even if people had stronger moral claims in some areas, it could in principle still turn out that in yet other areas it was cows that had the stronger claims. If something like that were the case, then it might not be particularly helpful to think of either cows or people as having an overall higher moral status than the other. On the other hand, if one of these had stronger moral claims with regard to a wide *range* of normative features, then talk of having a higher moral status might well be helpful and appropriate. And of course, even if it did turn out that cows had a lower moral status than people do, it could still be that case that cows nonetheless have a higher moral status than that had by snakes, say, or flies.

I have suggested using the term "status" to pick out the various normative features that govern our treatment of the given being. Strictly, however, this is probably too broad a use of the term for our purposes. After all, the particular moral restrictions that happen to apply to how we are to treat a given individual may well vary, depending on the specific circumstances of the situation in which we happen to find ourselves. Yet we would not normally think of this sort of highly situation-dependent feature as part of the thing's moral status per se.

Suppose, for example, that it is generally wrong to kill cats, even if this is done painlessly. Then it certainly does seem appropriate to think of this feature as an important part of the moral status of cats. In contrast, however, if there is normally nothing wrong with killing cats painlessly, and it just happens that I have made a promise to you not to kill *your* cat, then despite the fact that my treatment of your cat is now morally governed by this further feature—I may not kill it—it does not seem appropriate to say that this is now part of the moral status of the cat in question. Similarly, if I give you permission to borrow my car, your normative profile now includes an element that was not there previously, but that feature does not seem to be part of what we would normally have in mind in talking about your moral status.

Intuitively, it seems, the moral status of a given being is restricted to those more general and relatively stable features of its normative profile that do not turn on highly specific accidents of the particular situation. Admittedly, the distinction I've just drawn may not be a sharp one (it could certainly stand to be made more precise), but I hope it will suffice for present purposes. We can then say that something's moral status consists in the elements of its broad normative profile that are highly general and relatively stable, rather than being particular and situation specific. When I talk of someone's moral status, I have in mind these more general and fundamental normative features.

One further point. I have suggested using the term "status" to pick out the relevant fundamental features of one's overall normative profile. But often enough people use the term in a related, but slightly different fashion—to refer abstractly to that which is the ground or basis of those normative features. Thus, on this alternative usage, rather than saying that someone's status simply *is* the set of basic normative features that essentially govern how the being is to be treated, we would say instead that these normative features are in place *by virtue of* the creature having the moral status that they do.

As far as I can see, nothing substantive turns on which usage we settle upon. Either way, we will still face a pressing philosophical question, namely, what exactly provides the underlying explanation for why the creature has the particular moral status that it does? What properties of the creature explain why it has one possible status rather than another? Regardless of whether we adopt the first or the second use of the term, the significant philosophical questions remain the same.

I do find, however, that sometimes it is more convenient to use the term the one way, while at other times it is more convenient to use it the other way, depending on the context at hand. Accordingly, since, as I believe, nothing of philosophical significance turns on which way we talk, I will feel free to resort to whichever usage seems most convenient in the given case.

1.2 Sentience

Eventually, we will want to examine the idea that some animals have a higher status than others. But I think it would be helpful to begin by asking, which animals have moral standing of any sort at all?

Here is a familiar sort of case (in the philosophical literature, at least) to get us started. Imagine that I take a cat, douse it with gasoline, and set it on fire. It shrieks with agony, and then it dies.

I imagine that pretty much anyone reading this book will agree that I have done something wrong. It is immoral to gratuitously cause such agonizing pain. What's more, it seems clear that in performing this horrendous act, I wrong the *cat*. It may or may not be the case that the cat belongs to someone else; if it does, I presumably wrong its owner as well. But no matter, for even if the cat is a stray, I owe it to the cat *itself* not to cause it pain in this way. Morally speaking, the cat counts in its own right. It has moral standing.

Historically, we know, there have been people who would resist this description of the case. Some would claim that cats don't actually feel pain. Despite the shrieks and despite the other bits of bodily behavior on the part of the cat that seem so strong an indication of its suffering, some have argued that cats—and more generally, other nonhuman animals—feel no pain at all. They are not sentient. They are, instead, mere automata, fancy cuckoo clocks that simulate and imitate the sort of vocal and bodily behavior that would indeed indicate pain were it done by a human. But in this case, nonetheless, such sounds and behavior reveal nothing of the sort. Cats, the claim goes, actually feel nothing "on the inside" at all.

I will not take the time to attempt to refute this view. Others have already done it.[3] And if there still are some who deny sentience to cats and other animals nothing I can say here is likely to sway them. My concern is solely with those who agree with what almost everyone will insist upon in any event—that cats can feel pain.

Similarly, I will not take the time to refute those who recognize that setting a cat on fire *will* cause it pain but who insist nonetheless that doing this is not wrong, or—alternatively—that it is wrong, but not by virtue of any claim that the cat itself has upon us. Some would insist that if it is in fact immoral to set a cat on fire, this can only be by virtue of its effects on others. Perhaps seeing the cat suffering will cause distress to some sympathetic passersby, or maybe it will coarsen my own character making it more likely that eventually I will maliciously harm some other human. For these and other reasons, it might be suggested, it could still be wrong to set the cat on fire, even though, strictly speaking, the cat has no moral standing in its own right.

As I say, I won't attempt to refute this sort of view either. Almost all of us agree that it is wrong to cause this kind of pain to a cat, and that it is wrong precisely because the cat does indeed matter in its own right. Setting a cat on fire is abuse of the cat, and the cat has a moral claim against us not to mistreat it in this way. The cat has moral *standing*—it counts in its own right. And more particularly, of course, its moral *status* is such as to rule out the legitimacy of

---

[3] See, for example, DeGrazia, *Taking Animals Seriously*.

such gratuitous infliction of suffering. But in any event, my goal here is not to convince those who think otherwise. Rather, I want to raise the question, for those of us who readily recognize the overwhelmingly obvious thought that the cat counts morally in its own right: by virtue of what fact *is* it that the cat counts? What is it about the cat that grounds its moral standing?

The obvious answer, of course, is that the cat counts precisely by virtue of the fact that it can (and in this instance does) feel pain. Nothing more is required for the cat to have moral standing than for it to be true—what almost all of us recognize to be true—that cats can feel pain. This fact suffices, all by itself, to give cats moral standing: they can feel pain.

And once that thought occurs to us, it generalizes immediately. Any creature of any sort whatsoever that can feel pain will also have moral standing, by virtue of that very fact.

Notice how relatively modest this claim is. We need not yet take a stand on whether, morally speaking, all creatures that can feel pain are such that their pains count in precisely the same way. That question can come later. For the time being it is sufficient to recognize the overwhelming plausibility of the more minimal thought that if something can feel pain, then it does in fact count in its own right.

We can generalize a bit more. Not only can cats feel pain, they can also feel pleasure. This too seems relevant to moral standing, in more or less the same way, though of course it would take a different particular example to bring the point out. Regardless, it seems plausible to suggest that it is this same underlying capacity to feel pleasure and pain that suffices to ground the moral standing of cats and other animals: such animals count *by virtue of* their ability to feel pleasure and pain. Or, putting the point in slightly different terms, *sentience*—the capacity to feel or experience—suffices for moral standing.

This idea, that sentience suffices for moral standing, is an extremely common one in the literature on animal ethics. Indeed, it is very common to find the suggestion that moral standing *coincides* with sentience,[4] so that the ability to feel pleasure and pain is not only sufficient for moral standing, it is necessary as well. Cows and cats and camels are all sentient, and they all have moral standing; stones and streets and scissors all lack sentience—not a one of them can feel pleasure or pain—so they all lack moral standing. Or so the thought goes.

Admittedly, some are less confident as to whether sentience is indeed necessary for moral standing, or merely sufficient. Some are attracted to the idea that

---

[4] For example, Singer, *Animal Liberation*, pp. 7–8; Nussbaum, "Beyond 'Compassion and Humanity,'" p. 309; DeGrazia, *Taking Animals Seriously*, pp. 50 and 226–31.

plants may have moral standing after all, or at least ecosystems might, or perhaps animal species (as opposed to individual animals). These are interesting claims, but I won't consider them further. I suspect that many of us would agree that there may be some moral restrictions governing how we treat at least some of these things. Yet at the same time I imagine that most would nonetheless insist that even if we violate the relevant principles in some such case we are not *wronging* the plants, or the ecosystems, or the species, if we do; we do not owe anything *to* an ecosystem, for example, even if there are moral principles that restrict how we are to treat it. All of which is just to say, we are not inclined to think that ecosystems, or species, or plants (and so on) have moral standing in the sense of the term that we are employing.

So it isn't all that surprising when we find so many theorists saying that sentience is both a necessary and a sufficient condition for moral standing.

Actually, though, despite the frequency with which this idea gets put forward, I wonder whether it is really what people mean. One qualm I have is small and perhaps a bit nitpicky. The other seems to me to be significantly more important.

The relatively small qualm is this. The standard proposal is that sentience is both necessary and sufficient for moral standing. But is it actually *sentience* per se that people have in mind when they say this, or something rather narrower? After all, sentience is typically used in philosophical writing for the entire capacity for subjective experience and feeling. I take this to mean, in terms of yet further philosophical jargon, the ability to have conscious, qualitative experiences of any kind, not simply experiences of pleasure and of pain. Thus, for example, any being capable of experiencing the color blue, the particular sweetness of pineapple, or the unique smell of coffee, and so forth, would count as sentient, regardless of whether such a being were capable of feeling pleasure and pain. Pleasures and pains are among the sensory experiences which can be had by those who are sentient, those with an inner mental life with a qualitative aspect—a creature such that it makes sense to ask "what is it like to be" such a creature[5]—but there is *more* to sentience than simply the experience of pleasure and pain.

So what is it that actually grounds moral standing, according to the common proposal? Is it indeed sentience per se? Or is it, more narrowly, precisely the ability to experience pleasure and pain (or, perhaps, if one could have one without the other, the ability to experience either pleasure *or* pain)?

---

[5] Nagel, "What is it like to be a Bat?"

One way to get a fix on this question would be to imagine a creature that had qualitative mental states but was incapable of experiencing either pleasure or pain. (As a loose analogy, consider the fact that someone blind—incapable of experiencing color—can nonetheless experience the other sensory modalities.) Such a creature, we can suppose, might well have complex visual or auditory or olfactory experiences, for example, but it would not experience any of them as pleasant or painful. It might, for example, have a qualitatively distinct experience when seeing a sunset, say, but it would not experience those sensory states as *pleasant*. Indeed, it might even have various qualitatively distinctive experiences when different parts of its body were undergoing damage or trauma—for example, when its foot was being stepped on—but it would not experience those inner states as *painful* (or pleasant). Similarly, for its various other qualitative mental states as well.

For creatures like us, of course, pleasure and pain are so deeply intertwined with the other qualitative aspects of our mental life that we may find it difficult to fully imagine what it would be like to be such a being. But in principle, as far as I can see, it should be possible for someone to be sentient while nonetheless being utterly incapable of experiencing pleasure or pain.

So suppose we had such a creature. In fact, to make the example even more stark, imagine a creature that could occasionally experience blue, but had no other qualitative states at all. Would it *count*? Would it have moral standing? Would it be possible to *wrong* such a creature?

Thinking about this case allows us to ask whether it is really correct to say that sentience of any sort at all is truly sufficient for moral standing. Perhaps, on reflection, we might decide that what is really required for standing is the ability to feel pleasure or pain, full stop. Mere sentience, in the absence of the ability to feel pleasure or pain, may not actually suffice.

I am not at all confident as to what most people would judge about the moral standing (or lack of standing) of a creature of this simple sort, though I suspect that many at least would deny it standing. But I do want to forestall one possible line of thought. Some might worry that whatever uncertainty we may have about moral standing in this case is simply due to the fact that the creature in question has such an absurdly restricted range of qualitative experiences. Perhaps the problem isn't really the lack of the ability to feel pleasure or pain per se but rather the simple fact that the creature can only experience blue, nothing more. Maybe so limited a range of sentience is too limited to count.

This suggestion is tempting, but I suspect that it misses the mark. Imagine a different creature, equally simple in that it too has an extraordinarily limited range of subjective experience, except that in this new case the only experience of which the creature is capable is that it can occasionally feel a mild pain. In this case, I think, we would much more readily ascribe moral standing, even if only of a limited sort. There may not be much that we can do to harm or benefit such a creature, but there is something, and if we gratuitously cause it to feel the mild pain that it is capable of feeling (in the absence of some special justification for doing so), then I take it that we wrong it. So it seems that even highly restricted forms of sentience are compatible with moral standing, provided that they involve the ability to feel pleasure or pain.

Arguably, then, despite the fact that people frequently say that sentience suffices for moral standing, it is at least possible that what many of them really mean is that it is the ability to feel pleasure and pain that suffices. Mere sentience, on its own, may not be enough.

Furthermore, it is easy to see the appeal of a narrower account of this kind. If our simpleminded creature experiences pain, after all, it is hard to escape the thought that this is *bad* for it. Similarly, if a different simpleminded creature— one that could only experience certain mild pleasures—were to experience one such pleasure, it would be hard to escape the thought that that would be *good* for it. In this way, the ability to experience pleasure or pain underwrites the possibility of undergoing benefit or harm. And it seems plausible to think that the very possibility of this sort of benefit or harm is relevant for having moral standing. Creatures that can experience pleasure and pain have moral standing precisely because we can affect their welfare. That thought, or at any rate something close to it, is one that many will find attractive.

In contrast, when we consider the creature that can only experience blue, the connection between that experience and its welfare is broken. Indeed it is not at all immediately clear—in the absence of further detail—whether such a creature even has a welfare. But in any event, it certainly doesn't jump out at one that experiencing blue, in and of itself, could be either good or bad for it. And that very fact may go a long way toward explaining why many would hesi- tate to ascribe moral standing to a creature—even a creature that by hypothesis is stipulated to be conscious or sentient—when all we know about it is that it is capable of experiencing the color blue.

On the other hand, our hesitation about ascribing moral standing might well disappear were we to learn that the creature has *preferences* with regard to its conscious experiences—if we were to learn, in particular, that it wanted to have its occasional experience of blue, and if it behaved in such a way as to maximize its chances of undergoing these experiences. Mere sentience alone may not suffice for moral standing, but sentience backed by this kind of pattern of preference and behavior might well suffice. But this brings us in turn to the second, more important, qualm I have about the common claim that sentience is both necessary and sufficient for moral standing.

1.3 Agency

To approach this point, I want to consider a different thought experiment. Imagine that you have been kidnapped by aliens from another planet, who—let us suppose—plan to keep you in their intergalactic zoo, or perhaps to experiment on you, or worse. Suppose that you are able to communicate with them (maybe they've learned our language), and you are trying to persuade them that keeping you would be wrong, that they should let you go back to your life on Earth. What might you say? I want to quote at length from the writer on animal ethics who first proposed this scenario. She suggests that you

> might express your desire not to be held captive, that being held against your will is wrong, and that it prevents you from doing not just the things you want to be doing at home, but the things you are supposed to be doing. These aliens are frustrating your desires and preventing you from fulfilling your obligations to others. You might explain that you are a rational and sensitive individual who has immediate desires and long-term plans that you hope to satisfy. You don't think you should be treated as a means to some alien ends. You might try to bargain with them, telling them you will do something for them if they do something for you. You have relationships to others that you want to continue to pursue, and you would be willing to develop a relationship with them if they respect you. You value your freedom and your ability to make choices. You need to be with your friends, family, and others of your kind. If you are forced to stay with the aliens, you will become bored, frustrated, lonely, angry, and depressed. You may even die. Holding you captive, against your will, harms you in many, many ways.[6]

Now I must confess, I find this sort of answer fairly persuasive. It seems to me that these are indeed the sorts of considerations that others should be moved by. If we imagine that the aliens are moral agents, capable in principle of recognizing when others have moral standing and then being moved by the various moral requirements that follow from someone's moral status, then it seems to me that in principle at least the aliens should find an answer like this compelling.

It won't surprise you to learn that our author goes on to suggest that many remarks parallel to these can then be made on behalf of *animals*. If this imaginary

---

[6] Gruen, *Ethics and Animals*, p. 26.

plea to the aliens is compelling, she argues, then thinking about an analogous plea on behalf of animals should help us recognize that much of our current treatment of animals is unacceptable as well. And I think that some kind of argument along these lines may well be right.

But what I particularly want to draw your attention to is just how little of this imaginary speech to the aliens has anything much to do with the fact that you are *sentient*—where we continue to mean by that term the fact that you are capable of having conscious experiences, with a qualitative aspect. On the contrary, what the proposed answer primarily dwells upon is the fact that you are a being with your own preferences and plans, desires concerning how your life should go, and a will that is opposed to what is now being done to you. As far as I can see, sentience per se plays very little role in any of this. (Indeed, the word itself isn't even used.)

To be sure, it isn't as though references to conscious experiences don't appear in the plea at all. There is a passing reference toward the start of the reply to your being a "sensitive" individual, and that is probably intended to be a way of alluding to your sentience. And toward the end there are references to the possibility of your becoming bored, frustrated, lonely, angry, or depressed—and these states certainly do typically involve conscious experiences of various unpleasant kinds as well. So sentience is certainly part of what is being mentioned here.

But as I say, it doesn't seem to be the focus of the argument. The main complaint doesn't seem to be that if you are held against your will you will suffer some painful experiences, but rather precisely the fact that you *have* a will, that you have desires about what you want to do and what you want to happen, that you have plans and goals that you intend to act on, given the chance—and that being abducted in this way frustrates your plans, violates your will, and interferes with your ability to act as you choose. It is these facts about you, rather than your sentience per se, that seem to provide the core of the argument that there are limits to how you are to be treated, that abduction by the aliens fails to take into account the fact that you are a creature with moral standing.

It would be useful to have a name for this second, interrelated set of facts about you, that is, on the one hand, the fact that you have desires and plans, preferences concerning how your life goes and what you want to do with it, and—beyond this—the further fact that these preferences are normally no mere idle and impotent set of evaluations, but rather are things you act upon, choosing which goals to promote and behaving accordingly. I propose to use the term *agency*.

With this stipulation in place, we can summarize the point I have just been making by saying that in your imagined attempt to persuade the aliens that their treatment of you is wrong, the appeal to the fact of your sentience actually plays at best a minor role. What seems far more central is an appeal to the fact of your agency.

It must be admitted that my using the term "agency" in this way isn't ideal. Sometimes philosophers use the term more narrowly than I plan to use it, so that someone or something has agency (in this narrower sense) only if they meet some further conditions as well, beyond the relatively minimal conditions of having preferences and acting on them. In this narrower sense of the term, to have agency—to be an agent—one must have free will, or perhaps one must self-consciously deliberate about what there is reason to do, or one must be capable of responding to moral reasons, or perhaps one must view what one intends to do as good in some way. These various proposals (and there are, of course, still others) are obviously not all identical to one another, and depending on the details of how they get spelled out, a wider or narrower set of individuals will count as having agency. But what these various proposals have in common is that if we adopt one or another of these uses then there are far fewer agents—in the relevant sense—than there are if instead we use the term in the very wide way that I have in mind. Accordingly, there is at least some danger that in using the term as widely as I propose, we will sometimes inadvertently slip into thinking in terms of one or the other of these more "sophisticated" notions of agency. Hopefully, however, having noted this danger, we can avoid making this kind of mistake.

Note, in any event, that if we do indeed find ourselves moved by the thought that a speech similar to the one I've quoted can be provided on behalf of a wide range of animals—and if we agree as well that the core of that speech is devoted not to noting your sentience but to emphasizing your agency—then we need to be thinking in terms of a notion of agency that is expansive rather than restricted. For although it seems almost uncontroversial that animals display agency in my wide sense of the term, it is far less obvious whether many (or any) of them have free will, or self-consciously deliberate about the balance of reasons, or act under the guise of the good, and so forth. So if the parallel speech on behalf of animals is to be plausible, it had better be one that appeals to the agency of animals in a suitably broad sense of the term.[7]

---

[7] Other terms that we might have used instead, like "rationality" or "intelligence" have similar limitations. Take the term "rationality." Sometimes this term is used broadly, to mean a general capacity—which we share with animals—for deliberation and intelligent choice. That might make it suitable for our purposes. But often enough philosophers use it more narrowly, so that it is appropriate to talk of rationality only with regard to the special capacity for self-conscious deliberation about reasons that we make use of when we reflect in a highly deliberate way about which desires to act on (or how best to achieve our goals). Arguably, few if any animals are rational in this more narrow sense of the term. But if we are to move from the original speech to one on behalf of animals, it is the more general, shared capacity that must be the focus of our plea.

Admittedly, in the original speech, some of the more narrow notions of agency do appear as well. For example, one suggestion mentioned is that you should complain to the aliens about the fact that if you are abducted you cannot fulfill your obligations to others. Clearly, raising that sort of consideration brings in your ability to consciously respond to moral reasons, in a way that the mere appeal to agency in the wide sense does not. But it seems to me that at best this *strengthens* your case; it isn't essential to it. The crucial point, or so it seems to me, remains the simple idea that you have a wide variety of desires concerning what you want to do, and how you want to live your life, and that your abduction systematically interferes with your ability to act on those desires. Accordingly, even if we imagine your pleading with the aliens by means of emphasizing that point alone (perhaps combined with an appeal to your sentience), there would still be considerable force to your speech. The mere fact of agency in the broad sense—having desires and wanting to act on them—carries considerable weight in establishing your moral standing.

Accepting this point needn't be incompatible with the earlier suggestion that sentience is necessary for standing. It might be, for example, that agency *presupposes* sentience (a point we will consider below), in which case, of course, emphasizing someone's agency is simply an effective way of drawing attention to their sentience—the real basis of their having any moral standing in the first place. Or it might be that, strictly speaking, sentience is indeed required if one is to have any kind of moral standing at all, but facts about agency are nonetheless relevant to one's particular moral *status*—so that how it is, exactly, that others are required to treat you depends in part, perhaps in large part, on details about the nature of your preferences, plans, intentions, and so forth. After all, since your goal in pleading with the aliens is to persuade them that it is wrong to abduct you, merely establishing that you have moral standing wouldn't really suffice for your purposes. What you need to convince them of as well is that your particular moral status *rules out* that sort of treatment. Perhaps that is what the appeal to agency accomplishes, and why it seems so essential to the speech. So acknowledging the significance of agency is certainly something that can be done even by those who insist that sentience is a requirement for moral standing.

Nonetheless, recognizing the central role that agency plays in your speech to the aliens does at least suggest, if nothing more, that perhaps we err if we insist that sentience is indeed a *requirement* if one is to have moral standing. Perhaps agency suffices as well. That is to say, perhaps there are two potentially distinct bases for moral standing, sentience and agency, and either one is sufficient for grounding some sort of moral standing. This is, at the very least, a possibility worth entertaining, and I must say that it surprises me how regularly writers on animal ethics seem to overlook it. Or perhaps I should say, a bit more cautiously, that it surprises me how frequently writers on animal ethics announce their belief that sentience is required for standing, even though much of what they actually care about—it seems to me—falls more straight-forwardly under the seemingly distinct category of agency.

Of course, as I have already noted, there will only be a significant difference between the standard, familiar proposal (that sentience is required for standing) and the more "liberal" proposal (that either sentience or agency suffices) if it is indeed possible to have agency without sentience. Is that so?

This is, I suppose, a controversial question within the philosophy of mind. I've characterized agency in terms of having various preferences and desires and acting on them (or, perhaps we should add, wanting to act on them, if your ability to do so is stymied). So at a minimum, agency requires desires, and it requires beliefs about how to satisfy those desires, and—roughly speaking—it requires behaving in keeping with one's beliefs about how to satisfy one's desires. In contrast, as I have noted, sentience is a matter of having conscious experiences, subjective states such that there is something that it is like to be in those states. So what we need to know is this: can one have the first of these (preferences, beliefs, behavior) without the second (conscious experiences)? Can one have agency without sentience?

Just to be clear, the question is not whether in our *own* mental lives the con-stituents of agency typically involve sentience. For I take it to be plainly the case that frequently, at least, our desires do have a qualitative aspect, such that there is something that it feels like ("on the inside") to have the desire in ques-tion. And something similar holds for beliefs as well. That is to say, it often feels like something to believe something. But our question is not whether creatures with minds like our own always or typically experience our beliefs and desires in a qualitative fashion, but whether there is a conceptual connection between having beliefs and desires and sentience, such that a creature that lacked sentience simply could not have agency at all.

When I think about this issue, I find myself strongly inclined to think that agency does *not*, in fact, presuppose sentience. I tend to favor accounts of belief and desire that analyze these concepts in behavioral functional terms, where beliefs and desires interact in familiar ways so as to generate action. (Roughly speaking, beliefs are representations of the world; and desires are dispositions to act in ways that tend—according to one's beliefs—to bring about specified states of affairs. This is indeed rough, but spelling out the details would need-lessly take us very far afield indeed.) As far as I can see, the ingredients of agency can be present even in a mind that altogether lacks conscious mental states—in the sense that there is no qualitative aspect to the possession of these states, nothing that it "feels like" to have these beliefs or these desires or for them to join together to produce action.

What's more, it seems to me that this idea—that agency is possible even in the absence of sentience—is one that finds frequent enough expression in the corners of popular culture where the imagination conjures up futuristic scenarios involving robots and hyperadvanced computers.

Take, for example, the rogue computer HAL, who attempts to kill Dave—in the movie *2001: A Space Odyssey*—after having first successfully killed the other astronauts on the ship. I find it straightforward to say that HAL is displaying agency: he (or it) wants to eliminate the humans, given his beliefs about the importance of the mission and how humans are likely to screw things up; and he has various beliefs about how best to eliminate the humans, beliefs that he proceeds to act upon (unsuccessfully, as it happens, in the case of Dave). It seems to me overwhelmingly obvious that HAL has agency.

In contrast, I haven't the slightest idea whether HAL is sentient, whether he experiences colors, say, or sounds (as opposed to merely being able to identify them). I have no idea at all whether HAL undergoes any qualitative experiences. Indeed, having been primed by countless other, similar examples to worry about whether mere robots and computers can possibly be conscious in the sense of having qualitative experiences, I suppose I typically find myself thinking of HAL as though he is not sentient at all. He is an agent, but he is not a *sentient* agent.

Sometimes, of course, terms like "sentient" and "conscious" are used more broadly than I have been using these terms, so that having any mental states at all counts as being sentient, and having any kind of awareness at all of one's environment counts as being conscious. In this broad usage of the terms it follows trivially that any being with agency is sentient, and that HAL would count as conscious as well. But I am using the terms more narrowly, so that sentience and consciousness require mental states with a qualitative aspect. And typically, at least, I find myself thinking with regard to HAL that he lacks subjective experiences in that sense. There is nothing that it is like to *be* HAL— even though HAL has beliefs and desires and acts upon them.

Or so it seems to me. I certainly have to admit, however, that not everyone sees things the way I do. I frequently find that some of my students are unprepared to describe the case in anything like these terms. They are simply unwilling to ascribe genuine beliefs or desires to HAL. When I ask them why they refuse to do so, the most common reply is precisely that HAL is not conscious or not sentient, and so he cannot truly possess either beliefs or desires. To be sure, they add, he "acts" like something that has beliefs and desires, and it is easy enough to "personify" him (though perhaps it would be more precise in this context to talk about "sentiencifying" him) and all of this tempts and misleads us into ascribing agency. But in strict literal truth, they hold, HAL has no agency, even in the broad sense of the term that I have introduced, since in strict literal truth he has no beliefs and has no desires, and so, trivially, he never actually acts upon beliefs and desires.

If this more conservative view is correct, then agency really does presuppose sentience after all, and nothing will have changed if we say that agency suffices for moral standing, since it will turn out that agency itself requires sentience. On the other hand, at this point we might begin to wonder whether agency— strictly so called—is really the notion we should be focusing on. Instead, we might start to look for an even more expansive notion, one that could comfort- ably apply to cases like HAL. For it is clear (I think) that *something* akin to belief and desire and action is happening here. Call it *agency**, if you want to, rather than agency. The real question, then, will be whether agency* suffices for moral standing.

I am inclined to think it *would* suffice. That is to say, if having beliefs and desires (and the like) really does require sentience, then I believe that it would actually be sufficient for standing that one be an *agent**. Being a full- blown *agent*, in contrast, would be more than is required. Of course, given my own sympathies for the idea that agency doesn't actually require sentience at all, I have no personal need for the idea of agency*. But even if I were to become convinced that I am wrong about this, and that sentience really is a require- ment for agency, I would still find myself drawn to the idea that sentience is not actually a requirement for moral *standing*. I would then avail myself of the agency* locution, and suggest that we take seriously the possibility that either sentience or *agency** suffices for standing.

Accordingly, we need not try to settle here the question of whether agency requires sentience or not. The real question, for our purposes, is what is required for *standing*. Given my own views, of course, about the possibility of agency in the absence of sentience, I think we can legitimately express the question I want to pose this way: does mere agency suffice for standing? But as far as I can see, those who disagree with me about this can still raise the same underlying question, asking instead whether mere agency* suffices.

Perhaps, then, I should cast the discussion that follows in terms of agency*, rather than agency. Nonetheless, having now noted the possibility of adopting this special terminology, in what follows I propose to neglect it. I think it will be easier on the reader's eyes (if nothing more) if I continue to talk about "agency" simpliciter rather than "agency*." As far as I can see, anyone who thinks I am making a mistake here—that is, anyone who rejects the possibility of agency in the absence of sentience—can simply imagine that an asterisk has been provided wherever they think that one is needed.

1.4 Agency without Sentience

So our question is whether agency suffices for moral standing or whether sentience is required. And as I have already suggested, it seems to me that people often overlook the question, even when some of their own other remarks might easily have brought it to mind.

Here is an example of the sort of thing I have in mind. One author defends her view that sentience is required for moral standing by arguing that

> moral rights are protections designed to protect rights holders from harms or to provide them with benefits which matter *to them*. Only beings capable of sentience can be harmed or benefitted in ways which matter to them, for only such beings can like or dislike what happens to them or prefer some conditions to others.[8]

Arguably, this passage runs together sentience and agency in just the way that I have been warning against. Our author tells us that what matters is sentience, but what she actually seems to especially care about is agency, your having preferences, for example, about what happens to you. To be sure, talk of what one *likes or dislikes* is ambiguous between the idea of having preferences for or against various states of affairs, and experiencing those states of affairs as pleasant or unpleasant. But for all that, the key point here seems to be that of having something matter to you, having preferences for one outcome rather than another. Which is just to say, the key point isn't really sentience at all, but agency.

Admittedly, the passage just quoted doesn't gloss the idea of sentience, and it is possible that our author doesn't mean by the term what we are here taking it to mean—namely, being the subject of qualitative experience. But we can put such exegetical concerns to one side. The crucial philosophical point remains the same, namely, that anyone moved by the idea that having preferences concerning what happens is the key to moral standing should wonder whether sentience (in *our* sense of the term) is really required for standing at all.

---

[8] Warren, "Difficulties with the Strong Animal Rights Position," p. 171; emphasis in the original.

Here's another example. Recall the imaginary plea to the space aliens. The philosopher who offered this speech takes it to have established the importance of sentience for moral standing, but it seems to me possible that she too fails to distinguish, in the way I have suggested, between sentience and agency. She says, for example, that all beings "that have interests, wants, and desires are sentient, that is, they are capable of experiencing pleasures and pains."[9] But I have argued that in principle, at least, this need not be the case. So it may be a mistake to emphasize sentience rather than agency. Similarly, when looking back on that earlier speech, she says that in arguing with the aliens you

> expressed the value of being sentient, of having interests and desires that were frustrated, of suffering physically and emotionally from being away from your home and family. These are values that we share with other sentient beings.[10]

But what I have claimed, of course, is that there is far less emphasis on sentience in that speech than this summary would suggest, that the emphasis instead is on agency (having your "interests and desires" frustrated), and that in any event we should not run together questions about the significance of sentience with potentially distinct questions about the significance of agency.

Other examples could easily be offered, but I hope I have said enough at this point to at least have made it clear why it is worth asking whether it is really the case that sentience is indeed an essential requirement for moral standing, or whether, instead, agency might suffice. And speaking personally, when I directly consider the question in this way, I find myself inclined to the conclusion that agency really is sufficient, that one need not be sentient at all. Provided that one has desires about how one wants one's life to go, preferences with regard to what happens in the world, and provided that given the chance one acts on these desires and preferences—in a word, provided that one has agency, in the broad sense of the term—then it seems to me that one counts, morally speaking. Your preferences and desires need to be taken into account. You have moral standing.

I know that many will find this suggestion outlandish. Isn't it simply obvious that nothing lacking sentience can count in its own right? To take two examples of nonsentient entities, chosen more or less at random, surely stones and books lack moral standing! As one writer puts it:

> Sentience is not the only thing that matters for basic justice, but it seems plausible to consider sentience a threshold condition for membership in

---

[9] Gruen, *Ethics and Animals*, p. 32.   [10] Gruen, *Ethics and Animals*, p. 33.

the community of beings who have entitlements based on justice. Thus, killing a sponge does not seem to be a matter of basic justice.[11]

I do find myself agreeing that a sponge lacks moral standing; we do not wrong it if we kill it. In contrast, killing a squirrel, say, wrongs it, for squirrels count in their own right. So there is a crucial difference between a squirrel and a sponge. And squirrels, we should all agree, are sentient, while sponges are not. But none of this shows that sentience is required for moral standing, for in moving from the squirrel to the sponge we eliminate not only sentience but agency as well. Yes, the sponge cannot feel pleasure or pain; but neither does it have beliefs, desires, or action. So thinking about the lack of standing of sponges cannot establish the necessity of sentience. (It is remarkably easy to make this slip. Unless we are being especially careful when we think about things without sentience we are likely to eliminate all aspects of the mind altogether.)

Suppose we were to agree that agency suffices for moral standing, that sentience is not required. What practical significance would this have?

One thing it might do is to extend the set of beings that we recognize as having standing. For if the more traditional view were really correct, and sentience is required for standing, then we immediately face the worrisome fact that we have trouble being confident about the presence of sentience in creatures that are too different from us. Like you, I don't doubt that the other people I meet in daily life are sentient (that is, there is something that it is like to be them), and like you (as I imagine), I am confident that other mammals are sentient as well: cows, dogs, whales, mice, and so on, are all capable of feeling pleasure or pain. But once we leave mammals behind, my confidence wanes, and it does so rather rapidly. (It isn't a coincidence, I think, that more than one prominent writer on animal ethics focuses their attention almost exclusively on mammals.[12])

The further down the evolutionary tree of the animal kingdom we go, the less I know what to say. Reptiles, I imagine, are conscious, and so, I suppose, are birds, amphibians, and fish. But I don't say this with tremendous confidence. And when we get to insects or crustaceans, for example, I really don't know what to say at all.[13]

---

[11] Nussbaum, "Beyond 'Compassion and Humanity,'" p. 309.

[12] For example, Regan in *The Case for Animal Rights*.

[13] For a survey of some of the relevant evidence, see DeGrazia, *Taking Animals Seriously*. A more recent (and technical) discussion of consciousness in insects can be found in Barron and Klein, "What Insects Can Tell Us about the Origins of Consciousness."

Eventually, no doubt, sentience gives out, even within the animal kingdom. I may not know what to say about fruit flies and cockroaches, but I am confident that sponges feel neither pleasure nor pain. But how far down the evolutionary tree does consciousness extend? Most of us, I imagine, find it impossible to say. And while it is presumably possible to add to our stock of scientific evidence on the subject, the sheer interior nature of consciousness may leave us worried that the question will never be satisfactorily resolved.

But if agency suffices for standing, then there are different (or additional) questions we need to ask, and at least some of them may be easier to answer with confidence. I am uncertain whether frogs or fish feel pain, but I find that I have no doubts at all about ascribing agency to them, and the same thing is true, of course, for birds and reptiles. In all of these cases it seems straightforward to say that the given creature has beliefs and desires and acts on them. For example, a bird may want food, have beliefs about how to find it, and then act accordingly. A fish may sense danger, and then proceed to take appropriate evasive action.

That's not to say, of course, that it is never uncertain whether it is appropriate to ascribe agency to a given animal. Speaking personally, I find it natural to ascribe beliefs and desires of an extremely rudimentary sort to insects, for example. But I know that others may not, and I certainly think the matter open to reasonable debate. Here too, obviously, various bits of evidence can be brought to the discussion, and currently we may be rather far from resolving the relevant questions. But for all that, it seems to me that questions about agency are fundamentally more tractable than questions about sentience. Precisely because questions about sentience are questions about what it is like "on the inside"—whether, indeed, there is anything that it is like at all—they seem particularly elusive. In contrast, questions about agency are questions about whether the given creature is disposed to act in relevant ways, in keeping with its representations of the world, and these questions, it seems to me, turn on facts that are significantly more "out in the open," and so are more amenable to resolution.

All of which is just to say that there may well be cases where we can agree— or come to agree—that the animals in question possess agency, even though we remain uncertain as to whether or not they are sentient. In this way, then, acknowledging that agency can suffice to ground moral standing may serve to extend the circle of animals with regard to which we recognize that we have moral obligations of one sort of another.

That's not to say that there *are* any animals that display agency while nonetheless lacking sentience. Perhaps evolution simultaneously selected for both of these, whenever it selected for either one of them. As one author remarks:

> There are strong evolutionary reasons for thinking that the capacities for locomotion, perception, and sentience evolved in tandem... This means that even insects can feel pain. (If you think you doubt this, consider your reaction to seeing children pull wings off flies.)[14]

This seems a plausible enough conjecture, as far as it goes. But for all that, it might be wrong. Perhaps agency and sentience really have sometimes come apart. Perhaps the inclination to cringe when seeing someone pull the wings off a fly is due to nothing more than a natural tendency to *assume* sentience—even in its absence!—wherever one sees agency. Or maybe something rather different is going on. Maybe the inclination to cringe when a fly's wings are pulled off is due instead to a largely unacknowledged recognition of the fact that agency suffices to ground moral standing all by itself—regardless of whether or not there is sentience there as well.

Whether or not there really are cases in the animal kingdom of agency in the absence of sentience, it does seem as though this possibility is routinely entertained in science fiction literature and movies, where it is common enough to imagine androids, robots, and computers all manifesting agency to a degree comparable to our own. In some of these examples, to be sure, it is also stipulated that the robots, say, are sentient in our sense—capable of subjective experiences with a qualitative aspect. But in many other cases nothing is said about sentience at all, and no assumption is made one way or the other as to whether the robots and computers have any kind of "inner" life. And in still other cases, I think, we are supposed to understand that the robots *lack* sentience in our sense. Sometimes part of the very point is to come to see how a machine could display *agency* even though there is nothing that it is like to *be* the machine.

Suppose that there could be such machines. For example, suppose that there could be robots that were not sentient but which nonetheless manifested a high degree of agency. We don't have anything very much like that today, but I see no reason to assume that such inventions may not lie ahead in our future. If so, then of course if it really is the case that agency suffices for moral standing, machines like this would *count* from the moral point of view. They would have rights, of the relevant sorts, and if we violated the principles governing our interactions with them then we would be wronging the robots themselves. Machines like this would have moral standing. To offer an obvious possibility,

---

[14] Anderson, "Animal Rights and the Values of Nonhuman Life," pp. 288–9.

it might simply be immoral, full stop, to turn such a machine off—the moral equivalent of murder.

Here's a little fable to illustrate the idea. Imagine that in the distant future we discover on another planet a civilization composed entirely of machines—robots, if you will—that have evolved naturally over the ages. Although made entirely of metal, they reproduce (via some appropriate mechanical process), and so they have families. They are also members of larger social groups—circles of friends, communities, and nations. They have culture (literature, art, music), and they have industry as well as politics. Interestingly enough, however, our best science reveals to us—correctly—that they are not *sentient*. Although they clearly display agency at a level comparable to our own, they lack qualitative experience: there is nothing that it feels like ("on the inside") to be one of these machines. But for all that, of course, they have goals and preferences, they have complex and sophisticated aims, they make plans and they act on them.

Imagine that you are an Earth scientist, eager to learn more about the makeup of these robots. So you capture a small one—very much against its protests—and you are about to cut it open to examine its insides, when another robot, its mother, comes racing up to you, desperately pleading with you to leave it alone. She begs you not to kill it, mixing angry assertions that you have no right to treat her child as though it were a mere thing, with emotional pleas to let it go before you harm it any further.

Would it be wrong to dissect the child?

I know that different people will react in different ways to this story, but speaking personally I find that I have no doubt whatsoever that it would be wrong to kill (or, if you prefer, to destroy) the child in a case like this. It simply doesn't matter to me that the child and its mother are "mere" robots, lacking in sentience. What matters, rather, is that they are full-blown *agents*, with plans and hopes for their own lives, desires and ambitions for the future. For you to destroy such a machine really would be morally horrendous, just as it would be if you were to decide, instead, to painlessly kill and then carve up some human child in its place.

If that judgment seems implausible, it is worth noting just how readily machines like this would fit into some extremely popular theories concerning the foundations of morality. According to some versions of contractarianism, for example, moral rules are the principles governing our interactions with one another that would be agreed upon by rational bargainers. Yet if there really could be robots with levels of agency comparable to our own, it would seem that they too would take a place among the relevant bargainers. And the output of such a bargaining session would presumably include moral principles that protect robots just as they protect you and me. Roughly speaking, after all, just as it is rational for me to agree to a principle that rules out my killing you, in exchange for your agreeing to a principle that rules out your killing me, it will also be rational for us to agree to a principle that rules out our "killing" robots—turning them off against their wishes—in exchange for the robots agreeing to a principle that forbids their killing *us*. Worrying about sentience doesn't really seem all that relevant when it comes to contractarianism; what matters is whether an entity displays the appropriate degree of agency.

Or consider certain Kantian approaches to morality, where the essential question is sometimes said to be whether one is the kind of creature that can set goals for oneself, rationally choosing among the various alternatives and then acting accordingly. Anything that has this kind of autonomous end-setting ability (perhaps to a sufficiently high degree) is said to count as "an end in itself," a uniquely high form of moral status. But here too, it is hard to see why *sentience* should be thought to play any particularly important role in any of this. What matters, as far as I can see, is agency, or at least agency of a sufficiently sophisticated sort. Accordingly, even if robots had no inner subjective experiences, it seems that they might well count as end setters of the relevant kind, and thus warrant moral standing from the Kantian point of view. It is agency, not sentience, that should matter to the Kantian. (We'll return to some of these ideas in 8.2.)

Presumably, some will conclude that if contractarianism and Kantianism imply that nonsentient entities like robots could count morally, then that simply shows the inadequacy of those views. But others, I think, may find that these theories have sufficient plausibility in their own right—whether or not, at the end of the day, one accepts one of them as the best account of the foundations of ethics—so that the very fact that they seem to support granting moral standing to entities that lack sentience helps to render more attractive the idea that agency may suffice.

But at this point an objection suggests itself. It is one thing to claim—as the contractarian or the Kantian may claim—that agency of a sufficiently sophisticated sort may suffice to give one moral standing. It is quite another to claim, as I have of course been suggesting, that agency of *any* sort may suffice. After all, agency comes in degrees, and it is clear that the sort of minimal agency displayed by frogs or snakes—let alone insects!—is a far cry from the sophisticated versions I've been conjuring up while discussing the robots and computers of the distant future.

The point is well taken. Even if we are prepared to grant moral status to highly intelligent computers of the right sort, we certainly needn't agree that agency of any sort whatsoever suffices for moral standing. Perhaps agency has to be rather sophisticated before it can ground standing. (As it happens, contractarians and Kantians don't typically accept views quite as restrictive as this; but some might.)

But for all that, it does seem to me that the correct conclusion to reach here is not the restricted one—that although agency of a very high sort may count even in the absence of sentience, it is indeed only agency of a *very high sort* that will do the trick—but rather the more expansive one: agency of *any* sort suffices for moral standing of *some* kind. Arguably, of course, agency of a more sophisticated kind may result in a higher moral status than agency of a less sophisticated kind. That's a possibility we will want to consider later. But even minimal forms of agency should count for something.

This inclusive sort of position is analogous to the view that most of us find persuasive when thinking about sentience and the ability to feel pleasure and pain. It is a familiar point that people are capable of feeling highly complex pleasures and pains, and it is at least arguable that these may help generate a moral status distinct from that had by creatures that can feel only more rudimentary ones. But for all that, it seems to suffice for moral standing that one can feel pleasure or pain of any sort at all. Status may vary with the precise nature of the experiences of which we are capable, but the mere ability to feel pleasure or pain suffices to ground moral standing of *some* kind.

I want to endorse a comparable position with regard to agency: status may vary with the precise nature of one's agency, but any level suffices to ground moral standing of *some* sort.

1.5 Welfare and Standing

Return now to a point I made earlier. The thought that there is a connection between the ability to feel pleasure or pain and moral standing is virtually irresistible. But more than that, the connection seems to go by way of the welfare or well-being of the creatures in question. That is, when we raise or lower the pleasure or pain of a sentient being this seems to matter morally precisely because we are affecting its *welfare* in a morally relevant way. Is there, then, a *necessary* connection between standing and welfare, such that in order to have standing at all, one must be the sort of entity that *has* a welfare (something that can be better or worse off)? Suppose for the moment that there is. Then if I am correct in thinking that agency also suffices for moral standing, shouldn't we similarly expect to find a connection between *agency* and well-being? And if so, do we find such a connection?

Several points here merit discussion. First of all, if we do posit a necessary connection between *standing* and well-being, then it seems to me that we would want to be careful to distinguish between two claims. The first holds, broadly, that if you have any kind of welfare at all, you count morally. The second holds, more narrowly, that you count only if you have the kind of welfare that *matters* to you.

Conceivably, these two claims come apart, since, arguably, the notion of welfare is sufficiently broad in ordinary usage that many things that lack moral standing nonetheless have a welfare, in the sense that things can be good or bad for the objects in question. Thus, for example, if I take glue and pour it into the gas tank of my car, that is bad for the car, and if I water my houseplants after being away for several days, that is good for the plants. Given this broad notion of welfare or well-being, it would seem that virtually any object at all has a welfare that can be altered (in principle, at least).[15] And yet, for all that, most of us are not at all inclined to ascribe moral standing to the car, or to the plants.

Why not? That isn't easy to say, but at least one promising idea is that for cars and plants (and for many, many other things), such welfare-altering changes simply don't *matter* to them. Cars and plants (and stones and books) don't *care* about things that harm them or benefit them.

In contrast, of course, sentient creatures do care about whether or not they are in pain, or whether they are experiencing pleasure. This matters to them in a straightforward and undeniable fashion. (Hence the bafflement we sometimes find ourselves in when someone claims to not mind a given pain *at all*. We wonder: are they genuinely in pain?)

For something to matter to you, you have to care about whether or not it happens. And that involves beliefs and preferences of various sorts. Which is just to say, the sort of welfare that matters morally may well necessarily involve agency, of at least a minimal sort. When you are in pain, for example, you want the pain to *end*, and that is an important part of the reason why what is happening to you counts, morally speaking. And even though a newborn infant in pain will not have the concept of the pain's *ending*, it still seems appropriate to say that it *cares* about the pain (while the car does not care about the glue in its engine).

Arguably, then, agency may be even more fundamental than sentience for moral standing! If what is crucial for standing is whether or not you have a welfare that matters to you, then agency of at least a minimal sort may well be required for any kind of moral standing at all.

---

[15] Cf. Belshaw, "Death, Pain, and Animal Life," pp. 32–5.

Of course, many people find it more natural to use the terms "welfare" or "well-being" in a more narrow fashion, so that it is only in those cases where changes to you or to your life *matter* to you that it is appropriate to talk about welfare or well-being in the first place. But this doesn't affect the essential point, which is that insofar as some minimal level of agency is required for something to matter to you at all, then if it really is true that having moral standing requires that one have a welfare in this narrower sense, standing will require agency.

As it happens, it seems to me that this narrower use of the terms "welfare" and "well-being" is the more common one among moral philosophers (similarly for related terms, like "harm" and "benefit"). Perhaps this shouldn't surprise us. After all, much moral philosophy is concerned with working out the details of what is owed to those with moral standing. That's certainly our own goal, for example, in the present book. So it is easy to see why those doing ethics often find it more convenient to focus on a concept of welfare that entails standing straightaway.

Indeed, I am going to avail myself of this common practice as well. Hereafter, when I refer to the welfare of a given entity I should be taken to have in mind welfare of the sort that suffices for moral standing. I'll disregard the broader sense of the term in which even cars and television sets can be said to have a kind of welfare. Despite my doing this, however, it was still worth pointing out the existence of this broader sense of the term, for that helps us recognize what we might otherwise easily overlook—that even when moral standing is based on welfare (in the narrower sense), this may in turn presuppose agency.

The second point is this: if we do accept a connection between standing and welfare (narrowly construed), then that should give most of us pause with regard to the standard view that the ability to feel pleasure or pain is required for standing. Indeed, I wonder whether this common assumption is due (at least in part) to an unwitting presupposition of *hedonism*—the view according to which well-being consists solely in the presence of pleasure and the absence of pain. Obviously enough, if standing requires that one have a welfare (in the narrow sense), and if one's well-being is simply a matter of the proportion of pleasure to pain that one experiences, then only beings that can experience pleasure or pain can have standing. But most people are not, in fact, hedonists at all. On reflection, most judge hedonism to be an overly restrictive account of well-being. Pleasure and pain may well be relevant to one's welfare, but they don't actually exhaust its contents.

At the very least this realization should make us hesitate before embracing the claim that standing requires the ability to feel pleasure or pain. After all, if there are other things that can affect one's well-being besides pleasure and pain, then even if having a welfare is a requirement for standing, it might well be possible to have a welfare (and thus standing), even in the absence of the ability to feel pleasure or pain.

Exploring this point with care would require a lengthy survey of the leading theories of well-being. I'm not going to undertake that here. But let me make some quick observations about two familiar alternatives to hedonism. According to *preference* theories of well-being, your welfare consists in the extent to which you have, or fail to have, the objects of your various desires and preferences. Obviously, since those of us capable of experiencing pleasure and pain *care* about having pleasure and avoiding pain, it follows trivially on this sort of view that pleasure and pain are relevant to our well-being. But it is equally true that most of us have desires and preferences with regard to all sorts of other things as well, so these too will be relevant to our well-being, not just pleasure and pain. And since it seems possible—in principle, at least—that even a creature incapable of experiencing pleasure or pain could nonetheless have some of these other desires, it would seem to follow that according to preference theories such a creature would have a welfare.

On another significant alternative to hedonism, the *objective list* theory, there are certain goods with objective value, such that one is simply better off for having these goods. (Similarly, there are objective bads, such that one is worse off for having these bads.) Lists vary, of course, but virtually everyone would include pleasure on the list of goods, and pain on the list of bads. But the crucial point is that there are further things that typically appear on these lists as well. Thus, for example, the list of objective goods may also include knowledge and achievement and meaningful personal relations, among other things. And so here too it seems possible—in principle—that a creature incapable of experiencing pleasure or pain could nonetheless have some of these other goods (or their corresponding bads), in which case once again it would seem to follow that according to objective list theories such a creature would have a welfare.

Each of these theories has it variants, of course, and there are, as well, even more exotic alternatives. But I would hazard the opinion that for most plausible alternatives to hedonism, facts involving agency have at least as central a place in fixing whether a given entity has a welfare (in the relevant, narrow sense) as do facts about the ability to feel pleasure or pain. So at the very least, anyone attracted to the thought that there is a deep connection between having standing and being the sort of creature that can have a welfare, who nonetheless rejects hedonism as an overly narrow account of well-being, should hesitate before insisting that it is the ability to feel pleasure and pain, and this ability alone, that is necessary for moral standing. Indeed, going further, I think it is plausible to claim that for most nonhedonistic theories of well-being it follows that if one has *agency* one has the kind of welfare that may suffice for moral standing.

Still—and this is the third point—the connection between welfare and the ability to feel pleasure and pain seems relatively uncontroversial. Pain is, in and of itself, bad for you; pleasure, good for you. Few would deny that. Does a similar direct connection obtain between *agency* and well-being? Can we really say, for example, that the mere fact that you have not gotten something that you desire is bad for you, in and of itself? When the space aliens interfere with your ability to satisfy your desires, does that very fact constitute a harm?

One's answer, I think, depends on the details of the particular theory of well-being one accepts. Friends of preference theories of well-being should answer yes (putting aside certain complications in the theory that needn't concern us here). If well-being consists in getting what I desire, then when the aliens stop me from achieving my various goals, that very fact lowers my welfare. Similarly, if friends of objective list theories include, for example, achievements and meaningful relationships among the objective goods (the possession of which constitute my being well off), then when the aliens keep me from achieving my goals or interacting with my family and friends, they deprive me of some of the most important goods, directly lowering my welfare. On views like these, it seems, interfering with my ability to act on my desires harms me, pure and simple.

At the same time, however, I think it should be admitted that not all theories of well-being will posit this kind of direct connection between agency and welfare. Furthermore, it must be admitted that in at least some cases it seems as though getting what one wants needn't constitute any kind of boost at all to one's well-being, strictly so called. After all, we often take an interest in something that goes *beyond* our self-interest, narrowly construed. Because of this, in some cases it seems more illuminating to say that if someone interferes with your ability to promote the satisfaction of your preferences and desires, then this is more a matter of their failing to show you the sort of *respect* to which you are entitled, rather than necessarily harming you or lowering your level of well-being. Broadly speaking, then, perhaps interfering with a creature's ability to pursue its own ends is more a matter of failing to respect it, rather than harming it per se.

Accordingly, some may find it more plausible to think that the connection between agency and standing is to be explicated in terms of the concept of respect, rather than welfare. This would, of course, still be compatible with thinking that agency suffices for standing, along with sentience: perhaps standing arises whenever one's welfare is on the line *or* whenever one is owed respect.

Of course, on certain views it will be more natural to absorb one or another of these two bases under the rubric of the other. For example, those who prefer to emphasize respect might well argue that if we fail to take into account the well-being of those creatures that have a well-being, then we fail to show those creatures the respect to which they are entitled. Conceivably, then, anyone sympathetic to a view like this can argue that it is always respect that provides the real basis of moral standing. And on the other hand, those who prefer to emphasize welfare have it open to them (on at least some accounts of well-being) to suggest that if others fail to show someone the respect to which they are entitled, then this directly constitutes a reduction in their welfare. Here too, then, it may be claimed that standing has a single, unique basis. It's just that those sympathetic to a view like this will argue that it is welfare—not respect—that always provides the ultimate basis for moral standing.

Nonetheless, on still other views the gap between respect and welfare will remain a real one. So it may well be preferable to insist instead that there are indeed two potential bases for standing, and neither extends far enough to fully encompass the other.

For our purposes, I don't myself feel the need to settle the question whether standing has two distinct bases—welfare and respect—or just one (and if only one, which it might be). However, it will be convenient, in much of what follows, to cast the discussion in terms of well-being, and well-being alone. After all, when we turn to discussions of our moral obligations with regard to one another, it would quickly grow tiresome to be constantly having to make what would effectively be the very same point twice over, once in terms of welfare and once in terms of respect. Accordingly, if someone interferes with your ability to satisfy some desire, I will simply say that this *harms* you, even though others might prefer to say—in at least some of these cases—that what this really involves is a failure to show you the respect to which you are entitled. Similarly, I will frequently talk about the extent to which a given action frustrates your *interests* and I will view this as a sort of harm as well, even though others might prefer to say—in at least some of these cases—that the moral offense involved is more a matter of failing to respect, rather than harming per se. While it would certainly be possible in each such case to offer a double set of descriptions ("the given act here either harms or fails to show respect"), I don't see any corresponding benefit in writing in this more cumbersome manner. The points that follow will be cast in the language of well-being alone. As far as I can see, this shouldn't substantively affect the arguments that follow.[16]

---

[16] Throughout this discussion, I have been construing pleasure and pain in sensory terms, that is, as a matter of having the relevant sensations. But on an alternative account, they should instead be understood in terms of having the relevant propositional *attitudes* (e.g., being pleased that something is the case). On this alternative, the difference between thinking of sentience as the basis of standing and thinking of agency as the basis grows smaller, though the claim of agency to being central to standing may grow stronger. (See Feldman, *Pleasure and the Good Life*, especially pp. 55–90, for an account of pleasures and pains as attitudes.)

2

Unitarianism

2.1 Unitarianism

Imagine that we were to agree upon the ultimate basis (or bases) of moral standing. Even if we were to do this, that would still leave unresolved the question of whether all individuals with standing also have the very same moral *status*, or whether, alternatively, statuses can differ from one another.

My own view—the position for which I will be arguing in this book—is a hierarchical one. That is, I believe that statuses can vary, and that some individuals have a higher moral status than others. But there is a simpler alternative that deserves careful consideration. According to this alternative view, all creatures with standing have the very *same* moral status, so that talk of having a higher or a lower moral status is confused, inappropriate, or pointless. On the contrary, there is only the one single moral status, shared by all beings with any sort of moral standing at all.

Here's an expression of this second, simpler view. As one author puts it:

> Moral status is not a matter of degree, but is rather on/off: a being either has moral status or lacks it.[1]

That is to say: On the one hand, if you have standing you have a certain moral status, and *all* beings with standing have that very same moral status; there are no levels or degrees of status to be taken account of. And on the other hand— obviously enough—if you lack standing then you have no moral status at all. So you either have that common status, or you lack status altogether. Status is, as this author puts it, on/off. You either have it, or you don't.

Although this alternative view has a significant place in much contemporary writing on animal ethics, as far as I know it doesn't have anything like a standard name. I propose to call it *unitarianism*. This is in recognition of the key unitarian claim, that there is only a single moral status, common to all beings that have any sort of moral standing at all. (Of course, as I noted in

---

[1] Harman, "The Potentiality Problem," p. 183.

the introduction, this view could also plausibly lay claim to being called "egalitarianism"—since it holds that the status of any being with standing is precisely the same as the status of any other being with standing. But for better or worse that label is unavailable to us, having already been put to work elsewhere in moral philosophy.)

It is difficult to say how many of those currently working in animal ethics should be construed as unitarians, though I suspect it is a fairly common position. Comparably explicit statements, however, are relatively rare. In part, no doubt, this is because those who accept unitarianism will typically find themselves with little use for a notion of *status* in the first place! After all, talk of status in a given domain almost always goes hand in hand with the idea of there being a higher or a lower status, greater or lesser, more advanced or less advanced status, and so on. Accordingly, those who think that no such differentiation is appropriate when it comes to the moral standing of animals are unlikely to avail themselves of status talk at all. They may simply proceed apace, counting otherwise similar interests in exactly the same way, regardless of whether the interest is that of a person, a dog, or a mouse. In many such cases, then, the unitarianism is at best implied, or it must be inferred from other things that are said.

Of course, that's not to say that the unitarianism is normally hidden, or that it's located especially far below the surface. It's just that the unitarianism may not be asserted explicitly in terms of the language of "status." For example, many unitarians appeal to something like a *principle of equal consideration of interests*,[2] whose purpose is precisely to insist that "similar" interests are to be given the same weight, or are to be counted the same way, morally speaking. And the thought, of course—sometimes explicit, sometimes not—is that it can make no morally relevant difference whether the given interests are had by a person, say, or a cow. Clearly, to embrace a view like this is to embrace unitarianism, since in saying that it makes no difference whose interests are being considered we are saying that everyone's moral status is exactly the same. (Or, more precisely, everyone's moral status is exactly the same *provided* that they have any sort of moral standing at all.) There is no need to distinguish higher and lower forms of moral status: if one counts at all, then one has the single, common status shared by all beings with moral standing. Thus, although a position like this may not be *described* using the language of status, it is, for all that, a unitarian one.

---

[2] See, e.g., Singer, *Animal Liberation*, pp. 5–6, and DeGrazia, *Taking Animals Seriously*, pp. 44–53.

As I say, then, it seems to me that unitarianism is a common strand in much contemporary writing about our treatment of animals. And if we don't always see this, part of the explanation may be that the unitarianism is not necessarily right there on the surface; it may not be asserted explicitly. But there is a further, related explanation that seems relevant as well. Unitarianism is compatible with a wide range of other positions within normative ethics. Because of this, two people can agree about unitarianism—this can be part of their shared outlook—while still disagreeing wildly about other normative issues. And when those various points of *disagreement* are in the foreground, as they will be for many discussions of animal ethics, any bits of agreement or common ground—including unitarianism—may receive little or no discussion. As a result, an assumption of unitarianism may be present but simply recede from our notice.

In any event, unitarianism seems to me a sufficiently common position that it is important for us to decide whether it should be accepted. My own view is that it is mistaken, and that an acceptable normative theory will incorporate hierarchy, assigning a higher moral status to people than to animals, and a higher moral status to some animals than to others. Eventually, I will be offering various arguments in support of this idea, and I will try to indicate as well a few of the many issues that would need to be resolved if we hope to arrive at an adequate hierarchical theory. But before I do that, it will be worth our time to take a closer look at the unitarian alternative, for I think it must be conceded that this view has a lot to be said in its favor.

That last remark—that there is a lot to be said in favor of unitarianism—may surprise some readers. For I imagine that many will think it a matter of simple common sense that people count morally in a way that mere animals do not, and that only a hierarchical view can capture some fairly self-evident (or, at least, widely embraced) moral judgments. Ultimately, I suppose, I agree with this assessment. But for all that, commonsense views are often mistaken and should not be given a free pass. The truth in ethics, like the truth in any other area, may turn out to be rather different from what we initially take it to be. Beyond this, the simple fact of the matter is that unitarians are better able to accommodate many of our intuitive judgments than we might initially realize. Thus we will be in a proper position to choose between unitarianism and hierarchy only after we have laid out the unitarian position more fully, so that we can see the range of philosophical moves that are available to those who accept it.

There is, however, one point that should probably be acknowledged from the start. The contrast upon which I am putting so much weight—that between unitarianism and a hierarchy approach—is probably less crisp than it might initially appear. That's because it isn't always clear when it is appropriate to describe a given view as holding that one individual has a higher status than another. Indeed, as we will see, there are probably some cases where it seems appropriate to describe a particular view as unitarian, even though it also seems reasonable to hold that according to the very same view some beings have a higher status than others! Obviously enough, given the current state of our terminology that is a simple contradiction in terms. So when the time comes, a bit of further refinement and clarification is going to be necessary. I want to acknowledge that fact right here.

But acknowledging this fact is still compatible with finding our rough and ready distinction—is there one moral status or several?—a useful one. For there certainly does seem to be a significant difference between holding that all otherwise similar interests are to be given the same weight—counted in the same way—and holding (on the contrary) that otherwise similar interests can indeed differ in terms of how they are to be appropriately taken into account depending on *whose* interests they are. Intuitively, at any rate, it is one thing to say that everyone's interests count equally, and quite another to insist that the interests of some count more than the otherwise similar interests of others. We may need to refine our understanding of the issue as we go along, but something like this distinction should suffice to get us started.

However, when we do begin to consider the unitarian position more carefully it may seem as though we must come to recognize its inadequacy almost immediately. For at first glance, if nothing more, the unitarian position seems saddled with implications that virtually no one can accept. If these appearances stand up under scrutiny, then almost everyone will find that they have reason to reject unitarianism.

Here's an example of the sort of worry that I have in mind. (Examples could easily be multiplied.) Suppose that a mouse and a person are both drowning. Happily, you can save either one of the two. But unfortunately, you are not in a position to save both; by the time you have successfully saved one, the other will have drowned. Which, then, should you pick? The mouse? Or the person?

It seems as though a unitarian should be committed to the following line of argument: Normally—as we almost all believe—there would be some kind of moral obligation to save a drowning person. Accordingly, when someone is drowning there is (special circumstances aside) a strong moral reason to save them. Of course, sometimes that reason is balanced out by an equally strong reason to perform some alternative act instead. This is what we would face, for example, if—tragically—there were *two* people drowning, and we could only save one of them. Then there would be strong moral reason to save the one, and equally strong moral reason to save the other. So if we really were not in a position to save both there would be a kind of moral tie. Given all of this, perhaps we should flip a coin to determine which person we save.

Of course, in the case we are actually considering, we don't have two *people* drowning; we have, instead, one person and one mouse. But given the truth of unitarianism, it seems, where people have no higher a moral status than mice do, the reason generated by the chance to save the drowning mouse must be every bit as strong as the reason generated by the chance to save the drowning person. Or, putting the point in slightly different terms, the mouse's claim to being saved is every bit as strong as the person's claim. So here too we face a kind of moral tie. But this means that here too we should flip a coin to determine who to save. And if it turns out that the mouse is favored by the coin toss, then saving the mouse, rather than the person, is the morally right thing to do. At the very least, if we were to simply plump for saving the person—as though this choice was backed by a stronger moral reason—then that would be nothing more than an expression of prejudice, the kind of prejudice that unitarianism is intended to steer us clear of. Despite what we might initially think, then, there is no more reason to save the person than the mouse.

That, as I say, is what the unitarian apparently must assert. But that is a conclusion that virtually no one will be prepared to accept. Almost all of us believe that in this case it is not only permissible, but indeed morally obligatory (again, special circumstances aside) to save the person rather than the mouse. (If you think otherwise, try substituting some other animal even further down the evolutionary tree—a fish, perhaps, or an insect—making sure only that you think the animal does indeed have moral standing. Then consider the choice again.)

I say that "virtually no one" will accept this conclusion. I add this qualification because I find it conceivable that there may be some who actually *are* prepared to follow the argument all the way to its surprising conclusion. Presumably, I imagine, they won't do so without misgivings. Such people—if there are any—may be prepared to admit that this conclusion is at odds with their own direct intuitions about the case. It's just that on reflection they cannot see any way of consistently *avoiding* this result. And since the truth in ethics may well lie at a considerable distance from what we initially take it to be, they may be prepared to affirm—intuition to the contrary notwithstanding—that there is indeed no more reason to save the person than the mouse.

If there is in fact someone tempted by this line of thought, then I don't want to simply dismiss them out of hand. I certainly do agree that moral reflection can appropriately lead us to some rather surprising conclusions. But for all that, we should not embrace this sort of wildly unintuitive result without first making sure that there are no coherent (and preferable) alternatives. It might be, for example, that instead of following the unitarian all the way to this end point we should rather simply *reject* unitarianism and embrace instead some appropriate form of the hierarchy view. That would certainly be my own choice.

But there is a further alternative that it is important to consider as well, for even unitarians need not accept the argument that I have just sketched. Appearances to the contrary notwithstanding, it is in fact perfectly compatible with unitarianism to insist that there is indeed far greater moral reason to save the person than the mouse. And if that's right, then unitarians have it open to them to insist that in the example described it is indeed morally *obligatory* to save the person rather than the mouse. There is no tie here at all, they can insist, and coin flipping would be morally unjustified. In short, even the unitarian can insist that in the absence of extraordinarily special circumstances one must simply save the drowning person, full stop.

In point of fact, this is probably the approach that most unitarians accept. So it is important for us to understand just how it is that the unitarian can consistently take this position. For if there is indeed a way for unitarians to do this consistently, then the example provides no objection to unitarianism at all. One can simply retain the intuition that the right thing to do is to save the person (rather than the mouse) without feeling any corresponding pressure to abandon unitarianism along the way.

2.2 The Greater Harm

Here's the basic insight that allows the unitarian to avoid the unpalatable conclusion that there is no more reason to save the person than the mouse: under almost all realistic circumstances the person will lose more if she drowns than the mouse will lose if *it* drowns.[3]

It is of course true that both the person and the mouse face a threat of drowning. From that perspective, then, their situations seem similar. But this surface similarity masks a much more significant point of dissimilarity. For the simple fact of the matter is that the loss involved if the person drowns is far, far greater than if the mouse drowns. After all, what each stands to lose is the future well-being that would come their way if only they were saved from drowning—and it is almost always the case that when a person drowns this involves a tremendously larger loss of future well-being than when a mouse drowns.

---

[3] See, for example, Harman, "The Potentiality Problem," pp. 179–82, or DeGrazia, *Taking Animals Seriously*, pp. 251–4. Though not a thoroughgoing unitarian, Regan makes the same point in *The Case for Animal Rights* at pp. xxix and 324.

The truth of that last claim is likely to strike you as obvious. But just in case it's not, here's a very quick argument for it. First of all, then, since mice live for only two or three years at most, while humans can live for 80 years or more, if the person drowns she is likely to be losing many more years of life than the mouse will lose if it drowns instead. But beyond that, second, each one of those years in the life of the person is almost certain to contain a tremendously greater amount of well-being than a year in the life of the mouse (since the life of a person generally involves a significantly larger and more valuable array of goods than the life of a mouse). Bottom line: the well-being that is at stake for the drowning person is almost inevitably going to be *immensely* larger than the well-being that is at stake for the drowning mouse.[4]

Because of this, if the person drowns then she undergoes a tremendously greater harm (a greater loss of future well-being) than the mouse would undergo if *it* drowned. And that fact suffices, all by itself, to justify saving the person rather than the mouse. There is no need to appeal to some notion of a "higher" moral status purportedly had by the person as compared to the mouse. We need only recognize the simple fact that the person will be harmed more (if we don't save her) than the mouse will be (if we don't save it). What justifies saving the person rather than the mouse is simply the moral requirement to prevent the greater harm.

The crucial realization, then, is that decisions to aid one individual rather than another needn't turn on claims about differential status at all. They can be straightforwardly justified by a simple appeal to the question of which of the two has more at stake, who will be harmed more.

Obviously, the ideas at work here aren't limited to cases where we must choose between a person and an animal. They are relevant when we are dealing with interpersonal cases as well—and it is, of course, this very fact that allows the unitarian to appeal to these ideas with equanimity when dealing with the sort of conflicts between people and animals which our original example is meant to illustrate.

Suppose, for example, that you must choose whether to aid Jonathan or Rebecca—both of whom are people having some sort of painful experience— and suppose as well that here too you can only aid one of the two. (Perhaps you have a powerful painkiller which cannot be divided.) Finally, suppose that Jonathan is suffering from a severe migraine, while Rebecca only has a paper cut. In a case like this, must you view the situation as some sort of moral tie,

---

[4] Realistically speaking, the only exception will be in the unusual case where the person is *so* (irredeemably) badly off that it would be better for them not to be saved in the first place.

where each person's claim has the exact same strength? Is this a case where coin flipping is called for?

Of course not! It is clear that in a case like this (again, as always, special circumstances aside) the right thing to do is to aid Jonathan, simply by virtue of the fact that the pain he is undergoing is so much greater than the pain Rebecca is undergoing. The harm you will prevent if you aid Jonathan is significantly greater than the harm you will prevent if you aid Rebecca. And that fact, by itself, suffices to justify the decision to aid Jonathan. Indeed, it is perfectly clear that in a situation like this it would be *wrong* to aid Rebecca instead of Jonathan.

But note that in saying this we certainly are not making some claim to the effect that Jonathan has a higher moral status than Rebecca has! On the contrary, the two of them have exactly the same moral status. But status doesn't really come into it. Or, if you prefer, we can say that *despite* the fact that the two have the very same status it is appropriate to aid Jonathan rather than Rebecca, by virtue of the fact that the harm he faces is greater than the harm that she faces.

Similarly, then, with regard to the choice between the drowning person and the drowning mouse. It is clearly appropriate to save the person rather than the mouse, but this has nothing at all to do with some purported difference in the moral status of the two. Status really doesn't come into it. Or, if you prefer, we can say that despite the fact that the person and the mouse have the very *same* moral status, it is appropriate to save the person rather than the mouse, by virtue of the fact that the harm the person faces is greater than the harm that the mouse faces.

That, at any rate, is the position that can be put forward by the unitarian, and I think it must be conceded that it has a great deal of force and plausibility. What's more, similar remarks can obviously be made in a wide range of other cases as well, where we might face a similar need to choose between people and animals. Precisely because people's lives are generally so much more valuable than those of animals—longer, in many cases, and virtually always containing more good—it is almost always the case that the person has more at stake than the animal. So it seems that we can justify our intuition that in such conflicts it is better to favor the person rather than the animal, and we can do this while remaining comfortably within a unitarian framework. As it turns out, then, the unitarian position isn't nearly as easy to dismiss as it might initially have seemed.

What's more, once we see how the unitarian can go about defending the choice of a person over an animal, it is clear how a similar approach can also guide us when we must choose between different *types* of animals.

Here, for example, is a unitarian making essentially the same point as the one I have just been rehearsing, except that her example involves killing (rather than saving), and the choice is between two different types of animals. She begins by noting what almost all of us will agree is obviously the case, namely, that in *some* sense certain animals count more than others:

> Almost all ethical views of animal entitlements hold that there are morally relevant distinctions among forms of life. Killing a mosquito is not the same sort of thing as killing a chimpanzee.[5]

(I assume here—for the sake of illustrating a choice between two animals— that chimpanzees are not persons. If you think that's wrong, then substitute a different animal, such as a dog or a cow. It won't affect the point that follows.)

On the basis of remarks like these, a hasty reader might come away thinking that what is being endorsed here is some sort of hierarchy view. How else to explain the fact that killing a chimpanzee is worse than killing a mosquito? But that would be a mistake. What justifies the commonsense judgment is not an appeal to hierarchy, but rather recognition of the significant difference in harm that befalls the chimpanzee as opposed to the mosquito if we kill each. As the writer we are quoting puts it:

> More complex forms of life have more and more complex capabilities to be blighted, so they can suffer more and different types of harm. Level of life is relevant not because it gives different species differential worth per se, but because the type and degree of harm a creature can suffer varies with its form of life.[6]

In sum, it seems that unitarians can go a considerable distance toward accommodating our commonsense judgments that people count more than animals and some animals more than others. If there is a problem with unitarianism, it is going to take more work to identify it.

2.3 Comparing Lives

The defense of unitarianism that we have been examining makes essential use of the claim that the lives of people are typically more valuable than those of animals, and the lives of some types of animals more valuable than those of other types. What sort of value is being compared here? The answer is: welfare,

---

[5] Nussbaum, "Beyond 'Compassion and Humanity,'" p. 308.
[6] Nussbaum, "Beyond 'Compassion and Humanity,'" p. 309.

or well-being. That is, the relevant claim is that people are generally *better off* than animals (and chimpanzees, than mosquitos); they have lives of higher quality, providing greater benefit to the individuals whose lives they are. Putting the same point in slightly different terms, by virtue of the tremendous differences in their capacities for welfare and flourishing a person generally has a significantly higher level of well-being than a dog, say, or a cow; and a dog, in turn, has a significantly higher level of well-being than a snake or a fish. It is because of facts like these that a loss of life, for example, harms a person more than it harms a mouse. The person would normally be incomparably better off than the mouse; so what she stands to *lose* is incomparably greater as well.

As I have remarked, I imagine that most people will find claims of this sort uncontroversial: the life of a person is better than the life of a mouse. But I also know that some are uncomfortable making these sorts of comparisons. Who are we to say what it is like to live the life of a mouse? Isn't it mere prejudice for us to assert so baldly that our lives are superior to those of other animals? Anyone reading this book, after all, is a person. So isn't it a remarkable "coincidence" that we end up so confidently asserting that the life of a person is more valuable (to us) than the lives of mice and snakes and cows are (to them)? What other answer did we expect, when we only ask the opinions of other people? If only we could ask a dog or a squirrel, say, how *they* would make the relevant comparisons, no doubt we would get a different set of answers.

Perhaps the first thing to say, by way of a reply, is that if dogs or squirrels could understand the question, then they too would be people. So they wouldn't necessarily offer a distinct perspective after all. (The claim is only that *people* have richer lives than animals—that is, animals that are not themselves persons—not that *humans* alone have richer lives of this sort.) That may seem like a silly remark, but it makes a significant point: that only people are capable of understanding the sorts of questions we are here raising, only a person can so much as ask whether one sort of life is more valuable than another. So it can hardly be a telling criticism to point out that those of us posing and answering the question are all people! (Should we similarly dismiss the judgment that it is better to be alive than dead, on the ground that the question is only being answered by the living?) It is, of course, important that we do our best, in thinking about these comparisons, to entertain the issues without prejudice or parochialism. But the mere fact that it is inevitably a person doing the judging cannot by itself provide sufficient reason for dismissing the answers we arrive at.

To be sure, many judgments that we make here must be tentative. We are still in very early days indeed when it comes to learning about the inner (psychological) lives of animals. And for that matter, we know relatively little about their social lives as well. So it might well turn out that some of our beliefs about the nature and quality of a given animal's life might be mistaken. Perhaps squirrels, or salmon, or spiders have significantly richer lives than we currently appreciate.[7] Indeed, it seems virtually inevitable that as our empirical knowledge of these matters increases, at least some of our current comparative judgments will need to be refined or revised. In extreme cases, some may need to be overturned altogether.

But for all that, it seems extremely unlikely that we will ever learn anything to make us question the judgment that the life of a person is generally a more valuable one than the life of a squirrel, say, let alone the life of a fly. As one author aptly observes, "a fly's life doesn't amount to a lot, even at the best of times."[8] To be sure, our judgments are conditional: given that animal lives are more or less what we *take* them to be, here's how they seem to stack up against one another. But it is hardly prejudice to make what comparisons we can, in light of our best empirical evidence. And when we do try to make such comparisons, certain judgments seem virtually undeniable. As another philosopher remarks:

> The fullest mouse life there has ever been, so science would seem at the moment to suggest, does not approach the full life of a human; the difference in capacities, and what these additional capacities make possible by way of further dimensions to human existence, is just too great.[9]

If people have more valuable lives than animals, and some animals have more valuable lives than others, this is true by virtue of the contents of those lives, what they are like, and what they are capable of being like. To put the point simply, if a bit crudely, there are goods which people are capable of possessing—and which, in a reasonably full life, they do possess—that animals either lack altogether, or, alternatively, possess in smaller quantities, or possess in less valuable forms. And something similar holds when it comes to comparing significantly different forms of animal life as well. If we think that dogs have more valuable lives than fish, say, that is because we think that the goods available to dogs are, overall, better (in quantity and quality) than the ones available to trout or salmon.

What are these various goods? In a fuller discussion of this question it would be worth trying to spell these out with some care. Here, however, I will content

---

[7] Balcombe's *What a Fish Knows* is a wonderful attempt to show exactly that, with regard to fish.

[8] Kitcher, "Experimental Animals," p. 298. He continues: "maybe there will be the chance to fly around in the wild and copulate a bit…"

[9] Frey, "Response: Autonomy, Animals, and Conceptions of the Good," p. 13.

myself with quickly rehearsing some obvious proposals, claiming neither comprehensiveness nor precision.

First of all, then, people have deeper and more meaningful relationships than animals, with more significant and valuable instances of friendship and love and family relations, based not just on caring and shared affection but on insight and mutual understanding as well. Second, people are capable of possessing greater and more valuable knowledge, including not only self-knowledge and knowledge of one's family and friends, but also systematic empirical knowledge as well for an incredibly wide range of phenomena, culminating in beautiful and sweeping scientific theories. Third, people are capable of a significantly greater range of achievements, displaying creativity and ingenuity as we pursue a vast range of goals, including hobbies, cultural pursuits, business endeavors, and political undertakings. Fourth, people have a highly developed aesthetic sense, with sophisticated experience and under-standing of works of art, including music, dance, painting, literature and more, as well as having a deeper appreciation of natural beauty and the aesthetic dimensions of the natural world, including the laws of nature and of mathe-matics. Fifth, people have greater powers of normative reflection, with a heightened ability to evaluate what matters, a striking capacity to aim for lives that are meaningful and most worth living, and a remarkable drive to discover what morality demands of us. Relatedly, sixth, people display greater and more complex forms of virtue and virtuous behavior, acting deliberately and self-consciously out of moral conviction, even when this involves aiding others that we have never met and will never see. Finally (and perhaps more contro-versially), people are capable of experiencing the sacred and the holy, striving for spiritual understanding and then working—alone and with others—to give it a significant place in our lives.[10]

Perhaps you won't agree with all the items I've listed here. And no doubt there are still other items you would want to add to the list as well. But there is no need for us to arrive at a single, fixed list. The point is only that almost all of us recognize that our lives are richer and more valuable by virtue of our having goods *like* these in our lives. To have fewer of such goods—or to have less valuable instances of them—is to live a less desirable life, a life at a lower level of well-being.

Of course, different theories of well-being will accommodate this thought in slightly different ways. On some theories of well-being, for example, the sorts

[10] I draw heavily on similar lists to be found in McMahan, *The Ethics of Killing*, pp. 195–8; Frey, "Moral Standing, the Value of Lives, and Speciesism," pp. 287–90; Bramble, "The Case Against Meat," p. 148; and Regan, *The Case for Animal Rights*, pp. xxxv–xxxvi.

of things I have just listed count as the very *constituents* of well-being, the possession of which directly constitutes being better off. On other theories, in contrast, they are only necessary *components* of well-being, and must fit into one's life properly if one is to be well off. And on still other theories they are simply the essential *means* to well-being, instrumental to having the very best sort of life but not valuable in and of themselves. These points of theoretical disagreement are philosophically interesting, but for our purposes they needn't detain us. What is important is only the recognition that it is because our lives can have these things and other goods like these to a significant degree that our lives are more valuable than the lives of animals—that we are better off than birds and frogs and cows.

But this is not to say that animals lack these goods altogether. That may be true for some of the items I mentioned, but for the vast majority of goods on any list like this it would be more accurate to say that animals can have them, but only to a lesser degree. I would never want to claim, for example, that dogs cannot be friends (with one another, or with us), but it does seem clear that the depth, quality, and richness of the friendships that are available to a dog are simply less significant than they are for the friendships that people can have with one another. Similarly, I would not want to claim that only people can have significant and difficult accomplishments in their lives. When a beaver builds a damn, for example, or a spider spins a web, these seem to me to be remarkable achievements indeed. Nonetheless, I would still want to claim that the range, difficulty, and significance of human achievements routinely (even if not always) exceed that to be found in the achievements of animals. And while it is clear that animals are capable of attaining empirical knowledge (especially of a local sort), I think it is also clear that they have nothing close to the systematic knowledge of universal laws which our best empirical science provides.

In all these ways and more, then, the life of a person is a more valuable one than the life of an animal. To be sure, many of the goods of well-being are ones we share with animals, but it is plausible to hold that on the whole we have more of these goods, and higher quality versions of these goods, than they do.

And for similar reasons it is plausible to insist that some animals have more valuable lives than others. Dogs may not be capable of friendships with the richness and emotional depth of the friendships available to us, but I take it to be clear that the friendships that they can have are deeper and more valuable than the friendships available to squirrels, or snakes. Similarly, the squirrel's accomplishment in remembering where it has stored its nuts may not compare to your achievement in composing a poem, but it is still a greater achievement,

I presume, than anything a housefly achieves. It is better to be a person than a fox; but for all that, it is still better to be a fox than a goldfish.[11]

It is worth repeating the point than in making judgments like this we must do our best to avoid parochialism. We should not blithely assume that the particular forms of a given good which we happen to possess are the only forms with genuine value. We must be careful to recognize value in its different forms, especially when those forms are alien to the forms the values take in our own lives. Indeed, we should be open to the possibility that some animals may possess goods distinct from our own, or superior to ours in one or another way.

Here is an example. I have suggested that we have a deeper and more developed aesthetic sense than animals do. But consider the fact that dogs have an incomparably more sensitive sense of smell than humans have. Conceivably, then, dogs have a correspondingly rich aesthetic appreciation of the olfactory aspect of the world, something well beyond anything that humans approximate. While we have a highly developed appreciation of the visual beauty of our surroundings perhaps dogs have something similar with regard to smell. I certainly have no idea whether anything like this is remotely the case, but I am open to the possibility. And if something like this *were* the case, then to that extent, at least, it would certainly be appropriate to revise upwards our overall assessment of the value of canine life.

Here's a different sort of case. I have claimed that among the goods which make our lives especially valuable are deep relationships with others, something that snakes and squirrels and spiders don't come close to matching. Certainly any human who lacks friendship and love, for example, is less well off, in that regard, by virtue of that very fact. But isn't it possible that friendship, say, is a good for us only by virtue of the fact that we are social animals? Should we really insist that the members of species that are solitary by nature also have lives that are correspondingly the poorer?[12]

I am indeed inclined to say just that. Friendship is a tremendous good, and if some animals are incapable of friendship, then that is simply one more way in which it is better to be one of us than to be an animal of that kind. But perhaps this judgment is made in ignorance of a corresponding good which is to be had (uniquely, or in a more valuable way) by animals that have evolved to live largely alone. Perhaps there is some sort of good akin to a noble self-sufficiency, and moles, sloths, or wolverines possess this good to a high degree. As I say, that

---

[11] Cf. Mill's famous claim in *Utilitarianism* that "it is better to be a human being dissatisfied than a pig satisfied." For further discussion of this sort of comparison—which relies on both experience and imagination—see Singer, *Practical Ethics*, pp. 90–3.

[12] DeGrazia raises this question in *Taking Animals Seriously*, pp. 244–5.

seems to me unlikely; but perhaps this judgment simply reflects a failure of imagination and insight on my part.

So I am open to the possibility that some animals may possess goods we lack, or possess goods in forms that we might be in danger of overlooking or failing to properly appreciate. But being open minded in this way to revising or refining some of our judgments is not at all the same thing as being skeptical about the very idea that people have more valuable lives than animals, or that different types of animals differ, one from another, with regard to the values of their respective forms of life.

And yet, for all that, I know that some people remain skeptical in just this way. They insist that all such judgments are nothing more than expressions of prejudice.

It is difficult to know what more to say in the face of such skepticism. But perhaps there is one further point that can be made. Imagine a human who is *severely* cognitively impaired, with a mental life that is roughly the equivalent of that had by, say, a cat. Virtually everyone agrees this would be a tragedy, to be averted or corrected if this could be accomplished. But *why* would it be a tragedy? Surely part of the answer lies in the fact that we think that such a person would be much less well off than they could be, if only they had a normally functioning brain, capable of the sort of cognitive and emotional processing that the rest of us constantly engage in. To live a life at this reduced level is to live a life at a tremendously lower level of well-being than that available to almost all of the rest of us.

As one author puts it, while giving voice to what is essentially the same idea:

> Some human lives are so very deficient in quality that we would not wish those lives upon anyone, and there are few lengths to which we would not go in order to avoid such lives for ourselves and our loved ones. I can see little point in pretending that lives which we do everything we could to avoid are of equal value to those normal (adult) human lives that we are presently living.[13]

Now, the reason that someone with such a life would be at a lower level of well-being is precisely that their life would inevitably lack the goods that the rest of us possess. That is, a life without these goods (or with smaller amounts, or with less valuable kinds) is a less valuable life, and the smaller and poorer the array of goods, the worse off the individual is. Yet if something like this holds when comparing different individual human lives—and it seems almost undeniable in such cases—then it is difficult to see why it won't similarly hold when

---

[13] Frey, "Moral Standing, the Value of Lives, and Speciesism," pp. 293–4.

comparing our lives to the lives of animals, or comparing one type of animal life to another.

You wouldn't trade your life for the life of the severely cognitively impaired individual. Nor would you trade your life for that of a deer, or a sparrow. But your resistance to such trades is puzzling—unless at some level you already acknowledge the plain fact that those other lives are simply less valuable than your own.

2.4 Hierarchy

I have been arguing that there is a reasonable way for the unitarian to avoid commitment to the implausible thesis that there is no more reason to save a drowning person than, say, a drowning mouse. This requires asserting that a person's life normally possesses more good than a mouse's life—and, more broadly, that animals in general normally have lower levels of well-being than people do. But these are claims that unitarians are typically ready to embrace. Similarly, given that almost all of us will want to insist that it is more important to save some animals rather than others, the unitarian will also need to claim that we can rank typical animal lives as well, with some animals being acknowledged to be better off than others.

Admittedly, some people resist or want to reject the requisite comparisons between our own lives and the lives of animals, or between one form of animal life and another, but in the last section I argued that the relevant comparisons are actually quite plausible. My own belief, in any event, is that we should all accept judgments along these lines, whether we are unitarians or not.

If I am right about this, then it seems as though unitarianism is well positioned to answer the objection we initially raised against it. Despite what we might initially have thought, it appears that the unitarian can accommodate various widely held judgments about who to aid or who to harm, all the while insisting that no individual with moral standing has a higher moral status than any other individual with standing as well.

There is, however, a complication that should be considered at this point. Return to the example, introduced earlier, where we had to choose between aiding Jonathan (who has a migraine) and aiding Rebecca (who has a paper cut). I imagine that no one would be tempted to say that since we should help Jonathan rather than Rebecca this somehow shows that Jonathan has a higher moral *status* than Rebecca does. On the contrary, their status is the same, and it is the simple fact that Jonathan stands to undergo a greater harm than Rebecca does that justifies choosing to help him rather than her.

But imagine that this sort of disparity between the two were regular and systematic. Imagine that whenever we needed to decide whom to aid, Jonathan or Rebecca, it was always Jonathan who had more at stake, Jonathan who stood to suffer the greater harm, Jonathan who had the greater claim to aid, by virtue of having stronger or more valuable interests on the line. Suppose that Jonathan's life was so much richer and more valuable in any given case that we would always benefit Jonathan more (if we aided him) than we could benefit Rebecca (by aiding her instead).

If anything close to this were true then it seems that the same requirement that the unitarian has already appealed to—the requirement to aid whoever has more at stake—would lead us to be forever favoring Jonathan over Rebecca. Given the need to choose between the two, there would be a standing presumption (at the very least) to favor Jonathan. And at that point it might not really seem all that strained to say that Jonathan had a higher moral status than Rebecca.

We can push the example further. Suppose that this sort of systemic disparity existed not just between Jonathan and Rebecca, but between men and women quite generally. Suppose, for example, that men had sufficiently different psychological capacities from women (thanks to genetic differences) so that it turned out that their lives were always incredibly richer in terms of their levels of well-being. Suppose that whenever one faced a choice between helping a woman and helping a man it was always the case that the man had more well-being at stake, and the man would undergo the greater harm if you helped the woman instead (than the woman would, if you helped the man). The same requirement to aid the person with more at stake would then direct us to always favor the man, rather than the woman.

Or—pushing the example in a slightly different direction—suppose that Jonathan is white, while Rebecca is black, and that whites *always* had more well-being on the line than blacks did (thanks to genetic differences). Here too, it seems, the principle in question would lead us to have a standing presumption (if nothing more) to favor whites over blacks.

Obviously, nothing like this is remotely the case. There are no systematic differences in the innate capacities for welfare that would make it true that men always (or typically) have more at stake than women, or whites than blacks. But suppose that something like this *were* the case. What would it show?

One natural suggestion is that it would show that the principle requiring aid to the individual with more at stake may need revision or supplementing, to take into account whether some individual or group of individuals routinely and systematically ends up being on the losing side of our various choices. That's an important possibility, and we will return to it later. At the moment, however, what I particularly want to note is that if morality did direct us to systematically favor one such group over another (men over women, whites over blacks), then it would be rather natural to describe this situation as one in which the favored group had a *higher moral status* than the other group. After all, morality would be telling us to systematically favor the members of the one group over the other in response to their systematically stronger claims, and it seems natural to describe this sort of systemic difference as a difference in moral status.

As I say, no general differences like these actually hold between men and women, or blacks and whites. But for all that, this is precisely the situation that the unitarian was suggesting does indeed hold between people and animals. (And as we have now discussed, the claims in question are extremely plausible ones.) Due to the systematic differences that exist between the levels of well-being that people typically have at stake and the levels of well-being that animals typically have at stake, it turns out that people almost always have stronger claims than animals do in cases of the sort we have been considering. According to the unitarian position, then, we should almost always favor people rather than animals in such cases. But as we have just seen, if that's right then it seems perfectly natural to describe this sort of theory as one in which people have a higher moral status than animals have.

That seems to leave the unitarian in a somewhat uncomfortable position. Unitarianism is the view that there are no higher or lower moral statuses, only the one single moral status shared by all individuals with moral standing. At first glance, this appeared to have the implausible implication that forced to choose between saving a drowning person or saving a drowning mouse the situation would be a tie, and what we should do is to flip a coin. To escape this result, the unitarian emphasized the systematic ways in which a person almost always has more welfare at stake than an animal does (other things being equal). That avoids the unwelcome implication. But now it seems that it avoids it at the cost of reintroducing differences in moral status of precisely the sort that the unitarian is committed to denying! In short, the most promising response to our initial objection to unitarianism actually appears to be incompatible with retaining a commitment to *unitarianism*.[14]

---

[14] DeGrazia has emphasized the point that a commitment to the idea of giving equal weight to otherwise similar interests is nonetheless compatible with—and may actually entail—recognizing differences in moral status. (See "The Distinction Between Equality in Moral Status and Deserving Equal Consideration.") A similar idea is entertained by Harman ("The Potentiality Problem," pp. 197–8, note 17). Of the possibility that a trout has no lower a moral status than a normal person has, DeGrazia—a unitarian in my sense—writes that he "simply cannot believe this." ("Response," p. 80.)

There are, however, at least two possible replies available to the unitarian. Most obviously, I imagine that not everyone will share the intuition that if one group systematically has more welfare at stake than another—with the result that other things being equal one should always favor the members of the first group—then this situation is appropriately described as one in which the first group truly has a higher moral *status* than the other. After all, it isn't as though any interests of the first group are being counted more heavily than the *comparable* interests of the second group. Yet that's what it takes, some may feel, before talk of higher and lower status is really justified.

It isn't, for example, as though the unitarian thinks that two otherwise simi-lar *pains* should be given different weights in our moral calculations, by virtue of the fact that the one pain is had by a person, while the other is had by an animal. Any view like *that* would certainly qualify as involving some sort of hierarchy with regard to moral status. But that's not what we have in the case at hand. On the contrary, otherwise similar interests are being given precisely the same amount of weight. It just turns out that people frequently have more significant interests on the line than animals do (because they have greater goods at stake). That's a striking fact—it might be suggested—but recognizing this fact isn't at all the same thing as asserting that one group has a higher moral status than another. Claims about higher status are only legitimate if we coun-tenance giving greater weight to a given individual's interests than we do to someone else's otherwise *similar* interests. Or so it might be said.

Speaking personally, I find myself of two minds with regard to whether the sort of situation we are envisioning is indeed one that is appropriately described by saying that the members of the one group (people, say) have a higher moral status than the members of the other group (animals). I feel the pull in each direction. On the one hand, it does seem peculiar to call a theory hierarchical, if it always counts otherwise similar interests in precisely the same way. But at the same time, it also seems peculiar to deny that a theory is hierarchical, when it tells us to systematically favor one group over another.

I suspect that my ambivalence here is due to there being a fair bit of vague-ness with regard to what exactly counts as giving one group a higher moral status than another. As it turns out, it just isn't always clear when it is appropri-ate to describe a given view as holding that some individuals have a higher status than others.

But this points to a second possible unitarian response. Instead of arguing over whether the unitarian position can legitimately be described as involving hierarchy of *some* sort, unitarians can simply insist that *this* sort of hierarchy— if hierarchy it be—was never the kind of hierarchy that unitarians intended to deny the existence of in the first place. All along (they might reasonably assert), the crucial question was simply whether otherwise similar interests ever count for more, just by virtue of the fact that they are the interests of a person, say, rather than an animal. It is only hierarchy in *this* sense that unitarians are committed to rejecting. And the crucial point, of course, is that even if it is true that people generally have more at stake than animals do, and so there is systematic reason to favor people over animals (other things being equal), this still doesn't constitute giving more weight to the otherwise *similar* interests of people. So the unitarian's position remains nonhierarchical, it can reasonably be claimed, given the *relevant* sense of hierarchy.

All of this suggests, of course, that we shouldn't put too much weight on the question of whether any particular view can be legitimately described as assigning higher or lower statuses. The really interesting question, rather, is whether unitarians are right that it never makes a difference whether a *given* interest is had by a person rather than an animal (or what kind of animal the animal might be). My own view is that this often *does* make a difference, contrary to what unitarians claim. That is to say, I believe in hierarchy even in the more restricted sense that we've just introduced, hierarchy according to which how much a given interest counts depends on *whose* interest it is.

In light of all of this, we might wonder whether it would be better to avoid any further talk of moral status at all. Perhaps, for example, we should simply avoid remarks to the effect that a given theory does or does not assign a higher status to some groups than to others. But to accept this suggestion, I think, would needlessly complicate the discussion that follows. The fact of the matter is that when we are describing hierarchical theories of the sort that I intend to be discussing, the language of higher and lower status is simply too convenient for us to try to do without.

Happily, however, there is no need for us to forswear terms like "status" and "hierarchy." Instead, let me simply stipulate that in all that follows my talk of hierarchy—or of higher and lower status—is to be understood as involving precisely the sort of clear-cut hierarchy that we've just identified, the sort that even the unitarian must count as such. And similarly, then, when we say that unitarians are committed to the denial of hierarchy in moral status, let us hereafter understand that claim to be one concerned only with hierarchy in this more restrictive sense as well.

In particular, then, as I go on to argue for hierarchy in animal ethics, it is to be understood that I am indeed claiming that it matters *whose* interests we are talking about. My view is that people have a higher status than animals (and some animals have a higher status than others), and that the weight we should give to a given interest—the way we should count it in our moral deliberations—does indeed depend in part on the status of the individual whose interest it is. In short, the sort of hierarchy that I intend to defend is of a kind that unitarians unambiguously dismiss.

Of course, as we have now seen, unitarianism is a more plausible theory than it might initially seem. I certainly haven't offered any arguments yet for the sort of boldly hierarchical position I've just described. I turn to that next.

3

The Argument from Distribution

3.1 Distributive Principles

Pretty much everyone thinks that the value of an outcome turns, to a significant degree, on the well-being of the various individuals involved. Other things being equal, at the very least, one outcome will be better than another if the individuals in the first outcome are better off than they would be under the alternatives.[1] Putting the point simply—too simply, but perhaps acceptably for our purposes—the more well-being the better.

Of course, other things are not always equal. Sometimes we find that one outcome strikes us as worse from a moral point of view, even though it actually contains a greater total amount of well-being than its alternatives. There are various reasons why this might be the case, but one important set of reasons involves distribution: most people are attracted to the idea that the *distribution* of well-being matters, and not just the total amount. That is, although one outcome will normally be better than another when the first outcome contains a greater total amount of well-being, we may feel otherwise if something is amiss in terms of the distribution of that well-being.

We can illustrate the point by returning to the example of the imaginary world where men always have more well-being at stake than women do, so that we always provide a greater benefit, or avoid more harm, if we aid men rather than women. As we noted, if we were to always benefit the person who has more well-being at stake, then in a situation like this we might well find ourselves forever favoring men over women. The ultimate result could be an outcome with a greater total amount of well-being than could otherwise be had, but where the men are all extremely well off and the women are all extremely *badly* off. This disparity in level of well-being would obviously be

[1] Here, and in all that follows, I put aside the special vexing questions that arise when we start comparing outcomes where *different* individuals exist, so that a given individual might exist in one of the relevant outcomes but not in another. (The seminal treatment is Parfit, *Reasons and Persons*, part IV.) Discussions of the problems of population ethics—as the topic is called—usually focus exclusively on people, but similar issues arise for animals as well. See Singer, *Practical Ethics*, pp. 85–90 and 104–19, and my "Singer on Killing Animals," for an introduction to a few of the relevant questions.

tremendously troubling, but if it really were the case with regard to each choice we faced that we could benefit men more than we could benefit women, a requirement to be forever aiding the individual who stands to benefit the most might well lead us to this outcome.

As a result of thinking about examples like this, most people conclude that bringing about the greatest total amount of well-being isn't the only thing that matters. We need to be sensitive to the *distribution* of well-being as well. It is one thing to say that, other things being equal, we should normally aid the person who stands to lose (or gain) the most. But if someone routinely turns out to be on the losing side of such distributions, through no fault of their own, then that fact also needs to be taken into account. Putting the same point in slightly different terms, when evaluating the goodness of an outcome we need to take into account the way the welfare is distributed in that outcome. And if the distribution is sufficiently askew, we might well decide that some alternative outcome would be morally superior, even though the total amount of well-being might be lower—provided that the well-being in that alternative was distributed more evenly or fairly.

In short, an adequate moral theory will need to include a relevant *distributive* principle. And morality will then enjoin us to avoid outcomes where the distribution is problematic (in the relevant way). It will tell us to take steps to eliminate or reduce inappropriate distributive disparities, if we can.

Unsurprisingly, moral theorists differ over what exactly the relevant distributive principles come to. Many philosophers, of course, favor an *egalitarian* principle, according to which an outcome is morally objectionable to the extent that the people in one group are significantly worse off than the members of another group. Other things being equal, then, an egalitarian principle tells us to bring about an outcome in which the various individual levels of well-being are the *same*—or, failing that, one in which the amount of inequality is as low as possible. And since a world where men have everything and women have almost nothing is clearly a world with staggering (but reducible) inequality, commitment to an egalitarian principle will tell us to refrain from forever favoring men, even if such favoritism would have resulted in a greater total amount of well-being.[2]

Egalitarianism (in the sense just described) is probably the most familiar type of distributive view. But there are alternatives. For example, some people argue that the problem isn't really with inequality in and of itself—as if it were problematic when someone "only" has one billion dollars, while others have two or

---

[2] See Temkin, *Inequality*.

three billion!—but rather when someone ends up at an *unacceptably low level* of well-being, with a life that would be acknowledged as inadequate and limited by any objective reckoning. So what we really need to do, according to such accounts, is to specify a minimal level of well-being that will count as *good enough*. We need to identify a "baseline" level of well-being such that anyone at that level or beyond has a sufficiently decent quality of life. And the idea, then, is that it is indeed a moral priority to bring people *up* to this baseline level. But once someone has reached it, there is no longer a pressing moral mandate for the rest of us to try to improve their lives even further.[3]

Since a view like this turns on identifying a kind of life that is sufficient in this way, this position is sometimes known as *sufficientarianism*. This is, of course, still an expression of our distributive concern, since a world in which men have everything and women have almost nothing will be a world in which women are far below the baseline "good enough" level, and so we will need to avoid constantly favoring men at the expense of women. But for all that, it is clear that sufficientarianism is a different distributive view from egalitarianism, strictly so called. (Egalitarianism is a *comparative* view, since the relevant question is always whether some people are worse off than others, while sufficientarianism is a *noncomparative* view, in that the question is simply whether any given individual is below the baseline or not.)

Still others depart from strict egalitarianism in yet other ways. *Prioritarians* hold that what really matters is helping those who are at the lowest levels of well-being. Given the chance to increase someone's level of well-being by a fixed amount, we do more *good* (from the moral point of view) the worse off the person is that we choose to aid. According to prioritarianism, then, an increase in well-being of a fixed size does not always make the same addition to the value of a given outcome. If the boost goes to someone who is badly off (at a low absolute level of well-being) then this makes the outcome better by a significant amount. But if the very same boost in well-being goes to someone who is already at a higher level of well-being, then the good done is less, there is a smaller addition to the goodness of the outcome. And if that same boost goes to someone who is at an even higher level of well-being, then the additional value added to the outcome is even smaller. Thus, how much good is done by adding a given amount of well-being depends on the level of well-being of the person it is given to. The lower the level they start off at, the greater the increase in the value of the outcome. Given a sufficiently robust prioritarian view, it will often

---

[3] See Frankfurt, "Equality as a Moral Ideal," pp. 146–56, or "The Moral Irrelevance of Equality," pp. 87–96.

do more good to give a smaller increase in well-being to those at the bottom rather than a larger increase in well-being to those at the top.[4]

Accordingly, prioritarianism is also a distributive view in our sense, telling us to avoid the outcome where men have everything and women nothing. For even though it may be true that we can benefit men (boost their well-being) by a greater amount than we can benefit women, given the truth of prioritarianism it may still turn out that we can do more *good*—make the outcome morally better—if we aid the women rather than the men. Total well-being isn't all that matters; it also matters where the well-being is going.

Thus, prioritarianism is a distributive view as well. But it differs nonetheless from both egalitarianism and sufficientarianism. On the one hand, unlike sufficientarianism, the priority view continues to give priority (albeit reduced priority) to those above the "good enough" level. But on the other hand, like sufficientarianism and unlike strict egalitarianism, prioritarianism is, in the relevant sense, noncomparative. Prioritarians don't really pay any direct attention to the question of whether any given person is better off or worse off than someone else. All that matters is what the given individual's absolute level of well-being comes to. It is this absolute level—not the comparative fact of being better or worse off than another—that fixes the size of the increase in *value* that will occur if the person's level of well-being is increased.

So we have at least three distributive principles that have often been found attractive. And there are still others. Some argue that what really matters is not equality per se, but only whether people are getting, or failing to get, what they *deserve*. In many cases, of course, people will turn out to be equally morally deserving, and in such cases it will indeed be important that they also be equally well off. But in other cases, conceivably, the inequality may be deserved: perhaps, for example, those who are worse off are at fault in some way, so that they deserve to be worse off than the others. In such cases the inequality may not be troubling after all. So a desert sensitive theory differs yet again from our other distributive principles, though it too may find the world where women have virtually nothing an objectionable one, if—as could certainly be the case—the women are every bit as morally deserving as the men.[5]

Although it is an important question within normative ethics which, if any, of these distributive principles are correct, that will not be our concern here. For our purposes the crucial point is that many people, perhaps most people, are attracted to *some* sort of distributive principle along these lines, either one

---

[4] See Parfit, "Equality or Priority?"   [5] See my "Equality and Desert."

of the principles we've just considered, or something else that works in at least a somewhat similar fashion. And what I want to argue is that anyone who does accept this kind of distributive principle will have compelling reason to abandon unitarianism.

3.2 The Argument from Distribution

To see the problem for the unitarian, reconsider the claim with which I began this chapter. Pretty much everyone agrees that, other things being equal, the more well-being the better the outcome. To be sure, as the discussion of distribution has reminded us, other things are not always equal. But put that point aside for the moment, and just think about the significance of well-being.

Now when you do this, if you aren't careful, you may find yourself doing what most of us would do, and slip into thinking only about the well-being of *people* (or, perhaps, of all humans). Of course, an assumption running throughout this book is that it just isn't true that it is only our own well-being (the well-being of people or of humans) that matters, morally speaking. But it is easy enough to forget this point if one isn't making a special effort to bear it in mind. Still, the error is easily corrected. Once we recall the moral standing of animals we readily *extend* the thought about well-being so that it covers animals too. What we really believe (or at least, what we should believe) is that, other things being equal, *all* well-being counts, so that the more well-being—including animal well-being—the better.

A similar mistake is easy to make with regard to our distributive principles as well. As we'll see, a version of this problem arises for each of the principles we've mentioned, but for concreteness let's focus initially on the egalitarian principle. If we tell ourselves, then, that equality matters, we may find that if we aren't being careful we slip into thinking about equality and inequality only among *people* (or, perhaps, among humans).

But what happens when we recall, once more, the moral standing of animals? Should we extend our commitment to equality so that it covers animals too? Do we believe, for example—or rather, *should* we believe—that inequality matters, not just between people, but between people and animals (and animals and animals) as well?

It certainly does seem as though the unitarian, at any rate, is committed to just this sort of claim. Or rather, more precisely, unitarians who also believe in a principle of equality are committed to this conclusion. For unitarians believe that all those individuals with any sort of moral standing at all have exactly the same moral status; and egalitarians believe that it is a significant part of the moral status of a *person* that they have egalitarian claims against others, so that an outcome is worse (other things being equal) if there is an unequal distribution of well-being. Putting these two ideas together, this seems to imply that unitarians who are also egalitarians should believe that animals too have a moral claim to equality. After all, if one person is significantly worse off than another then the egalitarian says that this is a feature of the world which lowers its value from the moral point of view and we may well have a pressing moral obligation to do what we can to eliminate or at least ameliorate the situation. Consequently, once we recall that animals too have moral standing it seems as though the unitarian must also conclude that if one *animal* is significantly worse off than another, or if animals are significantly worse off than people are, then that too is a situation that we are obligated to try to correct.

But now, it seems, this really is the situation that we find ourselves in. That is, it really is the case that people are normally at a tremendously higher level of well-being than animals are. That, after all, was precisely the point of the penultimate section of the previous chapter. As I argued there, the virtually undeniable fact is that under almost all normal circumstances people are significantly better off than animals are, and some animals are better off than others. There is a vast array of goods that people can and typically do have in our lives which animals lack or at best have in lesser amounts (or in less valuable forms). And even among animals, there are huge differences in the kinds and extent (and forms) of the goods that are possessed. So people simply have much more valuable lives than animals do, and some animals have more valuable lives than others.

Certainly the unitarian, at any rate, won't want to deny this claim. For it was precisely the thought that our lives are so much better than the lives of animals that made it possible for the unitarian to avoid the implausible suggestion that if we are forced to choose between saving a person and saving a mouse, we must flip a coin. On the contrary, the unitarian reasonably replied that since the life of a person is so much more valuable than the life of a mouse, the person has more at stake; and it this fact—they claimed—that justifies our decision to save the person rather than the mouse. But this means, it should go without saying, that unitarians cannot now dismiss the comparative judgment that they themselves were earlier insisting upon. And even if they were so inclined, it wouldn't really matter. For as I have already argued, the thought is virtually undeniable in its own right: people have better lives—incomparably better lives—than mice do.

Yet if people really are so tremendously better off than mice (and for that matter, than other animals as well), and if as unitarians we now insist that mice (and other animals) really do have egalitarian claims of exactly the same sort that people have, then it really does seem to follow that a world like ours, a world in which people are incredibly better off than mice and other animals, is a world that is tremendously objectionable from the egalitarian perspective. If we can do anything about it—it would seem the unitarian must say—then we have a significant moral obligation to try to correct, or at least ameliorate, the situation.

Of course, I haven't made any particular claims as to how much *weight* the egalitarian principle should have in our overall moral theory. I presume that those sympathetic to egalitarian concerns will think it relatively important to try to correct or reduce morally objectionable inequalities. But I have not taken a stand on *how* important that will be, how much we should be prepared to sacrifice so as to reduce inequality when this can be done. So I cannot say with any precision what kind of sacrifices the unitarian seems to be committed to. I can only suggest, somewhat more cautiously, that *to the extent that* one thinks that equality is a significant moral ideal, something to which we should pay close attention when choosing between alternatives, then the unitarian will need to find the vast inequality that obtains between people and animals (and for that matter, between different types of animals) to be a troubling and morally problematic state of affairs, something that we should strive to redress.

This would seem to mean, for example, that instead of favoring public policies under which we shift resources from those people who need them less to those people who need them more, we should instead favor policies under which we shift resources from people quite generally to mice—and snakes, and birds, and frogs, and perhaps flies—so as to do what we can (to the extent required by our egalitarianism) to reduce the vast inequality that currently exists between people and animals.

Admittedly, there may not be all that much we can do to improve the level of well-being for mice. But it isn't as though there is nothing at all that we could do. We might, for example, take to leaving expensive cheeses around for the mice to eat. Similarly, we could devote ourselves to putting out seeds for birds, or carrots for rabbits. There are myriad ways in which we could improve the welfare of animals, even if only modestly. And it seems to follow from the unitarian position that this is what we are in fact required to do.[6]

But that, I think, is an absurd conclusion. I do of course agree that our lives are tremendously more valuable than the lives of mice (and birds and rabbits).

---

[6] There is a complication that I here put aside, namely, that in certain cases it can actually make the overall level of inequality *worse* to help some of those who are worse off rather than others. (See Temkin, *Inequality*, for discussion of this point.) But I presume that some improvements to animal welfare—appropriately chosen—really would reduce inequality overall.

So the conclusion that there is *some* kind of inequality here is, I think, undeniable. But I find it impossible to take seriously the suggestion that this inequality is, in and of itself, morally objectionable—that the mere fact that mice are worse off than us is morally problematic, and so we are under a pressing moral obligation to correct this inequality. Yet that does seem to be the conclusion that is forced upon us if we embrace both egalitarianism and unitarianism. Accordingly, unless we are prepared to give up on our egalitarian distributive principle, what we must do instead is to reject unitarianism.

Of course, some unitarians might conclude that it is really our commitment to egalitarianism that should be abandoned at this point, rather than the commitment to unitarianism. There are, after all, other distributive principles that we might embrace instead, so the unitarian might hope that we can avoid absurdity—while still retaining a commitment to both unitarianism and distributive fairness—by endorsing one of the alternatives. Unfortunately for the unitarian, however, if we do try to combine unitarianism with one or another of our remaining distributive principles, rather than the egalitarian one, unacceptable conclusions still follow.

Suppose, for example, that we endorse prioritarianism. Here the idea is that morality tells us to give priority to providing welfare to those with the lowest absolute levels of well-being. Comparisons are, strictly, irrelevant. It doesn't matter whether you are worse off than anyone else, as it does with an egalitarian principle; what matters, rather, is how well off or badly off you are. Adding a unit of well-being simply does more good, unit for unit, when it is given to those individuals who have the lowest absolute levels of welfare.

But once we have agreed with the unitarian that the moral status of animals is exactly the same as the moral status of people, then it follows that we must similarly give priority to boosting the welfare of animals, if it should turn out that animals have the lowest absolute levels of well-being. And that, of course, is exactly the case. A cat has a lower level of well-being than a person does, and so priority must be given to increasing cat welfare, rather than offering comparable increases in well-being to people. The welfare of a mouse is even lower, and so adding an extra unit of well-being for a mouse will do even *more* to make the outcome better than would be done by adding a unit of well-being to a person. And if flies count, morally, then presumably their level of well-being will be even lower absolutely speaking, so even greater priority will be in order.

In effect, the problem is this. Prioritarians claim that the welfare of people who are doing badly counts more than the welfare of people who are doing well, in the sense that it simply does *more good*, morally speaking, to increase the well-being of someone badly off than it does to increase the well-being of someone well off (and the *worse off* the person is, the greater the extra amount of good done by increasing their well-being). This weighting scheme is supposed to be sufficiently strong that it has the result that a concern for appropriate distribution will lead us to favor aiding those people doing badly, even if the amount of well-being that we can provide to them is less—perhaps even substantially less—than the amount of well-being we can provide to those people who are already doing well. But if we combine this view with unitarianism then we are forced to apply this very same weighting schedule to animals as well. Thus, given that animals are doing worse on the whole than people are—indeed, tremendously worse—it follows that it will simply do more *good* to provide quite minimal increases in the welfare of mice and flies, say, rather than providing more substantial increases to the welfare of *people* (even people who are doing rather poorly as compared to other people).

In short, if we embrace prioritarianism and combine it with unitarianism we are led to the conclusion that to the extent that distributive concerns should weigh on our deliberations, then our concern here will have to be almost exclusively focused on helping those animals with the lowest levels of well-being. That too, I take it, is a conclusion that few if any of us will be prepared to accept. So those who accept prioritarianism will need to reject unitarianism.

We get a similar result if we try to combine unitarianism with sufficientarianism instead. Sufficientarians, recall, emphasize the importance of bringing people up to a specified level of well-being, a level that marks a life that, although perhaps modest, is nonetheless recognizably a decent enough life for a person to have. If, for the sake of illustrating the idea, we imagine that we can assign precise numbers to various levels of well-being, and if we suppose that a quite nice life for a person is at a level of well-being of, say, 100, then perhaps the "good enough" level will fall around something like 80. According to sufficientarianism, then, priority is to be given to bringing people up to a well-being level of 80—or, failing that, to bringing them as close to that baseline as possible.

But now imagine that we combine this view with a commitment to unitarianism. This means that it does not suffice for us to do what we can to bring other people up to this minimal level (in our example, 80). If animals have the very same moral status as people do, then it will follow that the idea of a baseline level of well-being—one that we need to bring individuals up to—will apply to them as well. What's more, and this is the crucial point, if animals have the very same moral status as people do, then it will be the *very same* level of well-being that provides the relevant baseline, regardless of whether we are dealing with people or animals. Not only must we do what we can to bring *people* up to a level of well-being of 80, we must do the same for animals— or, failing that, we must bring them as close to that level as possible.

So if it should turn out that animals generally (or always!) have a level of welfare that falls below the designated baseline, then we will have to prioritize doing what we can to bring them as close to that level as possible. And this, of course, is precisely the situation we find ourselves in. For if a nice life for a person is a 100, and an acceptable life for a person is an 80—so that 80 provides the relevant sufficientarian baseline—then I take it to be clear that animals have lives far, far below that level. Recognizing that any numbers assigned here will be somewhat arbitrary, still I take it that one would be hard pressed to think that dogs have lives higher than 40 (if 80 is the relevant number for a minimally acceptable *human* life); and most other animals will have a significantly worse level of well-being, with mice earning at best a 2 or a 3 (that's probably generous), and insects having mere fractions of a point.

The precise numbers don't matter. What matters is that we recognize that animals fall *far* short of any baseline that it would be plausible for the sufficientarian to settle on with regard to people. So if the unitarian insists that animals have exactly the same moral status as people do, it will apparently follow that animals also have a claim to be brought up to this very same baseline. And if, as seems inevitable, we cannot actually manage to bring them all the way up to a level of life of comparable quality, then at the very least it seems the unitarian will have to claim that we must do what we can to bring them as close to such a quality of life as is possible.

But that too, I take it, is an implausible position to maintain. While it does seem reasonable to suggest that morality tells us to bring people up to a certain minimal level of well-being, it is impossible for me to take seriously the suggestion that we must similarly strive to bring mice up to that very same level (or as close to that as possible). This too, I take it, is an idea that few, if any, will be prepared to accept. So those who endorse sufficientarianism, it seems, will need to reject unitarianism as well.

(Could the unitarian claim, perhaps, that all that sufficientarianism entails is a requirement to bring individuals up to a level of well-being that constitutes a decent life for beings *of that kind*? We'll consider that suggestion in the next section.)

Finally, what about those who appeal instead to the importance of people getting what they deserve? If we follow the unitarian in claiming that animals have the very same moral status as people do, and then combine this with a belief in the significance of desert, what are we to make of the vast inequalities that exist between people and animals (and between some types of animals and other types)? Matters are slightly less straightforward here, since inequalities can be justified from the standpoint of desert as long as those doing better are more *deserving* than those doing worse. However, although it does seem possible to make out a view according to which, for example, a person really does deserve a higher level of well-being (than a mouse, say) simply by virtue of the very fact that they are indeed a *person*, to say anything like this is to introduce differences in moral status of the sort that the unitarian is trying to avoid. We would be saying, in effect, that the weight to be given to some particular individual's interest depends on how deserving they are, and how deserving they are depends (if not solely, then at least to a considerable extent) on what kind of *being* they are—person, dog, mouse, or fish.

But if we insist with the unitarian that all individuals with moral standing have the very same moral status, then these sorts of claims—asserting categorical differences with regard to what a cow deserves, say, as compared to a person—must be rejected. So if the otherwise similar interests of a cow and a person are to be given the *same* weight, then there is no justification for the fact that people are so tremendously better off than cows (and other animals) are. Here too, then, anyone trying to combine unitarianism with a commitment to the value of desert will have to conclude that we have compelling moral reason to do what we can to bring animals as close to the level of people as possible (to the extent that undeserved inequalities are objectionable). This remains an idea that few, if any, will be prepared to accept. So even those who are committed to the significance of desert will have reason to reject unitarianism.

We have now considered four distinct distributive principles, and while the details differ, each of them leads to a similar, unacceptable, implication when we combine it with unitarianism. The underlying problem is this: the distribution of welfare that exists, once we remember to take animal well-being into account, is such that it would strike almost all of us as morally unacceptable if a comparable pattern existed among *people*. Accordingly, if unitarianism is right when it insists that animals really do have exactly the same moral status as people do, then it follows that the distribution of welfare that we find—when we consider both people and animals—is indeed morally *unacceptable*. So to the extent that correcting such distributive injustices is morally obligatory, we have compelling moral reason to try to eliminate or ameliorate the situation, doing what we can, for example, to improve the lives of mice. But this is a conclusion that few, if any, will accept. So if you do endorse one of our distributive principles, it seems, you will need to reject unitarianism.

There are, of course, still other distributive principles, and there is no need to pretend that every single one of them will generate a similar problem for the unitarian. But the crucial point remains that the pattern of distribution of welfare that we find, when we count both animals and people, is one that almost everyone would find deeply objectionable if it held among people alone. Yet any distributive principle that would be up to the task of condemning such a pattern (among people) must similarly condemn that pattern when it holds between people and animals (or between animals and animals)—*provided*, of course, that it really is true that animals have the very same moral status as people have. Thus, unless you are prepared to condemn the overall pattern of distribution of welfare that holds between people and animals, if you embrace a distributive principle that would condemn this pattern were it to hold among *people*, you will have reason to reject unitarianism.[7]

3.3 Replies

I have argued that if we accept any one of several plausible distributive principles and try to combine it with unitarianism we are led to conclusions that few if any are prepared to accept.

Why the qualification? Why not simply assert baldly that the conclusion is unacceptable? Speaking personally, I *do* think the conclusion is unacceptable, but I want to acknowledge that others may disagree. Impressed by unitarianism, some people—only a few, I imagine, but some—may be prepared to follow the argument all the way to its rather surprising conclusion, that we really do have a significant moral obligation to correct the various inequalities that exist between people and animals (and among animals themselves).[8] They will insist (or perhaps, merely concede) that we must do what we can to improve the quality of life for squirrels, snakes, houseflies, and the like. As I've indicated, I find that impossible to believe. But if some are prepared to accept the cost of maintaining this position, there may be little more to say. Nonetheless, I am confident that almost all of us will find the conclusion impossible to embrace and will insist instead that it just isn't true that we are obligated to eliminate the various disparities we find in animal welfare.

---

[7] As far as I know, the earliest version of an argument of the sort that I have been discussing in this section is to be found in McMahan, "Cognitive Disability, Misfortune, and Justice," starting at p. 8. The fullest discussion of the general problem is Vallentyne, "Of Mice and Men."

[8] After noting the extremely demanding implications of sufficientarianism if the same baseline is used for both people and animals, Crisp remarks that nonetheless he is "prepared seriously to entertain this view." ("Equality, Priority, and Compassion," p. 761.)

Others who are drawn to unitarianism may try to soften the force of the argument by reminding us that distributive concerns are only one value (or set of values) among several in our overall moral theory. Just as we introduced distributive principles so as to correct for the implausible conclusions that would follow if all we cared about was bringing about the greatest total amount of well-being (or helping the individual who has the most at stake), so we must now recognize that these very same distributive principles will themselves lead to absurd conclusions if we lose sight of the fact that it does still matter how our actions affect the total. And since almost any serious efforts to eliminate the objectionable distributive features of animal welfare would cost us a tremendous amount, significantly reducing our own welfare and that of other people for at best minimal gains from the perspective of distributive justice, it might turn out that we aren't really required to do all that much—if anything—to improve the overall welfare of animals.

According to this second position, then, it is indeed true that the distributive principles should be extended so as to cover all animals, in just the way the unitarian position implies; and it is indeed true that, so extended, the distributive principles identify various features of the pattern of distribution of welfare (between people and animals, and among animals) as being morally objectionable. Consequently, if these various distributive offenses could somehow be corrected *without* this involving an unreasonable cost to ourselves or to the total overall welfare, then making these changes would indeed be something we were required to do. But in fact the cost would be too high, the sacrifices required would be too great, and so the actual obligation (all things considered) is slight—*once* we remember to take into account our other moral values as well. In short, the results of combining unitarianism with our distributive principles are actually modest and acceptable, as long as they are worked out in the context of our overall moral theory. So there is no need to reject the unitarian position after all.[9]

Putting the point in a slightly contentious form, the idea is that our distributive principles are relatively *weak*, all things considered, weak enough to avoid generating the implausibly onerous obligations that unitarianism seemed to imply when applied to these same principles.

Now, it certainly must be conceded that if the moral force of our distributive principles were sufficiently weak then the obligations created when they are combined with unitarianism would be weak as well. But it seems to me unlikely

---

[9] In "A Basis for (Interspecies) Equality," Persson endorses a view like this, suggesting that it avoids the "patently absurd consequences" that he agrees would follow if the (legitimate) egalitarian principle were applied in isolation (p. 192).

that many will be prepared to give their favored distributive principles such minimal force. For as I have already suggested, if the overall patterns of distribution of welfare that we find once we take animal welfare into account were ones that held merely among *people*, those of us drawn to distributive principles would find the situation simply unacceptable. We would take ourselves to be under a pressing moral obligation to ameliorate the situation as best we could. So it isn't really true that our distributive principles are relatively weak, all things considered. Yet if, somehow, they seem to be relatively weak when we are dealing with *animal* welfare, this can only be because animals don't count, in precisely the same way people do, when it comes to applying the relevant distributive principles. That is, the distributive claims of people are stronger, somehow, than the distributive claims (if any) of animals. So the unitarians are wrong when they insist that the moral status of animals is precisely the same as that of people.

This is not to say that animals have no distributive claims whatsoever. For all that I have argued so far, there may well be circumstances in which it would indeed be appropriate to speak of distributive injustice or unfairness with regard to how a given group of animals is doing (either absolutely, or in comparison to others). My point here is simply that those who are independently drawn to demanding distributive obligations when the case concerns people and only people (as with, for example, the world in which men have everything, and women almost nothing), cannot suddenly pretend that the corresponding obligations would nonetheless be mild and untroubling if those very same distributive principles were then extended to animals in the way that the unitarian claims they should be.

Of course, one alternative still open to those sympathetic to unitarianism would be to reject the various distributive principles altogether. That would clearly solve the problem we've been discussing, since it is only when unitarianism is combined with one or more of those principles that it generates the particular obligations we've been considering. Accordingly, those unitarians who are prepared to reject the distributive principles are not themselves vulnerable to the objection to unitarianism that I've been discussing.

Nor should it be thought that a reply along these lines must be one that is made out of desperation, as though a position like this could only be undertaken precisely so as to avoid the objection. On the contrary, although it is true that most people do find themselves sympathetic to the sorts of distributive concerns that we've been considering, it is also true that this is not the case for everyone. Some will have denied the intrinsic significance of distribution right from the start—that is, even before any questions about distribution and animals were raised. Accordingly, I think it must be conceded that the retention of unitarianism remains (for the time being, at least) a coherent possibility—provided, of course, that one really is prepared to dismiss the various distributive principles altogether.

Speaking personally, I am not myself drawn to this particular solution, since I do find certain of our distributive principles compelling (though I won't try to defend any of them further here). But at any rate, assuming that one does indeed embrace a robust version of one of our distributive principles, what other positions remain open?

One might wonder whether a proper understanding of the *content* of the relevant distributive principles might allow one to embrace the importance of distribution while still avoiding the implausible claim that the welfare levels of animals are, on the whole, morally objectionable. Of course, any such proposal is likely to be specific to the particular principle in question. But it does seem to me that no such proposal will be both independently plausible and available to the unitarian. Here are a few examples to illustrate this thought.

First, then, a fan of the egalitarian principle might argue that one only has an egalitarian claim with regard to some particular good if one actually is capable of having (possessing, appreciating, deriving benefit from) a good of that particular kind. Thus, rather than holding out for equality with regard to overall well-being, one needs to demarcate individual "spheres" for distinct types of goods, and within a given sphere equality matters only if those who have less of the good in question could actually benefit from having more of that good. And so, for example, since mice cannot appreciate the visual arts, it doesn't matter that they have a lower overall level of well-being as a result of the absence of art in their lives. Similarly, even though dogs can have friendships, they cannot have friendships of the deep sort that people can have, so the fact that their lives are less valuable because of this doesn't result in any sort of egalitarian claim either. Generalizing, then, since the absence of goods like this (or the inevitable possession of what are, at best, less valuable forms of these goods) is the primary reason that animals have less valuable lives than people, the inequality that results from all of this is not, in fact, morally objectionable, once the egalitarian principle is properly understood.

A suggestion like this avoids the implausible claim that we must strive to correct the inequality between people and animals (or among animals), yet it does so in a way that appears to be consistent with a unitarian outlook. For the principle of equality, so construed, gets applied to people and animals in exactly the same way: if one has an *interest* in art, for example—if one can benefit from having it in one's life—then one has an egalitarian claim to art; if not, not.

Similarly for other goods. And if an evenhanded application of this principle results in animals being worse off than people, so be it. There would be no further distributive requirement arising from our egalitarian principle to correct the situation; the inequality would be real, but morally unobjectionable. Yet this wouldn't be due to any supposed differences in moral status. Rather, it would simply arise from uncontroversial differences in the natures of animals and people (with regard to which goods they can enjoy).

Unfortunately for the unitarian, however, the proposed interpretation of egalitarianism is unlikely to be one that the unitarian is actually prepared to endorse. To see this, it's helpful to consider the suggestion as it might apply to inequalities among *people*. Suppose, for example, that a blind person had a lower level of well-being than others, simply due to the fact that by virtue of her blindness she was incapable of enjoying the visual arts. I take it that our reaction to a case like this—a reaction that would be shared by unitarians—would not be to think that her resulting lower level of well-being was irrelevant to our egalitarian concern. On the contrary, we would presumably hold that, other things being equal, she had a claim to be compensated by being given more of some *other* sort of good.

Contrary to the proposal being considered, then, egalitarian claims are not in fact limited to particular "spheres" of goods. If someone cannot have (or benefit from) one particular type of good, then they may well have a claim to being given more good of a different type, one which they can indeed enjoy. And once we acknowledge this point, it undermines the suggestion being made on behalf of the unitarian that mice (and dogs, and bluebirds, and so forth) simply have no claim to being given more of the goods that *they* can enjoy.

Here's a different proposal, this one involving sufficientarianism. Sufficientarians believe that people have a special claim to be brought up to the designated welfare baseline. And as we have seen, if we accept the unitarian position this seems to entail that animals too would have a claim to be brought up to this very same level. But it might be suggested that a proper understanding of sufficientarianism can avoid this result. Perhaps what each individual is entitled to is not some particular absolute level of well-being (for example, 80 units of well-being on some appropriate scale), but rather a minimally *decent* life. And since a decent life for a person will involve a considerably higher level of welfare than a decent life for a dog, let alone a mouse, the sort of inequalities that we find (with animals far below the levels of well-being that would be acceptable for people) may not be troubling from a sufficientarian perspective after all.

Unfortunately for the unitarian, however, to interpret sufficientarianism in this manner is to introduce hierarchy of a sort that the unitarian cannot accept. For in relativizing the sufficientarian baseline in this way, we would be saying that people, for example, have a stronger moral claim to welfare, simply by virtue of the fact that they are, indeed, people, while mice, in contrast, have a weaker claim to welfare (or only have a claim to a lower level of welfare) simply by virtue of the fact that they are mice. As a result, an otherwise similar interest in having some pleasurable experience, say, might count for more if the pleasure would belong to a person rather than a mouse (if, for example, the mouse were already at its baseline, while the person—though far better off than the mouse— was not). Any such view would involve a hierarchy, with people having a higher moral status than that of animals, and some animals having a higher moral status than others. So relativizing the sufficientarian baseline is not a proposal of which the unitarian can avail himself.

The situation here is similar to one we have already considered in connection with desert. I noted earlier that a view according to which animals are said to be less deserving than people (or, alternatively, are said to deserve a lower level of well-being), might suffice to make the pattern of unequal welfare that we find between people and animals (and among animals) acceptable from the standpoint of a desert sensitive distributive principle. But it would do so at the cost of assigning a higher moral status to people than to animals. As such, whatever its plausibility, this idea cannot be embraced by the unitarian. Similarly, then, for the suggestion that the sufficientarian principle should assign different baselines to different types of animals. The proposal may well be a plausible one, but it is not available to the unitarian.

Here's one more example, this one again involving egalitarianism. Someone might suggest that equality matters not across species, but only *within* species. So it isn't morally objectionable that people are better off than snails or squirrels or eagles; the only objectionable forms of inequality would be inequality *among* squirrels, or among snails, or among eagles (and so on).

I think it must be conceded that if the egalitarian principle were interpreted in this way, it would avoid the implausible claim that there is something deeply morally objectionable about the fact that people are so much better off than animals. But that hardly makes the proposal an attractive one. It is, after all, difficult to see why squirrels should have egalitarian claims with regard to one another, and yet it should matter not at all from the egalitarian perspective how squirrels are doing in comparison to eagles. But be that as it may, regardless of whether the proposal is an attractive one or not, interpreted in this way the egalitarian principle would be one that the unitarian could not embrace. For if a squirrel has an egalitarian claim only with regard to how its welfare compares to that of other squirrels, while eagles have egalitarian claims only in comparison to other eagles, then clearly the status of squirrels differs from the status of eagles—since they have egalitarian claims with regard to different sorts of animals—contrary to the unitarian assertion that all those with moral standing have the very same moral status.

(In an interesting variant on the idea just considered, it might be suggested that inequality only matters among individuals who are in principle capable of attaining *comparable* levels of well-being.[10] This formulation avoids an appeal to species per se, though its practical effect would be largely the same. But here too the proposal is incompatible with unitarianism, since those individuals capable of higher levels of well-being would have different egalitarian claims than those individuals capable only of lower levels; so not all creatures with moral standing would have the very same moral status.)

Other proposals could be mentioned as well, but perhaps these suffice to make plausible the thought that no interpretation of our distributive principles will be both plausible in its own right and acceptable to the unitarian, while still avoiding the implausible claim that we must try to correct the pattern of welfare that obtains with regard to people and animals. Details will differ, of course, but the underlying reason is essentially the same as the one that we have already noted: The pattern of welfare that actually obtains among people and animals would be morally objectionable if it held merely among people, so any interpretation of the relevant distributive principle that suggests otherwise is implausible. Yet if that very same pattern of distribution is *not* to be considered morally objectionable when animals are involved (rather than people alone), then it must be that the distributive claims of animals differ from the distributive claims of people. And that's a conclusion that the unitarian cannot accept, since it would mean that the status of animals differs from that of people (and the status of some animals differs from that of others).

The problem for the unitarian, in effect, is this. Any distributive principle compatible with unitarianism must treat any given pattern of distribution the same way, morally speaking, regardless of whether the individuals involved are people or animals. Yet when we look at the pattern that actually obtains (counting both people and animals) we find ourselves drawn to quite different judgments, depending on whether we "fill in" that pattern with both people and animals, or with people alone. The very pattern that seems quite unobjectionable in the actual case, where animals are relatively badly off

---

[10] A view like this is mentioned in passing in McMahan, *The Ethics of Killing*, p. 161.

(both absolutely, and compared to people), would seem utterly unacceptable if it only involved people. So the two ways of filling in the pattern cannot plausibly be treated the same way after all. Yet any principle that accommodates these divergent judgments—as I think one must, if one is to have an intuitively acceptable position—will do so by assigning different moral statuses to animals and to people. And that means, of course, that it cannot be combined with unitarianism.

If I am right about all of this, what follows? Most obviously, we need to reject unitarianism since, as I have just argued, acceptable distributive principles will assign different distributive claims to people and to animals. But how exactly should this be done? What alternatives remain open to us?

The simplest approach, presumably, would be one that denies distributive claims to animals altogether. On this approach, whatever our favored distributive principles might be, they only apply to the distribution of the welfare of *persons*. Animal welfare simply isn't a concern of the relevant distributive principles at all. Obviously enough, if we accept a view of this sort, then there is nothing morally troubling about the fact that animals have the low levels of well-being that they do (both comparatively and in absolute terms), since the distribution of animal welfare isn't governed by any valid distributive principle in the first place. It isn't so much that the pattern of animal welfare that actually exists happens to be acceptable (according to the appropriate distributive principles), but rather, it is irrelevant. According to this view, questions about the legitimacy of a given distribution of welfare only arise in connection with the welfare of people.

It is worth explicitly noting the point that someone who accepts a view like this certainly needn't deny that animals have moral standing. The claim being made is not that animals don't count, nor that animal well-being isn't significant from the moral point of view, but only the more limited one that the pattern of distribution of animal well-being (both comparatively and in absolute terms) is not a moral concern. Accepting this view is thus perfectly compatible with holding, for example, that animal pain *is* a significant moral concern, that other things being equal one should take animal welfare into account when choosing among alternative outcomes, or even that one should avoid harming animals whenever one can. In short, accepting the view in question would still leave open the possibility of assigning a significant moral status to animals. One would only be claiming that the particular moral status had by animals is such that *distributive* claims of the sort that we have been discussing simply cannot arise for animals. Only people—and not animals—have a moral status that allows for claims to reasonable or just distribution.

Although this is a perfectly coherent possibility, it is not, as it happens, the particular view I find most attractive. Part of my reason for resisting it is that I cannot see good reason to accept the idea that questions of distribution don't arise at all when it comes to animal welfare. If distribution is a legitimate and significant moral concern when it comes to the welfare of people—and I take it that it is—then it is difficult to see why it should suddenly become utterly irrelevant when it comes to the welfare of animals. To be sure, animals may not have exactly the *same* claims with regard to distribution as people have. If, as I believe, animals have a lower moral status than people do, then it is reasonable to expect that their distributive claims will be weaker as well. But that's not the same as expecting animals to have no distributive claims whatsoever. Absent some special argument, we shouldn't expect distributive claims to disappear altogether when it comes to animals. Rather, we would expect the strength or scope of their distributive claims to be appropriately *reduced*—discounted, in some way, so as to take their lower status into account.

To be sure, someone sympathetic to the first approach might well insist that there is in fact a special argument that explains why concerns about distribution are irrelevant when it comes to animals. Plausibly, illegitimate distribution is a kind of *injustice*, and perhaps only creatures of the right sort are such as to fall within the particular sphere of morality where questions of justice and injustice can even arise. In particular, then, it might be suggested that one must be a person before one can legitimately lay claim to being treated justly, or complain about being treated unjustly. Animals, in contrast, lie completely outside the domain of justice. Accordingly, no distribution of animal welfare can be rejected simply by virtue of its *distributive* features, since no such distribution can be legitimately said to be unjust.[11]

Of course, an argument of this sort is no stronger than its central claim that animals fall completely outside of the domain of justice. I see no reason to believe this claim, though I will postpone discussion of it until later, when we turn to a view I will call "restricted deontology" (see 8.1). There is also reason to wonder whether it is really the case that distributive concerns can only be legitimate if construed as among the demands of *justice*, rather than as being part of some other corner of morality. But I will let this point pass as well. For now, let me simply register my belief that the right way to handle our distributive concerns is indeed one under which animals do fall under the principles in question—whether or not we think of these as part of an adequate account of

---

[11] Cf. McMahan, "Cognitive Disability, Misfortune, and Justice," pp. 29–31.

justice—so that animals too can make claims (or have claims made on their behalf) based on the relevant distributive features of a given outcome.

Thus the position which strikes me as most plausible is one according to which the relevant distributive principles also govern the distribution of animal welfare, and not merely the welfare of persons. But for all that, the distributive claims of animals are weaker, in a way we have yet to work out, than the corresponding claims of people. More particularly, the strength of a given animal's distributive claim depends in part on its individual moral status, with lower animals having proportionately weaker claims.

A suitable approach along these lines should allow us to recognize that animals too can make claims (at least in principle) with regard to unreasonable or unfair patterns of distribution, while at the same time allowing us to avoid the implausible position that the *current* pattern—with mice, say, so much worse off than people—is necessarily itself an unreasonable or unfair one. In sum, by introducing an appropriate form of hierarchy in moral status we can recognize the importance of distributive principles and recognize that animals too fall under these principles, while still avoiding the implausible implications that have led us to reject unitarianism.

4

Hierarchy and the Value of Outcomes

4.1 Hierarchy in Distribution

I have been arguing that if we are to retain a plausible view about distribution, while extending our moral theory so as to cover animals, we're going to need a theory that involves hierarchy. The basic idea behind such a theory is clear enough: distributive claims are sensitive to one's moral status, so that a lower status results in claims that are reduced or weakened in some appropriate way (relative to the claims of those with a higher status). And the accompanying thought, of course, is that within this general framework animals have a lower moral status than people do, while some animals, in turn, have a lower status than others.

As I say, the basic idea is clear enough. But the details remain to be worked out, and doing this isn't always a trivial matter. One central remaining task, of course, involves developing the relevant hierarchy. But beyond this, it turns out that it isn't always a straightforward matter to see exactly how the relevant adjustments in the various distributive principles are to be made. Unsurprisingly, the details depend on the particular distributive principle in question.

Let's start by considering the sufficientarian principle. As we have already noted, a plausible suggestion here is that the relevant baseline depends on what constitutes a *decent* life (or perhaps, alternatively, a *minimally* decent life) for the individual in question. Since a decent life for a dog, say, will presumably be at a considerably lower overall level than a decent life for a person, sufficientarianism so construed will ground a "weaker" claim for dogs than for people, in the sense that when priority is appropriately given to bringing individuals up to their respective baselines, the level of well-being to which the dog has a sufficientarian claim will be considerably lower than the level of well-being to which the person can lay claim. And similarly, of course, since a decent life for a bird or a fish will be at a lower level still, birds and fish will have even weaker sufficientarian claims than dogs.

To be sure, the notion of a "decent life," or a "minimally decent life," on which the current proposal turns, remains somewhat indeterminate. But the indeterminacy at work here isn't created by the introduction of hierarchy and relativized baselines; it is present even in those views that restrict themselves to granting sufficientarian claims to people. For even in these restricted versions, the baseline is tied to the idea of a life that is "good enough" or "adequate" for someone to live—that is to say, a decent life for a person—and it is difficult to say with any precision what exactly the idea of a "good enough" life comes to. Presumably it falls significantly short of the *best* life a person could conceivably live, while still being far above the *worst* such life as well. Yet even if we were to precisely fix the range of lives available to persons (or, perhaps, human persons), it isn't plausible to think that the notion of a *decent* life can be fixed through any simple mathematical expedient, like taking a life three fourths of the way up from the bottom of the range, or one third of the distance down from the top of the range to the neutral or zero point (a level of well-being neither better nor worse than nonexistence). Nor can we stipulate that the baseline is simply the *average* life actually lived by people (since it is easy enough to imagine worlds in which everyone has a more than decent life, or a less than decent one). We may get somewhat closer if we try, instead, to capture the idea in qualitative terms, perhaps saying that a good enough life is one in which the person's basic needs are reasonably met. But things remain imprecise even here, since the relevant notion of "need" (not to mention "reasonably meeting" those needs) remains difficult to pin down. (After all, it isn't as though a life of bare subsistence counts as good enough.)

So the notion of a (minimally) decent life remains a difficult one to make precise. But for all that, we do seem capable of judging certain human lives as good enough, others as better than that, and still others as falling short of any level reasonably considered adequate for a person. And it seems clear that comparable judgments can be made about animals as well. We have a tolerably good sense of what a decent life for a dog comes to, for example—and we know as well that it falls far below the kind of life that would constitute a decent life for a person. And presumably a decent life for a cow, say, would be at a lower level still; all the more so for snakes and fish. To be sure, speaking personally I know far too little about the kinds of lives available to most animals—very much including cows, snakes, and fish—to render precise judgments here with much confidence. But many others know far more than I do, and in principle, at least, it would seem possible to arrive at appropriate baselines for different types of animals.

In fixing these baselines, what is it that makes it true that one kind of animal (a rabbit, say, or a fish) has a baseline that is lower than that had by another (a dog, or an elephant)? Why is it that an adequate life for an animal of one sort is different from an adequate life for an animal of another sort? Why is a decent life for a person so much higher in quality than a decent life for an animal? The answer, clearly, has to do with the psychological capacities of the different types of individuals. Animals differ from one another, and people differ from animals, in terms of the sophistication and complexity of their respective psychologies, with huge differences in terms of the kinds of cognitive processing that are possible, and the types and depths of emotional responses that are available to them. These differences underlie the radically different types of lives that are available to animals and to people, and help make it clear that a decent or good enough life for one sort of creature will be rather different from (and differ in value from) a decent or good enough life for a quite different sort of creature.

Armed with relativized baselines of the sort I've been describing, the sufficientarian avoids a blanket condemnation of the distributive fact that fish live lives that are significantly worse than those lived by people. Yes, fish have less valuable lives than people do, but for all that, those lives may still constitute decent lives for *fish*. If so, then despite being worse off than people are—and despite having lives that would never be considered even minimally adequate for a person—no distributive claim to the effect that priority must be given to improving the lot of fish will yet follow. Similarly, of course, for other animals. In this way, then, the sufficientarian who accepts hierarchy can avoid the implausible implications that plagued the unitarian.

At the same time, however, it should be noted that a view of this sort does not exclude animals from ever making distributive claims of any sort. Although the broad generalizations ("fish have it so much worse than people do!") will not be morally objectionable, it remains the case that specific individual animals may still fall short of their respective baselines. If some particular mouse, for example, has a life that cannot be said to be a minimally decent one—not even for a mouse—then perhaps we should indeed prioritize doing what we can to bring that mouse's level of well-being up somewhat.

No doubt, some will find even this more modest conclusion implausible. If so, they may prefer the more radical hierarchical view mentioned in the previous chapter (in 3.3), according to which animals are excluded from having any distributive claims at all. Personally, however, I find the more moderate position more congenial. For if animals count (and surely they do), and if distribution matters (as I think it must), then it is difficult to see why animals could never conceivably be in a position to make a distributive claim.

It should be noted, however, that for various reasons the cumulative force of such claims is likely to be comparatively modest. First of all, and most importantly, only those animals with lives that fall below their respective baselines will have complaints from the standpoint of sufficientarianism. So even if *all* mice were worse off than people, that fact would simply be irrelevant; only those mice with lives that are unacceptable *for a mouse* would have any sort of sufficientarian claim to aid. Second, even those mice that do have legitimate complaints from the standpoint of sufficientarianism will only have a claim to be brought up to the baseline level for *mice*—not to the level that would constitute a decent life for a person! So the distributive claim, even when it exists, will be for less. (And if the sufficientarian principle is stated in terms of a *minimally* decent life—rather than a decent life, simpliciter—the relevant baselines will be that much lower, with correspondingly fewer claims, and with claims for that much less.) Finally, it is important to bear in mind that a plausible version of sufficientarianism will tell us to give the greatest priority to those who fall the farthest from their respective baselines. Since it seems likely that when people fall short of their baseline this will frequently be by a greater amount than when mice fall short of theirs, hierarchical sufficientarianism is likely to instruct us to give greater priority to aiding people who fall short, rather than to mice (or other animals).

In sum, under hierarchical sufficientarianism animals have claims to a reasonable distribution of well-being, but the obligations emerging from such demands may end up being rather limited. Except perhaps for rather unusual cases, it may turn out that the distributive claims of animals are generally not especially pressing ones.

Turning next to distributive principles based on desert, recall that according to such views inequalities are acceptable if they are deserved. Consequently, if the claim can be made out that people are more deserving than, say, wolves, and wolves than fish, then the kinds of inequalities that actually exist among animals, and between animals and people, may not be morally objectionable.

Can claims of this sort be defended? At first glance, the prospects of doing this successfully may not seem particularly promising, since it isn't clear whether animals can be appropriately evaluated (as we do evaluate people, when assessing what they deserve) in terms of their moral and immoral deeds, or their virtuous and vicious motives. But further reflection suggests that an approach like this may be more plausible than we might initially think.

The issues are complicated, and I won't do more than sketch the basic thought here, but consider the fact that what a given person deserves is often thought to be a function not merely of their particular thoughts and deeds, but also—behind or underneath all of this—of the very fact that they are indeed a *person*. That is, one common view concerning desert holds that there is a kind of initial or baseline level of well-being that one deserves simply by virtue of the fact that one is a person. To be sure, one's moral track record may modify what it is that one deserves overall, raising or lowering the deserved level of well-being, for example; but the baseline against which such modifications take place is set by the very fact that one is a person.

Now the fact is, there are several aspects of what one deserves that may be affected in this way by the fact that one is a person. As I've just suggested, being a person may give you an initial claim to some given level of well-being (even though your actions and motives may raise or lower what you deserve *overall*). But beyond this, being a person may also set a lower bound to what you can deserve, such that no person can deserve to be worse off than that. And there are, as it happens, still other ways in which how generally deserving you are may be affected, at least in part, by being a person. (It is also conceivable that being a person affects as well the *amount* of good that is done when you get what you deserve.) But spelling all of this out would be a complicated under-taking, and lead us rather far afield. So for simplicity I will limit our discussion to the idea that there is some particular level of well-being that you initially deserve by virtue of being a person.[1]

But if a person can lay claim to deserving some initial (or baseline) level of well-being by virtue of being a *person*, then it doesn't seem implausible to sug-gest that a dog may also lay claim to deserving some initial or baseline level of well-being by virtue of being a *dog*, and a rabbit to some baseline level by virtue of being a rabbit. At the same time, it may also be plausible to suggest that the absolute level of well-being that one will (initially) deserve by virtue of being a person will be higher than the level deserved by virtue of being a dog, which in turn is higher than that deserved by virtue of being a rabbit. And so on and so forth, for the various other kinds of animals.

What is the precise level of welfare that any given animal or person initially deserves? A natural enough proposal to make at this point is that these will be the same levels as (or, at least, closely related to) the sufficientarian baselines that we have already considered. That is, what a rabbit deserves is a decent life for a rabbit, while a dog deserves something higher, a decent life for a dog, and a person deserves something higher still, a decent life for a person. To be sure, one need not fix the particular initially deserved levels of well-being in just this

---

[1] I examine some of the different ways in which what one deserves can vary in *The Geometry of Desert*. However, that discussion focuses solely on desert for people, and doesn't explore questions of animals and desert at all. Indeed, I know of no sustained discussion of the latter topic.

way, but I suspect that many will find some proposal along these lines an intuitively attractive one.

Of course, even if we do accept this proposal, there remains the further question of whether individual animals can alter the level of welfare that they deserve *all things considered* from the baseline level that is initially deserved. People presumably can do this, but it remains controversial whether the same is true for animals. I am inclined to think so (since it seems to me that at least some animals can, like people, have virtuous or vicious motives), but I won't pursue the matter here. For our purposes it suffices to note that whether or not animals can *alter* what they deserve—away from the "initial" baseline—it does seem possible to maintain that animals deserve less than people do (on the whole), with higher animals deserving more than lower animals. So here too, a suitable hierarchical view can recognize the distributive claims of animals, without automatically condemning the distributive disparities that exist among animals, or between animals and people.

A slightly different approach suggests itself with regard to the *priority* view. The idea here, recall, is that the amount of good done by increasing some individual's level of well-being a given amount depends on how well off or badly off the individual in question actually is. And here too, it seems plausible to suggest that something similar should hold for animals. That is to say, unit for unit it does more good to increase the welfare of a mouse (or a squirrel, or a chicken) the worse off the mouse (or squirrel or chicken) is. But at the same time, if we are to avoid the implausible claim that absolute priority is to be given to aiding mice and squirrels and chickens rather than people—given that animals are so much worse off than people—we need to somehow relativize these prioritarian claims. That is, in assessing how "badly off" a given animal is, this cannot be done in terms of the absolute level of well-being that the animal is at. Rather, the assessment has to be done in such a way as to take into account the fact that it is acceptable for animals to have lives at lower levels of welfare. Morally speaking, it is legitimate for animals to be doing worse than people; it is only when they are doing *disproportionately* worse than that, that prioritarian claims are generated.

In short, in assessing how badly off an individual is for the purposes of determining the relative priority of aiding them, we need to "recalculate" their level of welfare in a way that appropriately takes into account the higher or lower status of the individual in question. It is only this *status adjusted level of well-being* that should play a role in determining one's prioritarian claims.

There are different ways to accommodate this thought, but perhaps the simplest approach works like this. We start with a relative ranking of the moral statuses of different types of creatures, arbitrarily assigning some convenient number to one of these statuses, and then fixing appropriate numbers to each other status in such a way as to reflect its comparative standing. If, for example, we assign 100 to the status that goes with being a person, then perhaps dogs will have a status of 30 or 40, and mice 2 or 3. Equivalently, we could set the status of a person at 1, and then give dogs a status of 0.3 or 0.4, with mice at 0.02 or 0.03. (In the examples that follow I adopt the latter numbering system.)

Of course, I offer these numbers merely for the sake of illustration; I don't mean to defend here any precise view about the relative status of dogs or mice compared to people. That would require a greater knowledge of dogs and mice (and other animals) than I possess. But in fixing the relevant numbers we will doubtless be guided here—as we were earlier with the other distributive principles—by our assessment of the differing psychological capacities of the various animals, and by the comparative value of the different lives that animals have available to them. So animals with ever simpler psychologies will have lower and lower statuses, represented by numbers approaching zero.

Now, in assessing how badly off an animal is (for the purpose of prioritarian calculations), we want to take its moral status into account, so that the same absolute level of well-being will count as "less bad" for a creature with a lower status than it would for a creature with a higher status. In terms of the jargon just introduced, we want to find a suitable way to calculate the animal's status adjusted welfare, where, other things being equal, the lower your status the less badly off you are from the standpoint of the prioritarian principle.

The most straightforward proposal for doing this tells us to calculate the adjusted level of well-being as follows: simply divide the *absolute* level of well-being by the number representing the individual's *status*. This yields the desired result that for any given level of well-being, the lower one's status, the *higher* one's *status adjusted* well-being. Let's call this method of calculating status adjusted welfare *simple division*.

To illustrate this approach at work, suppose that some person's level of well-being is 80 (on some appropriate scale for measuring welfare), while a dog is at 36. And imagine that we can either raise the dog's well-being or the person's well-being by exactly one unit, but we can't do both. At first glance it might seem that prioritarianism will direct us to aid the dog, since it is worse off—so an extra unit of well-being should do more good, morally speaking, when given to the dog. But that initial judgment fails to take status into account, something we must do before deciding whose prioritarian claims are stronger. So suppose, instead, that we use simple division to find the relevant adjusted levels. Upon dividing each individual's absolute level of well-being by their respective status we find that it is actually the *person* who has the stronger claim to priority, not the dog. (80/1 yields 80 as the status adjusted level for the person; while 36/0.4 yields 90 as the status adjusted level for the dog.) In short, introducing hierarchy allows the prioritarian to say that more good will actually be done by aiding the person (in this particular example) than by aiding the dog, despite the dog's lower absolute level of welfare.

Of course, without further, detailed information about the precise ways in which the priority principle gives extra weight to lower levels of (status adjusted) well-being, we cannot say how *much* more good will be done by increasing the person's welfare rather than the dog's. Unsurprisingly, prioritarians differ among themselves about the exact shape of the weighting function. The point here is simply to note that prioritarian views can be extended to animals, without it trivially following that animals have stronger claims to greater priority by virtue of their having lower absolute levels of well-being. Here too, then, distributive claims can be granted to animals, without it automatically following that we should devote ourselves to raising the welfare of animals rather than people—despite the vast disparities in welfare that actually obtain between animals and people.

A similar approach seems promising for the egalitarian principle as well. Here, of course, the idea is not the noncomparative prioritarian one, that an increase in well-being does more good the worse off the individual who receives it, but the *comparative* one, that it is morally objectionable if some are worse off than others. As we have seen, if this idea is extended to animals without taking differences in status into account, it leads to the implausible conclusion that it is morally objectionable that animals are so much worse off than people are and that we have a significant obligation to do what we can to correct this situation. But here, too, we can avoid this implication while still allowing animals to have egalitarian claims, if we find a suitable way of adjusting for status, so that a creature with a lower status has to be disproportionately worse off before an egalitarian claim gets generated. And the obvious proposal to make at this point is that what we need to equalize are not *absolute* levels of well-being, but rather *status adjusted* levels of well-being, where status adjusted welfare is again calculated by means of simple division.[2]

Suppose, then, once again, that the person's level of well-being is 80, but this time imagine that the dog's level is 32. Since the person is obviously better off than the dog, at first glance it might seem that an egalitarian must identify the situation as a morally objectionable one, something we should try to correct

---

[2] A proposal like this is adopted as a "working assumption" in Vallentyne, "Of Mice and Men," p. 426.

(perhaps by moving resources from the person to the dog, bringing their two levels of well-being closer together). But here, too, this fails to take status into account, something that must be done before deciding whether a given distribution constitutes a morally relevant form of inequality. So we need to recalculate, using simple division. And when we do this, dividing each individual's absolute level of well-being by their moral status, we find that the adjusted levels of well-being are actually the same. (The person's status adjusted well-being is still 80/1, or 80. The dog's is 32/0.4, which is also 80.) So the dog does not actually have an egalitarian claim after all. Indeed, if we return to the earlier example, where the dog's absolute level of well-being is a bit higher, at 36, we find that it is actually the person that has an egalitarian claim now, not the dog (since the dog's status adjusted level of welfare will now be 36/0.4 = 90, which is, of course, greater than the person's status adjusted level of 80). And what all of this means, of course, is that by taking differences in status properly into account, we can once again extend distributive claims to animals, without it trivially following that we have an obligation to reduce the disparities in welfare that currently exist between people and animals (or among animals themselves).

4.2 Problems for Priority

I hope I have said enough to render plausible the claim that suitably revised (or perhaps reinterpreted) the various distributive principles can be extended to cover animals, while at the same time avoiding the implausible implications that would follow if we tried to do this within a unitarian framework. The key, of course, is to recognize the existence of a hierarchy of moral statuses, and to understand the distributive principles in such a way as to take these differences in status into account. When this is done properly we find ourselves in a position where we can recognize the vast differences in welfare that exist among animals and between animals and people, without necessarily viewing these differences as morally problematic or objectionable. Once relevant differences in status are taken into account, the distributive claims of animals—despite initially appearing widespread and pressing—may actually turn out to be minimal or nonexistent.

In the previous section I sketched some promising ways of introducing hierarchy into several familiar distributive principles. But I would not want to claim that it is a trivial matter to work out the details of any of these proposals, and in some cases, at least, I think it fair to say that difficult questions remain unresolved. It may turn out that a suitable version of any given principle will need to be developed along rather different lines from the ones we've just considered. Although I am confident that an adequate moral theory will be a hierarchical one, I am also confident that extending our various moral principles—not just the distributive ones, but others as well—so as to take hierarchy into account will often turn out to be a difficult and complicated undertaking. After all, working out the details of any given moral principle is almost always a puzzling and elusive matter; I certainly see no reason to think it should be any less so when the details happen to concern animals and status.

Since I do think it important for us to recognize that extending ethics to animals is a more complicated undertaking than we might initially realize, I want to quickly mention a few problems that arise for one of the proposals that I introduced in the last section. Recall, however, that my goal in this book is not at all to present a finished account of animal ethics, only to make the case for the importance of hierarchy. Consequently, having noted the problems, I won't try to resolve them. That is work for another occasion. Nor will I pause to point out corresponding difficulties for the other principles. A single illustration should suffice.[3]

Suppose, then, that we take a closer look at the priority principle. I noted the plausibility of suggesting that in determining whose well-being is such that a unit increase counts for more, what we need to attend to is not the absolute level of well-being, but rather the status adjusted one; and I suggested as well that we might arrive at a proper measure of status adjusted welfare through simple division—dividing one's absolute level of well-being by (a suitable numerical representation of) one's status.

That approach gives plausible answers for a wide range of cases. More particularly, it gives plausible answers so long as the relevant levels of well-being are all positive and none of them are too close to zero. Unfortunately, if one or another of these conditions isn't met then simple division quickly leads to results that are either troubling or altogether unacceptable.

Consider, for example, a case involving negative levels of well-being (where the lives lived are worse than not existing at all). Imagine, as before, that a person's status is 1, while a dog's is 0.4, and imagine that both are at the *same* negative level of well-being, say, −10. Dividing this absolute level by their respective statuses, we find that the dog's status adjusted welfare is −10/0.4, which comes to −25, while the person's status adjusted welfare is −10/1, which comes to −10. According to the proposal under consideration, therefore,

---

[3] Several different proposals for adjusting distributive principles in light of status are critically examined by Vallentyne in "Of Mice and Men."

where status adjusted welfare is calculated by means of simple division, the dog has a lower status adjusted level of well-being. This implies that it is the dog that should have priority if we can aid either one of the two (but only one of them) by a few units of well-being. Intuitively, however, that's the wrong answer. Given the higher moral status of the person as compared to the dog, and given that both are at the same absolute level of well-being, it is the person rather than the dog who should have the stronger claim from the prioritarian perspective.

Worse still, imagine that the dog is at -10, but the person is actually at -15. Here it is all the more obvious that a suitable version of the priority view will give greater priority to aiding the person, yet here too the proposal as it currently stands is at odds with this judgment. (The dog's status adjusted welfare remains -25, while the person's is $-15/1$, which comes to -15; so the person's adjusted welfare remains higher than the dog's.)

Clearly, then, we need to modify our approach to calculating status adjusted welfare, so as to handle cases like this involving negative levels of well-being. Simple division can't possibly be the right approach all the way across the board.

It isn't impossible to come up with a reasonable suggestion for cases like this. Intuitively, a negative level of well-being counts less (unit for unit), when the individual in question has a lower status. Dividing by status in such cases gets this exactly backwards, with lower status making for an adjusted level that is lower still. Perhaps then in such cases we should *multiply* by status, rather than dividing.[4] That will make the negative welfare of individuals with lower status count for proportionately less, and gives the intuitively appropriate answers in our two cases. (When the dog and the person are both at -10, for example, the dog's adjusted welfare will be $-10 \times 0.4 = -4$, while the person's adjusted welfare will be $-10 \times 1 = -10$. Since the person has a lower status adjusted level of well-being, she will have the stronger prioritarian claim. And if the person were instead at -15, her status adjusted welfare would now be -15 (since $-15 \times 1 = -15$), which would of course give her an even stronger prioritarian claim as compared to the dog's.)

Unfortunately, while this modification of the proposal helps, it doesn't yet handle all the problematic cases. Suppose the dog and the person are both at *zero* (that is, at the level of welfare where life is neither worth living, nor worse than nonexistence). Intuitively, the person should have the stronger prioritarian claim here, given her higher status. But simple division won't yield this

---

[4] Vallentyne notices the problem with simple division for negative levels of welfare, and suggests this correction ("Of Mice and Men," p. 426, note 14).

answer, since if we divide absolute level of welfare by status, we find that both the dog and the person have the very same status adjusted level of welfare (since both 0/1 and 0/0.4 equal 0). Nor are we any better off if we extend the recent modification (multiplication, rather than division) to cover this case as well, for here too both the person and the dog end up with the same status adjusted level (since an absolute level of 0 yields the same adjusted level of 0 as well, regardless of whether we multiply it by 1 or 0.4).

Clearly, we will need yet another modification to our method of calculation if our priority principle is to properly handle cases like this. But it isn't at all obvious what the appropriate modification should look like.

The problem of how to handle a zero welfare level is especially pressing given the likelihood that there are animals that will frequently be at this level. (After all, animals with a very low maximum possible level of welfare probably hit or cross the zero level relatively often, since it takes so very little by way of bad luck for them to be pushed down to the zero point or beyond.) But even if we restrict ourselves to *positive* levels of well-being, there will still be problems that arise in connection with animals that have extremely low limits to how well off they can be.

Imagine an animal that can have no greater a level of well-being than a tiny fraction of the level of well-being that can be had by a person—perhaps a ten thousandth as much, or even less. If, as we've been assuming, a good human life is 100 on a suitable scale of welfare, then we are imagining an animal that can have no greater welfare than 0.01 or less. What kind of animal would that be? Perhaps a fly. Let us suppose that a fly's level of well-being can be as high as 0.01, though no higher. In point of fact, I suspect that this is actually an overly generous estimate of the quality of life that flies can attain as compared to what people can attain,[5] but for the sake of concreteness let us suppose that a fly can indeed attain a life as high as 0.01. (If you think that insects lack moral standing altogether, just substitute some other animal with standing but a maximal level of well-being of 0.01. And if you agree with me that some animals—maybe flies, maybe something else—will have even lower maximum levels of well-being than 0.01, then note that using an even lower maximum would simply strengthen the argument that follows.)

Next, let's ask ourselves what sort of status a creature like this is likely to have. Presumably, any creature so tremendously limited in terms of the

---

[5] The average human life span is about 79 years, or more than 28,000 days. Divided by ten thousand that's still more than 2.8 days. If, like me, you wouldn't give up even a *single* day as a person for an entire extra lifetime as a fly, then you agree that the welfare to be had within a fly's life is less than one ten thousandth the welfare to be found in a person's life.

well-being that it can acquire will be correspondingly limited in terms of the sophistication and complexity of its psychological capacities as well. So if, as I have suggested, an individual's status is largely proportional to the level of its psychological capacities, then our creature will also have to possess a correspondingly low moral status. Therefore, if we continue to set the status of a person at 1, the status of our fly will be something like 0.0001.

Finally, suppose that the fly is a *very* small amount worse off than the maximal level of well-being that it can attain. Instead of being at its upper limit, perhaps it is five thousandths of a unit of well-being worse off than that—an almost negligible difference. And now compare the prioritarian claims of this fly to those of a *person*, who is, let us imagine, almost *50* units of well-being worse off than the 100 that would constitute a good life for a human.

Given all of these stipulations, who has the greater prioritarian claim? The fly is 0.005 worse than its maximum of 0.01, which is to say it is at an absolute level of well-being of 0.005. Its status, we are supposing, is 0.0001. So if we use simple division to calculate status adjusted welfare, its adjusted well-being is 0.005/0.0001, which comes to 50. If the person's level of well-being is, say, 51, then simple division yields a status adjusted level of well-being of 51/1, which of course comes to 51. In short, the status adjusted well-being of the fly turns out to be lower than that of the person.

But think about what this means. Even though the fly is only negligibly worse off than the best life it can have, while the person is *very* far below the level of a good *human* life, it is nonetheless the fly who has the greater prioritarian claim to aid! That seems to me to constitute yet another unacceptable implication of the proposal to calculate status adjusted welfare in terms of simple division. Yet this is a case where all the welfare levels are positive.[6]

The problem arises, of course, from the fact that the fly's level of well-being is so very low in absolute terms. So even though the number we arrive at (when calculating its status adjusted welfare) is significantly higher once we divide the fly's very low absolute level of well-being by its extremely low status, nonetheless, for all that, the resulting adjusted welfare is very low. Thus, if we calculate status adjusted welfare using simple division, the fly retains a huge prioritarian claim as compared to the person. But the thought that a person would have to be at a lower level of well-being than 50 before she had a stronger prioritarian claim than the fly is just not a credible one. So here too simple division yields unacceptable results.

---

[6] I take this argument to be a variant of one given by Vallentyne in "Of Mice and Men," at pp. 414–15.

I need hardly point out that the very reason we originally introduced status sensitivity into our prioritarian principle was precisely so as to block the thought that animals have larger prioritarian claims by virtue of their strikingly lower levels of well-being. But it seems that we have not yet managed to find a way to take account of status properly. Arguably, simple division provides an adequate way of calculating status adjusted welfare for those animals with reasonably high levels of well-being. But as we have now seen, it certainly doesn't provide an adequate approach for animals with very low levels of welfare. Accordingly, considerably more work will need to be done before we can confidently claim to have a suitable method of extending the priority principle so that it covers animals as well as people.

(I perhaps should note, in passing, that still further difficulties would arise for the proposal to calculate status adjusted welfare through simple division if statuses could be negative or zero. But since it is plausible to hold that any creature with moral standing will have a moral status appropriately represented by a *positive* number, I won't pause to spell out the details.)

It is certainly possible that an appropriate way of calculating status adjusted welfare will retain the use of simple division at its core. Alternatively, it might be that an altogether different approach will be required. Let me quickly mention one such alternative, if only to make clear that here, too, finding an adequate version would be a nontrivial undertaking.

Some might think that a preferable way to calculate who has the stronger prioritarian claim will appeal to the *range* of well-being available to the given individual. Instead of considering where an individual's well-being falls in absolute terms, perhaps we should ask where it falls within the range of possible levels of well-being that are, in principle, available to him. Given the plausible thought that individuals with higher status will have a greater highest possible level of well-being (as well as, perhaps, a lower bottom), by seeing where the individual's actual well-being falls *relative to* his range of possible levels, we will in effect be generating a measure of well-being that is relativized to status. We can then use this alternative method to decide who has the greater claim to priority; the worse one is doing relative to one's respective range, the greater one's prioritarian claim.

The basic idea being proposed here—a range-relativized method of calculating status adjusted welfare—seems like a promising enough approach. But here too it must be admitted that the details are obscure, and many initial attempts prove unacceptable. Since my immediate goal is simply to establish this point, nothing more, let me just note a few initially attractive, but ultimately unsuccessful, proposals.

First, then, suppose it is suggested that the right way to calculate someone's status adjusted welfare is to look to see how many units of well-being they are shy of the upper limit of their range. Arguably, the individual who is the furthest down from their respective maximum is the one who has the largest prioritarian claim.

Unfortunately, any approach as straightforward as this has unacceptable implications. To see this, let us suppose that the range of lives available to humans goes from +200 at the top to −200 at the bottom. (That seems a reasonable enough suggestion, if—as we have assumed—a good life for a human is placed at 100.) In contrast, as we can also suppose, a mouse's range may only go from +4 to −4. Next, imagine that some person has an incredibly good life, at +192. That would be a mere 8 units shy of the best life a human could possibly have (perhaps a better life than any human has ever yet attained). And compare this to a mouse who is near the very *bottom* of the range of lives available to it, at −3.

Intuitively, in a case like this it is the mouse who should count as being worse off for the purposes of prioritarian claims. Indeed, if animals are not to be excluded from the priority principle altogether, then presumably cases like the one just described—where the animal is not only worse off in absolute terms, but is also near the very bottom of its available range with a life not worth living, while the person is near the very *top* of hers—should be among those where the animal has a stronger prioritarian claim to aid. But this is not at all the result we have if we accept the current proposal to measure adjusted welfare in terms of the units of well-being that a given individual falls short of the very top of their available range. For in our example the mouse, at −3, is a mere 7 units down from the top of its range (+4), while—as we have already noted—the person is fully 8 units of well-being down from the top of *her* range. So on the "top down" approach, as we might call it, it is the person who has the stronger prioritarian claim here, not the mouse. And that claim seems quite implausible.[7]

Happily, we can have a more plausible position with regard to this example if instead of adopting a top down approach, we take a "bottom up" approach to calculating status adjusted welfare. On this approach, instead of looking to see how far down the given individual is from the top of his range, we measure how far *up* he is, from the *bottom* of his range. The individual who is less far up has the greater prioritarian claim. This gives the intuitively right answer in our example—that it is the mouse rather than the person who has the stronger

⁷ Cf. Vallentyne, "Of Mice and Men," p. 416.

claim to priority—since the mouse is a mere 1 unit up from the bottom of its range (−4), while the person is an incredible 392 units up from the bottom of *her* range (−200).

Unfortunately, the bottom up approach runs afoul of a different sort of example. This time, imagine that it is the mouse who is better off, with a welfare level near the top of *its* range—say, +3.9—while the person is quite near the very bottom of her range, at −190! Here, I take it, it is obvious that a plausible prioritarian principle will say that now it is the person who has the greater claim to priority, since the mouse is not only better off than the person, but almost at the top of its range, while the person is near the bottom of hers. Yet the bottom up approach cannot accommodate this judgment, since the person is in fact a full 10 units up from the bottom of her range, while the mouse is only 7.9 units up from the bottom of *its* range. Since we get the wrong answer if we measure status adjusted welfare in this bottom up manner, we still don't have an acceptable way to relativize to the given individual's range.

It might be suggested, of course, that the problems we have identified arise not from the basic idea of relativizing to the individual's range, but from the further decision to measure distance (whether from the top or from the bottom), in terms of units, rather than percentages. That is, perhaps what we should do is ask which individual is a smaller *percentage* of the way up from the bottom of their range. Arguably, that's the individual with the greater prioritarian claim.

An approach of this sort avoids both of the problems I've already mentioned. In the first case, where the mouse is at −3 while the person is at +192, it is clearly the mouse who is a smaller percentage of the way up from the bottom of its range: 12.5% for the mouse, as compared to 98% for the person. So the percentage approach appropriately identifies the mouse as having the larger prioritarian claim. And in the second case, where the mouse is at +3.9 while the person is at −190, it is the person who is a smaller percentage of the way up from the bottom: 2.5% for the person, as compared to 98.75% for the mouse. So the percentage approach correctly identifies the person as the one with the larger prioritarian claim in our second example. So far, then, so good.

Nonetheless, the percentage approach faces its own problems. Up to this point our examples have all involved ranges that are "symmetrical" in the sense that the top of the range is as far above the zero point as the bottom of the range is below it. For example, we have assumed that the mouse's range goes from +4 to −4, while the range for humans goes from +200 to −200. But it isn't at all obvious that all animals will have ranges that are symmetrical in this way. It is easy to believe that some may be capable of going much further above the zero point than they can go below it—with a range, for example, of +20 to −5—while other animals may be capable of going much further *below* the zero point than they can go above it. (Of course, for still other animals a symmetrical range may well be the correct one.) Unfortunately, however, when the percentage approach is applied to such asymmetrical ranges it can easily generate unacceptable results.

Suppose that one sort of animal has an asymmetrical range that goes from +20 to −80, while a second sort has a symmetrical range that goes from +20 to −20. And imagine that the first animal is at −5, while the second is at +8. If we use percentages to calculate status adjusted welfare we are forced to say that despite initial appearances it is actually the second animal that has the greater prioritarian claim to aid, since the first animal is fully 75% of the way up from the bottom of its range, while the second animal is only 70% of the way up. But it seems quite unacceptable to suggest that the first animal is "better off" from the perspective of a prioritarian principle appropriately relativized to status. The first animal, after all, is worse off in absolute terms, and no reason has been given to assume that it has a lower moral status than the second. Indeed, it might well have a *higher* moral status than the second (perhaps it has more sophisticated psychological capacities, which make it more vulnerable to significant forms of suffering). Since it is plausible to think that it is the first animal, rather than the second, that has the greater prioritarian claim, it turns out that the percentage approach is also flawed. So we still don't have an appropriate way to relativize prioritarian claims to the given individual's range.

I want to be clear. In noting these various difficulties for the attempt to relativize prioritarian claims to one's range, I do not at all mean to be suggesting that no such approach can succeed. Until considerably more work is done constructing and evaluating views of this sort, any such judgment would be premature at best, and unwarranted. Similarly, when rehearsing the problems for an approach based instead on simple division, I did not mean to be making any suggestion at all with regard to whether or not a view along this basic line can be successfully developed. Perhaps with sufficient effort and ingenuity adequate versions of one or the other of these two approaches can be worked out. Or perhaps we will need to go in some other direction altogether, before arriving at a suitable way of calculating status adjusted welfare. We just don't know yet.

My point, rather, is the more limited one, that even once we decide that prioritarianism should be extended so as to cover animals and not just people, and even once we agree that the only acceptable way to do this involves finding a version of the principle that takes into account differences in moral status, a tremendous amount remains to be done. Working out the details of a suitable version of the principle is not at all a trivial undertaking.

The same thing is true, more generally, for our other distributive principles as well. Here too, I think, suitable versions will have to cover animals and not just people—and the right way to do this will inevitably involve taking proper account of differences in status. But to recognize all of this is not yet to have a detailed understanding of how, precisely, any given distributive principle will best take status into account. For the time being, at least, correctly extending our distributive principles so as to cover animals remains a complex and open challenge.

4.3 Well-Being

I have argued that in order to properly extend distributive principles we will need to recognize that not all individuals with moral standing have the very same moral status. However, as I have also noted, not everyone accepts distributive principles of the sort that we have been discussing. Some think that when assessing the goodness of an outcome we need only attend to the (total) amount of well-being to be found within that outcome, questions about the distribution of the well-being having no direct bearing on the outcome's value.

People who are skeptical about distributive principles might wonder whether they too have reason to embrace a hierarchical approach to moral status. So suppose we put aside questions about distribution, and simply focus on the value of well-being itself. Virtually everyone agrees that an outcome is better, other things being equal, if it contains a greater amount of well-being. So what then should we say about the connection, if any, between status and the value of well-being? Might status make a difference even here? Or can we agree, at least, that when it comes to the value of well-being in and of itself, status is irrelevant?

Of course, those who believe in the significance of distribution will think that things are not always equal, that sometimes one outcome is a better one, despite having a smaller total amount of well-being, because the well-being is distributed in a more fair or just fashion. But what we are here asking about is the value of well-being in its own right, questions about distribution aside. And what we want to know is this: does status make a difference to the value of well-being itself?

Presumably, regardless of what one thinks about status and distribution, one might accept a unitarian position with regard to the value of *well-being*. That is, one might hold that in assessing the contribution to the goodness of an outcome made by an increase in welfare for a given individual, it makes no difference *whose* well-being we are talking about. On this view, an extra unit of well-being has the same moral significance—makes the same contribution to the value of the outcome—regardless of the status of the individual.

But it might be that we should reject unitarianism here as well. Perhaps the contribution that an increase in welfare makes to the goodness of an outcome depends in part on the status of the individual whose welfare it is. More particularly, perhaps a given increase in welfare makes a larger addition to the goodness of the outcome when the welfare is going to an individual with a higher, rather than a lower, moral status. On this alternative view, status makes a difference to the *value* of well-being.

Of course, posing the issue this way—asking whether status makes a difference to the value of well-being—is a bit contentious. Those who deny the significance of distributive principles, or who deny that adequate distributive principles must be sensitive to differences in status, may not yet concede that there *are* any differences in status in the first place (to potentially make a difference to the value of well-being). So it might be better to limit ourselves to asking, somewhat more cautiously, whether the value of well-being varies depending on *whose* well-being it is. Nonetheless, having now belabored the point, I think that no real damage will be done if we continue to pose our new question in the way I just did, by asking whether status makes a difference to the value of well-being. Anyone who has read this far will understand perfectly well the question that I mean to be raising. (And if they find themselves uncomfortable with the way I am framing the question, they can always substitute a suitable paraphrase.)

There is a further point of clarification that may be helpful as well. In asking whether status makes a difference to the value of well-being I am not asking whether status makes a difference to the amount of good done *to the individual*. Indeed, it is not at all clear to me whether a question like that even makes sense. If your welfare has gone up by three units, say, then it has indeed gone up by three units. The intrinsic value *to you* of having the increase in well-being has already been stipulated, as has its size: an increase in well-being of three units just *is* a benefit *to you* of precisely three units (of well-being). So if we meant to be asking about the value *to the individual* of increases in well-being, there would be no point in asking whether the size of that benefit varied with status.

However, our question is not about the size of the benefit to the individual, but rather about the increase in the value of the given *outcome* that is directly brought about by any given increase in well-being. And here, I think, there is room to wonder whether this is indeed fixed. Almost all of us agree that it makes an outcome better (other things being equal) if someone's welfare has gone up—but this point of agreement still leaves it open whether the *amount* by which the outcome is made better turns solely upon the amount by which the individual's welfare has increased, or whether, instead, it turns in part on the *status* of the individual who has undergone the increase in well-being. Putting the same point in slightly different terms, a one unit increase in well-being necessarily benefits the individual by one unit, but that doesn't yet tell us whether the difference in the moral value of the *outcome* produced by that one unit increase in welfare is always the same, regardless of the status of the individual in question. It is conceivable, at least, that status makes a difference here, so that the higher the status of the individual whose welfare is at issue, the greater the impact of the given change (in welfare) on the value of the outcome.

Is this indeed the case? Does status affect the value of welfare? I find myself inclined to think that it does. But I have to admit that others may be unpersuaded.

Unsurprisingly, part of the reason I find myself thinking that status matters in this way is because I have already concluded that status matters elsewhere, in connection with distribution. As we've seen, a plausible account of distributive principles requires us to say that the distributive claims of animals are weaker, in appropriate ways, than the distributive claims of people would be, in what would otherwise constitute similar patterns of distribution. The distributive claims of animals are *genuine*, but weaker because of differences in status. But if that is indeed the case—and I believe it is—then it is plausible to think that these selfsame differences in status should weaken other moral claims that animals have on us as well, at least in comparison to the corresponding claims of people. It particular, it seems to me implausible to think that status would be significant when it comes to the *distribution* of welfare, but not when it comes to the moral value of welfare itself. On the contrary, just as the distributive claims of animals have to be adjusted so as to take into account their lower status, the claims of animals to greater welfare have to be adjusted as well. Here, too, then, their claims should be genuine, but weaker. Which is to say, a given increase in welfare will be morally less significant—it will make a smaller contribution to the overall goodness of an outcome—when the relevant individual has a lower rather than a higher moral status.

That's a rather abstract argument, I suppose, but I do find it rather persuasive. It may similarly move some of those who have agreed with me that a proper account of distribution will be a hierarchical one. Once we have acknowledged the significance of status in matters of distribution, it may seem implausible—and more than a bit ad hoc—to deny its significance when it comes to the value of welfare itself.

Of course, this argument, whatever its value, will have little or no persuasive force for those who have not yet been persuaded of the need for hierarchy in distribution. To be sure, it may show them the plausibility of extending the hierarchical approach once it has been adopted; but they may still think there is no compelling reason to adopt such an approach in the first place. In any event, we may still wonder how the issue of status and welfare strikes us when we consider it directly, in its own right. That is, questions of consistency aside, does it seem plausible or not to suggest that status affects the value of welfare?

Here's a case to check your intuitions. Suppose that two individuals have toothaches, equally intense, and I have enough painkiller to put an end to either one of the two toothaches but not both. Suppose, next, that unless I stop one of the toothaches they will last equally long. Finally, imagine that one of the two individuals is a normal, adult human—that is, a person—while the other is a mouse.

What I have tried to do here, of course, is to describe a case in which the two toothaches are equally bad, in the sense that they have an identical impact on the welfare of the mouse and the person. So the very same quantity of well-being is at stake, regardless of who I decide to help.

And yet, for all that, when I think about this case, I find myself strongly inclined to judge that it is more important to help the person than the mouse.[8] More particularly, the outcome in which the person's toothache comes to an end seems to me to be a better one than the outcome in which it is the mouse's pain that is eliminated. And if I ask myself why this is so, why greater good is accomplished if I raise the welfare of the person rather than the mouse, the answer I am drawn to is this: the person is a more valuable sort of being than the mouse is, she counts more, she has a higher moral status—and one of the ways in which this status reveals itself is precisely in the fact that there is greater moral reason to aid the person than the mouse. A world in which a *person's* toothache has been relieved is a better world than one in which the same has been done for a mouse instead.

Perhaps you share my intuition about this case. Then that provides at least some support for the idea that status matters here too, that the value of welfare depends in part on the status of the individual whose welfare it is. Combined with the earlier abstract argument, I find that these two considerations together add up to a fairly compelling case for the claim that status affects the value of

---

[8] Kazez considers a similar example, and reaches a similar conclusion, in *Animalkind*, pp. 91–3.

welfare. But at the same time, I realize that not everyone will be persuaded. I have already acknowledged that the "consistency" argument will have little force for those who reject my conclusions about status and distribution, and I must now acknowledge as well that there will doubtless be many people who simply don't share my intuition about the toothache case either.

What's more, even if one does share my intuition about this example, one might reasonably worry whether I have really constructed a case in which the two potential increases in welfare are genuinely the same size. It is arguable, after all, that the person's welfare will take a greater hit if her toothache is left untreated than the mouse's welfare would (if it were the mouse's toothache that was left untreated). Among other reasons, the person presumably has a much better memory than the mouse has. Once the mouse's toothache is over it may immediately be forgotten; but the person will remember hers—and the longer it goes on, the more painful the later memories may be. So even if one does have the intuition that it is better to aid the person, this may simply show that one actually thinks that a greater increase in welfare will be brought about if one aids the person rather than the mouse. Status may play no role whatsoever in explaining why the result will be better if we aid the person. (Similarly, if it were a matter of *preventing* the toothache—rather than merely curing it—there would be the related possibility that the person would unpleasantly anticipate their future pain, while the mouse would not.)

I do think that such concerns about the example are legitimate. To be sure, it is difficult to be confident that the person has more well-being at stake than the mouse has, but this does seem a real possibility. Of course, in still other ways it might turn out that it is actually the mouse that undergoes the greater loss in welfare. After all, the person can recall the fact that toothaches sometimes come to an end on their own, while the mouse may be utterly caught up in its suffering, unable to "think its way through" the pain.[9] But in any event, given all of this, one may be quite uncertain as to whether the two toothaches really do involve the same quantity of welfare, and if not, which is greater. (Indeed, I find it difficult to be confident that I am really imagining that the mouse has a toothache that is every bit as intense as the one I am ascribing to the person.)

So the example of the two toothaches may be less well constructed than it might initially have seemed.

In principle, of course, we could deal with this worry by offering a different example in its place, one where we had no serious reservations about the truth of the key claim that the person and the animal have the same amount of

---

[9] As Thomson notes, *The Realm of Rights*, pp. 292–3.

well-being at stake. But I find it impossible to construct a case that does any better in this regard. It is easy enough to *stipulate* that some example involves equal quantities of well-being; but when I actually try to spell out the details it becomes far from clear that I have really accomplished what I set out to do.

So I conclude this section a bit more tentatively than I would like. It does seem to me that when I do my best to try to imagine cases in which a person and an animal have the same amount of well-being at stake that I really do find myself inclined to judge that it would be better to aid the person rather than the animal—that doing this makes for a greater increase in the goodness of the relevant outcomes from the moral point of view. And it does seem to me that this same conclusion is reinforced by consideration of the views I have already defended in connection with distribution. Taken together, as I have remarked, these seem to me to add up to a reasonably strong case for the view that status affects the value of welfare. The case will become even stronger later on, as we see further places where status matters. But I admit that for the time being, at least, one can instead reasonably refuse to embrace this conclusion.

4.4 Dismissing the View

I have just argued for a hierarchical, status sensitive approach to the value of well-being. But it is sometimes suggested that this sort of view is utterly implausible on its face. How could one possibly think that status affects the moral significance of *welfare*? After all, as skeptics have sometimes noted, "pain is pain."[10]

Of course, despite the catchiness of this slogan, it does not really support the unitarian position here rather than any other. For while it is certainly true that pain is pain, it is also true that not all pains are equally significant; some matter more, morally speaking, than others. Thus, for example, some pains last longer than others, or are more intense.

Now, everyone agrees that eliminating pains that are worse in this way (longer or more intense) makes for a larger improvement in the overall value of the outcome. No one would think that a claim to the effect that it is more important to eliminate intense pains, say, rather than mild ones, is somehow shown to be unacceptable by virtue of the fact that "pain is pain."

But then, obviously enough, it is equally true that a hierarchical approach to the value of well-being cannot be shown to be unacceptable by virtue of this fact either. What is at issue is precisely the question of whether differences in

---

[10] Singer, *Animal Liberation*, p. 20; DeGrazia, *Taking Animals Seriously*, p. 234.

status are among those features that make a difference to the moral *significance* of a given pain (or pleasure, or other alteration in well-being). If they are, then of course no simple appeal to the uncontroversial observation that pain is pain will show otherwise.

In effect, in the context of a debate over whether status makes a difference to the value of well-being, to insist that pain is pain does nothing more than reveal that you yourself happen to think that status makes no difference here. That's interesting; but it offers no reason to agree with you.

Of course, we should not lose sight of the fact that there are differences in the *way* that status affects significance, and the way intensity and duration do so. If a pain is more intense, say, or lasts longer, then it makes a bigger difference to your *welfare*. And it is by virtue of that fact that it also makes a difference to the value of the given outcome: the intensity of the pain affects the *amount* of welfare at issue, and the amount of welfare affects the value of the outcome. In contrast, if status makes a difference here it isn't via making a difference to your welfare; a one unit change in welfare is still a one unit change in welfare, regardless of whose welfare it is. Nonetheless, for all that, it could still be the case that this one unit change in welfare makes a *larger* difference in the overall value of the outcome if it is a person's welfare that is at issue, say, rather than that of an animal.

To be sure, the unitarian may be tempted to insist that the *only* way that welfare can plausibly be thought to affect the goodness of an outcome is by coming in larger or smaller *quantities*. If so, then status will be irrelevant to the value of any given change in well-being.

For if status doesn't alter the quantity of well-being at stake—a one unit change being a one unit change, regardless of whose it is—then status won't affect the value of the change.

But it just isn't true that the only way that welfare can be plausibly thought to affect the value of an outcome is by coming in larger or smaller quantities. At the very least, anyone sympathetic to distributive principles must reject this claim. Suppose, for example, that you embrace the priority principle, according to which the size of the contribution that a given increase in well-being makes to the overall goodness of an outcome depends on how well off (or badly off) the individual is who will receive that increase. To say this, obviously enough, is to say that the impact of a given increase in well-being depends not just on the quantity of well-being at stake, but also on where the well-being is going. So when the value of an outcome is affected by increases in welfare this may be the result of other features besides the *quantity* of welfare at stake. Similarly, of course, if you embrace an egalitarian principle, according to which the value of an outcome may be improved by reducing inequality. An increase in welfare that goes to someone who is worse off than others may make the outcome better, while the same increase given to someone better off than others may make it worse. Here too, then, the impact of a given increase in well-being depends not just on quantity, but on where the well-being is going.

In saying all of this, I have not lost sight of the fact that we are currently focusing on the value of well-being itself, and not on the significance of distribution. But what thinking about distribution reminds us of is the fact that there are indeed other features of well-being besides its quantity that can potentially affect the impact of that well-being on the goodness of an outcome. Accordingly, anyone sympathetic to distributive principles must reject the idea that the *only* feature of welfare that can make any difference to the goodness of an outcome is the quantity of welfare at stake. Quantity aside, distributive features of the welfare can also make a difference. And once we have recognized that fact, the door is similarly open to suggesting that questions about *status* can make a difference as well.

Admittedly, those who reject distributive principles may find this a less compelling line of thought than it will seem to those who accept them. But it is not without force, I think, even here. For the question, strictly, is not whether any given theorist does in fact believe that distributive features affect the impact of welfare, but simply rather whether they are open in principle to the possibility that something like that *might* be true—or whether, instead, they think that it is somehow appropriate to dismiss distributive views out of hand, as it were, on the grounds that nothing could *conceivably* affect the impact of welfare other than the quantity of welfare at stake. Provided that they are at least willing to entertain the possibility that distributive features might matter in this way (even if, at the end of the day, they don't think that they do), then they should similarly be prepared to entertain the possibility that status affects the value of welfare as well (or instead).

It is, to be sure, easy to feel the appeal of the thought that what matters about pain is the sheer fact of how *painful* it is. And while intensity and duration can alter this, it is clear that one's status cannot. So it may seem obvious that status—or the psychological capacities that ground it—cannot have any bearing on the significance of pain. As one author understandably protests,

> How can one's intelligence, sensitivity, and the like be relevant to *how much a certain amount of pain or suffering matters?*[11]

---

[11] DeGrazia, *Taking Animals Seriously*, p. 249; emphasis in original.

The rhetorical force of remarks like this cannot be denied. But it is important to see that the analogous question would be considerably less compelling if it were offered as an argument against the significance of, say, equality. If someone were to ask, "How can the mere fact that one person is worse off than another be relevant to how much a certain amount of pain or suffering matters?" it would be perfectly reasonable to reply that while the fact that one is worse off than another doesn't alter how much a given pain *hurts*, nonetheless it does affect the value of eliminating or reducing that pain. That is, it may be more important to eliminate one person's pain rather than another's precisely because the one is so much *worse off* than the other is. But similarly, then, it is reasonable to answer our author's protest by noting that while status may not affect how much a given pain *hurts*, nonetheless, it too may affect the value of eliminating or reducing that pain.

In effect, the question is really this: must the bearing of some "bit" of welfare (positive or negative) on the value of an outcome depend solely on the features of that bit of welfare (such as intensity and duration) that affect the *amount* of welfare involved, or can it depend in part on other features of the welfare as well (such as *where* the welfare falls within an overall distributive pattern, or *whose* welfare it is)? And what I want to suggest is that, absent some special argument to the contrary, there is no good reason to assume that all such further features—including status—must be irrelevant.

It might be suggested, however, that just such an argument can be provided by means of an appeal to the *principle of equal consideration of interests* (introduced in 2.1). According to this principle, recall, similar interests are to be given the same weight and counted the same way.

Here's a typical statement of the principle in question:

the interests of every being affected by an action are to be taken into account and given the same weight as the like interests of any other being.[12]

And here's another:

Equal consideration, whether for humans or animals, means in some way giving equal moral weight to the relevantly similar interests of different individuals.[13]

It might seem a trivial step from acceptance of this principle to the conclusion that status cannot make a difference to the value of well-being. Indeed the first of the two authors I've just quoted pretty much says as much:

[12] Singer, *Animal Liberation*, p. 5.   [13] DeGrazia, *Taking Animals Seriously*, p. 46.

> It is an implication of this principle of equality that our concern for others
> and our readiness to consider their interests ought not to depend on
> what they are like or on what abilities they may possess.[14]

I takes this to mean (at least in part), that given the principle of equal consideration of interests, the irrelevance of status to the significance of well-being follows more or less automatically. If like interests are to be given the same weight, then it cannot matter *whose* welfare is at stake, only how *much* welfare.

But of course the inference cannot be quite as trivial as that. For equal consideration does not require us to treat all interests the same—only those that are "like" (in the words of the first statement of the principle) or "relevantly similar" (in the words of the second).

This point is essential. As we have already noted, no one would think it illegitimate to give more weight to a more intense pain, or one that lasts longer. But that's obviously not an objection to the principle, for equal consideration only requires that we give the same weight to interests that are similar in all morally relevant ways—and these are clearly morally *relevant* differences. So what we need to ask is this: What about status? Might differences in status count as morally relevant as well?

If so, then here too it is no violation of equal consideration of interests to count one increase in well-being as more significant than another, even though both are the same size—provided that the first would go to someone with a higher moral status. For if status matters, then the interests that the two individuals have in increasing their well-being will not actually be *relevantly* similar, initial appearances to the contrary notwithstanding: the first interest may involve the welfare of a person, for example, while the second involves the welfare of an animal.

Of course, it may seem perfectly obvious to some that status is not, in fact, the kind of feature that matters when deciding whether two interests count as relevantly similar or not. Speaking personally, I don't actually think that it *is* obvious. But the point right now is simply that this is indeed a *further* claim—not something that follows from the principle of equal consideration considered all by itself. And while it is certainly true that you might be prepared to make that further claim—insisting that status is simply irrelevant to the moral significance of any given interest—to do so already *presupposes* (or, perhaps, constitutes) a denial of hierarchy. The appeal to equal consideration provides no *independent* support for rejecting the significance of status.

---

[14] Singer, *Animal Liberation*, p. 5.

That, at least, is the situation we find ourselves in if we interpret the principle as I have been interpreting it—as requiring only that we give equal weight to interests that are similar with regard to all morally relevant characteristics. So construed, the principle provides no guidance whatsoever on the question of what features count as morally relevant, and so, in particular, it cannot be used to argue for the irrelevance of status.

But there is an alternative interpretation of the principle that might seem better suited for the job. Perhaps the principle is to be understood as requiring us to give equal weight to any two interests that are similar *qua interests*—that is, that are similar with regard to the features of the interest that make it have a bearing on one's welfare. Interpreted in this second manner, the principle still tells us that if two interests are similar in relevant ways they must be given the same weight, but it further specifies that the relevant similarities or dissimilarities are only those that have a bearing on how the welfare of the given individual will be affected if the interest is satisfied (or frustrated). In short, if two interests would have the same impact on well-being, they are to be given equal weight.

Understood in this second way, the principle of equal consideration of interests does indeed suffice to rule out the view that status affects the value of welfare. In deciding whose well-being to promote, we need only ask how much welfare is at stake in each case; it is irrelevant who the welfare is going to. As the author of our second statement of the principle remarks,

> If a human and lizard lose equally much from death, they have relevantly similar life interests meriting equal moral weight.[15]

That's not at all to suggest, of course, that a lizard really does have as much to lose from death as a (normal) human. That will presumably never be the case. But it is a dramatic way of expressing the irrelevance of status. What matters is only the *amount* of well-being at stake, not who the well-being is going to; any appeal to the purported higher moral status of humans (or persons) as compared to lizards is simply irrelevant.

Undoubtedly, some would like to use the principle of equal consideration, understood in this second way, to argue for the irrelevance of status to the value of well-being. Unfortunately, however, so construed the principle does little more than beg the question. This is in striking contrast to the principle under the *first* interpretation, for it does seem undeniable that if two interests are the same in *all* morally relevant ways, then they must be given the same weight.

---

[15] DeGrazia, *Taking Animals Seriously*, p. 233.

But if we build into our understanding of the principle the further assumption that the only ways in which interests can relevantly differ are those that have an impact on the amount of well-being at stake—and this is, after all, precisely what the second interpretation does—then to accept the principle one must first have decided that nothing else affects the moral significance of a given interest other than its impact on welfare. And that, of course, is exactly the issue under debate. No one sympathetic to the idea that status can affect the value of welfare will be prepared to accept the principle of equal consideration under the second interpretation. To put forward the principle when it is understood in this way is not so much an argument against the relevance of status as a bald *assertion* of its irrelevance. Here too, then, the principle cannot provide independent support for the rejection of hierarchy.

Indeed, it is worth noting that no one sympathetic to our distributive principles can accept the principle under its second interpretation. For if interests that have the same impact on welfare must be given the same weight in our moral deliberations, then it is must be *irrelevant* to ask whether a given boost in well-being would go to someone who is worse off than others. We cannot legitimately hold that it will do more good to give the increase to someone who is worse off, rather than give an increase of the same amount to someone who is better off. Yet these are exactly the sorts of considerations that anyone drawn to egalitarianism will think relevant in assessing where a given increase in well-being will do the most good. Thus, despite the similarity in names, anyone who accepts an egalitarian distributive principle must reject the principle of equal consideration of interests, when it is understood in this second way.

Similarly, anyone who accepts the relevance of desert must also reject the principle of equal consideration, so understood. For sometimes, in choosing whose welfare to increase, it is relevant to ask not just how great the given increase might be, but whether one individual *deserves* it more than the other—even though questions of desert may have no bearing on the *amount* of welfare at stake. And something similar is true, of course, for those who accept the priority view: in deciding where a given boost in welfare will do the most good, it is important to ask how *badly off* the individual is who will receive it, and not just how much welfare is at stake. So those drawn to the priority view must also reject the principle, if it is understood in the second way.

In short, the principle of equal consideration is unacceptably narrow when it is interpreted the second way. In contrast, of course, on the first interpretation, features like whether someone is better or worse off than another (or whether they deserve an increase in well-being, or whether they are badly off, absolutely speaking) can count as being among the morally relevant features of a given interest. That's one clear reason for preferring the *first* interpretation: it appropriately tells us to treat relevantly similar interests similarly, but it doesn't implausibly restrict the set of relevant features to those affecting the amount of well-being at stake.

But as we have already noted, if we do interpret the principle in this first, more expansive fashion, then we no longer have any independent reason to insist that status cannot be among the morally relevant features. One can embrace the principle of equal consideration of interests, all the while still insisting that a given increase in welfare is more significant when the individual receiving the increase has a higher moral status. (I might add, in passing, that it is because of this possibility that I refrained from defining unitarianism (in 2.1 and 2.4) in terms of acceptance of the principle of equal consideration of interests. As we have now seen, even those who reject unitarianism can embrace that principle, in its more plausible interpretation.)

The bottom line, then, is this. Status may well affect the value of welfare. The arguments for thinking that it does may not be decisive (though they do persuade me), but at the very least this possibility cannot be simply dismissed out of hand.

4.5 The Status Adjusted Value of Well-Being

Suppose you agree with me that the contribution that a given individual's welfare makes to the value of an outcome depends on the moral status of that individual. In assessing the value of an outcome we need to take status into account, even when we are focusing solely upon the contribution made by well-being itself (that is, leaving distributive features aside). This means that it won't suffice to merely measure the *amount* of well-being, since the value of that quantity can vary, depending on whose well-being it is. In effect, then, what we need is another *status adjusted* measure of welfare.

What would such a measure look like? We need to take the quantity of welfare at issue and discount it by a suitable amount—where the discount is greater, the lower the status of the given individual. No doubt there are various ways to accomplish this, but the simplest, I imagine, would be to multiply the quantity of welfare by an appropriate fraction, a fraction that is lower for animals than for people, and lower still for some animals than for others.

Since the multiplier should vary in a way that is proportional to status, the obvious suggestion to make at this point is that we should avail ourselves of the same numerical representation of status that we used earlier (in 4.1) when extending the priority view. Arbitrarily assigning a value of 1 for the status of (human) people, we imagined assigning suitable fractions of this amount to various animals. Of course, I made no attempt to actually work out the relevant numbers, but for the sake of illustration I proposed that dogs might be assigned a status of 0.3 or 0.4, while mice might be assigned 0.02 or 0.03. (Later I imagined that a fly might have a status of 0.0001.) The idea, then, is that we can arrive at a suitable measure of the amount of welfare for the purposes of determining its value by multiplying the absolute level or quantity of well-being by (this numerical representation of) status. Call this proposal *simple multiplication*.

Suppose, for example, that two animals each have a level of well-being of 20, measured in absolute terms. If one of the two—let us suppose it is a dog—has a status of 0.3, while the other—a rabbit, perhaps—has a status of 0.1, then although each has the same *amount* of welfare, the value of their *having* this welfare differs from the moral point of view, from one to the other. Since the dog has a status that is three times as great as that of the rabbit (0.3 as compared to 0.1), each unit of well-being possessed by the dog counts three times as much. Similarly, if we had the chance of increasing either animal's welfare by 5 units, three times as much good would be done if we were to aid the dog rather than the rabbit.

If we accept simple multiplication then sometimes it will do more good to give a smaller increase in well-being to an animal with higher status, rather than a larger increase to an animal with lower status. Thus, for example, giving an extra 2 units of well-being to the dog will add more value than giving an extra 5 units to the rabbit (since $0.3 \times 2 = 0.6$, which is more than $0.1 \times 5 = 0.5$). On the other hand, simple multiplication certainly does not entail that increases in welfare should *always* go to the individual with the highest status. Even if we continue to focus exclusively on the value of welfare itself (that is, disregarding questions of distribution), a large enough increase to a lower status animal can be a greater contribution than a sufficiently small increase to a higher status animal. Thus, for example, if we could give either 1 unit of extra well-being to the dog or 5 to the rabbit, it would do more good to aid the rabbit, despite the fact that the dog has a higher moral status (since $0.1 \times 5 = 0.5$, which is more than $0.3 \times 1 = 0.3$). The crucial idea remains this: other things being equal, the greater the status of a given individual, the more value there is in any given unit of welfare obtaining for that individual. Simple multiplication readily accommodates this thought.

By this time, however, a question will have suggested itself. When looking for a suitable way to adjust welfare for the purposes of determining priority under the priority principle, I suggested simple division. (To be sure, I also noted difficulties with this proposal, but those problems don't speak to the question I am about to raise.) Here, however, in looking for a suitable way to adjust welfare I am suggesting simple multiplication instead. What explains the difference? Why multiply by status in the one case, while dividing by it in the other?

The answer lies in the different ways that status is appropriately taken into account in the two cases. The intuitive idea behind status-relativized accounts of the value of well-being is that the lower one's status, the less value there is in one's welfare. So for the purpose of calculating the value of welfare we have to adjust the absolute level of welfare (or quantity of welfare) by *reducing* it an appropriate amount—where the lower one's status, the greater the amount of the reduction. That, of course, is precisely what is accomplished by multiplication (since multiplying by a fraction of 1 has the result of reducing the product). A similar intuitive idea was at work when it came to finding a status-relativized version of the priority principle: the lower one's status, the smaller the prioritarian claim generated by one's welfare. But since the prioritarian principle gives greater claims to those with *lower* welfare, a properly relativized version of the principle has to adjust the absolute level of welfare by *inflating* it for lower status, rather than reducing it. And that, of course, is what division accomplishes (since dividing by a fraction of 1 has the effect of multiplying by the *inverse* of that fraction—with the result that the lower one's status, the greater the amount of inflation).

In both cases, then, the underlying thought is the same: individuals with lower status count for less, one way or the other. It's just that accommodating that shared thought requires different mathematical operations in the two different contexts.

It may be worth pausing for a moment to note that simple multiplication does not run afoul of the particular problems that plague an unqualified appeal to simple division (see 4.2). For example, we still get intuitively plausible results if we move from positive levels of welfare to negative ones. If the dog and rabbit are both at -20, say, rather than $+20$, simple multiplication yields the appropriate hierarchical conclusion that the dog's suffering reduces the value of the outcome more than the rabbit's suffering. (The dog's status adjusted welfare is $0.3 \times -20 = -6$, which is worse than the rabbit's $0.1 \times -20 = -2$.) Similarly, if both are at the zero point of well-being, then it seems intuitive to suggest that each animal's neutral level of welfare neither adds to the value of the outcome nor subtracts from it (disregarding, of course, any sufficientarian claims that might be made), and this intuitive result is retained under simple multiplication. (The dog's status adjusted welfare is 0 as is the rabbit's, since $0.3 \times 0 = 0$ and $0.1 \times 0 = 0$ as well.) Finally, no special problem arises for levels of welfare that are positive, but extremely close to zero. (Recall the fly with its level of well-being at 0.005. If its status is 0.0001, then simple multiplication yields a status adjusted level of welfare of a mere 0.0000005! Appropriately enough, this will add a vanishingly small amount of value to the outcome.)

Of course, in noting these relative advantages I do not mean to suggest that simple multiplication has no unique problems of its own. Until the proposal is examined with greater care, I don't think we are in a position to say that with any confidence. Nor do I even mean to claim that it is the *best* approach to calculating status adjusted levels of welfare. Perhaps some other approach will turn out to be superior; I don't think we know that yet either. I offer it simply by way of showing what a status-relativized approach to the value of welfare might conceivably look like. That's worth doing, even if further reflection might ultimately lead us to an approach that ends up being rather different from this first one. For the thought that status might affect the value of welfare is an unfamiliar one—typically dismissed by those working in animal ethics—and it is worth recognizing the fact that while the details may prove difficult to work out, in principle at least the idea need not be a particularly complicated one.

One final point. In thinking about the moral significance of well-being, there are, broadly speaking, at least two different ways we might proceed. We can talk, as I have largely done here, about the value of welfare, and how well-being adds to the *value of an outcome* (or reduces it, in the case of negative welfare). Speaking personally, I find that a congenial way to think about these issues. But others may prefer to think, instead, in terms of *the claims that individuals can make* to have their welfare increased or maintained. Here the focus isn't so much on the value of outcomes per se, but rather on individuals and their claims to welfare (and the reasons we thus have to increase or maintain that welfare). It will have been noted that I have occasionally helped myself to locutions of this second sort as well, since I think that the difference between these two ways of talking is more apparent than real. (Comparable remarks apply to the discussion of distribution, where, as it happens, I have emphasized the second way of talking rather than the first.) But others may disagree, and some may find it unhelpful at best for me to have spoken so frequently of the value of welfare, or of the contribution that welfare makes to the goodness of any given outcome.

Accordingly, anyone so inclined is invited to recast the foregoing discussion in language that they find more congenial. But I hope the following is clear: questions about status and welfare arise regardless of whether we choose to discuss these issues in the first way or the second. However we prefer to talk about the matter, we must be open to the possibility that status affects the moral significance of well-being.

5

Status

5.1 Grounds of Status

If people have a higher moral status than animals do, then presumably this is by virtue of having certain features that animals lack or have in a lower degree. Similarly, if some animals have a higher status than others, then the former too must have some features that the latter lack, or that the latter have to an even lower degree.

What sort of features might these be? A complete theory of moral status would need to offer a full and satisfying account of this matter. I am not going to try to provide that here. But I take this much to be clear: it isn't as though all features whatsoever are the sort of features that make a difference to status. Intuitively, for example, height, body shape, or weight simply have no bearing on one's moral status. Similarly, physical strength, speed, or the sound of one's voice are irrelevant, as is hair color—or, for that matter, whether one has any hair at all.

So what sorts of features are the ones that make a difference? Think about how people differ from bears, or pigs from fish. What are we responding to when we find ourselves intuitively inclined to assign higher moral status to people than to bears, or to pigs than to fish? As I have already suggested, the relevant characteristics here seem to be psychological ones. More precisely, we seem to be responding to differences in *psychological capacities*. Of course, upon more careful reflection it may turn out that psychological capacities aren't the whole story here; it may be that there are further features that have a bearing on one's moral status as well. In fact, I think this will indeed turn out to be the case. But psychological capacities are surely a central part of the story. People have various psychological capacities—both cognitive and emotional— that bears either lack or have in lesser degree. The same thing is true for pigs as compared to fish, or, for that matter, for fish as compared to bees. It is clear that these differences in capacities go a long way toward explaining why it is that people have a higher moral status than animals do, and why there are relevant differences in status among animals as well.

A quick word of explanation may be in order about this focus on *capacities*. Intuitively, at least, one's status doesn't seem to be so much a function of which particular thoughts one happens to be thinking, or which emotions one happens to be feeling. Rather, status seems to turn more on an individual's general *capacities* for thought and emotion. It isn't as though one's status flutters up and down as particular thoughts and emotions enter and then leave one's mind; it isn't as though a person in dreamless sleep has no higher a moral status than a sleeping mouse. What matters is the fact that people are *able* to think thoughts or feel emotions of various kinds while animals cannot (or cannot to a comparable degree of sophistication). Similarly, what matters is the fact that wolves, say, have psychological capacities that go beyond the capacities of fish or bugs.

(Note that the mere fact that one could come to possess a given capacity isn't the same thing as *already having* that capacity. Whether the *potential* to gain a capacity has a bearing on status is an issue we will come to later.)

Intuitively, then, the picture we have is this. Psychological capacities play a role in grounding one's status. And statuses differ, precisely because these capacities seem to come in varieties that differ in terms of their complexity and sophistication. That is to say, some types of animals have a greater capacity for complex thought than others, or can experience deeper and more sophisticated emotional responses. And as a first approximation, at least, it seems as though animals that have higher capacities of one sort also have higher capacities of other sorts as well. If something like this is correct, then we can arrange animals into a hierarchy, assigning a higher moral status to those with the more advanced sets of capacities. (More accurately, of course, what we are really doing here is simply *recognizing* the higher status that they already have, by virtue of those higher capacities.) And given that people have the most advanced and developed set of psychological capacities with which we are familiar, we end up with a system in which some animals have a higher moral status than others, and people have a higher moral status still. Thus, to pick just a few members of the resulting hierarchy, people have a higher moral status than cats, while cats have a higher moral status than salmon, and salmon in turn have a higher moral status than butterflies.

Of course, as always, any particular judgments we might make about how one type of animal ranks in comparison to others will be subject to revision in light of further advances in empirical science. We may well discover that we have overestimated or underestimated the psychological capacities of any given type of animal. Unsurprisingly, then, any such ranking will remain tentative (and perhaps a bit rough as well). But in principle, at least, a suitably informed ranking could be produced, and that ranking could then be improved upon as science reveals more about the details of animal psychology.

Nonetheless, it is not my aim to produce that ranking here. I know too little about the capacities of animals—including what's already been established by science—to think there is any value in my trying to work out a detailed ranking. That task must be left to others. In what follows, therefore, I will continue to confine myself (just as I have been doing up to this point) to examples where the differences in capacities are both stark and (I hope) uncontroversial. I won't try to decide whether horses, say, have a higher status than zebras; instead, I will limit myself to comparing either of them to, for example, insects or fish.

There is, however, a potential complication that should be noted here, even in the absence of a detailed ranking. I have been writing as though statuses can be ranked along a single dimension, so that it makes sense to simply talk—as I have been talking—about "higher" or "lower" status. This same thought lies behind the earlier suggestion that we may be able to represent status with a single number, where people have a status of, say, 1 and animals have a status that is some fraction of that number. That sort of idea makes sense if psychological capacities tend to come as a package, so that animals with more advanced versions of one relevant capacity also tend to have more advanced versions of other capacities as well.

Conceivably, however, the reality is more complicated. It could be that some animals are more advanced in connection with certain capacities, but less advanced with regard to others. Of course, in principle this could still be compatible with status being something that could be represented with a single number. Perhaps, for example, a creature like this would have a status that reflected some kind of average of the differing levels of the diverging capacities. But it might be, instead, that certain capacities are relevant for a given set of moral claims, while other capacities are the basis of different claims. If so, then a creature with advanced capacities of the one kind, but less advanced capacities of the other, would have a relatively high moral status with regard to the first set of claims, but a low moral status with regard to the second set.

If something like this were the case, then it could turn out that it was inappropriate (or, at best, a rough approximation of the facts) to rank statuses along a single dimension. It could turn out, for example, that animals of kind A and of kind B could not be ranked along a single scale, as though one of these two types must have a higher moral status than the other (or else have the very same status). Rather, we might be limited to saying something more like this: with regard to normative features x, y, and z, type A has a higher status, while with regard to normative features p, q, and r, type B has the higher status.

If the relevant psychological capacities could "come apart" like this, with moral status being fragmented as a result, then instead of representing status with a single number, we might need to make use of ordered pairs, or n-tuples. Instead of saying that animals of a certain kind have a status of, say, 0.4— implying by this that they have a status of 0.4 across the board—perhaps the best we could say is that animals of a given kind have a status of, say, (0.2, 0.4), meaning that they have a status of 0.2 with regard to some first set of normative features, while having status 0.4 with regard to a second set.

Indeed, depending on just how much the relevant underlying psychological capacities could vary independently of one another, and how much, as a result, the relevant normative features could vary, we might need an even more complicated representation of status, with three or more places, each place marking out one's status with regard to some narrow band of normative features. The more independent variation there could be, the larger the number of places needed in the n-tuple that would be required for adequately representing moral status. (Indeed, in the most extreme case it could turn out that we would need to assign a separate score for each normative feature that can vary with one's status.)

As I say, all of this seems to me a coherent possibility. In principle, at least, it may be a mistake to think that status can be adequately represented with a single digit, arrayed along a single dimension. Nonetheless, having noted this possibility, I intend to put it aside. After all, before deciding that this sort of multidimensional approach to moral status was appropriate we would first need to get clearer about several difficult issues. We would need to know which normative features vary with status. And we would need to determine which particular psychological capacities (or sets of capacities) provide the basis for one's claims with regard to each such normative feature. Finally, we would also need to establish that the relevant psychological capacities can indeed vary independently of one another, and do so to a significant degree. But I take it to be clear that we are nowhere near knowing enough about any one of these points—let alone all three—to yet make out the case that we really do need to represent status in this more complicated fashion. So while we may someday conclude that it is an oversimplification to think of status as falling along a single dimension, for the time being, at least, I think we are justified in making use of the simpler model.

There is a second potential complication that is worth noting as well. I have suggested that status depends on psychological capacities, such that the possession of more advanced and sophisticated forms of these capacities raises one's moral status, in comparison to the status of those who lack the relevant capacities altogether, or who possess them only in simpler or less advanced forms. On this picture, in effect, what the relevant capacities serve to do is to *raise* one's status, albeit by differing amounts, depending on their level and sophistication. Less advanced versions of the given capacity will raise status by a smaller amount than more advanced versions, but one's capacities never *lower* one's status in absolute terms. In this sense, the status-generating features are all positive.

In principle, however, it seems that one's status could also be in part the result of still other features, features that would have the effect of actually *lowering* one's status (rather than merely failing to raise it, or doing so only minimally). Features of this second sort would be robustly *negative*. Conceivably, even features like this could come in different degrees, with more "advanced" versions of the negative features pushing one's status lower than "less advanced" versions would do (while lacking the negative feature altogether would leave one's status unaffected). If there are such negative features, then presumably one's overall moral status will be a function of both the positive features one possesses (if any) and the negative ones that one possesses (if any) as well.

This in turn would raise the possibility of there being individuals with a moral status that was actually negative overall, rather than positive. That too would be a departure from the picture we've been developing, for up to this point I have assumed (albeit largely implicitly) that everyone's status is appropriately represented by a positive number. That thought was at work, for example, in the suggestion that we might use 1 to represent the status of people, and then assign smaller numbers, fractions of this, for animals with lower statuses. Animals with minimal moral status might have that status represented by numbers close to zero—recall the fly with a status of 0.0001—but while statuses could in principle *approach* zero, I assumed nonetheless that they were all positive.

But if there are features that can lower one's status, rather than merely failing to raise it, then it might well turn out that animals with a sufficient array of negative status-generating features (in suitably "advanced" versions) might end up with a status that was appropriately represented with a negative number, rather than a positive one.

If there could be such animals, then what we owed them would be an interesting inversion of the duties we normally have toward people and other animals. Instead of thinking that, for example, increases in their welfare added value to the outcome, we would have to hold that it actually lowered the value of the outcome, other things being equal. Similarly, instead of thinking that there is a minimally decent life for that kind of creature, such that it was important to make sure that the animal was brought up to that level of well-being, perhaps we would have to say, instead, that it was important to make sure that the animal never did *better* than the relevant level. Our other moral principles would similarly need to be inverted and modified, so as to properly take into account the implications of having this kind of negative status. From a theoretical point of view, at least, negative status must be considered a fascinating and intriguing possibility.

But that's not to say that we have any good reason to believe that an individual's overall moral status ever can in fact be negative in this way. Indeed, as far as I can see, there is no good reason to think that there are any status-generating features that are negative at all. Intuitively, at any rate, when I think about the various psychological capacities that seem to have a bearing on moral status, they all seem to be robustly *positive* in the sense that we've now identified; they can raise one's status, but they never lower it. I simply find myself unable to identify any psychological capacities—or for that matter, any other features at all—that strike me as being negative in the relevant sense, features where I find myself inclined to judge that if only the individual lacked the relevant capacity altogether, that would directly result in a higher moral status. So while I have no special argument against the possibility of such negative status-generating features, I am inclined to put this possibility aside as well, on the ground that such features simply don't seem to exist.

(Admittedly, the idea of negative status has a striking resemblance to certain retributivist views in the theory of moral desert, according to which it may be good for a sufficiently vicious person to suffer or undergo punishment. I am inclined to think that even here the person's *moral status* remains positive, despite the fact that they now deserve to suffer. But I won't take the space here to explore this question more carefully.)

Accordingly, in what follows I will continue to assume that one's moral status, whatever it is, can be appropriately represented with a positive number. The moral status of animals with minimal psychological capacities may come extremely close to zero—and if we wanted to we could even say that animals that lack moral standing altogether have a moral status of zero itself—but let us proceed on the assumption that no individual of any sort has a *negative* moral status, and that no individual with *standing* has anything other than a positive one.

5.2 Individualism

In at least one important way, the discussion up to this point may have been misleading. I have talked repeatedly about the status of dogs or pigs or fish, and so on, as though status is something that one has by virtue of one's species (or other biological grouping). But strictly speaking, that's not really correct. What matters, I think, are the capacities that any given individual has in their own right. That is, the issue isn't really what capacities pigs have, either on average or stereotypically, but rather what capacities this particular pig, or that particular pig, happens to have. The status of a given individual depends on the possession (or absence) of the relevant features by that very individual—so that to the extent that psychological capacities are relevant to status, what matters are the capacities had by that particular individual.

Of course, if it happens that all members of a given animal species have more or less the same set of psychological capacities (or, more precisely, similar *levels* of the relevant capacities), then no harm is done by speaking about the status of rainbow trout, say, as a group, rather than referring more particularly to the status of this or that individual trout. Similarly, if members of larger taxonomic groupings share similar levels of the relevant psychological capacities, then no harm is done by speaking about the status of pigs, or wolves, or even snakes, fish, or insects. I have assumed that, for the most part, large groups of animals do share at least roughly similar capacities in this way, and so I have spoken indifferently about the status of fish, for example, without making any attempt to distinguish between different species of fish,[1] let alone distinguishing between different individual fish. For our purposes, I trust that no harm has been done, and I have actually pointed to something morally important, when I have claimed that, for example, dogs have a higher moral status than fish (because the former have more advanced psychological capacities). It is certainly possible that some of these generalizations have been mistaken, but since I have offered them primarily as a way to illustrate certain general philosophical ideas, for the most part nothing significant would be lost if it should turn out that certain particular examples needed to be revised or replaced.

Nonetheless, strictly speaking, what matters are the particular capacities had by particular individuals. And this means that in at least certain cases this kind of sweeping reference to an animal's species (or larger grouping) could be importantly misguided. For we can readily imagine the possibility of an animal whose individual psychological capacities differed *significantly* from those had by other members of its species. In such a case, generalizations about the typical member of the given species would be irrelevant and misleading; for what really matters are the capacities of the particular individual in question.

---

[1] Of which there are more than 30,000! Balcombe, *What a Fish Knows*, p. 11.

To take an extreme example, suppose that after taking a remarkable "supervitamin," what had previously been a normal golden retriever turns into a person. It isn't that the dog is now *human*; it remains a dog. But it is now a dog with the full range and level of psychological capacities that normal adult humans have. Among other things, it is rational and self-conscious, capable of abstract thought and deliberation, aware of itself as having a future and possessing detailed preferences for that future. It is, in a word, a person. At this point, it would be morally inappropriate to treat the dog as though it had the moral status of a "mere" dog—that is, the status had by more typical dogs. For the fact that dogs normally have much more limited psychological capacities than people do has no direct bearing on the status of *this* dog. What matters, rather, is the fact that this particular dog is a person, and as such it has the same moral status as other people do.

Of course, any example like this is extremely fanciful. We don't have any prospect at all of developing a pill of this amazing sort. The example is also extreme in a second way, since the jump from the capacities of a normal dog to the capacities of a person is a huge one. But it is conceivable, at least, that less extreme cases might sometimes arise naturally. Perhaps there have been instances where genetic anomalies of the right sort have resulted in individual animals possessing psychological capacities that significantly exceed those had by more normal members of their species. If so, then it is possible, at least, that such animals have actually had moral statuses that are greater than the ones we would have normally assigned to them, had we made our assessments solely on the basis of their respective species. Such animals would have a moral status equal to that of their "psychological peers" (other animals with comparable capacities), rather than having the lower status shared by the other members of their species.

I don't know whether such cases of "superanimals," as we might call them, ever actually do occur. But as I say, they seem to me at least conceivable. Also conceivable is the possibility of animals that diverge from what is typical for their species in the other direction, that is, having capacities that are significantly *less* advanced than those normally had by their conspecifics (or lacking some of those capacities altogether). Indeed, I think it's clear that this second sort of case is not merely conceivable, but one that actually arises, presumably across a rather wide range of species. For as we all know, there are various ways in which the brain can be damaged (either genetically, developmentally, or through later accident) resulting in severe cognitive and emotional impairment. This happens, tragically, with certain humans (hence the need to distinguish between being a human and being a person), and presumably it happens with various other animal species as well.

Here, too, I think individualism is the proper position to take. Animals that are significantly impaired with regard to their psychological capacities have a lower moral status than that had by normal members of their species. Although I will later qualify what I am about to say (see 5.5 and 6.3), as a first approximation, at least, we can say that individuals that are significantly impaired have the status not of their conspecifics, but rather of their psychological peers.

To this extent, then, I have been a bit imprecise when I have talked about the status of dogs, mice, frogs and fish, and so on. Strictly speaking, what I had in mind might have been more accurately described as psychologically normal (adult) dogs, mice, frogs and fish.

If in some instance I misled you or you misunderstood me on this point, that is certainly unfortunate. But I suspect that the chances are good that you realized all along that, although I wasn't being explicit, what I had in mind were dogs, mice, and fish (and so on) that were indeed normal in just this way. And having now clarified the point, I will resume my practice of ordinarily leaving the relevant qualifications implicit. Unless context suggests otherwise, when I talk about a given type of animal, it should be understood that I mean individuals with the psychological capacities that are normal or typical for an animal of that kind.

There is, however, a more troubling issue that gets generated by the existence of significant psychological impairment. Take a severely impaired human. Depending on the extent of the brain damage, it seems possible to imagine this human having the psychological capacities of animals that are extremely limited indeed. Such an individual will still be human, to be sure, but it may only be the psychological peer of a chimp, or a dog, or even worse. So if status turns solely on the individual's actual psychological capacities, the severely impaired human will have a significantly lower moral status than the rest of us have. That's an intuitively troubling thought at best, and it will strike many as unacceptable. But if status turns on one's actual capacities, and these humans are not persons (in the technical sense of the term that we have adopted), then it seems virtually inevitable that a sufficiently impaired human will have a lower moral status than you and I have.

Conceivably, one might have similar misgivings about the analogous judgments concerning impaired sheep, or lizards, or birds. That is, one might be uncomfortable with the suggestion that impaired animals of any kind can have a lower status than that had by normal members of their species. However, I suspect that most would be willing to embrace this conclusion, after due reflection, if only there were a motivated way to avoid saying something comparable about severely impaired *humans*. Unsurprisingly, that's the case that really troubles us.

I will eventually offer a proposal that may go a certain distance toward softening the force of this worry. As I have already suggested, I think that the position I have been describing up to this point—according to which status turns solely on one's actual capacities—is only a first approximation. The full story is more complicated. My own view is that even impaired individuals have a *further* feature that is relevant to their status as well—so that they actually possess a status that is at least somewhat higher than that of their psychological peers in lower species. But the discussion of this idea will have to come later. The problem of severely impaired individuals is an issue to which we will need to return.

5.3 Which Capacities?

To say that it is psychological capacities that provide the basis for status is not yet to say that all such capacities are relevant. Perhaps it is only a particular subset that play a role in grounding one's moral status. If so, which capacities are the relevant ones?

I think we don't yet have a good answer to this question, and I am not prepared to put forward a precise proposal with any real confidence. Although, as it seems to me, we have a reasonably decent intuitive feel for which capacities are relevant for status, a tidy abstract account of what unites these features remains somewhat elusive.

Here is one potentially promising suggestion. As we have already noted, there seems to be a connection between an individual's status and the value of the life that the individual is capable of achieving. Animals with higher status are capable of attaining more valuable lives than animals with lower status. Presumably, however, an important part of what makes it possible to achieve a more valuable life is the possession of sufficiently advanced forms of the relevant psychological capacities; otherwise one cannot desire, pursue, attain, and enjoy the given goods. So lives that are more valuable by virtue of involving a greater array of goods, or more valuable forms of those goods, will require a greater array of psychological capacities, or at least more advanced versions of those capacities. And the thought, then, is that it is precisely these differences in capacities that are relevant for *welfare* that are also relevant for fixing *status*. More advanced capacities make possible more valuable forms of life, and the more advanced the capacities, the higher the moral status grounded in the possession of those very capacities.

In effect, an account along these lines takes what otherwise would have been a mere correlation—that animals with higher status generally have more valuable lives—and it eliminates the appearance of coincidence, by suggesting that the very same set of psychological capacities underlie both status and welfare. One's status is grounded in the very capacities that make one's welfare possible.

As far as I can see, a proposal like this does a reasonably good job of identifying the capacities that actually do seem to play a role in fixing one's status. And it has a certain amount of direct intuitive appeal as well.

I suspect, however, that a suitably refined version of this basic approach would encourage us to avoid focusing exclusively on the upper limits of the range of lives available to any given individual. Indeed, as I noted earlier (albeit parenthetically, in 4.2), it seems possible that certain psychological capacities might actually make one vulnerable to particularly *low* levels of welfare as well; and it is conceivable, at least, that such capacities might still enhance one's status, even if they play no role (or don't play a comparable role) in making possible the attainment of more valuable *goods*. Arguably, then, what matters isn't so much the upper limit of welfare of which one is capable, but rather, somewhat more precisely, the *kinds* of welfare of which one is capable, positive or negative. If something like this is right, then it would be more accurate to say that the psychological capacities relevant for fixing status are relevant by virtue of their potential impact on one's well-being, whether for good *or* for ill.

Another refinement—or, perhaps, clarification—that may be helpful is this. We must avoid taking an overly narrow approach when thinking about the psychological capacities that make welfare possible. Welfare is the result of desiring, pursuing, acquiring, and enjoying possible goods (and avoiding possible bads). Intuitively, I think, the capacities that come into play in *each* of these stages can play at least some role in fixing one's moral status. That's an important point to keep in mind, as we can see by considering the possibility of cases in which a given individual lacks some psychological capacity that is needed for the obtaining or enjoyment of a given good, but nonetheless recognizes that very lack, and wishes it were the case that they had the requisite capacity (or capacities) so that they too could try to acquire the missing good. In such a case, we can say that the individual "aspires" to having the good (even if they realize that they have no realistic chance of attaining it), as well as aspiring to the various psychological capacities needed to possess and enjoy the good. And it seems to me that the very ability to have such aspirations may well be relevant to fixing one's status as well. What matters isn't just the kind of welfare that one can in principle achieve (given one's capacities), but the kind of welfare to which one can aspire. Thus, even if one lacks some psychological capacity or capacities needed to attain or enjoy a given good, provided that one can *want* the good that one cannot have (or want the capacities needed to attain and enjoy the good), that very capacity to want it plays a role in determining one's status.

Would a view more or less like this truly identify all the capacities that intuitively play a role in fixing an individual's moral status? I'm not sure. Consider the following worry. It seems plausible to suggest that one of the things that gives people a higher moral status than animals is the fact that we care about and can attend to morality and its obligations. Yet some might insist that this capacity has no direct connection to welfare. To be sure, conformity to morality can enhance the welfare of others; but some would claim that it has no direct bearing on attaining the constituents of welfare for oneself. If so, then the proposal to identify status-generating capacities with the capacities that make one's welfare possible is overly narrow.

Of course, the matter is far from straightforward. My own view, you will recall (see 2.3), is that our ability to reflect on and act upon our moral obligations is indeed one of the very goods that make it true that people have, on the whole, more valuable lives than animals do. Along with such goods as deep relationships, more sophisticated and advanced knowledge, and more significant achievements, our ability to act out of moral conviction is one of the goods that give our lives their special value. So my own view is that the psychological capacities that make one capable of moral agency are indeed among the capacities that directly contribute to one's well-being. And if that's right, then the thought that the capacities relevant for generating status are those that make one's welfare possible may remain a plausible suggestion after all.

Still, as I noted, not everyone accepts this sort of direct connection between morality and well-being, and so some may prefer to look for an additional or alternative way of identifying the capacities relevant for fixing one's status. So let me mention a second natural proposal, which is that the relevant capacities are those that determine one's level of *agency*. I have of course argued that a vast range of animals exhibit agency in some form or the other, but it is clear that animals differ from one another, and from people, in the degree of sophistication of that agency. Some animals are limited to very rudimentary desires, and are capable of only minimal choices about how to act upon those desires. Other animals can have more fine-grained and complex preferences, and can make correspondingly more sophisticated plans. And people, of course, are the most sophisticated agents of all, capable of highly abstract reflection, detailed evaluation of a wide range of alternatives, and careful control over which of their preferences they choose to act upon. The suggestion, then, is that it is these capacities—the capacities that make possible the particular forms and levels of agency of which one is capable—that play a role in fixing one's moral status.

Clearly, any account along this second line will largely overlap in its verdicts with the first proposal, since more advanced forms of agency also make possible more advanced forms of well-being as well. So it is likely that to a considerable extent the two accounts will agree about which capacities are relevant for fixing one's moral status. But that's not to say that they will agree across the board. After all, while some deny any direct connection between moral agency and *well-being*, it is, I think, perfectly clear that our capacity for moral agency is a central and significant aspect of our agency more generally, turning as it does on our underlying capacities for normative reflection and self-governance. So at least some people may find certain capacities relevant under the second proposal that they may not be prepared to count under the first proposal. Similarly, there may be some capacities that at least some people would be more ready to count under the first proposal than the second. Either way, some may find themselves drawn more to one of these proposals rather than the other.

My own view is that an adequate account will inevitably incorporate both ideas (though one could, of course, try to subsume one of the two under the rubric of the other). This seems particularly plausible to me, given that both figure in the most promising accounts of what it takes to have any kind of moral standing at all. After all, it should hardly surprise us if the considerations relevant for making one count in the first place should also turn out to be relevant for fixing one's precise *status*. Put another way, given that welfare and agency both seem important for thinking about *who* counts, it is plausible to think that both will also play a role—direct or indirect—in determining how *much* one counts as well.

Nonetheless, I believe that agency is the more fundamental notion here, with regard to determining which capacities are relevant for status. The real payoff in thinking about moral agency in connection with status lies in the fact that it reminds us of our ability to aim at things *other* than our own welfare (even though, as I believe, it is also an ingredient in our welfare). Our status is enhanced precisely because we have a form of agency which allows us to take on a wide range of aims, to self-consciously evaluate the reasons for and against acting on each of these, and to restrict our behavior, overriding some of our initial desires, when we recognize compelling reason (moral or otherwise) to do so. Even if these very same capacities all turn out to play a role in making possible the having of lives with a particular kind of well-being, I suspect that the ultimate reason that these capacities enhance our status is by virtue of the role they play in constituting the particular kind of agency that we possess.

Imagine that we had resolved this issue. Ultimately, of course, we would like to know not just what the various capacities that help fix one's moral status have in common (whether it's their connection to agency, or welfare, or some third thing), but what the relevant capacities actually are. Thus, a complete theory of the grounds of status would presumably list the various capacities in question and then indicate how the particular ones that are had by any given individual together determine the status of that individual. Unfortunately, I don't think we are yet in a position to offer an account of this sort either; I'm certainly not prepared to do so.

What I can do is say a bit more about at least a few of the relevant capacities, by contrasting the form they take in people and in animals. I have of course already argued that the lives of persons have greater value than the lives of animals: we possess goods that they either lack altogether or have only in less valuable forms. And I take it that the reason people are able to have lives that are richer in this way is because of our having more advanced forms of agency than those had by animals. So let me quickly mention a few of the very general psychological capacities that play a role here, in making our lives so much richer than theirs. No doubt a more thorough discussion would note still other capacities and eliminate potential redundancies (areas where the capacities I list overlap). But no matter; I offer these examples more by way of illustration, rather than as part of any attempt to be systematic or exhaustive. At any rate, all of the following seem to me to play a part in explaining why we have the high moral status that we do, and why animals are lower in this regard (though it might well be that a more systematic account would break some of these capacities down into more basic constituents).

First of all, then, people have a considerably more developed capacity for abstract and complex thought and emotion. This manifests itself in almost every aspect of our existence, from self-reflection and understanding of the external world, on through deliberation and choice. Second, people have a more developed capacity for creativity and imagination. Our thoughts and decisions are informed not just by what we have experienced, but by what we can imagine, and our imaginations are very wide-ranging indeed. Third, we have a tremendously greater capacity for thinking into the further future, and into the distant past. This includes not just the ability to have thoughts and desires that *concern* the future or past, but also the more sophisticated ability to explicitly *locate* events temporally. Thus, for example, not only can we want something that won't actually occur until tomorrow, we can want it *to happen* tomorrow—or next week, or next year, or in a thousand years. Fourth, we have the capacity to make and carry out more long term and complicated plans, many of which involve highly sophisticated, skilled, and noninstinctive actions. Fifth, we have a greater capacity for self-awareness and self-consciousness. We are better able to identity our choices and actions, our mental and bodily states, our environment, and so on, *as our own*, better able to explicitly think of ourselves *as* ourselves. Sixth, we have a greater capacity for normative reflection and motivation (including, but not limited to, moral reflection and motivation). We are able to respond to reasons, not just in fact, but under that very concept—evaluating, comparing, and acting on reasons *as* reasons, even when they conflict with intensely felt desires and preferences. Relatedly, then, seventh, we have a greater capacity for self-governance and autonomous choice. And finally, eighth, we have a greater capacity for individual and idiosyncratic choice. When we make a choice, fewer of our decisions are instinctive; and in making that choice we deliberate over a wider range of importantly distinct alternatives. This results in a tremendous amount of variety, both between the lives of different persons, and over the course of any single such life.[2]

In all these ways and more, the capacities that underlie or constitute our agency are more developed and occur in more sophisticated forms than can be found in animals. Note that it is the *comparative* claim that is crucial here. I am not suggesting that animals have none of these capacities (though no doubt some animals do lack some of them), only that people have them in more sophisticated and advanced forms. That's why people have a higher moral status than animals do. And since animals themselves differ from one kind to the next, with regard to the extent to which they have capacities like this, or with regard to the level or sophistication of their versions of the relevant capacities, this is also why some animals have higher moral status than others.

Some may complain that the list of capacities I've just identified is objectionably anthropocentric, as was the procedure used to arrive at them. In effect, I started out by asking what makes people special, particularly with regard to our agency. I identified a group of relevant capacities, and I then concluded that animals have a lower moral status because they lack or have less advanced forms of these very same capacities. But it should hardly surprise us—the objection would go—that animals look worse in terms of our moral theory, if we simply start out with the assumption that people are superior!

---

[2] Much of this paragraph is inspired by a similar discussion in Frey's "Moral Standing, the Value of Lives, and Speciesism," though he wouldn't agree with me about all the details, and he puts it to a different use.

There is clearly something to this charge. It certainly isn't as though I started out by independently identifying a set of capacities that seemed intuitively relevant for grounding a high moral status, and only then discovered—what a remarkable coincidence!—that people have them to a high degree. Rather, I *began* with the view that people have a high status and I attempted to identify some of the features that make it so. Inevitably, this involved reflecting on features that differentiate people from animals—capacities that we have to a greater degree or in a more advanced form. And so it was indeed inevitable that the features so identified would be ones that we (normal adult humans) have to a relatively high degree, more so than animals.

But that's not to concede that there was anything objectionable about this process. For people are, in fact, the beings with the highest moral status with which we are uncontroversially acquainted. That is, there are no other beings with regard to whom is clear both that we are genuinely acquainted with them and that they have a higher status than us. Thus, while we may be able to imagine creatures with a higher moral status than our own, as far as we can tell animals don't fall into this group; and while a deity certainly might have a higher moral status than we do, it is highly controversial whether such a deity exists (and what it might be like). So if we are trying to identify capacities that ground relatively high moral status, there is nothing misguided about focusing on features that *people* have in more advanced forms than can be found among animals. People are, as I say, the highest status beings with which we have (uncontroversial) acquaintance.

Furthermore, nothing that has been said rules out the possibility that there may be further capacities, beyond those already listed, that also particularly enhance status, and that certain animals might have some of those to a greater degree than people have. I am certainly open to the possibility of discovering that various animals have particular status-enhancing capacities that people have only to a lesser degree (or lack altogether). For even if it is true that people have an overall higher moral status than animals do, it could still be the case that some animals have certain relevant capacities to a greater degree, or in more sophisticated forms, than we have.

Are there such capacities? I don't know. As I have previously remarked (see 2.3) it seems to me possible that dogs, say, have an olfactory aesthetic sense beyond anything that humans have, owing to their considerably more sensitive sense of smell. Conceivably, if there were such a heightened olfactory aesthetic sensibility, this might be among the capacities that raise a given individual's status.

On the other hand, it also seems plausible to suggest that merely having a particularly acute and sensitive sense of smell won't suffice to ground an *aesthetic* sensibility with regard to that sensory modality: that may well require sufficiently sophisticated emotional and cognitive capacities as well. So if dogs lack these further capacities (or fail to have them to a sufficiently high degree), then they may also lack the corresponding aesthetic sensibility; and so they may *not* have a capacity that especially boosts their moral status (as compared to people) after all. Still, while this or other similar proposals may remain contentious, it seems to me that in principle at least we should remain open to the possibility that some animals may have status-enhancing capacities that people lack, or have only to a lesser degree.

In any event, it is worth bearing in mind the point that the list of capacities that I gave above was deliberately constructed with an eye toward identifying some of the capacities that particularly help to ground the relatively higher moral status of people as compared to animals. I certainly did not intend to suggest that these are the only capacities that play any sort of role at all in fixing one's moral status. In particular, then, it should be noted that there may well be still other capacities that are common to people and to animals that play a significant role in fixing one's status. For example, the sheer capacity to feel physical pleasure and pain may play an important role in determining one's moral status, yet there is no obvious reason to assume that this capacity is one that humans have to a higher degree than animals have. (Or rather, somewhat more precisely, while it does seem plausible to suggest that *some* animals have this capacity to a significantly lesser degree, there is no reason to assume that people have it to a higher degree than *all* other animals do. Indeed, some animals may have it to a higher degree still.)

On the other hand, I think it should be conceded that if we turn from bare physical pleasure and pain to emotional elation and suffering, or to the propositional attitudes of taking pleasure or displeasure in some state of affairs, it once again becomes plausible to suggest that these are capacities that people have in much more sophisticated and advanced forms than can be found among animals. So to the extent that these further capacities are themselves among those that play a significant role in fixing one's moral status—a claim that does strike me as plausible—then we find ourselves once again with part of the explanation for the fact that people have a higher moral status than animals do.

I trust it is clear that the sorts of remarks I have been offering are no substitute for a more systematic account. Psychological capacities of the right sort may or may not be the only features that help play a role in fixing one's moral status, but they are certainly among the most important such features. So we need a better understanding of these capacities and their bearing on status.

Not only do we need to know which capacities count at all, but we also need an account of how the different forms that the relevant capacities can take enhance one's status to varying degrees. And we need an account as well of how the relevant capacities interact, not just psychologically but normatively, so that together they jointly help to determine the overall moral status of any given individual. Almost none of this, I think, has yet been adequately worked out.

Let me close with one more question that deserves a fuller discussion than I can provide here. I have suggested that possession of the relevant psychological capacities plays a central role in fixing one's moral status. But is mere *possession* of the given capacity truly sufficient? Or must the capacity actually be *exercised*? Would an individual who had a relevant capacity but never actually used it have the same moral status as an otherwise similar individual who did, at least on occasion, put that capacity to work?

Imagine, for example, someone with the capacity for normative self-governance who never actually uses it, someone who perpetually acts without pausing to reflect on whether there is adequate reason to act as they do, someone who never overrides his initial desires as a result of judging that they are morally objectionable, and so forth. But stipulate that they really do have the capacities in question: in principle, at least, they *could* undertake the relevant reflection, make the requisite judgments, alter their behavior in light of those judgments when that was called for, and so on. It is simply that the capacities are never, in fact, put to work; they are always left idle. Would an individual like this really have the same moral status as someone who not only had the capacities, but used them?

Intuitively, at least, it seems to me that the *exercise* of the relevant capacities is indeed relevant for fixing one's status. Someone with status-enhancing capacities who never uses them would, I think, have a lower status than someone who actually puts them to work. But does this mean that unactualized capacities have no role at all in fixing one's status? If one never uses a given capacity is one's status the *same* as an otherwise similar individual who simply *lacks* the capacity in question? That seems to me wrong as well. I suspect—though I won't try to argue for it here—that mere possession of a relevant capacity does in fact raise one's status, even if it is indeed the case that the actual exercise of that capacity would raise it even further.[3]

Yet even if we were to agree about all of that, further questions would still remain. For example, if the exercise of relevant capacities matters, does it

---

[3] Cf. Arneson, who wonders whether having capacities that were never exercised would boost one's status. ("What, if Anything, Renders All Humans Morally Equal?" p. 111.)

matter how *frequently* they are used? Would a single instance of normative self-governance, say, suffice—even if the capacity was never used again? If not, must the given capacity be used on a regular basis? (What, precisely, would that come to?) Would more frequent use of a status-enhancing capacity elevate one's status more than less frequent use?

These are difficult and delicate questions, and the answers are far from obvious. Here, then, as elsewhere, we are very far indeed from having a complete and adequate account of the grounds of moral status.

5.4 Potential

Although psychological capacities (and, perhaps, their exercise) play a central role in fixing one's moral status, they are not, I think, the whole story. What should we say about an individual who does not actually *have* a relevant capacity, but can eventually *develop* that capacity? A normal newborn human baby, for example, does not yet have the various psychological capacities that people have (it is certainly not yet a person, in our technical sense of the term), but of course under ordinary circumstances it will eventually come to have those capacities. It is not a person yet, but it has the *potential* to be a person, and to have the capacities that ordinary people possess. So we need to ask: what bearing does this potential have on the moral status of the infant?

It is important to note that this is not a case of the sort we were just considering, where some individual has the relevant capacities but simply does not exercise them. It isn't as though, for example, a newborn is *capable* of rational and abstract thought, long term planning, and normative self-governance—and merely fails to exercise these various capacities. No, the newborn does not yet possess these psychological capacities at all. It can of course come to have them, and we can, if we like, express this point by saying that it has the second-order capacity to develop the relevant first-order psychological capacities. But possession of this second-order developmental capacity is not in itself the same thing as already having the first-order capacities. It is, instead, merely a matter of having the *potential* to gain the relevant first-order capacities. So we still need to ask: what bearing, if any, does the possession of this potential have on moral status?

(Of course, as we have already seen, it may be that status depends not only on the possession of the relevant capacities but also on their exercise. So in addition to the question just raised—about the bearing on status of the potential to gain capacities—perhaps we should also raise the corresponding question about the significance, if any, of having the potential to *exercise* these capacities as well. However, since the potential to gain the relevant capacities will also entail the potential to exercise them, I won't give this second kind of potential separate treatment.)

There is, of course, a corresponding question that arises for infant animals as well. A (normal) newborn kitten does not yet have the full set of psychological capacities that it will have if it becomes a normal adult cat. And even with regard to the capacities that it does have from birth, it may not have them in their more developed forms. But, of course, the kitten has the *potential* to attain the capacities typical of adult cats. Similarly, a newborn chick may not yet have all the psychological capacities it will have as an adult hen (or may not have them in comparably developed forms), but normally it will have the potential to gain them. So for animals too we need to ask: what bearing, if any, does this sort of potential have on moral status?

Apparently, then, the question we are interested in is a quite general one. What we want to know is this: if the possession of a set of psychological capacities would suffice to ground an individual's having a particular moral status, what bearing if any does the mere *potential* to gain these capacities have on the status of an individual? Speaking loosely, but intuitively, we could phrase the question this way: what bearing does the mere *potential* to have a certain status have on one's *actual* status?

This question should not, I think, be confused with a different one, with which it might easily be conflated, namely, what bearing, if any, does one's *future* status have on one's *current* status? This new question asks whether the fact that you *will* have various capacities in the future has any bearing on your moral status *now*. That's certainly an interesting question, too. My own view is that it has no bearing: your current moral status depends on your *present* properties, not the ones you will come to have in the future. But whether or not I am right about this, it's a different question from the one I mean to be posing, which is whether your current moral status depends only on the psychological capacities that you currently possess or also on the fact that you (currently) have the potential to gain further particular capacities. That potential, after all, is among the properties you do already have. So even if only present properties can help fix one's status, it might still be the case that the fact that you currently have a certain potential might be among the present properties that are relevant for fixing your status.

As I say, the two questions are easily run together. When we think about a newborn baby, for example, and we point out that it has the potential to become a person, one way to establish that fact is by noting (as I did, above), that under normal circumstances it will in fact *become* a person. Clearly, if it *will* come to have a set of capacities (in the future), that entails that it already has the *potential* to come to have those capacities. And ordinarily, at least, a child that has the potential to become a person actually does become one as well. So the issues are easy to conflate. But for all that, talk about the individual's potential and talk about its future need to be distinguished, since, for example, if the infant should die in an accident the next day, it will still be true that it had the *potential* to become a person, even though (in this scenario) it will never, in fact, become a person at all.

All of which is just by way of clarifying that the question I mean to pose is indeed the one about potential, rather than the one about the future. What I want to ask is whether the mere potential to have a certain status has any influence on an individual's *actual* status.

This is, of course, a question that has been widely debated in philosophical discussions about the morality of abortion. The developing embryo or fetus, after all, is not yet a person; but on most views it has the potential to become one.[4] Understandably, then, those wishing to develop an adequate account of the morality of abortion have felt the need to take a stand on whether the mere potential to be a person itself suffices to ground an elevated moral status.

(Note, incidentally, that the topic of abortion is one concerning which it is especially important to distinguish between the relevance of potential status and the relevance of future status. If the fetus is aborted it never actually becomes a person; but for all that, it still had the potential to be one.)

The topic is far too complicated for me to do justice to here, but let me quickly note two familiar positions, and then sketch an alternative. On the one hand, it is sometimes suggested that the potential to become a person suffices to ground *exactly* the same moral status as that had by someone who is already a person. So not only is potential personhood relevant to one's status, it is every bit as significant as actually having the relevant capacities themselves.

If one takes this first view, what should one say about the more general case? Does the analogous claim hold for animals as well? To be sure, adult animals have a lower moral status than people do, but is it at least the case that an infant animal's potential to gain the capacities of a normal adult animal of the relevant kind already suffice to give the infant animal the moral status of an adult? Does a kitten, say, already have the status of an adult cat, simply by virtue of having the potential to become one? Or is there something special

---

[4] To be sure, on certain views concerning the nature of personal identity an embryo or fetus in sufficiently early stages of development is not the right *sort* of entity to ever become a person at all; so it won't actually have that potential. (See McMahan, *The Ethics of Killing*, pp. 267–9.) For our purposes we needn't try to settle the question.

about the potential to become a *person* that gives potential personhood special normative force, so that not only does it ground a higher status (the status of a person), but it is unique—as compared to other mere potentials—in grounding the corresponding status at all? (Perhaps a potential person has the status of a person, while a kitten does not yet have the status of an adult cat.) Unsurprisingly, discussions of abortion rarely pursue this more general question.

A different familiar position with regard to potential takes the other extreme, and denies that mere potential personhood has any status-enhancing properties at all. To have the potential to become a person indicates nothing more than that you *could* become a person. If and when you do so, of course, you will then have the status of a person. But the mere fact that you have the *potential* to become a person does nothing at all to enhance your status.

(Someone who takes this view could nonetheless hold that *future* status affects current status. So if you are not yet a person but *will* become one, that may already give you the status of a person *now*. Still, the mere fact of being a *potential* person does not enhance one's status, so a potential person that dies before becoming an actual person never has the status of a person at all.[5])

Here too we face the question of how to generalize, but here at least the answer seems obvious. If potential personhood has no bearing on moral status, it is unlikely that other forms of potential will do any better. Thus a kitten, despite being a potential adult cat, gains no increased status from that fact.

It is, of course, important to bear in mind that even if having a potential status does nothing at all to increase one's actual status, it certainly doesn't follow that one's actual status is particularly low (or that one currently lacks moral standing altogether). Many newborn animals, for example—and certainly newborn humans—will already have some psychological capacities that are relevant for moral status. So even those who deny the relevance of potential to status will want to take those capacities into account. The bare potential to gain relevant capacities may do nothing to enhance one's status, but for all that, one's actual current capacities will of course still be relevant.

So there we have two more or less familiar views concerning the relevance of potential to one's moral status. But I am attracted to a view intermediate between them. Unlike those who accept the second view, I find it plausible to think that potential does make a difference to status. But unlike those drawn to the first view, I don't think it gives one the very same status as an individual who already *has* the relevant capacities. So a normal newborn human, for

---

[5] Cf. Harman, "The Potentiality Problem" and "Creation Ethics."

example, counts more than an animal that is its psychological peer (that is, one with the same actual capacities) but who lacks the potential to become a person. Still, such a newborn doesn't count as much as someone who is *already* a person. Potential increases status, but not by as much as actually having the relevant capacities.

And I see no reason to think that something like this holds only with regard to being a potential person. As far as I can see, something analogous should hold across the board, for animals as well. Thus, for example, a kitten is a potential adult cat, and thus has a higher status than would be had by a different animal that was its psychological peer but that didn't have the potential to gain the capacities that a normal adult cat possesses. Still, for all that, the kitten has a lower status than an adult cat (given that kittens don't have the full capacities had by adult cats). Similarly for other animals. In each case, potential increases status (subject to the qualification I describe below), but not by as much as actually having the relevant capacities themselves.

Since this is an intermediate view, there remains the further question: how *much* does potential increase one's status (over the status one would have if one lacked the potential)? A minimal version of the view would come close to the second position described above, holding that potential increases status only a very little, barely anything at all. A maximal version would come close to the first, holding that potential increases status a great deal—almost as much as actually having the capacities would do. Here too I find myself thinking that neither extreme is right, so that the difference potential makes is significant, but not close to the full difference made by actual possession of the relevant capacities. But I won't try to answer the question with any further precision than that.

For all that, of course, it does seem right to suggest that the *size* of the boost depends on the status that one has the potential to attain. Thus, if we were to imagine two psychological peers, who differ only in terms of their potential, if one only has the potential to gain the capacities typical of adult dogs, while the other has the potential to be a person, then the current status of the two individuals would not at all be the same: the enhancement to status due to the potential to be a person is significantly greater than the enhancement due to the potential to be an adult dog. So the status of the potential person will be higher than the status of the potential adult dog. Still, be that all as it may, the question remains: how *much* of an enhancement does each get? I won't try to answer that.

If potential really does enhance or boost one's status, how exactly does that work? One obvious proposal is that it does this by raising one's status a particular amount, with the precise amount of the boost depending on the status that one has the potential to attain. So the potential to acquire the capacities of an adult dog will raise one's current status by a particular fixed amount, while the potential to acquire the capacities of an adult bat would presumably raise one's status by a *lesser* fixed amount, and the potential to be a person would raise one's status by a *larger* fixed amount. On this model, the boost to one's current status would be solely a function of the status that one had the potential to attain; it wouldn't depend at all on one's current, actual capacities. So two individuals with the same potential would get the same size boost to their status, regardless of whether their actual capacities differ.

But I am attracted to an alternative model, where one's potential functions more like an amplifier, multiplying the "signal" generated by the capacities one already has. So if two individuals with the same potential differ in terms of their actual capacities, the one with the more advanced set of capacities will ordinarily get a larger boost to their status, despite the fact that the potential in question is the same for both.[6] Speaking loosely, the individual who "starts out" with the higher status (based on current capacities alone) has a stronger "status signal" to be amplified, and so status is enhanced by a larger amount. On this model, therefore, the size of the enhancement due to the amplification depends not just on the potential itself, but also on the underlying capacities being amplified.

Of course, even here, it remains true that the size of the enhancement is *also* a function of the status that one has the potential to attain. The potential to be a person is a more powerful amplifier than the potential to be an adult dog, let alone the potential to be an adult bat. So the size of the enhancement depends not just on the nature of the signal (one's current, actual capacities), but also on the nature of the amplifier as well (what it is that one has the potential to become).

Still, even the most powerful amplifier needs a signal to amplify. This means that if something currently has none of the capacities sufficient to ground moral standing, then even if it has the *potential* to attain some of these capacities that fact by itself will not suffice to give that entity moral standing. If there is no "underlying" status to be amplified, mere potential cannot create one. In effect, the mere potential for standing does not suffice to generate standing;

---

[6] This will only *ordinarily* be the case. Since potential cannot raise one's status to a level higher than what one would have if one already actually had the relevant capacities, if a developing individual gets sufficiently close to having those capacities in their fully developed form, the incremental *boost* to status from the remaining potential will necessarily start growing smaller.

potential can only enhance one's status when there is something already there to work on.

(A view like this clearly has implications for the morality of abortion. Embryos and early fetuses lack both agency and sentience; they have none of the capacities relevant for moral status. By my lights this means that they lack moral standing altogether, since mere potential personhood cannot give status to something that would lack standing in the absence of that potential. So even if it is true that an early fetus, say, has the potential to become a person, there is no "signal" here to amplify, and no moral status is generated. It is only at later stages of development that the fetus gains standing, though even then the relevant capacities are initially quite limited, so there is at best only a weak signal to be amplified. It may only be at late pregnancy, or after birth, that potential personhood has a significant effect on status. Unfortunately, it would take us too far afield to pursue this topic any further here.)

There is one further point about the bearing of potential on status that should be noted. Although I have been writing as though a given individual either has the potential to gain certain capacities or else lacks it altogether, the truth of the matter is that potentiality actually comes in degrees. Speaking abstractly, a given entity has the potential to gain certain features if it would come to possess those features under the right circumstances. So in principle, it seems, even if those circumstances are remote and unlikely to come to pass, it would still be correct to say that the *potential* was there. Thus, for example, even a puppy may have the potential to become a person, if (as seems possible) there is some complicated (not yet discovered) medical technique that would vastly enhance its psychological capacities, turning it into a person.[7] Even if this technique is never discovered, there will be a sense in which each puppy is already a potential person.

What this shows, of course, is that we need to grade the *strength* of a given potential, where a weaker potential is one that will be actualized only in relatively remote or unlikely circumstances. A newborn human baby is a potential person, and so, perhaps, is a puppy. But that potential is ordinarily a very strong one for a human infant, since the circumstances required to turn the infant into a person are not at all remote or unlikely to occur, while it is an extremely weak one (for the time being, at any rate) in the case of the puppy. Strictly speaking, then, we should not talk in an unqualified way about the amplificatory power of one's potential; we also need to take into account the *strength* of

---

[7] The process would also have to preserve identity—so that it was the very same animal that emerges as a person. (McMahan, *The Ethics of Killing*, pp. 302–5 and 308–9.)

the potential, since the weaker any given potential is (other things being equal), the less its amplificatory power. Of course, for obvious practical reasons we will typically limit our attention to potentials that are relatively strong. Thus, for example, the potential for personhood is strong in the case of a normal human newborn, and the amplificatory effects of that potential should, accordingly, be taken into account; but the potential is *negligible* in the case of a puppy, and so under ordinary circumstances its amplificatory effects there can safely be ignored.

5.5 Modal Status

The question of whether potential has a bearing on status is a familiar one, sufficiently so that even those who deny the relevance of potential recognize the need to discuss the issue. But I want to turn now to a different feature—similar to potential, though not identical to it—which has not received comparable attention. Like potential, this new feature is concerned with possibilities, but unlike potential, which is a matter of what could *become* the case (if the right conditions obtain), the new feature is a matter, rather, of what *could have been* the case (*had* the right conditions obtained).

Consider, for example, a 20 year old human who suffered irreparable brain damage as an infant, so that she never became a person, but remains, instead, at the cognitive level of a four month old. This individual does not have the *potential* to become a person, since there is nothing that we could do now for her that would allow her to become one. But for all that, it is still the case that she *could have been* a person (now), had the accident not occurred when she was a baby. (Strictly, of course, it may well be the case that she actually *does* have a potential to become a person, albeit a very weak potential, if there is some undiscovered medical technique that would undo the brain damage and allow her to develop the capacities had by normal adult humans. But as I have already explained, any such potential will be so weak that for all practical purposes we can justifiably ignore it—and for simplicity of exposition that is exactly what I will do.)

In effect, it is too late for the individual in question to become a person. Although she *had* the potential as a newborn to become a person later, she lost the potential when she had the accident. So she does not have potential personhood now. Nonetheless, the following remains true of her: she could have been a person now, since she *would* have been a person by now had the accident never happened. So although she lacks *potential* personhood, she has another modal property in the same neighborhood. As far as I know, this second modal property does not have a standard name. Let's call it *modal personhood*, and let us say of someone who is *not* a person but who *could* have been a person (now), that they are a *modal person*.[8]

As we have just seen, someone can be a modal person without being a potential person. Similarly, someone can be a potential person without being a modal person. A newborn human, for example, is a potential person, but it is not a modal person, since there is nothing that could have happened earlier that would have made it be the case now that the infant was *already* (currently) a person. So modal personhood needs to be distinguished from potential personhood. Nonetheless, I want to suggest that modal personhood is like potential personhood in an important way: it too can raise one's status from what it otherwise would have been.

Indeed, it seems to me that the parallel is a fairly close one, with modal personhood's bearing on status being very similar to that of potential personhood. First of all, then, modal personhood enhances one's status, so that if there are two individuals who are otherwise similar, including being psychological peers, but one of them is a modal person while the other is not, the former will have a higher moral status than the latter. However, although the modal person's status will be higher than it would have been had she not been a modal person, nonetheless, she still does not have as high a status as she would have if she actually were a person. Modal personhood increases status, but not by as much as actually having the relevant capacities.

Of course, this still leaves the question of how *much* modal personhood increases status. Once again, a minimal view would say that it does so by a very small amount, while a maximal view would say that it comes close to giving one the same status as is had by someone who already is, in fact, a person. My own view is that (as with potential) neither extreme is right: the contribution is significant, but not enough to bring one close to having the status of an actual person.

Second, here too I see no reason to think that the sort of enhancement to status that I am describing holds only with regard to being a modal *person*. I presume that, for example, there are brain damaged adult dogs, who lack the capacities typical of adult dogs, but who *could have* had those capacities in the present, had things gone differently in the past. So they are *modal dogs*, as I will call them, and their status is higher than that had by any otherwise similar psychological peers who lack modal doghood (though it is a lower status than that of normal adult dogs). Similarly, for various other types of animals. In each case, a modal animal of a given type will have a higher status than its

---

[8] I introduced this notion in "What's Wrong with Speciesism?"

otherwise similar psychological peers who are not modal animals of the given type, but a lower status than that had by animals with the full set of capacities had by normal adult animals of the type in question.

(Just to be clear: as I am using the term, a modal dog is not an animal that is not a dog but could have been one; rather it is an animal that does not have the capacities had by normal adult dogs, but could have had them. Similarly for other types of modal animals.)

It will be helpful to have a general term for this status-enhancing feature. I propose to call it *modal status*. To have a given modal status is for it to be true of you that you could have had the status in question (or, alternatively, the capacities that would ground that status). And what I am claiming then, quite generally, is that one's modal status affects one's *actual* status. If the status you could have had is greater than your "underlying" status (the status you would have, based on your actual capacities alone), then your actual status is higher than it would be in the *absence* of having that modal status.

Third, I take it that the size of the boost to status created by one's modal status depends on the particular capacities that one could have attained. Roughly speaking, the higher the status that one could have had, the greater the boost to one's actual status. If we imagine two psychological peers, who differ only in terms of their modal status, if one is a modal person while the other is a modal dog (that is, could only have had the capacities typical of adult dogs) then the modal person will have a higher status than the modal dog.

Fourth, like potential, modal status works like an amplifier. The boost it provides is a function not just of the status one could have had, but also of one's actual current psychological capacities. Other things being equal, the greater the "signal" provided by one's current capacities, the greater the boost generated by any given modal status. In particular, then, if there is no underlying signal, then there is no amplification of status. Thus, something that would lack moral standing altogether but for having some particular modal status will still lack moral standing, *despite* having that modal status; modal status needs something to "work on" if it is to enhance status.[9] Still, as I have already noted, if there *is* a signal to work on then the amount by which that signal gets amplified depends

---

[9] I thus erred in my essay "What's Wrong with Speciesism?" when discussing an example (at p. 18, but cf. p. 17) of an anencephalic child who was a modal person. I claimed there that modal personhood gave such anencephalics a higher moral status; but I forgot to take into account the fact that such a child would have no moral standing generated by its actual capacities (if—as I assumed—they don't even have the ability to feel pleasure or pain, nor do they possess any agency), so modal personhood would have no "signal" to amplify. For the purposes of that paper, I would have done better to use examples of adult humans who were brain damaged—either because of genetic defects or because of an accident in infancy—but who retain the minimal capacities of newborns. (Thanks to Doran Smolkin for this point.)

on the particular status that one could have had. Other things being equal, being a modal person provides more amplification than being a modal dog, which in turn provides more amplification, than, say, merely being a modal bat.

Finally, modal status also comes in degrees, so here too we need to distinguish between varying degrees of strength. Strictly speaking, a modal person is an individual who *could* have been a person now, had the right circumstances obtained in the past—no matter how remote or unlikely a possibility it was that those circumstances would occur. Thus even a dog will count as a modal person if there is some complicated medical technique (perhaps never to be discovered) that *could* have been used to turn it into a person (had the technique been discovered sufficiently earlier, and had it been applied to the growing puppy in time, and so forth). Clearly, however, the case of the dog needs to be distinguished from our earlier example of an adult human who accidentally suffered brain damage as an infant. The circumstances that would have allowed the dog to be a person now were extraordinarily remote and unlikely; in contrast, the circumstances that would have allowed the adult human to be a person may not have been remote or unlikely at all (perhaps all that was needed was that the child not have been accidentally dropped). Thus even if a dog is a modal person, its modal status is at best extremely weak, while the modal personhood of the adult human is quite strong.

Accordingly, we also need to take into account the *strength* of one's modal status, with weaker modal statuses providing proportionately less amplificatory power. And here too, for obvious practical reasons, we will typically and justifiably ignore modal statuses that are weak, confining our attention to those that are relatively strong. The modal personhood of the adult human in our example is strong, and her status is, I believe, significantly increased; but the modal personhood of the dog is negligible at best, so under ordinary circumstances the amplificatory effects of that modal status, if any, can justifiably be ignored.

Actually, there is one further way in which modal status is similar to potential, though this particular feature is not one that I have previously mentioned. Modal status, like potential, appears to affect one's actual status in an *asymmetrical* way. What matters are the (relevant) possibilities that concern *higher* or more advanced sets of capacities, not the various possibilities that concern *lower* or less developed ones. Presumably, after all, for any given individual, not only is it true that in principle at least it could have had a *more* sophisticated set of capacities (had things gone the right way), it is also true that—in principle, at least—it could have had a *less* sophisticated set than its actual set (had things gone the wrong way). Yet intuitively, at least, it is only the first, "positive" modal status that has a bearing on actual status. A normal adult human, for example, does not seem to have a lower status by virtue of the fact that they *could* have suffered brain damage earlier, and so not been a person right now! A "negative" modal status—the fact that one could have been at the cognitive and emotional level of a cat, say—seems irrelevant, unlike a positive modal status. Similarly for potential: under the "right" circumstances (however remote) the puppy could become something even less cognitively and emotionally sophisticated than it already is; yet this negative potential seems irrelevant, unlike its positive counterpart.

Presumably part of the difference here can be explained by appeal to differences in the *strengths* of the various potentials and modal statuses. For example, a puppy is normally more likely to develop in the direction of higher capacities than in the direction of lower ones. But I doubt that this sort of consideration will fully explain the asymmetry. For even when a negative modal status is reasonably strong—say, when one has narrowly escaped an accident that would have left one brain damaged—this doesn't seem to lower one's actual status. Similarly, a negative potential of a given strength doesn't seem relevant in the same way that a positive potential of the same strength would be.

Of course, it may be too extreme to claim that negative potentials and negative modal statuses don't count *at all*. But at the very least they do seem *less* significant than correspondingly strong positive potentials and modal statuses, and that fact remains puzzling. I have no ready explanation for this asymmetry. Perhaps it is an illusion. But whatever it is that one makes of this apparent asymmetry—regardless of whether it is real, or merely apparent—it does at least seem true that in the *positive* case, if nothing more, modal status, like potential, is relevant to actual status: a positive modal status, like a positive potential, will enhance one's status.

Presumably, however, some will object to my various claims about the significance of modal status, suggesting that they run afoul of the individualism about status that I endorsed earlier (in 5.2). After all, I asserted then that a given individual's status depends solely on the capacities that are had by the particular individual. Yet here I am now, asserting that it also depends on capacities that one *could* have had, rather than capacities that one actually has. A similar objection could of course also be raised with regard to my views about the significance of potential, since I hold that one's status also depends on capacities one could *come* to have, and not just on those one actually has.

But of course at that earlier point in the discussion I was merely trying to make clear that despite the fact that I had been talking about the status of dogs, cats, snakes, and so forth, one's membership in a given species (or other biological grouping) was not really what mattered. What mattered, rather, were the capacities of the particular individual—not the capacities that might be typical of members of its species.

In any event, when I endorse individualism with regard to status, all I mean to claim is that what matters for the status of a given individual are the (relevant) features of that very individual (and not, per se, the features of members of groups to which the individual might belong). And it should be clear that a commitment to individualism in this broad sense does not yet tell us *which* features of the individual are relevant. Thus individualism actually leaves open the possibility that other features of the individual, besides their actual capacities (and, perhaps, the exercise of those capacities), might be relevant to fixing status.

In particular, then, it is no violation of individualism to maintain, as I do, that one's modal status and one's potential are relevant to fixing one's moral status. Recall our earlier example of the adult who was brain damaged as an infant. It is certainly a feature of that very woman that she is a modal person. Indeed, this is every bit as much a genuine feature of the woman as that she has red hair, or that she was born 20 years earlier, or that she has the capacity to feel pain. Similarly, it is a genuine feature of a normal human newborn that it is a potential person. There is simply nothing in one's acceptance of individualism per se to give one reason to rule out the relevance of modal status or potential.

Indeed, recognizing the significance of modal status and potential can go a long way toward explaining why it has often seemed so *tempting* to think that species membership does matter—even though, as far as I can see, one's membership in a given species actually has no moral significance in itself at all. Starting with the obvious point, in a typical case, at least, knowing an adult's species (whether human or animal) will give you a pretty good sense of their actual capacities. But less obviously, even in the atypical case, such as when you are dealing with an infant or a brain damaged individual, species membership is still a useful guide. For it will ordinarily provide you with a pretty good sense of the individual's potential (in the case of infants), or modal status (in the case of brain damage or other cognitive impairments). To be sure, there will be exceptions—for instance, science fiction examples where an individual has capacities far beyond those typical of its species or where the individual lacks the potential or modal status normally associated with its species. But in ordinary cases, at any rate, knowing the individual's species will tell you a lot of what you need to know to determine the individual's status. No wonder then that it is so tempting to think that species membership matters in its own right.

Of course, what really matters are one's actual capacities, one's potential, and one's modal status. But species membership is normally an extremely useful bit of relevant evidence about all of that. Hence the common confusion.

Conceivably, however, concern about modal status and potential isn't really about individualism per se, but rather involves a more demanding claim, namely, that status must turn solely on the *intrinsic* properties of the given individual. If we were to accept this claim, then that would indeed rule out the sort of views I have been putting forward. For I have claimed that one's actual status depends on the strength of one's potential or the strength of one's modal status—and neither of these turn on one's intrinsic properties alone.

An example should make the point clear. Take the potential to be a person. As I have already noted, even a puppy may have this potential—in a very weak form—if there is some undiscovered (and perhaps never discovered) therapy that would allow it to develop into a person. But imagine that we do indeed eventually discover the therapy, and we routinely deliver it to puppies. Then a puppy who is soon to get the therapy is also a potential person—and in this case the potential is a strong one. Clearly, however, the availability (and standard use) of the therapy is not an intrinsic fact about any given puppy. So having potential personhood of a given strength is not an intrinsic feature of the puppy, though it does of course depend on intrinsic features of the puppy as well. Similar remarks apply to other potentials. Consequently, if, as I claim, one's status is affected by the strength of one's potentials, one's status does not turn solely on one's intrinsic properties. Putting the same point the other way around, if status does turn on intrinsic properties alone, then I am wrong to suggest that the strength of one's potential has a bearing on one's status.

A similar argument works, of course, for modal status as well. Suppose the remarkable therapy exists but is never discovered. Then a puppy is a modal person (it could have been a person had the therapy been discovered and been applied), but this modal status is extremely weak. In contrast, if the therapy has been discovered, and is routinely administered to puppies, but this particular puppy has somehow been accidentally overlooked (and now it is too late to administer the therapy), then the puppy's modal personhood is rather strong. But the availability and normal use of the therapy does not alter the intrinsic properties of puppies. Therefore, having modal personhood (or, more generally, modal status) of a given strength is not an intrinsic feature either. So if status does turn on intrinsic properties alone, I am wrong to suggest that the strength of one's modal status has a bearing on one's status.

Very well, we must choose. Should we insist that it is indeed the case that status turns solely on intrinsic properties—and so conclude that modal status and potential are irrelevant to status? Or shall we reject that claim, and thus allow for the relevance of potential and modal status?

(Is there a third alternative? Might one try to develop an account of potential or modal status where these actually do turn solely on intrinsic properties? My own view is that the prospects of doing this successfully are dim.[10])

I know that some will find it simply obvious that status must turn on intrinsic properties and intrinsic properties alone. They will point out that unless we embrace this thesis one's status will partly be an accident of one's external circumstances, so that two intrinsically identical beings can nonetheless differ in terms of their moral status.[11] That, they will insist, is absurd.

But for myself, I see no compelling reason to agree that status must turn on intrinsic properties and nothing else.[12] To be sure, we must be on guard to dismiss the pretentions of *irrelevant* properties; but such false contenders are hardly limited to extrinsic ones. Nor am I troubled by the realization that two individuals who are similar in terms of their intrinsic properties may nonetheless differ in terms of their moral status. That seems to me acceptable—provided, of course, that the difference in status is grounded in some suitable underlying difference. So the question simply becomes whether there is intuitive support for the idea that potential and modal status are among the features that can affect one's status. And in my own case, at least, when I ask that question the answer is clear: both do seem intuitively relevant. If you, too, share those intuitions, then you have at least some reason to reject the unargued assumption that status must turn on intrinsic properties alone.

Admittedly, I haven't really offered much by way of argument for my different claims about modal status or potential. Indeed, much the same thing might be said about the claims I've made throughout this chapter. But my goal here hasn't been so much to defend a particular view about the basis of status as much as it was to simply sketch a possible view. To be sure, I believe that the various claims I have made about the grounds of status do a good job of matching common intuitions (concerning which individuals have higher status than others, and why those individuals have the higher status that they do)—but I haven't taken the time to run through a suitable range of cases so as to vindicate that judgment. In any event, I certainly haven't attempted to lay out and defend a full account of the basis of status. My goal here was more modest: to

---

[10] See McMahan, *The Ethics of Killing*, pp. 308–16.

[11] For example, McMahan, *The Ethics of Killing*, pp. 309–11.

[12] Some of the appeal of the claim may be due to viewing status as a kind of intrinsic value, combined with the assumption that intrinsic value must turn on intrinsic properties alone. I have argued against one version of that assumption in "Rethinking Intrinsic Value."

sketch in broad outlines one possible view that has at least a reasonable amount of initial plausibility.

As I have emphasized, then, even if one accepts a view of this general shape, there remain many details to work out.[13] No doubt, in the course of doing that, some of what I have tentatively endorsed here may need to be modified or abandoned. Still, since I believe that an adequate account of animal ethics will inevitably involve hierarchical claims about status, it seemed important to at least sketch one potentially promising approach to thinking about the basis of that status. But here, as with all the other topics I discuss in this book, a tremendous amount of work remains to be done.

---

[13] For example, imagine an infant that suffers brain damage, and so loses its potential to become a person. It is not a potential person (it can no longer become a person), nor is it a modal person (it couldn't have been a person yet), but it is a *modal potential person* (it *could* have been the case that it was a potential person now). Does that property raise one's status as well?

6

Worries about Hierarchy

6.1 Elitism

Some people will be prepared to dismiss out of hand the sort of hierarchical view I have been describing. After all, they may insist, hierarchical views of any kind are elitist, opening the door to practices that are utterly unacceptable from the moral point of view. Hierarchical views are "morally pernicious."[1]

It is unclear how best to reply to this objection, since it is unclear what exactly the objection is supposed to be. It is certainly true that hierarchical views of one kind or another have been used to defend a wide range of unjust and morally abhorrent practices. Among many other instances, appeals to theories involving moral hierarchies have been used to support claims that slavery and caste systems are justified, that women have fewer moral rights than men, that monarchs and the nobility have moral privileges that ordinary people utterly lack, and that God's chosen have a moral standing to which the heathen cannot lay claim. These views are certainly all deplorable.

But it is difficult to see what conclusion we are entitled to draw from this fact. Surely the thought cannot be that if false moral views of a given kind have been used to defend horrific practices, then *all* views of that general kind must be false as well, or, at the very least, are to be avoided out of fear that the relevant notions may be put to ill use. For it is hard to see how any moral theory of any kind at all could escape condemnation on that ground. At any rate, we do not go around dismissing out of hand all appeals to moral *rights*, for example, on the ground that false and objectionable views about rights have often been used to justify morally abhorrent practices. We do not find ourselves ready to reject all appeals to the moral importance of freedom, say, or autonomy, or equality, or well-being, or the social good, or justice itself, on the ground that such notions have often been put to work to justify actions that we rightly condemn as morally appalling.

---

[1] Regan, *The Case for Animal Rights*, p. 234. In this passage, Regan is only explicitly criticizing hierarchical views (he calls them "perfectionist") that distinguish between different types of *people*; but his aim in doing so is to give grounds for rejecting hierarchical views of the kind I am endorsing as well.

So even if it is granted—what surely must be granted—that hierarchical views have often been used to defend morally pernicious practices, nothing will follow other than the uncontroversial thought that *false* hierarchical views will lead to false moral beliefs, and thus have the potential to lead to injustice (or worse). Accordingly, we should be careful here, as with any moral claim whatsoever, to subject our hierarchical claims to careful and conscientious scrutiny. But it certainly won't follow that we have good reason to reject any and all hierarchical views per se.

What about the worry that hierarchical views are inevitably elitist? I find myself inclined to say that this may well be the case—depending on what, exactly, we mean by that term. But what we still need to know is why that fact should be thought to constitute some sort of objection. Often enough, it seems to me, to say that hierarchical views are elitist is to do little more than to point out that hierarchical views are indeed hierarchical—all the while implying that this very feature somehow automatically renders them unacceptable.

Of course, whether hierarchical theories are indeed elitist depends in part on how we define the notion of "elitism"; but I suppose the following is a reasonable gloss:

the belief that certain persons or members of certain groups deserve favored treatment by virtue of their superiority, as in intelligence, social standing, or wealth.[2]

It does seem to me accurate to describe the view I have been defending as an elitist one—in *this* sense of the term. For I have been arguing that people have a higher moral status than animals do, and that some animals have higher statuses than others. These differences in status ground corresponding differences in the strength of relevant moral claims (for example, giving people stronger distributive claims), and in that sense those with higher status will receive favored treatment: their otherwise similar interests will be given more weight. And the members of these favored groups will have this higher status by virtue of having superior status-generating features—for example, more developed and sophisticated psychological capacities (or the potential to gain such capacities, and so on).

So the view I am defending is indeed an elitist one. To be sure, it doesn't assign status on the basis of social standing, or wealth. Nor does it do so on the basis of other features familiar from common elitist views, such as sex, skin color, religion, or family. Conceivably, it might be said to assign status on the basis of something roughly similar to *intelligence*—one of the features mentioned

---

[2] thefreedictionary.com. Definition accessed 3/28/17.

above—depending on how broadly we construe that term (it certainly isn't looking at anything as narrow as, say, IQ). But this is neither here nor there. Presumably, it suffices for a theory to qualify as elitist that there be *some* designated feature that purportedly grounds the differential treatment; and the appeal to psychological capacities (along with potential and modal status) certainly plays that role in the theory I've described.

So the theory is an elitist one. But why exactly is that a problem? Once we remember not to overgeneralize from the fact that most elitist views are mistaken (and, indeed, pernicious) to the conclusion that all of them must be, it is hard to see what exactly is supposed to be objectionable about embracing views that involve this sort of differentiation in assigning status.

Some might complain that such talk of "differentiation" is a contentiously anodyne way of describing elitist views; it would be better, perhaps, to say that elitist views are unacceptable precisely because they involve illegitimate *discrimination*—an unjustified refusal to treat similar interests similarly. But at this point the criticism of hierarchy has been reduced to little more than name calling. "Elitist" becomes a term that we apply to a moral theory only when it involves drawing a distinction among groups that we take to be unjustifiable.

Consider, for example, the commonplace thought that some pains are morally more significant than others, perhaps because they last longer or are more intense. If we find ourselves prioritizing those with more intense pains—giving them "favored treatment"—is that practice elitist? Of course not. No one would call it that, because of course everyone recognizes that it is *appropriate* to distinguish between more intense and less intense pains. To call views that discriminate between pains in this way *elitist* would be to suggest (without, perhaps, strictly entailing) that the distinction being drawn was somehow morally illegitimate. And no one believes that.

Similarly, consider a view according to which a convicted murderer's claim not to be imprisoned is less weighty than that of an innocent person who has never been so much as accused of murder. Such a view also discriminates between different groups, giving some (the innocent) favored treatment over others (the guilty). But here, too, no one would ever call such a view elitist, since we recognize the justification for the differential treatment.

In short, whatever the official definition of elitism might be, in practice we tend to reserve the term "elitist" for theories and practices that differentiate on grounds that we think morally irrelevant. So if one were to complain about a hierarchical view in animal ethics on the grounds that such views are elitist that wouldn't really be offering any kind of *argument* against the view in question; rather, it would simply be to presuppose that the view is mistaken. We would not yet have been told why others should share that judgment.

6.2 Superior Beings

Even if hierarchical views should not be rejected automatically—that is, simply by virtue of the very fact that they involve hierarchy—there may still be good reason to reject them. Accordingly, in what follows I want to consider three more substantive worries one might have about the sort of position I have been describing. My own view is that all three are legitimate concerns, in that they might reasonably give one pause before accepting a hierarchical approach to animal ethics, but only the last two are genuinely troubling.

The first of the three worries I have in mind involves the possibility of beings with a moral status that is *superior* to our own. I have of course been defending the idea that moral status can vary, with animals of different sorts having statuses lower than the one we have. But it seems plausible to suggest that a hierarchical view would also open the door to the possibility of recognizing statuses *higher* than ours as well. After all, if animals can have a lower moral status by virtue of their less developed or less sophisticated psychological capacities, then it seems that we must be open to the possibility (in principle, at least) of there being still other creatures with *more* developed capacities, creatures who would thus have a higher moral status than we do. And that, it may be suggested, is a sufficiently troubling prospect that it may give us reason to reject the hierarchical approach altogether. (As a cynical critic might remark, a hierarchical approach may seem tempting when it is *flattering* us, telling us that we have rights that animals lack or have only in weaker form, but once we recognize that the very same approach will also entail that beings of the right sort would be permitted to lord it over *us*, the appeal of hierarchy may simply disappear.)

So we need to face a pair of questions. First, could there really be beings with a higher moral status than our own? And if so, second, should that possibility trouble us? Let's consider these one at a time.

As to the first question, there certainly doesn't seem to be any compelling reason within a hierarchical framework to rule out the very possibility of statuses higher than our own. Admittedly, philosophers who write about moral status sometimes use the language of "full moral status" to describe the status that we have. But I trust it is clear that the question we are asking here—whether someone could have a status higher than our own—is a substantive one, not the sort of thing that can be settled by a simple appeal to the *label* we happen to use to describe our status.

Of course, it isn't especially problematic to talk in terms of "full" moral status when the question on the table is whether there are beings—such as animals—that might have moral standing but with a *lesser* status than our own. (Even unitarians could accept that terminology, simply insisting that any individual with any moral standing at all has full moral status.) But precisely when the question is whether there could be beings with a status *superior* to our own, it would be pointless to insist that the answer *must* be no, since, after all, it is stipulated that we have "full" status. Instead, when thinking about such questions, it would be better to simply avoid that sort of language in the first place.

In any event, nothing in our earlier talk of higher and lower status gives us reason to think that the status we happen to have cannot be surpassed. Although I proposed using a 1 to represent the status of normal human persons (with numbers between 0 and 1 representing the statuses of various types of animals), there is obviously nothing in that proposal that rules out the possibility of statuses that are higher still, statuses that can be appropriately represented by numbers *higher* than 1.

Suppose, however, that while you wanted to accept a hierarchical approach you nonetheless also wanted to *deny* the possibility of statuses higher than our own. How might this be done?

One way would be to insist that the psychological capacities that ground our own moral status cannot be surpassed. Is that at all plausible?

It is, I think, clear that most (or all) of the relevant capacities can come in different degrees. We easily see this when considering animals, who often have the same capacities that we do, but in less developed or less sophisticated versions. But, of course, that doesn't tell us whether the relevant capacities can also be imagined in *more* sophisticated versions, without limit. Perhaps, then, status-enhancing capacities have upper bounds, or perfect forms. If something like that were correct, then there might be an upper bound to moral status as well.

And it does seem plausible to think that some of the capacities relevant to status may have upper bounds of this sort. Memory, for example (which plays a crucial role in sophisticated forms of agency), presumably has an upper bound. Imagine someone who could instantly remember absolutely everything—every thought and experience from their life—effortlessly and flawlessly. It is difficult for me to see what could possibly constitute a better memory than that. So it is at least arguable that memory has an upper bound.

But does something similar hold for the other capacities that ground our status? Is there an inherent upper bound to aesthetic appreciation? To the capacity for normative reflection? To autonomy? To the ability to grasp abstract truths? To emotional depth?

I don't think the answers to these questions are at all obvious. So I see no reason to assume that there are such upper bounds for all status-generating capacities. But at the same time, neither am I confident that such upper bounds are lacking. So perhaps the relevant capacities really do have upper bounds after all.

However, even if that were the case, that wouldn't suffice to establish that our status is the highest possible. At best it would support the thought that there is an upper bound of *some* sort to moral status. It certainly wouldn't show that *we* have the maximum possible status. For it seems perfectly clear that even if the relevant capacities have upper bounds, our own versions of those capacities are far below the perfected versions. (To take an obvious example, our memories are far from the infallible version we imagined a moment ago; and even if there is such a thing as a perfect ability to grasp abstract truth, it is clear that we don't have it.)

Furthermore, even if we somehow persuaded ourselves otherwise on this first point—that is, even if we justifiably concluded that our own capacities are in the most highly developed forms those capacities could ever take—that still wouldn't settle the matter. For as I have previously noted (in 5.3), there may be still other capacities that would raise one's status, capacities that we simply lack altogether. It does seem to be the case, after all, that certain animals lack some of the status-generating capacities that *we* possess. So I find it difficult to see why there couldn't be still other status-enhancing capacities that we simply *lack*. If so, then even if it were true that the capacities we do have are ones that we possess in their most sophisticated forms, for all that, there would remain the possibility of individuals who had all the capacities we have (in their ideal forms) but who also possessed some of those further status-enhancing capacities as well. And those individuals, it would seem, would still have a set of capacities sufficient to generate a higher status than our own.

It might be suggested, however, that even if psychological capacities relevant to status can surpass ours, nonetheless moral status itself cannot continue to "grow" without limit. Perhaps there is an upper bound, not to the capacities that ground status, but to the normative possibilities for status itself. Perhaps at a certain point we reach a status such that the very idea of there being a status that is higher still no longer makes any sense.

However, while the bare logical possibility of a maximal moral status does seem coherent (when described in this abstract fashion), I see no compelling reason to believe that status does in fact have an upper bound in this way. For it is difficult to see why the various types of moral claims that can make up one's normative profile must each have an inherent limit with regard to its potential strength or scope.

It is conceivable, of course, that some types of moral claims do have upper bounds, so that it would be impossible to have a moral status that generated a stronger claim of the given type. On certain moral views, for example, it is morally forbidden to intentionally harm an innocent person, no matter *what* the circumstances may be (even if, say, this is the only way to avert a disaster). Clearly, any moral status that included this kind of "inviolability" could not be surpassed by a higher status in this regard; no stronger claim in this particular area is possible. But for all that, of course, there are still other moral claims that also play a role in one's normative profile, and for some of these, at least, it certainly does seem as though they can take ever stronger forms.

For example, recall the various distributive principles that we discussed earlier. I argued (in 3.2) that people have stronger claims in this area than animals do, so that, for example, a person can be at a higher absolute level of well-being than a rabbit, say, and yet still have a stronger prioritarian claim. As far as I can see, nothing stands in the way of positing the possibility of creatures that would have even *stronger* claims in this regard. Similar remarks apply to the other distributive principles as well. Or consider the claim (argued for in 4.3) that by virtue of our higher status a person's well-being may make a greater contribution to the value of a given outcome than would be made by the same amount of well-being if had by an animal. Here too, it is easy to imagine the possibility of a being whose well-being counted for even more.

In principle, then, there seems to be no good reason to rule out the possibility of creatures with a status higher than ours. Indeed, once we allow for the possibility of status-enhancing capacities that we simply lack altogether, it seems conceivable that utterly new types of moral claims might emerge as well, ones that we don't have even in weak form. So that too might be a way in which another being's status could be higher than ours. In short, while there may or may not actually be any individuals with a higher status than the one we have, as far as I can see, anyone who embraces a hierarchical approach has to be willing to at least entertain that possibility.

Very well, if we must at least allow for the possibility of beings with a status superior to our own, the next question we need to ask is this: what would their normative profiles look like, and is this in fact a morally troubling possibility?

As to the contents of their normative profiles, some parts of that may be easier to describe than others. A full answer would probably require an imaginative exercise beyond any I am prepared to undertake here. If, as does seem possible, there can be status-enhancing capacities that we completely lack, it may be far from obvious what sorts of normative features would be grounded in such unfamiliar ("alien") capacities. Of course, if we actually met such creatures, we might eventually come to grasp something of the nature of those capacities even though we lacked them (just as the blind can somewhat grasp the nature of vision)—and perhaps we could then come to understand which new types of normative claims these alien capacities supported. In fact, for all I know, we might even be able to work out some of the relevant possibilities a priori—even *without* encountering such creatures—simply through a suitable exercise of philosophical imagination and reflection. But as I say, I am not going to attempt that here.

(Would such superior beings be able to *explain* their superior status to us?[3] Perhaps, but perhaps not. We have a superior moral status to mice, but mice are too cognitively limited for us to explain that fact to them. Conceivably, then, we too might be too cognitively limited to fully understand why and how others have a status superior to our own.)

On the other hand, other aspects of the normative profile belonging to beings with a higher moral status than our own may be relatively easy to grasp. After all, to the extent that their superior capacities would also ground moral claims *similar* to those with which we are already familiar, but having greater weight, it is tolerably clear what would be involved in their having a higher status. They would be able to make the same *sorts* of moral claims that we can—but, other things being equal, their claims would be stronger.

Indeed, it is easy to see how some of the models I sketched in our earlier discussions could be easily and appropriately extended to beings with higher status than our own. Thus, for example, if we were to accept the idea of using simple division—dividing by the numerical representation of status—to calculate status adjusted levels of welfare for the purposes of determining prioritarian claims, then we could do this with statuses higher than our own as well. (As we saw when dividing welfare by numbers between 0 and 1, the higher the number, the stronger the prioritarian claim generated by a given level of welfare; dividing by numbers even higher than 1 would appropriately extend this result.)

Similarly, if we use simple multiplication—multiplying by the numerical representation of status—to determine the extent to which one's welfare contributes to the value of an outcome, then we can continue to do this as well for statuses even higher than our own. (Just as multiplying by a number between

---

[3] Cf. Nozick, *Anarchy, State, and Utopia*, pp. 45–7.

0 and 1 captured the thought that a given amount of welfare counted for more, the higher one's status, multiplying by numbers even higher than 1 would appropriately capture the thought that the well-being of creatures with a higher status than ours would count for even more.)

Finally, to take just one more example, consider the matter of setting relevant sufficientarian baselines. Just as the baseline is set higher for people than it is for animals, we can easily set higher baselines still for any creatures with statuses that are higher than our own. And this seems a reasonable thing to do. After all, as we have previously noted, a (minimally) decent life for a person involves more than does a (minimally) decent life for a cow, let alone a snake. Similarly, then, it seems likely that any creature with a higher status than our own would be such that a (minimally) decent life for such a being would be higher still. (Since their psychological capacities would be significantly greater than ours, it is reasonable to suspect that they might have significantly more valuable lives available to them as well.) Accordingly, it will be appropriate to assign them a higher sufficientarian baseline.

(I should perhaps acknowledge that it has sometimes been suggested that the kind of life that constitutes a (minimally) decent life for us would also be good enough for *any being at all*, no matter *how* much more valuable the lives that they could potentially have.[4] But I simply find that impossible to believe. I very much doubt that any single line suffices for *all* creatures, no matter how advanced they might be in their psychological and emotional capacities. And in any event, even if I am wrong about that and somehow there *were* a kind of life that would be sufficient (or better) for any being at all, it would be a remarkable coincidence indeed if a (minimally) decent life for humans just happened to fall at that precise level.)

So far, at least, none of these implications strike me as especially troubling. While it may not be altogether transparent what would be entailed by the existence of superior beings (that is, beings with a moral status superior to our own), my own view is that none of the implications that we have traced up to this point provide any good reason to reject the hierarchical approach.

But of course I have not yet addressed what are doubtless the most worrisome possibilities. Many, I imagine, will be concerned that if we do allow for the possibility of beings with a higher status than ours, then such creatures would be morally permitted—by virtue of their higher status—to trample

---

[4] For example, Crisp reports that his own intuition is that, say, "eighty years of high-quality life on this planet is enough, and plausibly more than enough, for *any* being"—including beings on other worlds who live lives "at a much higher level of welfare than even the best off on this planet." ("Equality, Priority, and Compassion," p. 762; emphasis added.)

upon the moral rights that we take ourselves to have. Their rights might simply outweigh ours—trumping them, overriding them, or otherwise silencing them. Even though we (normal adult humans) are not permitted to treat *one another* in various morally repugnant ways, it might still turn out to be true, for all of that, that beings with a superior status would indeed have the right to treat us in precisely those ways. That, at least, is the worry. If we open the door to the possibility of beings with a higher moral status than our own, how can we rule out the possibility that they might be morally permitted to treat us like mere things or resources, in much the way that we currently treat animals?

It is important to recall, however, that my own view is that our current treatment of animals constitutes horrendous moral abuse. Yes, I have argued for a hierarchical approach, according to which our interests count (in various ways) more than the otherwise similar interests of animals. But this should not be conflated with a view according to which the interests of animals don't count at all. Indeed, I believe that on any plausible hierarchical approach it will turn out that many of the most important ways in which we interact with animals (enslaving them, for example, or raising them for food) will turn out to be simply unjustified. Similarly, then, it would turn out to be equally unjustified for beings with higher status than ours to treat *us* as mere resources. Indeed, given the fact that our own moral status is even higher than that of animals, any such mistreatment will almost inevitably constitute an even greater moral horror. So while the specter of "superior beings" permissibly enslaving us may be a familiar one, I see no good reason to believe that an otherwise plausible hierarchical approach will actually allow this. We are, after all, intelligent, sensitive, rational, autonomous beings. These features help explain why enslaving one of us is a particularly horrendous thing to do. But we will continue to possess those features, even in the presence of beings with higher psychological capacities than our own. So slavery will remain morally illegitimate.

What does seem possible, of course, is that other beings might be even more intelligent, more sensitive, more autonomous than we are. If so, then it might well turn out that it would be even worse to enslave such creatures than it is to enslave one of us. But this implication strikes me as being an intuitively reasonable one. If there really were creatures with even higher degrees of autonomy than our own, then it might well be worse to enslave one of *them*. But that would hardly show that it was permissible for them to enslave one of *us*.[5]

---

[5] Of course, it isn't difficult to *construct* a hierarchical theory that does have the implication that sufficiently superior beings could permissibly enslave or otherwise "abuse" us. But I see no good reason to think that the most *plausible* hierarchical theory will allow this.

I conclude, then, that the possibility of beings with higher moral statuses than ours is one that we should allow. If there really are such beings, then in various ways their interests will simply count for more, morally speaking, than our own (other things being equal). No doubt, acknowledging this possibility may be, for some, a humbling thought. But as far as I can see, it doesn't provide any good reason to reject the hierarchical approach.

One final point. If there were superior beings of this sort, presumably they too would be persons: like us, they would be rational and self-conscious, aware of themselves as existing across time (and so forth). And this means, of course, that I have been imprecise, in earlier discussions, when I talked in an unqualified way about the moral status of "people," as though all people necessarily have the same moral status. What I meant to be talking about, rather, was something more like "people with capacities similar to ours"—that is, capacities like those had by normal adult human persons. Similarly, then, I was also imprecise when I suggested using the number 1 to represent the status of persons. What I had in mind, of course, was using it to represent *our* status—not the status of beings (if such there be) who are persons, but significantly superior to us.

If we wanted to, we could introduce a new term of art at this point, one stipulated to pick out only those persons with something like our capacities and our status. We could, for example, start talking about "human-like persons" when we wanted to refer only to members of this more restricted group— persons that (whether human or not) had the capacities and status typical of adult humans. Or we could distinguish between talking about persons in a *narrow* sense of the term (where it refers only to persons with capacities and status like ours) and talking about persons in the strict, *broad* sense of the term (where it applies to all persons whatsoever, including superior beings). No doubt there are other possibilities as well.

For the most part, however, instead of adopting one of these conventions I am going to let context do the relevant work. In what follows, when I use the term "person" (and its cognates), then unless context indicates otherwise, you should assume that I mean to be talking only about persons in the "narrow" sense (that is, I am referring only to human-like persons). In contrast, when I mean to include other sorts of persons as well—persons in the broader, more inclusive sense of the term—I will either say so explicitly, or the context will have already made this clear.

6.3 Marginal Cases

The most commonly discussed objection to adopting a hierarchical approach doesn't so much concern superior beings but something more like the opposite.

It is a familiar and heartbreaking fact that some humans are so severely impaired that their cognitive capacities fall short, sometimes staggeringly short, of those of typical adult humans. There are, for example, grown human beings lacking self-awareness or a developed sense of time, with only minimal memory and little or no ability to make and execute plans. Although they are conscious, and able to feel pleasure and pain, these are human beings who are so cognitively impaired that they lack the capacities necessary for being a person. They are the cognitive and emotional peers of animals, not normal adult humans. Yet if, as I have argued, an individual's moral status is a function of their psychological capacities, then it seems to follow that such impaired humans will have to be assigned a moral status that falls short of our own. If people have a status of 1, then these severely impaired humans will have statuses that are substantially less than 1. And that is an implication of hierarchy that many take to be troubling indeed—enough so, in fact, that many will conclude that it gives us decisive reason to reject a hierarchical approach of the sort I've been describing.

The idea that hierarchy's implications for the severely impaired provide reason to reject such an approach is sometimes called the argument from marginal cases. The "marginal cases" in question are, of course, the severely impaired humans who, it might be suggested, form a kind of intermediate group between animals and ordinary adult humans. Thinking about this intermediate group, it is said, allows us to see that the only morally acceptable view is a unitarian one; hierarchy must be rejected.

The basic argument goes like this: On the one hand, it is morally unacceptable to treat impaired humans worse than ordinary humans. But on the other hand, there are no morally relevant differences between impaired humans and animals. Accordingly, it must also be morally unacceptable to treat *animals* worse than ordinary humans. Thus, by thinking about marginal cases—severely impaired humans—we can see the necessity of embracing unitarianism, since a *hierarchical* approach will inevitably force us to the unacceptable conclusion that it is morally permissible to treat impaired humans badly.

Presumably, a parallel argument could be constructed about impaired animals as well. Thus, for example, a severely impaired wolf, say, might be the psychological peer of a snake. Conceivably, then, some might want to argue that since it is morally unacceptable to treat impaired wolves worse than ordinary wolves, and since there are no morally relevant differences between impaired wolves and snakes, it follows that it is morally unacceptable to treat snakes worse than wolves. Generalizing from this example, they would then conclude that any hierarchical view that assigns lower statuses to some animals than to others must be mistaken.

So an argument from marginal cases need not focus on impaired humans. Nonetheless, for obvious reasons this is the form the argument routinely takes, since it is the prospect of the mistreatment of some of our fellow *humans* that especially leaves us troubled and unsettled. (In contrast, we may be far less confident what would constitute mistreatment of, say, an impaired wolf.) Accordingly, in discussing this argument, I will follow the common practice and focus on its implications for impaired humans.

(Of course, even when focusing on severely impaired humans not all cases pose an equally troubling challenge to hierarchical views. For some of the severely impaired were people in the *past*. Arguably, then, although these individuals have undergone a loss of the cognitive capacities that make one a person, nonetheless, precisely because they once *were* people, there may be significant moral limits even now concerning how they are to be treated, limits that are grounded in the various interests and desires that they had at that earlier time. In light of the moral significance of past personhood, the cases of impairment typically thought to be most problematic for hierarchical views concern those individuals who by virtue of their impairments are not persons, never *have* been persons, and never will be—individuals who, at this point, do not have even the *potential* to become a person. Since our goal here is to consider the most pressing objections to hierarchical views, I am going to focus exclusively on severely impaired humans of this latter sort.)

Now some of the rhetorical force of the appeal to marginal cases derives from the implicit assumption that under a hierarchical view animals will barely count. So if impaired humans have a status no higher than the animals that are their psychological peers, they too will barely count. And it is the thought that it might be permissible to treat such humans so "badly" (as I put it above) that seems most troubling.

So the first thing to note is that even if a hierarchical view did have the implication that impaired humans have the same status as animals, that would hardly entail that it is permissible to treat such humans poorly. That conclusion would only follow if something like our current treatment of *animals* were morally legitimate. But I hope it is clear that a hierarchical view needn't—and shouldn't—take this position. To say that animals count less than people is not at all the same thing as suggesting that animals count for little or nothing. On the contrary, on any plausible hierarchical view it will turn out that very little of our current treatment of animals can be morally justified. So even if it were true that impaired humans should be assigned the same moral status as the animals that are their psychological peers, it wouldn't follow that it was permissible to treat them poorly.

But in any event, the second point to note is that on the particular hierarchical view that I favor, it isn't really true that severely impaired humans have the very same moral status as the animals that are their psychological peers. On the contrary, there is a morally relevant difference that warrants assigning a *higher* moral status to the impaired humans. For unlike animals, impaired humans are modal persons, and modal personhood enhances one's status.

It is easy to overlook this suggestion. It is often assumed that the only way in which one could maintain that impaired humans count more than their animal peers would be if one's *species* were relevant to one's status. After all, it is certainly true that if the mere fact of membership in the species *Homo sapiens* were sufficient to give one the very same moral status as normal adult humans, then severely impaired humans would have the same status as people, rather than having the status of animals. But it is of course difficult to find a compelling argument for counting species membership in this way. Indeed, it is often suggested that the view that species membership has this kind of moral significance should be dismissed as a mere prejudice. And once this sort of speciesist prejudice is rejected, it is claimed, we can see that impaired humans must indeed have precisely the same moral status as whatever animals happen to be their psychological peers.

As it happens, I do in fact agree that one's species has no direct moral significance (though I am not at all convinced that to think otherwise must be nothing more than a mere *prejudice*).[6] But it is a mistake to think that the only way that impaired humans could count more than their animal peers would be by virtue of their species. For there are other differences which may still matter from the moral perspective. In particular, as I just noted, impaired humans will normally be *modal* persons. And as I have previously suggested, modal personhood seems to me to enhance one's status. Thus, on the sort of view I am proposing, impaired humans will have a *higher* status than the animals that are their psychological peers, since the former, but not the latter, are modal persons.

At the very least, then, the original argument for unitarianism, based on an appeal to marginal cases, fails. That argument, recall, claimed that animals must have the same moral status as people, given that animals have the same status as impaired humans, and that impaired humans have the same status as the rest of us. But once we recognize that impaired humans will have a higher

---

[6] The charge that "speciesism" is a mere prejudice is made by Singer in *Animal Liberation*, pp. 1–9. I defend the claim that it needn't be a *prejudice* in "What's Wrong with Speciesism?" pp. 1–8. For some reasons to doubt the moral *significance* of species, see "What's Wrong with Speciesism?" pp. 14–17, and McMahan, *The Ethics of Killing*, pp. 209–28.

status than their animal peers, the unitarian conclusion (that animals have the same status as people) will no longer follow—not even if we grant the other premise of the argument (that impaired humans have the same status as unimpaired ones).

Nonetheless, even if the original argument for unitarianism fails, we might still be troubled by the thought that an appeal to modal personhood cannot suffice to ground a sufficiently *high* status for impaired humans. This points to a second way that unitarians might make use of an appeal to marginal cases. If it should turn out that the only way to avoid an unacceptably low status for the impaired is to embrace the idea that all with standing have the very *same* status, then some may conclude that an appeal to marginal cases suffices to justify unitarianism after all.

Of course, the force of this revised argument depends on questions we haven't tried to settle, concerning the *extent* to which modal personhood can enhance one's status. On a minimalist account, the status of the impaired might be only slightly higher than that of their animal peers. This, despite the fact that the impaired are modal persons. But my own view is that modal status should count for *more* than this. The gap in status between impaired humans and their animal peers may be considerable. Indeed, on sufficiently strong views concerning modal status, impaired humans might have a status quite close to that had by people. So it simply isn't true that a hierarchical view inevitably consigns the impaired to a moral status that is unacceptably low.

Still, some will be troubled by any view according to which impaired humans have a lower status of any sort at all. The only acceptable position, they will insist, is one according to which even the severely impaired have the same status as we have.

It is perhaps worth noting that even this last position can be accommodated within a hierarchical approach, provided that one was prepared to give sufficient weight to modal status. As we have previously noted (in 5.5), on an extreme view of the matter modal persons have the very same status as actual persons. Conceivably, then, some who are otherwise attracted to hierarchy, but who are unwilling to countenance lower status for the severely impaired, might find that this gives them reason to embrace the extreme view with regard to modal status.

Speaking personally, however, while I do believe in the significance of modal personhood, I am not inclined to accept the extreme view. I find myself drawn instead to a more moderate position, one where the status of a modal person is enhanced, but not by as much as would be required to generate the same status as is had by actual persons. Accordingly, it does seem to me correct to hold that the status of a severely impaired human will be lower than that of a normal, adult, human person.

Indeed, this very same conclusion is reinforced when we remember the point (also noted in 5.5) that the strength of the enhancement due to one's modal status will vary depending on how close or remote the circumstances were under which one would actually have had the capacities in question. And it is, presumably, plausible to think that the circumstances under which someone who is not a person would have *been* a person may be more or less remote. (For example, is the actual impairment due to an accident that could easily have been avoided? Or is it due to something having gone wrong during fetal development? Is it the result of a genetic anomaly?[7] And so on.) Accordingly, impaired humans will differ in terms of the *strength* of their modal status. So even if some cases of impaired humans will have an overall status that is close to that of a person, there will be still other cases where the difference in status will be more significant. Only a view of modal status that was utterly indifferent to this kind of difference in remoteness can readily avoid this implication. And that seems to me quite implausible (especially given that even animals will count as modal persons, if one is willing to entertain sufficiently remote possibilities).

So I do think that the most plausible version of hierarchy will be one according to which at least some of the severely impaired will have a moral status that is lower (perhaps significantly lower) than that had by persons.

(In light of all of this, perhaps I should explicitly add the following: even though impaired humans will have—by virtue of their modal personhood—a higher moral status than animals that are their psychological peers, this does not mean that each impaired human will have a higher status than any animal whatsoever. Modal personhood enhances one's status, but so does the actual possession of more developed or sophisticated psychological capacities. I see no reason to assume that the former always does more to enhance status than the latter. So not only will actual persons have a higher status than any given severely impaired human, the right sorts of animals— animals with sufficiently sophisticated sets of capacities—may have a higher status as well.)

---

[7] On certain metaphysical views, it is an essential property of any given individual that they came into existence with the particular set of genes that they actually had. Had *anything* been different in that regard, that particular individual would never have existed (rather, some sibling would have been born instead). If so, a human whose failure to be a person was due to a genetic abnormality would normally not even count as a *modal* person (in a sufficiently strong sense). As it happens, I am skeptical of the relevant metaphysical claims. But I won't try to argue the point here.

Is this conclusion unacceptable? Should we reject any view that assigns impaired humans a lower status than the rest of us have? Some will certainly take it to be so. They will resist any view according to which there is any kind of gap between the moral statuses of normal and impaired humans.

Yet this is a difficult objection for the unitarian, at least, to maintain, given that unitarians typically already recognize—indeed, insist upon—the fact that it is permissible (other things being equal) to favor people over *animals*, given that ordinarily animals have less valuable lives. (Recall the discussion from 2.2.) Once we acknowledge this fact, it seems equally plain that severely impaired humans *also* have less valuable lives than people ordinarily do. So if, as unitarians typically hold, it is permissible to save a person rather than, say, a dog, it should also be permissible to save a person rather than an impaired human who has the cognitive capacities of a dog. Like the dog, the impaired human simply has less at stake than a person is likely to have.

To be sure, this isn't yet the same thing as saying that impaired humans have a lower moral *status* than people do (at least, not in the sense of "status" identified in 2.4). But this is concession enough to leave it obscure why unitarians would be entitled to dismiss as unacceptable the suggestion that severely impaired humans may have a lower moral status as well.

It would be one thing if—aspiring to the moral "high ground," as it were—the unitarian could insist that it is never permissible to favor persons over impaired humans. But as we have just seen, the typical unitarian is committed (although perhaps only implicitly) to precisely this sort of favoring. So they cannot consistently insist that any such superior treatment for persons over impaired individuals is simply to be rejected out of hand. The question, rather, becomes which *sorts* of moral differences seem plausible on reflection. And here, I can only report, it does seem to me that it is intuitively plausible to assign lower status to marginal cases.

To see this, consider yet again the various distributive principles we have previously discussed, and bear in mind the fact that the severely impaired have lives that are considerably worse than the ones that people generally have (though, by virtue of their impairments, they may not suffer; indeed, they may not even recognize their situation). Now if this sort of pattern of distribution of welfare were one that held merely among *people*, we would take this fact to generate stringent moral demands to correct the situation. Yet, while we may be open to thinking that to some extent there are indeed obligations to do something significant to improve the lot of the severely impaired, few would think that those obligations are comparable to the ones we would have if it were ordinary *people* who had the relevant low levels of welfare. All of which is just to say that the distributive claims of the severely impaired, while real—and higher, no doubt, than the claims of their psychological peers among the animals—are nonetheless weaker than the corresponding claims that would be had by persons who were comparably badly off. That is, the severely impaired have a lower moral status than that had by persons.

In short, while it may leave us initially uneasy to contemplate the fact that the severely impaired have a moral status that is lower than our own, on reflection, I believe, we should find that this is nonetheless a reasonable position to maintain. I conclude, accordingly, that marginal cases don't give us reason to reject a hierarchical approach. While contemplating such cases may give us pause, on balance, it seems to me, a suitable hierarchical approach can generate acceptable answers.

It must be conceded, of course, that the hierarchical approach I have endorsed is revisionary, in that most of us would not have prereflectively recognized that the severely impaired have a lower moral status than the rest of us have. But we should not lose sight of the fact that the unitarian position is even *more* revisionary, insisting, as it does, that animals have the very *same* moral status as us. The simple fact of the matter is that there are no easy answers here. I suspect, in fact, that any coherent (and not ad hoc) view on the subject will inevitably run afoul of at least *some* of our intuitions.[8] When viewed from that perspective, then, I believe that the hierarchical approach I have proposed should prove to be an acceptable one, all things considered.

Admittedly, we could simply dig in our heels and insist that even the severely impaired have a moral status equivalent to that of ordinary people, while animals do not. That too, of course, would be a hierarchical view, and no doubt an even better fit with our prereflective intuitions than the more revisionary alternative I am putting forward. But unless one is prepared to insist that modal personhood has sufficient weight to ground a status equal to that of actual persons, such a view cannot, I believe, be defended. And it simply seems to me implausible to suggest that the significance of modal personhood is as great as that. (Alternatively, of course, one could claim that mere species membership suffices for attaining the status of actual persons. But that claim seems even *less* plausible.)

---

[8] Consider, in this light, Regan, much of whose language in *The Case for Animal Rights* might suggest to a hasty reader that he is (in our terms) a unitarian. Yet even Regan seems prepared to allow for the possibility that the correct moral view will give a lower moral status to animals and humans that lack a sufficiently complex mental life (see, e.g., pp. 243–7). If it does, then since some severely impaired humans will fall below the relevant level of psychological capacities, they will have a lower moral status than the rest of us have. It is difficult to avoid saying something like this about at least *some* marginal cases.

The situation, then, seems to me to be this. It is understandable and appropriate for us to hesitate before embracing a view according to which the severely impaired have a lower moral status than the rest of us. Nonetheless, ultimately this is precisely the sort of position that we should indeed endorse. In the end, the argument from marginal cases does not, I think, give us adequate reason to reject a hierarchical view of the sort I have been describing.

6.4 Normal Variation

There is one further worry about hierarchy that I want to consider. This last problem will probably strike many as the most troubling of the ones that I have been discussing.

Here's the worry. I have claimed that status is largely a function of one's actual capacities. Furthermore, as I have also frequently observed, these capacities are variable; many animals have them only in less developed or less sophisticated forms. Because of this, I have argued, animals have a lower moral status. But the fact of the matter, of course, is that there is variation in the level and sophistication of the relevant capacities not only between people and animals (and among different types of animals), but also among people as well. So it seems as though the hierarchical approach must also be committed to the existence of differences in moral status among *people*.

Now in raising this point, I do not mean to be returning to the bare possibility of people who have vastly superior capacities compared to us (that is, to the possibility of superior beings). I mean, rather, that there is variation even among ordinary humans, variation among people who have capacities that are more or less similar to our own. For even if someone else's capacities are *more or less* like mine, they still needn't be identical to mine. I might, say, have a somewhat better ability to plan than you have, while you have a somewhat greater capacity for normative self-governance. Similarly, *she* might have a smaller than normal capacity for abstract thought, while *he* has a somewhat greater than normal capacity for emotional insight and reflection.

This sort of *normal variation*, as we might call it—observed each day as we move from one person to the next—constitutes a different sort of problem from the ones we have already considered. It is all very well to allow for the possibility of incredibly superior beings (who might, consequently, have a higher status than our own), or to recognize the existence of humans who are severely cognitively impaired (and who thus might warrant a lower status). These sorts of variations in capacity are extreme, and it may not be too difficult to acknowledge, after suitable reflection, that such extreme differences in relevant capacities should underwrite corresponding differences in status as well. But if there is also variation in the status-generating capacities of *ordinary* people, then won't that mean that here too we should expect corresponding differences in moral status? The differences may not be huge, but shouldn't we anticipate that some of us will indeed have a slightly higher or a slightly lower status than others?

(If status is a *multidimensional* affair, better represented by an ordered n-tuple rather than a single number (see 5.1), then things are more complicated. Consider someone with a poorer emotional range, say, but a more developed capacity for, perhaps, abstract thought. Conceivably such a person's moral status will be lower along one relevant dimension, but higher along another. Normal variation would still generate differences in moral status, but the relevant differences wouldn't be appropriately represented by means of a single number. For simplicity, however, I continue to put aside this kind of multidimensional approach.)

But this really does seem a troubling and unpalatable prospect. Are we truly to accept a view according to which some ordinary humans really do count somewhat more than others, while others simply count for *less*? Consider someone with a slightly poorer memory—perfectly adequate for ordinary purposes, not in any way interfering with their ability to make significant long range plans, but for all that somewhat poorer than most people have. Are we really prepared to say that such a person counts less than others, that their interests are to be given somewhat lesser weight?

That seems unacceptable. We may be willing to entertain differences in status for individuals who differ *dramatically* from us, as with, for example, superior beings or the severely impaired. But if the sort of normal variation that we regularly observe between people means that according to a hierarchical approach there are genuine differences in how much each of us counts, then many really will take this to provide a compelling reason to reject hierarchy after all.

Note that to generate the problem of normal variation it isn't necessary that the capacities that underwrite our status be able to vary continuously. It could turn out that in some or all cases the relevant capacities can vary only by discrete amounts. What matters, rather, is that we actually do find variation in relevant capacities among different individuals. That is, as long as ordinary adult humans differ among themselves in the degree of one or more of the relevant capacities, that should suffice to generate the problem. And people really do seem to differ in precisely this way. (Similarly, even if each of the capacities relevant for establishing our status had an upper bound, this wouldn't avoid the problem either, unless each of us were *at* that upper bound—an utterly implausible supposition.)

One possible response to this concern, of course, is to insist that the sort of differences in status that we are envisioning here are nonetheless acceptable, despite whatever initial misgivings we might have on this score. The crucial idea here is to keep firmly in mind the fact that the relevant differences in status will be quite *small*, perhaps too small to make any real difference. For practical purposes, then, we may be justified in simply disregarding them.

At first glance, this might not seem an especially plausible thing to claim, given how large such interpersonal differences can appear to us. Your memory may seem *significantly* better than mine, his capacity for self-reflection significantly weaker. But we should not lose sight of the fact that these differences—though they loom large to us—may still be relatively trivial, when one considers them in comparison to the *overall* range of such capacities, from their least developed forms among the lower animals to their most developed forms. Viewed against the full extent to which any given capacity can vary, the variation on display among ordinary adult humans may be too small to have any significant impact on how we should treat one another.

Arguably, then, the answer to the problem of normal variation is that the actual amount of variation that one normally sees isn't, in fact, especially problematic. To take this position is to concede that there are or can be trivial differences in moral status from one person to the next, but to suggest that these differences are too small to concern us.

Speaking personally, I find this a plausible response. But I suspect that many people, perhaps most people, will be uncomfortable with any answer along these lines. Surely—it will be said—no acceptable moral theory will embrace differences in moral status, no matter how small, among ordinary, nonimpaired, adult human beings. To discriminate between people in this way is simply unacceptable, even when it has little or no practical import. Any such differentiation must run afoul of our fundamental moral commitment to equal respect for all people.

Interestingly, we are not similarly troubled when we find ourselves deciding to favor one person over another because the former has more *well-being* at stake than the latter. Intuitively, at least, that seems compatible with the common assumption that equal respect and regard is due to each of us. But to suggest that someone might have a stronger moral claim simply by virtue of the fact that she has a slightly better ability to plan for the future—that, as I say, will seem to many to be utterly unacceptable in a moral theory.

With hindsight, in fact, we may find ourselves wondering whether some or all of the concern about elitism (explored in 6.1) may have really been an attempt to point toward this problem, the problem of normal variation. While it may have been overblown to draw analogies to systems of thought under which some people have lacked moral standing altogether, or have had it only to a dramatically reduced degree, still, the underlying concern may simply have been this: people will always differ, one from another, in terms of whatever features are thought to ground one's moral status; so if *variation* in status is allowed at all, inevitably some people will end up with a higher status than others. While the differences in status may not be as extreme as they have sometimes been thought to be (under some of the most abhorrent historical examples of discrimination), any differences at all in the status of one person as compared to another is simply unacceptable.

For those who do find it intolerable to countenance the very idea of differences in status among people, what alternatives remain? Must one reject hierarchy? Not necessarily. For even if we acknowledge the existence of normal variation among the various status-generating capacities, what I am calling the *problem* of normal variation could still be avoided if such (small) differences could make no difference to one's *status*, or if, alternatively, once one was above a certain *threshold* level with regard to a given capacity—a level which all normal adult humans meet—any further increases in the level of that capacity simply made no *further* difference to one's status. If either of these positions could be maintained, we could recognize the presence of differences in our capacities but still deny that these result in differences in moral status.

Unfortunately, it is far from obvious what could justify adopting either one of these proposals. If a given capacity enhances one's status, such that *large* differences in the capacity support differences in status, it is difficult to see why *small* differences should be morally irrelevant. More plausible, it seems, is a view according to which small differences in capacities would *also* support differences in status, albeit only small ones. Similarly, if greater or more developed levels of a given capacity would normally support an increase in status, it is difficult to see why this sort of effect should suddenly disappear, simply because we have now reached a particular ("threshold") level of the capacity. Rather, if there really can be still higher levels of the capacity in question, then it seems more plausible to suggest instead that status would continue to vary, as one moved to higher and higher levels of the given capacity.[9]

---

[9] Cf. Arneson, "What, if Anything, Renders All Humans Morally Equal?"

So neither of these two solutions to the problem of normal variation seems particularly promising. Are there others? (We will return to some questions about thresholds in 8.4.)

If there were no adequate answer to the problem of normal variation, I imagine that that fact would move many to abandon the hierarchical approach. At the very least, most people would conclude that the problem points to a seriously unattractive feature of hierarchy. Conceivably, of course, one might still conclude that hierarchy in ethics was superior overall to the alternatives (that is, despite its shortcomings). But the problem of normal variation would still strike most of us as perhaps the most important shortcoming in the theory, a genuine mark against it.

Happily, however, I do think that there is a plausible solution that we have not yet considered. (Alternatively, it can be viewed as a way of making good on the first proposed solution, according to which small differences in capacities might make *no* difference in status.) The answer lies in an idea that I will call *practical realism*. But I don't want to give the details yet; that will come later (in 11.2). For the time being, then, we can consider my claim as something of a promissory note: the problem of normal variation has a possible solution, yet to be described, that should prove attractive to many.

If I am right about this, however, then I think we have acceptable answers to each of the worries that have concerned us in this chapter. Hierarchical theories may be elitist (in at least one sense of the term), in that they give higher moral status to some individuals than to others, but this, in and of itself, provides no reason to reject such views. And while some of the implications of hierarchy may be surprising or even concerning (the possibility of superior beings, for example, or the status of marginal cases), none of these implications gives us sufficient reason to reject the hierarchical approach.

Before (temporarily) leaving the problem of normal variation, I want to make two further observations. First, it should be noted that a similar issue might arise for animals as well. Presumably, after all, there will be normal variation among cows, say, or among swans. So here too we would expect that a hierarchical approach will generate differences—perhaps small, but nonetheless genuine—in moral status. Conceivably some will find this implication troubling as well, but I suspect that most will find the problem of normal variation worrisome only with regard to *people*. That's why I have chosen to discuss the issue only in terms of variation among normal, adult, humans.

Second, we should remember the possibility that some animals (other than humans) may be persons as well. For those animals (if any) that have capacities similar to ours, it should go without saying that a suitable hierarchical approach will view them as having the same status as we do. But what about the possibility of animals that are persons only in a greatly diminished or minimal way? If there are such animals,[10] with capacities that ground personhood but only in a considerably less developed form, then I think that they will have a moral status that is *lower* than the one that we have. Just as I think we should be open to the possibility of superior beings, persons with capacities significantly greater than our own, I think we should also be open to the possibility of *minimal* persons. And just as the former may merit a higher status than ours, the latter—if such there be—may merit a lower one. The problem of normal variation, as I conceive it, arises not from the large range of capacities that can be found across *all* persons (from minimal persons to superior beings), but rather from the much more limited range of capacities that can be found among ordinary adult humans.

---

[10] Or humans. Not all severely impaired humans fall completely short of being persons at all; some may be persons of this more minimal sort.

7

Deontology

7.1 Consequentialism and Deontology

An adequate moral theory will need to incorporate a hierarchical approach to moral status. But acknowledging this point does not yet tell us which parts of our moral theory will need to be modified or complicated so as to accommodate hierarchy. So far, I have argued for doing this in two main areas. First, I have argued that distributive principles should be modified in such a way as to give stronger distributive claims to those individuals with higher status. Second, I have suggested that the value of welfare itself may depend on the moral status of the individual whose welfare is being affected.

Both of these examples fall within value theory, or what is sometimes called the theory of the good—the part of our moral theory that describes the features that make one outcome a better or worse outcome than the relevant alternatives. In effect, then, I have been arguing that to the extent that a given moral theory instructs us to bring about morally better results—to promote or maintain outcomes that are better from the moral point of view—that theory will need to incorporate hierarchical elements.

Conceivably, there are still other ways in which an adequate theory of the good will need to reflect the significance of status beyond the ones we have already identified. But since it is not my goal in this book to develop a complete, status sensitive moral theory, I won't explore that question here. The crucial point for present purposes is simply that an adequate theory of the good will be a hierarchical one.

For some theories of morality, once the theory of the good is in place, the most central part of our moral theory is complete. For according to *consequentialist* theories, right and wrong is simply a matter of bringing about (or not bringing about) the best possible outcomes overall, so that an act is permissible if and only if the results of that action would be better than (or, in the case of ties, as good as) the results of any alternative action available to the agent. Of course, this consequentialist idea cannot stand on its own. Anyone who accepts a consequentialist theory of permissibility also needs to supplement it with a theory of the good, so that one can evaluate alternative outcomes and identify the optimal ones. But once an adequate theory of the good is provided, the main work in normative ethics is complete. (There will of course remain the crucial and challenging empirical task of determining the possible results of different actions. But for all that, the central question of normative *ethics* will have been answered: the right thing to do, in any given case, is to bring about the best available outcome, as identified by the correct theory of the good.)

In fact, however, most people are not consequentialists at all, but *deontologists*. That is to say, they believe that there is more to right and wrong than simply bringing about the best possible results. According to this alternative view, deciding the permissibility of an action isn't simply a matter of evaluating its consequences (as compared to those of its alternatives); there are or can be other features of the act that also play a role in determining whether it is permissible or not. In particular, and most pressingly, certain acts may be morally forbidden, even though they would bring about the best available results. In effect, deontologists hold that there are certain *ways* of bringing about results that are morally significant in themselves. Because of this, even when it is true that performing a given act would have better results overall, it may still be *wrong*, all things considered—if the act is of a morally objectionable sort.

Unsurprisingly, perhaps, deontologists differ among themselves as to which features, precisely, make an act objectionable in this way. Details aside, however, the most common deontological thought here is that there is something especially morally problematic about *doing harm*—or, somewhat more precisely, doing harm to the innocent. In particular, then, deontologists typically think that it would be wrong to (deliberately and knowingly) harm the innocent, even if doing so is required to bring about better results overall.[1]

Here's an example of the sort that is regularly used to illustrate and motivate the deontological perspective. Suppose that there are five innocent people who will die unless we kill some other (equally innocent) person. It might be, for example, that we need to kill and "chop up" the one, so as to provide organs to be transplanted into the five others who will otherwise soon die. Or it might be that the five have some rare infectious disease, and the only way to save them is to grind up the body of the one, since he is the only available source of a sufficient quantity of the relevant antibody. For our purposes we need not further specify the gruesome details, we need only stipulate that killing the one will save the five, and that there is simply no other way that the five can be saved. Let us also stipulate that no other features of the case are relevant. (Thus, for

---

[1] Most deontologists also reject consequentialism's insistence that one is always morally required to do as *much* good as one can (within permissible means). We'll briefly consider this view later (in 9.4). See my *Normative Ethics*, part I, for a fuller discussion of the differences between consequentialism and deontology.

example, it isn't that the one is about to find a cure for cancer, and if we kill him thousands will die who would otherwise have been saved; nor is it the case that if it were to come out that we have killed an innocent person this would lead to wholesale abandonment of the healthcare system, with countless more deaths in the long run; nor is it the case that the five are somehow partly responsible for the fact that their organs are about to fail or that they have the infectious disease; and so on.)

In our imaginary case, then, our choice boils down to this: kill the one and save the five, or refuse to do so, in which case the one lives, but the five die.

Now most people, when they think about this kind of case, have a firm and immediate response: killing the one would be wrong. Note, however, that in the case as we have described it, the results really would be better if we killed the one, since it is better to have five (innocent) people alive, rather than only one. But this is precisely why deontologists insist that morality is not simply a matter of bringing about the best results. It is crucially important—the deontologists explain—that in our case the only way to bring about the good of saving the five is by *killing* the one. There is, they say, something particularly morally objectionable about *doing harm* to the innocent. Indeed, doing harm is sufficiently objectionable that it is wrong, all things considered, to kill the one, despite the fact that if you don't do this the five will die.

In contrast, if you appropriately refrain from killing the one, you have not killed the five, you have only *allowed* them to die. And while allowing harm is hardly a matter of moral indifference, it isn't nearly as problematic as *doing* harm. Indeed, it is much worse to kill *one* than it is to allow *five* to die. That's why, in our example, killing the one is forbidden.

That, in a nutshell, is the position of the deontologist. And as I say, when they think about it, most people find that they agree with the deontologist on this score.

As it happens, I think that most people are wrong about this. I believe, in fact, that despite the strong intuitive support that admittedly exists for deontology, the consequentialist approach here is actually the superior one. But that is a very long and complicated debate, and I don't intend to rehearse the arguments for consequentialism and against deontology here. Instead I simply want to acknowledge the fact that most people are—for better or for worse—deontologists. Accordingly, it is important for us to ask whether hierarchy is also appropriate here. That is, assuming that one incorporates deontological elements into one's overall normative theory, is there a need to incorporate sensitivity to status into *those* elements as well? Should the deontological part of our moral theory (if there is such a part) *also* involve hierarchy?

In raising this question, I don't mean to suggest that deontologists don't care about results, and so needn't bother with a theory of the good. *Of course* they care about results: *every* plausible moral theory does that. So a hierarchical account of status is required for deontological theories as well, and not only consequentialist ones. But as I have just explained, deontologists think that there is more to right and wrong than a simple appeal to consequences; there are further elements that also need to be included in our moral theory. And what we don't yet know is whether these further elements should also be sensitive to differences in status. That's the question I want to explore next.

In what follows, therefore, I am going to adopt a deontological perspective. I want to ask whether hierarchy is appropriate for the deontological elements as well, the elements that are unique to the deontological point of view. Although I am not myself a deontologist, I am going to argue that those who *are* deontologists should *also* accept a hierarchical approach—not just with regard to the theory of the good, but with regard to the more distinctively deontological aspects of their theory as well.

I should note, however, that the discussion that follows should be of interest not only to deontologists, but also to consequentialists. For most consequentialists believe that in almost all ordinary situations it is appropriate to deliberate along broadly deontological lines. Doing so, they argue, is generally the best way to bring about the best possible outcomes overall.

Although this may sound paradoxical, the point is actually a simple one: although we are fairly good at identifying broad classes of actions that tend to have good (or bad) results, we are not nearly as good at identifying when we are in a situation that is an exception to these broad generalizations. Accordingly, we normally do better to guide our decision making by simply striving to perform the types of acts that generally do good, while avoiding the acts that generally do bad. And for the most part these are the sorts of acts that would be enjoined or condemned, respectively, by a suitable version of deontology.

Thus, for example, although we can readily *imagine* cases like our hypothetical example, where killing an innocent person would do more good (saving the five), in real life it is almost never the case that doing harm to an innocent person will *actually* have better results overall. And even if we think we have found ourselves in an exception to this broad generalization, it is actually far more likely that we are simply *mistaken* on this point. So we do better to guide ourselves by a rule that *forbids* killing the innocent—even when we think that the results might be better if we did otherwise. Conforming to such deontological prohibitions—consequentialists argue—will actually lead to better results, in the long run, than trying to identify the exceptions.

Of course, despite all of this, consequentialists still differ from deontologists with regard to the *intrinsic* moral significance of the various deontological prohibitions. Consequentialists view the deontologist's rules as merely being useful *heuristics* for identifying the acts which are likely to have the best results, while deontologists think that the relevant rules pick out features of our actions that have direct moral significance in their own right. This is clearly an important theoretical disagreement. Still, despite the philosophical significance of this disagreement the practical bottom line here will generally be much the same, regardless of whether one is a deontologist or a consequentialist. As I have suggested, even consequentialists will normally want to guide their everyday decision making by a suitable set of deontological principles. Because of this point, even consequentialists should find it of more than passing interest if it should turn out that the most *plausible* deontological rules will themselves involve sensitivity to status.

Either way, then, the question of whether deontological prohibitions should be sensitive to differences in moral status is an important one. Both deontologists and consequentialists should care about the answer. Nonetheless, in that follows I will discuss the issue from the perspective of someone who thinks that the deontological account of morality is simply the *correct* one, full stop. This will simplify the presentation. I won't pause to state the similar but not quite identical version of the argument that would be more directly aimed at those who view deontology instead as merely being a useful set of heuristics. (Those who accept this alternative view of deontology will know how to make the requisite corrections to what I say.)

7.2 Absolutist Deontology

Deontologists believe that there is something particularly morally objectionable about doing harm (as opposed to, say, merely allowing it). Accordingly, they embrace a prohibition against deliberately and knowingly harming the innocent. Killing the one to save the five, in our imaginary example, violates this prohibition, so even though killing the one would bring about a better result overall (five alive, rather than one), it would still be wrong to do this. The mere fact that the results would be better—say the deontologists—cannot justify killing someone.

Sometimes this same idea is expressed using the language of rights. Deontologists then say that each of us has a (deontological) right to life, or more generally a right not to be harmed, and killing the one to save the five would violate this right. Admittedly, if we don't kill the one, the five will die, but this doesn't violate their right not to be killed (or harmed), since failing to kill the one isn't actually a way of *killing* the five, it is merely refusing to save them. Here too, then, the basic idea is that despite the fact that if you did kill the one the results would be better overall, this cannot justify doing so. The mere fact that the results would be better cannot justify violating someone's right to life.

That, at least, is what deontologists say when thinking about our original example, where killing the one is the only way to save the five. But what if there were a larger number of people whose lives were at risk? What if killing the one could save not only *five* others, but ten, or a hundred, or a thousand, or a million or more? (Since there aren't enough organs in our one victim to save large numbers like this, it may be best to assume that there is an epidemic threatening thousands or millions of lives, and killing the one is the only way to extract and then synthesize the crucial antibodies needed to save all those others.)

What if a *billion* innocent people stood to lose their lives, and the *only* way to save all of those people was by killing the one? What then?

Interestingly, there are two schools of thought among deontologists in response to questions like this. Some deontologists are *absolutists* about the prohibition against killing the innocent. They stand firm in their assertion that it is wrong to deliberately kill an innocent—no matter *how* much good is at stake. It doesn't matter, they insist, whether killing the one would save a mere five, or a thousand, or even a billion. The right to life—the right not to be killed—cannot be outweighed by the mere fact that the results would be better. No matter how much good is at stake it is morally forbidden to kill an innocent person.

Other deontologists, however, disagree. As the number of lives increases, and the amount of good that will be achieved by killing the one grows ever larger, many deontologists find themselves thinking that it can become permissible to kill the one after all, if it is indeed truly the case that there is simply no other way to avoid the loss of that huge number of lives.

On this more *moderate* deontological view, the right to life has genuine moral weight, but it is not infinitely weighty; if *enough* is at stake then even the right to life can be outweighed. This isn't to say, obviously enough, that in such cases there is no longer anything morally troubling about the need to do harm to an innocent person. It is merely to say that there is also something morally troubling about allowing huge numbers of people to die. And as the number of people in the group that can be saved grows ever larger, the strength of the moral reason to save them continues to grow as well. Eventually, it becomes so strong that *on balance* there is more reason to kill the one than there is to refrain from doing so. In effect, the right to life has a *threshold*, a point at which *enough* good is at stake, so that the right to life gets outweighed and it is now permissible (all things considered) to infringe the right. (We can use talk of "infringement" to mark the fact that the act in question is of the sort that would *normally* be forbidden.)

Moderates thus reject the absolutist position, according to which it is never permissible to kill the one. On the contrary, according to the moderate position, whether it is permissible to kill the one depends on how much good can be achieved (or how much bad can be avoided). If the threshold has been met or surpassed, killing the one is no longer forbidden.

Of course, moderate deontologists can and do disagree with one another as to the precise *location* of this threshold. How *many* lives does it take, before the right to life is outweighed? Will one hundred suffice? A thousand? A million? That question will turn out to be important later on, but for the moment we can put it aside. For I want to start by considering the implications of being an *absolutist*. In particular, I want to ask about the implications of combining absolutist deontology with unitarianism. I believe that almost everyone will find the implications of this combination unacceptable. And if I am right about this, then anyone who is attracted to absolutist deontology will have reason to reject unitarianism and to embrace a hierarchical approach instead.

To see this, we should start by bearing in mind the absolutist claim that it is morally forbidden to kill an innocent person, no matter how much good this does (no matter how bad the results would be, otherwise). And now let us suppose that the absolutist is also a unitarian, thus holding that animals have the very same moral status as people have. This means, of course, that it is also morally forbidden to kill animals. Indeed, it is wrong to kill an animal no matter *how much good* this brings about. Deliberately killing an (innocent) animal is simply forbidden, period. Like people, animals have a right to life, indeed (given the assumption of unitarianism) the very same right to life as you and I have. So if it is wrong to violate that right, no matter how much good is at stake, when the victim is a person, then it is also wrong to violate that right, no matter how much good is at stake, when the victim is an animal instead.

And all I can say is that this result seems to me to be the wrong answer. When I think about cases where a large number of human lives (that is, the lives of a large number of human persons) could be saved but only by killing some suitable animal, perhaps a rabbit, I simply cannot take seriously the suggestion that this is morally wrong. Such a claim simply strikes me as incredible—not to be believed. If you agree with me about this, then you agree that absolutist deontologists must reject unitarianism.

Admittedly, my own intuitions on the subject are somewhat suspect. I have, after all, already confessed that my sympathies lie with consequentialism rather than deontology. I am especially unsympathetic to absolutist deontology. Perhaps, then, in reporting that I find the results of combining absolutist deontology with unitarianism unacceptable, all I am doing is revealing the fact that I never had much sympathy with absolutism in the first place. Perhaps it isn't so much unitarianism that is called into question by the argument I just gave, but my own nondeontological intuitions.

I suspect, however, that even those who do have a deep-seated sympathy for absolutism will find themselves incredulous at the claim that it would be wrong to kill a rabbit even if this were the only way to save the lives of a hundred people, let alone a thousand, or a million, or a billion. It is, after all, one thing to say that *people* are not to be deliberately sacrificed for the greater good—but quite another to insist that even a mouse or a rabbit or a snake cannot be killed, even when this is the only way to save hundreds or thousands of people or more. So even those committed to absolutist deontology should, and likely will, hesitate before extending such absolute deontological protections to mere animals. On the contrary, absolutists will want to reject the unitarian claim that animals have the very same moral status that people have. They will want to claim, instead, that people have a higher moral status than animals have, with different or stronger rights.

In fact, to make this point there is no need to resort to such fanciful examples, examples where, somehow, the lives of thousands or millions of people turn on the fate of a single rabbit! On the contrary, to establish the implausibility of accepting unitarianism when one already accepts an absolutist deontological position, much more modest examples will suffice.

Imagine, for example, that Tom has been shipwrecked, castaway on an uninhabited island. Imagine further that although there is vegetation on the island, it is not adequate to sustain him. But Tom needs to eat, of course; otherwise he will soon starve. Suppose he could keep himself alive by periodically catching and eating a fish. May he do that? (If you don't think that fish have moral standing, suppose instead that there are no fish, but Tom could catch and eat wild rabbits.)

As far as the unitarian absolutist is concerned, the answer is no: Tom may not kill an innocent animal, and that means, obviously, that he may not kill a fish (or rabbit, or deer, and so on)—even though there is no other way to stay alive! To kill a fish, after all, would be to violate its right to life, a right to life every bit as strong and significant as the right to life you and I have. And since the absolutist thinks that it is never permissible to kill an innocent *person*, the unitarian absolutist must similarly think it is never permissible to kill an innocent fish. Apparently, then, the only permissible thing for Tom to do is to allow himself to starve to death. In any event, what he must not do is to kill a fish so as to keep himself alive.

But that is a conclusion that few if any will be prepared to accept. Yet I don't see any way for the unitarian absolutist to avoid this result. It certainly won't help to point out that if Tom dies he will lose far more than the fish would lose were the fish to die instead (given the vast difference in the quality of life of a person—even a marooned person—as compared to a fish). That is indeed the case, but it has no bearing on the situation, for it merely reminds us of the fact that if Tom does kill the fish, the results will be better overall than if he lets it live, since it is better to have a person alive than a fish alive. That is all well and good, but it does nothing to alter the fact that according to the unitarian absolutist, killing the fish will be violating its right to life, and this is something that simply cannot be justified by the mere fact that the results will be better if one does it. Absolutists think that rights are not to be violated no matter how much good is thereby achieved, so unitarian absolutists must conclude that it is indeed forbidden for Tom to kill the fish, even if this is the only way to prevent his own death.

As I say, I find this claim utterly implausible, and I imagine that almost everyone will agree with me. Of course, like all philosophical arguments, this argument against unitarianism can be resisted, even if one insists on maintaining absolutist deontology as well. There is certainly no contradiction in the position of the unitarian absolutist, no hidden inconsistency that would force someone to recant the view. All I can do is to point out the costs of embracing this position. But these costs do seem to me to be incredibly high: I imagine that virtually no one will be prepared to insist that Tom must indeed allow himself to starve.[2] So if we are to avoid this conclusion while remaining absolutists, we must reject unitarianism.

It is worth noting explicitly that in making this argument I am not at all assuming that it would always be unacceptable for a moral theory to tell someone that she must allow herself to die rather than to take the steps necessary to save her own life. Most would find it unacceptable for you to kill a *person*, for example, even if this were the only way to acquire the spare heart needed for the heart transplant that would keep you alive. If these really are your only options—kill another innocent person, or allow yourself to die—then most would agree that, tragically, you must allow yourself to die. This, at any rate, is a common enough deontological thought. (Recall, after all, that most think it wrong to kill the one to save the five; presumably most would agree that it would remain wrong even if the one doing the killing were *one* of the five.)

---

[2] To be sure, there are those who in their daily lives reject eating any animal products whatsoever. But of course in *normal* circumstances it is possible to stay alive while on a strictly vegan diet. Very few people, I imagine, would forbid eating animals if there were truly *no other way* to avoid starvation.

What is absurd is not the suggestion that it may be wrong for you to kill someone, even if you will die otherwise; it is the suggestion that it would be wrong for you to kill a *fish* (or rabbit, or squirrel).

So absolutist deontologists should reject unitarianism. What should they accept in its place? A hierarchical view, of course, one according to which people, by virtue of their higher status, have rights of a kind (or strength) that animals do not possess. We'll consider some possibilities along these lines later. Before that, though, let's see whether unitarianism fares any better when combined with moderate rather than absolutist deontology.

7.3 Moderate Deontology

Moderate deontologists differ from their absolutist cousins in that, unlike the absolutists, the moderates believe that if enough good is at stake it is permissible to infringe a right. Moderates believe in *thresholds* for rights, and they hold that if the threshold is met it becomes permissible to do what would otherwise be forbidden: one can permissibly kill an innocent person, for example, provided that the amount of good at stake is *large* enough.

Conceivably, then, it might be possible for a unitarian deontologist to *agree* that it is permissible for Tom to kill the fish—provided that the unitarian is a moderate deontologist, rather than an absolutist. For killing the fish is the only way to save Tom's *life*, and we have already acknowledged the fact that the results would be better, indeed far better, if Tom were alive (and the fish dead) rather than if the fish remained alive and Tom were dead. Perhaps then a unitarian who was a moderate deontologist could argue that although killing the fish infringes its right to life, nonetheless it is permissible for Tom to do this, since there is *so much* at stake. Given how much worse the results will be, arguably the threshold for the right has been met.

Unfortunately for the unitarian, however—even a unitarian who is a moderate deontologist—it is one thing to note that a fish's right to life could be permissibly infringed provided that the threshold is met; it is quite another thing to show that the threshold actually *has* been met in the particular case we are considering. Everything turns, of course, on the precise location of the threshold. Just how much good does it take before the right to life can be permissibly infringed?

To try to arrive at an answer to this question, let's return to our earlier example, where the only way to save five people was by killing a sixth. As we know, most people agree with the deontologist that it is wrong to kill the one in a case like this. Although the results would be better (five alive, rather than only one), that isn't enough to justify infringing the right to life. Of course, we are now focusing on the position of a moderate deontologist, someone who thinks that the right has a threshold. So if *enough* good is at stake then it does become permissible to kill the one. But how much good is that? How many lives does it take?

I have discussed this question with thousands of people (mostly students) over the years, and I have found that there is a tremendous amount of disagreement about this question. Although most people agree with moderate deontology—accepting a deontological right to life, but one with a finite threshold—people nonetheless vary wildly in terms of how *many* lives it actually takes before the right can be permissibly infringed.

In principle, of course, the threshold could be very low indeed. In fact, in theory a moderate deontologist could believe that it actually was permissible to kill the one even to save a mere five. (Perhaps the threshold is set at three lives, and so saving five actually suffices.) Unsurprisingly, however, most think the threshold is far, far higher than this. When I ask my students about this question, I find that pretty much everyone thinks it is forbidden to kill an innocent person even if this is the only way to save 10, 50, or even 100 lives overall. As I continue to raise the number of lives at risk ("What if we could save 500? What if we could save 1,000? 10,000?"), most people do eventually decide that a threshold has been met—but the relevant number is usually rather high. Many think we don't reach the threshold until a hundred thousand or a million lives are at stake; others place it even higher, at a billion. But even those who place the threshold at the lower end of this range don't place it all that far down. Generally, it isn't until I get up to around 1,000 lives saved that I begin to find any deontologically inclined individuals who think that the threshold has been met. (Of course, there are often a few consequentialists among my students who think it permissible to kill the one as soon as the results would be better overall, just as there are sometimes a few absolutists, who refuse to recognize any kind of threshold at all; but I am here reporting the views of those who are moderate deontologists.)

Suppose, then, that we set the threshold at one thousand lives. As I have just noted, most moderate deontologists would set the threshold at a level considerably higher than this. But the higher the threshold, the more difficult it is to meet that threshold in any given case, and we are currently trying to determine whether the unitarian can plausibly claim that the threshold has been met in the example where Tom is marooned on the island. Since the lower the threshold, the greater the unitarian's chance of defending their position, let us suppose that the threshold really is as low as that: it is permissible to kill an innocent person if this really is the only way to save one thousand other people (though of course it remains forbidden if there is *less* good at stake than this).

Very well, according to moderate deontology we have to be saving one thousand people before it is permissible to deliberately kill an innocent person. But the unitarian claims that the moral status of animals is the very same as the moral status of people. If we combine the two views, what then does this imply about the threshold for an *animal's* right to life?

The simplest possible view here is quite straightforward. The threshold for any given animal's right to life should be at the very same level as the threshold for a person's right to life. Since it takes saving a thousand lives to justify killing an innocent person, it will similarly take saving a thousand lives to justify killing an innocent animal. This means, of course, that although we may now be able to imagine circumstances where killing an innocent fish would be permitted, we will only be able to say this of cases where a thousand lives or more could somehow be saved through the deliberate killing of the fish. And that, obviously enough, isn't remotely the case with regard to Tom's situation. It is true, we have agreed, that *more* good will be done if Tom kills the fish (than if he lets it live and he then dies of starvation), but not *enough* more good, not nearly enough to meet the threshold. If Tom kills and eats the fish then he has saved one person's life—his own. But he obviously hasn't come anywhere close to saving a *thousand* lives!

So the threshold for the right to life has not been met, and Tom is forbidden to kill the fish. Which is just to say, the implausible claim that Tom must allow himself to starve has not yet been avoided. And of course, if the threshold for the right to life is even higher than 1,000 lives saved—as most moderates think—then Tom's situation falls even further short of meeting it.

The bottom line is that if the view we have just sketched really is the correct way of understanding the implications of combining unitarianism with moderate deontology then the turn to moderate deontology does not actually manage to save unitarianism from its implausible implications. Not just absolutists but moderate deontologists too will have reason to reject unitarianism.

There is, however, an alternative way of understanding the moderate deontologist's position. According to this more complicated approach, the threshold for a right to life is not fixed at one single level. It depends, instead, on how much *harm* is involved in losing one's life. Arguably, the less one loses, the less good that must be gained before someone can justifiably impose this loss.

If a view like this can be made out, then given the fact that when a fish is killed it loses considerably less welfare than a person loses when *she* is killed, it should follow that the fish's right to life has a considerably lower threshold than a person's right to life. Conceivably, then, Tom really can justify killing the fish to avoid starvation. Although he is saving only one single human life—his own—perhaps this does still manage to meet the appropriately reduced threshold. Yet since the lower threshold would be the result of the simple fact that fish have less welfare at stake when they die than people do, acknowledging the resultant lower threshold should still be fully compatible with unitarianism. Thus, given this more complicated understanding of moderate deontology, it may be possible to combine unitarianism with moderate deontology after all—all the while still recognizing the permissibility of Tom's killing of the fish.

To get a better feel for this alternative approach to moderate deontology, recall the fact that there are countless other ways of doing harm to people besides killing them. Obviously, killing someone is usually one of the worst things one can do to them, but there are other, lesser harms one can impose instead. Thus, to name just a few examples, I could cut off someone's leg (horrible, but usually significantly better than death), cut off their little toe, punch them in the nose, give them a headache or an upset stomach, or stick them with a needle (causing a sharp but quickly subsiding pain). Moderate deontologists presumably think that each one of these harms can be justified if enough good is at stake, but here too we need to ask: how much good does it take? If I were to harm you in any of these ways with the threshold having been met, I would not violate your right not to be harmed. But where, exactly, is the threshold located?

One natural thought here is that the threshold *varies*, depending on which way I harm you. The pain of a pin prick is extremely modest, the pain from a punched nose is larger; the harm from a lost leg is still greater (and not at all limited to whatever pain might be involved), and from two lost legs, larger still. Although one could insist that all cases of doing harm involve the very same threshold—so that it takes the very same amount of good to justify slapping you on your cheek as it takes to justify cutting off your leg—a far more plausible suggestion for the moderate deontologist to make is that the threshold varies, so that the greater the harm being done to the innocent victim the greater the amount of good that must be involved before imposing that harm can be morally justified. After all, even if it does take saving a thousand lives (suppose) to justify killing an innocent person, it is not particularly plausible to think that it also takes saving a thousand lives to justify punching them in the nose instead. Presumably, fewer lives—a lot fewer lives—would suffice to justify infringing the right not to be harmed when the harm is so much smaller. (Of course, an absolutist deontologist might reject this entire line of thought; but we are here exploring the standpoint of the moderate deontologist.)

Plausibly, then, what the moderate deontologist will want to say is this: the level of the threshold is a function of the amount of harm being done. The smaller the harm, the lower the threshold. If I kill you, normally this does a *tremendous* amount of harm to you, and so the threshold will be, accordingly, very high. But if I harm you in some smaller way, the threshold will be correspondingly lower.

The details of this approach remain unsettled, but a simple example of the requisite function might look like this. Perhaps we find the threshold by multiplying the size of the harm being imposed on the victim by some suitable fixed amount. On this view, although the amount by which we multiply the given harm (so as to arrive at the threshold) is fixed, the level of the threshold itself will still vary: as the size of the harm being imposed gets larger, the product will be larger, and so the threshold will be higher; as the size of the harm gets smaller, the threshold will be lower.

In symbols, if we let h stand for the size of the harm being imposed on the victim, let m stand for the fixed multiplier, and let T stand for the threshold, we can say that

$$T = mh.$$

This is, of course, just a schema, until we have a concrete suggestion about the relevant value of m. We know that moderate deontologists will think that m is significantly greater than 1, since they believe that *much* more good must be done than the harm being imposed, before imposing that harm can be justified. But as we also know, moderates disagree about the precise location of the threshold, so they are going to disagree about the size of m as well.

Even without having settled the size of m, however, we can see how a view of this sort may give hope to the unitarian moderate deontologist. For if the level of the threshold is a function of the *amount* of harm being done when one harms someone, then it really does seem as though a person's right to life should have a threshold that is higher—indeed, significantly higher—than the right to life of an animal. For when we kill a person we normally do much more harm than when we kill an animal. This follows from the fact that normally the value of a given person's life is much greater than the value of a given animal's life. So when we kill a *person* (robbing them of the future life that they would otherwise have had), we normally harm them much more than we harm some animal when we kill *it* (robbing it of *its* future life).

This difference will certainly be significant when we compare the harm done by killing a person to the harm done if one kills a fish. The fish has so much less at stake, so the harm we impose on the fish when we kill it is tremendously smaller than the harm that is normally done when we kill a person. Accordingly, the threshold for the right to life is not at all the same when it is a matter of killing a fish as when it is a matter of killing a person. In both cases, of course, $T = mh$. But since the harm done is so much less when it is a fish being killed rather than a person, the threshold is tremendously smaller as well.

Note, however, that despite saying this, we are straightforwardly applying the very same function across the board. No one is claiming that the fish's right to life is somehow weaker by virtue of its having a lower moral status than a person has. No, the thought is simply that when one has less at stake, one is harmed less if one is killed, and so the threshold of the right not to be harmed is appropriately lower. So we can recognize that the right to life of a fish has a lower threshold than the right to life of a person without in any way appealing to a difference in moral status. Purported differences in status are simply doing no work here: the very same right to not be harmed is being appealed to, for both person and fish, with the very same threshold function.

That's why the unitarian who is also a moderate deontologist can reasonably hope to allow for the permissibility of Tom killing his fish. While it would certainly be forbidden to kill a *person* to keep Tom alive (the relevant threshold would not nearly be met), the fish has so much less at stake that the threshold will be much lower. Arguably, then, that threshold can indeed be met: the good of Tom's saving his own life will be great enough to justify infringing the fish's right to life, given the significantly lower threshold.

That, at least, is what the unitarian would like to argue. But unfortunately for the unitarian, when we actually try to do the calculations—as we will, in a moment—we find that the threshold remains too high. It cannot, in fact, be met, even given this more subtle approach to moderate deontology. If I am right about this, of course, then the moderate deontologist who accepts unitarianism remains saddled with the unacceptable conclusion that it is immoral for Tom to kill fish, rabbits, or deer to keep himself alive. Accordingly, even the moderate will have reason to reject unitarianism.

7.4 Some Calculations

I have just claimed that if we do the relevant calculations we will find that even with a variable threshold function of the kind we have just introduced (where $T = mh$, so the level of the threshold depends on the size of the harm imposed), it will turn out that Tom won't actually have met the threshold, so cannot justify killing animals to stay alive. Of course, this result, while still significant, will be less impressive if it happens to be an artifact of the *particular* animal we use in our example. That is, if the relevant calculations somehow support the conclusion that Tom cannot kill *certain* animals, but nonetheless (due to differences in the details) it is quite permissible for him to kill most other animals, we might well conclude that on balance the implications of unitarianism here are acceptable. It might be slightly surprising if this or that particular animal turns out to be off limits for Tom while others are not, but that still might be a result that the unitarian can accept. On the other hand, even if it turned out that for some animal or the other it was permissible for Tom to kill an animal of *that* sort (perhaps one with an unusually low threshold), if it was nonetheless wrong to kill *most* animals, we might still conclude that the unitarian position should be rejected.

Ideally, then, we would run through the calculations for a relatively large sample of animals: fish, rabbits, squirrels, birds, deer, and more. I won't take the time to do that. I will however consider two such cases: fish and deer. My hope is that these are sufficiently typical to make plausible the general claim that the unitarian deontologist, even if a moderate deontologist, cannot permit Tom to kill most animals even when this is needed for him to stay alive. That will be a problem for the unitarian, given the fact that almost all of us do believe that this is generally permissible.

The first question we need to ask is this: what is the value of m, the constant that we multiply the imposed harm by to determine the level of the threshold? As before, larger values will make for a higher threshold, meaning that it will be less likely that the threshold has been met. So let us once again err on the side of the unitarian and take a value on the lower end of the typical range of moderate views. Suppose then that it is permissible to kill one innocent person to save a thousand other people (but not less). If we also suppose that there is nothing particularly unusual about these people (it isn't that the thousand have especially long lives ahead of them, for example, or that the one has an unusually low level of welfare), then this means that in killing the one we will be producing one thousand times as much good as the harm we are imposing (a thousand lives saved at the cost of one life lost). So if this is indeed the point at which the threshold has been met, it follows that $m = 1,000$. (Since $T = mh$, if the threshold is 1,000 human lives saved when the harm imposed is 1 human life lost, this means that $1,000 = m1$, from which it follows that $m = 1,000$.)

Does this mean that Tom can permissibly kill a deer, say, only if this has the result of saving a *thousand* lives? (If so, then he is clearly forbidden to kill the deer in our example, since doing so saves only his own life, not that of any others.) Not at all, since a deer's life has less *value* than a person's. So when Tom kills a deer, he is doing less harm than he would be doing were he to kill a person. That's going to reduce the level of the threshold. What's more, deer do not generally live nearly as long as humans do. So when Tom kills one, he is depriving it of fewer years than he would be taking away from a human victim. That will lower the level of the threshold as well.

At the same time, however, it must also be recognized that killing the deer won't allow Tom to avoid starvation *forever*! Unless Tom is rescued in the interim, he will eventually need to kill another deer, and then eventually a third, and so on. Each such killing provides Tom with only a certain extra length of human life. So that needs to be taken into account as well, in deciding whether the good done in killing a given deer (preserving Tom's life for that period of time) is great enough to meet the threshold (the result of multiplying m = 1,000 by the harm imposed by depriving the deer of its otherwise remaining years).

So let's ask, first, if Tom does kill a deer, how much food is that likely to provide? How long will it keep him alive? Obviously, the answer will vary tremendously with the size of the particular deer, but let's try to be generous with the estimates here (so as to maximize the chances that the unitarian is right, and enough good is done to meet the threshold). A white tail deer can provide up to about 125 pounds of meat. If Tom can survive on 1/3 of a pound of meat a day, that means the meat from the given deer could last him about a year. (Obviously, the meat will have spoiled long before this unless Tom has some snow or ice to keep it frozen. For the sake of the example, suppose that he does.)

Very well then, killing the deer keeps Tom alive for a year. That's the amount of good that's done if he kills it and eats it.[3] But how much harm does he do *to* the deer? How much does the deer lose? A deer can live for 15 to 25 years, which means that the average deer lives about 20 years. So when Tom kills a random deer we can suppose it is 10 years old, and Tom is depriving it of 10 further years.

All of this means that Tom is taking away ten years of the deer's life (on average) so as to provide himself with one extra year of his own life. So if a year of a deer's life were every bit as valuable as a year of a human life, then this would be a poor trade indeed, from the moral point of view. But as we have already argued, the life of a person—even a person marooned on an island—is a more valuable one than the life of an animal. A year of life as a *deer* simply does not provide nearly as much welfare as a year of life as a person. I am not prepared to

---

[3] Some might object that I am grossly underestimating the amount of good done when Tom kills the deer. After all, doing this makes the *entire rest of his life* possible; if Tom goes on to live for, say, another 50 years, then killing the deer actually saves 50 years of his life, not just one. But this alternative way of approaching the issue is mistaken. If we are going to count the entire 50 years as the good accomplished, then we also need to take into account the fact that Tom will have to kill 50 deer, not just this one, to stay alive that long.

argue for any precise number here, but it does seem as though the unitarian could reasonably maintain that a year of deer life is *less* than *one tenth* as valuable as a year of human life. If that's right—and for the sake of argument, let's suppose that it is—then it will turn out that in killing the deer, Tom actually brings about a better result overall. Although he is eliminating ten years of deer life to gain only one year of human life, a year of human life is sufficiently valuable that the result is a better one overall.

So does this mean that Tom is justified in killing the deer, since the threshold for the deer's right to life has been met? Unfortunately for the unitarian, the answer is no. At best, all we have established so far is that Tom does *more* good (overall) by killing the deer. But we haven't at all shown that he does *enough* good to meet the threshold! Recall that according to our formula, T = mh. Since we are assuming that m = 1,000, this means that it doesn't suffice to meet the threshold for it to be the case that killing the deer does *more* good, overall, than letting it live (and having Tom die instead). Rather, the threshold will be met only if killing the deer does a *thousand* times as much good as the harm that would be done to the deer.

Think about what this means. In killing a deer, Tom takes away (on average) ten years of deer life. In order to reach the threshold, then, killing the deer has to do a thousand times as much good as that amount of harm. That is, it must bring about a good equal in value to 1,000 times 10 years of deer life. So the threshold for killing the deer is equivalent to 10,000 years of deer life!

But Tom himself only gains one year from killing the deer. So if the unitarian is going to claim that the threshold has been met, she will have to insist that a year of human life is at the very least equal in value to 10,000 years of deer life! Thus, to meet the threshold, it won't suffice for the unitarian to claim, as she might arguably claim, that a year of human life is more than *ten* times as valuable as a year of deer life. Rather, the unitarian has to claim that a year of human life is more than *ten thousand* times as valuable as a year of human life. The amount of welfare that a deer gains, in living a year, has to be less than one ten thousandth of the amount of welfare that a person gains.

And that claim, I think, is very hard to believe. It is one thing to suggest, reasonably, that human lives contain more well-being, indeed far more well-being, than the lives of animals, including the lives of deer. But it is quite another thing to suggest that a year of human life contains *ten thousand* times the amount of welfare contained in a year of deer life. Unfortunately for the unitarian, however, unless we are prepared to make this claim, we will have to recognize that the threshold for the deer's right to life has not been met. Or rather, somewhat more precisely, it won't have been met if the unitarian is correct and the very same threshold function is called for in dealing with both people and animals.

Putting the same point the other way around, if we try to combine unitarianism with moderate deontology, we are led to the conclusion that Tom may not permissibly kill a single deer—not even if this is the only way to keep himself alive for a full year. If, as I believe, almost everyone will find that an implausible thing to claim, then those who accept moderate deontology have reason to reject unitarianism.

I hope it is clear that while one might quibble with the particular values I've used in making these calculations (the average life span of a deer, say, or its weight, or how much meat Tom needs to stay alive), varying these values (within reason) isn't likely to be of much use to the unitarian. What forces the unitarian to the implausible claim that a deer's life has a minuscule fraction of the value of a human life is her insistence that we should calculate the threshold for the deer's right in the very *same* way we would calculate a person's right— that is, by multiplying the harm imposed by a *thousand*.

But for this reason it is also important to remember that this number—the value set for m—was chosen with an eye toward maximizing (within reason) the chance of the unitarian's being able to claim that the threshold had indeed been met. Most moderate deontologists will prefer a value for m far higher than the mere 1,000 that we have been working with. But a higher value for m would mean an even higher threshold—and would thus require an even less plausible claim about the comparative value of deer welfare.

Turning now to a different animal, the unitarian's prospects may initially look better if we imagine Tom killing and eating a *fish* rather than a deer. Most of us, after all, are probably prepared to believe that a year of a fish's life is even less valuable than that of a deer. Indeed, it probably strikes us as being considerably less valuable. That means that the harm done to the fish if Tom kills it is even smaller than the harm done to the deer, so the threshold will be correspondingly smaller as well. And since many fish live shorter lives than deer, even less of this (less valuable) life will have been eliminated. That too should result in a lower threshold. Perhaps, then, Tom may permissibly fish, even if he cannot permissibly hunt?

Here too, of course, the details will vary, depending on what sort of fish we imagine Tom catching. But let's suppose that there are rainbow trout in a lake on the island. Since rainbow trout live for about 5 years, if Tom catches and kills one, he will be depriving it (on average) of only about 2.5 years of life. That's several fewer years eliminated than in the case of the deer, so that should help to reduce the threshold as well.

On the other hand, the amount of *good* that will be done by killing a fish is considerably less, since a fish can only sustain Tom for a much shorter period of time. Rainbow trout range from 1 to 5 pounds, so an average trout might weigh about 2.5 pounds. If we assume, again, that Tom can survive on about 1/3 of a pound a day, this means that a given fish will keep him alive for only about a week.

Suppose, then, that $T = mh$, and m is set at 1,000. The harm to the trout is about 2.5 years, which means that if the threshold is to be met, the good that Tom achieves by killing the fish must be equal to or greater than 1,000 times the value of 2.5 years of trout life. That is, killing the fish will be permissible only if the good achieved is equal to at least 2,500 years of trout life. But eating the fish only preserves Tom's life for about a week! So the threshold will have been met only if a week of human life is equal in value to 2,500 years of trout life. Now, 2,500 years is the same as 130,000 weeks. So the threshold will have been met only if a week of human life is as valuable as 130,000 weeks of a trout's life. Human life has to be more than 130,000 times as valuable as the life of a fish!

Now as I have already admitted, it does seem plausible to think that a week or a year in the life of a fish contains less welfare than a week or a year in the life of a person. Indeed, I think it is quite obvious that it contains *far* less welfare. But that's not to say that the extreme comparative judgment needed by the unitarian is particularly plausible. It would imply, for example, that on average a person gains more welfare in *four minutes* than a fish swimming in a lake will normally gain over the course of an entire year! I find that very hard to believe. But unless one is prepared to endorse this kind of comparison, we have to conclude that the threshold hasn't been met. Or rather, if we agree with the unitarian that we should calculate the threshold of an animal's right not to be harmed in the very same way as we would calculate the threshold of a *person's* right not to be harmed—multiplying the harm imposed by a thousand—then we have to conclude that the threshold has not been met. And that would mean, of course, that it is wrong for Tom to catch and eat fish, even though he has no other way to keep himself alive. I think that almost everyone will find that an unacceptable conclusion. So, again, almost anyone attracted to moderate deontology will have reason to reject unitarianism. (And, of course, if we set the value of m even higher—as most moderates would do—then the requisite claims about the comparative welfare of fish would be even more extreme.)

Admittedly, even if the unitarian does have to insist, implausibly, that Tom may not kill a deer, or catch a fish, that doesn't show that unitarians have to forbid *all* cases of killing and eating animals. Indeed, by this point it is easy enough to imagine what type of animal might be such that Tom's killing it to survive would be permissible. Ideally, the animal would be one with a very short life span (so that little future life would be lost), and an extremely low quality of life (so that what life was lost would have little value), but the animal would nonetheless be large and nutritious, so that a single such animal could sustain Tom for a very long time.

Perhaps there are such animals. I don't know. If there are, then the unitarian may be able to point to at least some variants of our example and proclaim that Tom can permissibly keep himself alive after all, provided of course that he only kills and eats animals of the *right* sort.

But for reasons mentioned at the start of this section, even if there are such animals I don't think it would suffice to render unitarianism plausible. For as I suggested, it isn't good enough to show that one may permissibly kill certain *extraordinary* animals in order to keep oneself alive. If it remains the case that for *typical* animals this is forbidden, the view remains unacceptable. So if I am right in thinking that a moderate deontologist who is a unitarian must forbid catching fish, or hunting deer, even though the alternative is starvation, then I think that suffices to reveal the unitarian position as one that will be appropriately rejected by all, or almost all, moderate deontologists.

In short, the results of combining unitarianism with deontology—whether absolutist deontology or moderate deontology—are intuitively implausible. So it isn't just with regard to our value theory that we should embrace a hierarchical account, one according to which animals have a lower moral status than people have. Rather, even the *deontological* elements of one's theory need to be understood in such a way as to take into account the fact that animals simply count for less than people do. The right way to deal with animal ethics within a deontological framework isn't through unitarianism, but through hierarchy.

8

Restricted Deontology

8.1 Excluding Animals from Deontology

Most people sympathetic to deontology won't be especially troubled by my argument that deontologists should reject unitarianism. Indeed, to the extent that deontologists have thought about animal ethics at all, I suspect that most were never attracted in the first place to the claim that animals count in exactly the same way that people do. On the contrary, a more typical position is probably something like this: an adequate moral theory must contain deontological elements (rights, for example), but the protections afforded by these deontological elements are not to be accorded to animals, only to people. That is, it is only the part of morality that governs our treatment of *persons* that takes on a deontological form. The part of morality that governs the appropriate treatment of *animals* does not involve anything deontological. Animals do count—their interests must be given weight—but for all that, when it comes to animals a different moral framework is called for.

It is worth emphasizing this last point, that according to the view being described animals really do count morally. There are, of course, people who deny the moral claims of animals altogether (including some deontologists), but this is not the sort of position I have in mind. I am trying to describe a view according to which animals really do have moral standing, so that it is, for example, morally unjustified to simply disregard their interests. But for all that, the correct way to take animal interests into account is quite different from the correct way to do this when it comes to the interests of persons. *People* must be accorded the sort of rights that deontologists describe, but *animals* don't have these sorts of rights all. So while it is a mistake to think that animals don't count, it is nonetheless also a mistake to worry about *extending* deontology so that it covers animals as well. On the contrary, the scope of deontology is appropriately restricted.

What then is the right moral framework for thinking about animals? Perhaps a consequentialist one. On such a view, of course, inflicting *gratuitous* harm on animals will be forbidden. What's more, even if harming an animal brings about some good, this may still be wrong, if the good done is smaller than the harm imposed. But for all that, perhaps animals can be permissibly harmed if doing so really does bring about a better result *overall*.

In this way, then, the view under consideration provides a different normative profile to animals and to people. People, according to this view, have moral rights that animals simply lack. When it is a *person* that we are considering harming, it is forbidden to do the harm—either absolutely (if one accepts absolutist deontology for persons), or unless the relevant threshold for the right has been met (if one accepts moderate deontology). But when it is an *animal* that we are contemplating harming, it suffices if *more* good is done on balance than harm; it suffices if the results really will be better overall. There is no need to outweigh or overcome any deontological prohibition against harming animals, for animals simply do not fall under the scope of deontology. With regard to animals mere consequentialism suffices.

To see the intuitive appeal of a view like this, consider again the case where we can save five people, but only by killing a sixth. As we know, most find this unacceptable, and that was what led us to describe and explore the deontological approach to morality. But I imagine that most of us would have a rather different reaction to this sort of case if it involved animals rather than people. Suppose, for example, that we can save five rabbits, but only by killing a sixth rabbit. Here, I suspect, a deontological reaction won't seem appropriate at all. On the contrary, most will comfortably conclude that while it is unfortunate that we cannot save the five rabbits without sacrificing the sixth, still, on balance, killing the one rabbit is indeed the right thing to do, since this is the only way to save a larger number of rabbits overall.[1] In short, when it comes to thinking about animals most of us are quite comfortable thinking in consequentialist terms. Certainly, we must take into account the welfare and other interests of any given animal, but if the results really would be better if a given animal is sacrificed or harmed, then harming that animal will be permissible.

Admittedly, not everyone will feel this way. Some may feel uncomfortable with the idea that it is permissible to kill a rabbit so as to save five others. Such people won't be satisfied with consequentialism at all, not even just for animals. But most, I suspect, *will* feel comfortable embracing consequentialism when it comes to animals. It is only when we come to cases involving *people* that consequentialism suddenly seems inadequate and we are drawn to a deontological framework instead. Perhaps, then, we should adopt precisely this sort of two-tiered account of morality, assigning to animals the sorts of moral

---

[1] Cf. Thomson, *The Realm of Rights*, p. 292.

claims that get recognized by consequentialism, while assigning to persons—but only to persons—the stronger protections afforded by deontology.

For obvious reasons, we could summarize the kind of view that I have been describing as consequentialism for animals, deontology for people.[2] It will be helpful to have a name for this position. Although the label is far from perfect, let's call it *restricted deontology*. (It should be clear that the deontological portion of restricted deontology can come in both absolutist and moderate versions.)

Whatever we call it, it must be admitted that restricted deontology has a considerable amount of intuitive appeal. For example, note how restricted deontology immediately yields the intuitively attractive results about killing animals to save human life that eluded unitarian deontologists. For if the correct moral theory involves deontology for people, but consequentialism for animals, then animals don't have deontological rights at all. Obviously, then, we won't need to worry about whether killing the animals can produce enough good to reach the requisite *thresholds* for those rights. On the contrary, all we'll need to ask is whether killing a given animal will produce *better* results overall. But this was something we were already prepared to assert. Tom's killing a deer, for example, may deprive it of ten years of life while giving Tom only one, but if, as seems likely, a year of a deer's life contains less than a tenth as much welfare as a year of a person's life, then the result really will be better overall if Tom kills and eats the deer. Similarly, killing a fish may deprive it of 2.5 years, while keeping Tom alive only for a week, but if, as certainly also seems possible, a week of a fish's life is less than 1/130th as valuable as a week of a person's life, then the results will again be better overall, if Tom kills and eats the fish.

I hesitate to say that restricted deontology is the commonsense view of the matter. I doubt that most people have thought sufficiently hard about the moral status of animals to have in mind any view as determinate as the one I have just described. But for all that, it might be fair to suggest that restricted deontology is the sort of view that most people would move to, if they gave the matter more thought. It represents a rational reconstruction of the moral outlook that may lie behind a great deal of common moral thinking.

And restricted deontology is, of course, a hierarchical view. It acknowledges that animals count, but it insists that animals count in a morally less impressive

---

[2] Nozick describes a view he calls "utilitarianism for animals, Kantianism for people" (*Anarchy, State, and Utopia*, pp. 39–42). Since utilitarianism is a form of consequentialism, and Kantianism is a form of deontology, for our purposes the idea is pretty much the same. It should be noted, however, that although Nozick discusses the view, he dismisses it as inadequate.

way than people do. Unlike people, animals lack the sorts of rights generated within a deontological framework.

One further point. For the most part, I won't be distinguishing between different versions of restricted deontology in the discussion that follows. However, I do want to explicitly note one possibility that may be of particular interest given our earlier discussion of distributive principles. As I explained there (in 3.3), I am drawn to a view according to which animals can indeed have distributive claims, though weaker ones than people would have in similar situations. But I also noted an alternative view according to which distributive principles simply don't apply to animals at all, only to people. Conceivably, such a view could be defended as part of a suitable version of restricted deontology, if, for example, distributive principles are taken to be part of a theory of justice, and claims of unfairness or injustice can only be made by those (or on behalf of those) whose normative profiles include deontological elements.

I presume that a view like this will appeal to some (though not all) restricted deontologists. But I won't pause to ask whether the requisite further claims—those connecting distribution and justice, and justice and deontology—can be successfully defended. For present purposes there is no need to give this particular version of restricted deontology special consideration. The more pressing task, rather, is assessing the more general idea that lies behind restricted deontology per se. Is it plausible to exclude animals from deontology altogether?

8.2 Autonomy

Restricted deontology is a view worth taking very seriously. But I think it is mistaken. I don't think the sort of sharp boundary that lies at the heart of the account—where animals are simply excluded from the deontological protections that are afforded to people—can be defended. On the contrary, I think that if one is going to be a deontologist with regard to people one will need to be a deontologist with regard to animals as well. That doesn't mean that animals should have the very *same* deontological protections as people have, or have them to the same degree. I have, after all, already argued against unitarian approaches to deontology. But rather than excluding animals from deontology altogether, it seems to me that those attracted to deontology for people should instead accept a view according which animals simply have *weaker* deontological rights than people have. If one is going to be a deontologist at all, then *excluding* animals from deontology is unjustified. The sharp contrast between people and animals presupposed by restricted deontology cannot be maintained.

To see this, suppose we start by asking what is it about *people* that makes it appropriate to grant them deontological rights? More particularly, what feature is it that people have, but animals lack, that makes it appropriate to maintain that people have rights while animals do not? Presumably, after all, if restricted deontology really is correct—if people have deontological rights, but animals don't—this is because there is something about being a person which grounds or generates those rights, a feature that people have but animals lack. But what is the feature in question? Just what does it take to have *deontological standing* (as we might call it)?

There are really two questions being asked here. First, what is the feature that people possess which makes it appropriate to ascribe deontological rights to them? Second, is it really true that animals lack the feature in question? Restricted deontology presupposes that a plausible answer to the first question will identify a property for which an affirmative answer to the second question will be plausible as well. It won't do, for example, to propose some feature as the basis of deontological rights in persons if animals have that feature as well. Nor will it do to propose a feature that animals lack, if it is implausible to think that the feature in question is indeed the basis of people having rights.

So let's start by trying to answer the first question. What is the feature that grounds the possession of deontological rights? What does it take to have deontological standing?

Now, were it our goal to provide a complete philosophical defense of deontology, then it wouldn't suffice to name a particular feature as (purportedly) providing the grounds for possession of deontological rights. We would also need to defend the claim that it is indeed a *deontological* framework that best or most appropriately reflects the feature in question; we would need to show how and why the given feature was one whose significance is best accommodated within a deontological structure (rather than, say, a consequentialist one). Happily, however, this is a job that we need not take on for present purposes. My goal here is not to evaluate whether any particular feature really does support deontology, nor even to make the case that it is reasonable or at least prima facie plausible to think that it does. For our purposes we can simply put aside the question of whether the relevant feature genuinely supports deontology or not; we can just suppose (for the sake of argument) that it does. Instead, we only need to identify the sort of feature that those sympathetic to deontology are likely to *point* to. That will allow us to ask whether it is really true that animals simply lack the feature in question.

So what is the feature that deontologists are likely to point to? What is it by virtue of which (deontologists say) people have rights? There are of course different precise proposals that get made here, but I think the most common idea (or the core of the most typical proposals) is that the relevant property is *autonomy*: people are autonomous, and it is by virtue of their autonomy that they possess the deontological rights that they do.[3]

Of course, autonomy is itself a complicated and controversial concept, one whose precise contours are subject to continuing debate. But the basic idea, I think, is reasonably clear: an autonomous being has preferences about how they want their life to go, preferences that are neither simply imposed by external forces or circumstances, nor merely a matter of instinct rather than individual choice; furthermore, when free from outside interference autonomous beings are capable of *acting* on those preferences to a considerable degree, thus living (to at least some extent) the life that they have chosen for themselves. Obviously enough, to be autonomous certainly doesn't guarantee the lack of interference in the pursuit of one's goals, nor does it even guarantee the possession of sufficient resources and abilities to achieve one's goals in the absence of such interference. But autonomy does involve having the capacity for individually chosen action, where one's choices are made (in the light of one's circumstances) in keeping with one's individual preferences.

The thought, then, is that people are indeed autonomous in this sense, and that it is by virtue of this autonomy that people have deontological rights. These rights provide moral protection against being harmed against one's will even if the results would be better overall; they express the thought that autonomous beings should have significant *control* over how their lives go, and that this control is reduced if such an individual can be involuntarily sacrificed for the greater good of others.

Assuming that this is the sort of feature that deontologists will want to point to as grounding deontological rights, then the question we need to ask next is whether it is really true that animals simply lack autonomy. And what I am going to claim, of course, is that it would be a mistake to suggest that animals lack autonomy altogether. On the contrary, animals are or can be autonomous; it is just that they are *less* autonomous than people are. The crucial point here is to recognize that autonomy is not an on/off feature, one which you either have in full-blown form or else lack any trace of whatsoever. Rather, it comes in degrees. So if autonomy really does provide the basis for possessing rights, then the appropriate conclusion is that animals too should be granted such rights, in appropriately weaker forms. And that means, of course, that restricted deontology should be rejected: the correct view here is not one

---

[3] For example, McMahan, *The Ethics of Killing*, p. 256. Cf. Nozick, *Anarchy, State, and Utopia*, pp. 48–50.

according to which animals completely lack deontological rights altogether, but rather one according to which animal rights—though real—are *weaker*.

What I am going to do, then, is to argue that autonomy can come in varying degrees. Of course, strictly speaking, even if I am right about that it won't necessarily follow that animals too should be given rights. For conceivably, at least, it could turn out that although various lesser forms of autonomy are logically possible, in point of fact none of these lesser forms are ever actually exhibited by animals. Perhaps it is only growing human *children* that display reduced forms of autonomy—becoming more and more autonomous as they develop into adults—while mere *animals* never display any autonomy at all. If this were the case then the argument for granting animals genuine but weaker rights would be unsuccessful. But as we will see, it isn't merely that lesser forms of autonomy are logically possible, nor is it the case that only human children possess these more limited forms of autonomy. On the contrary, it is plausible and natural—once one starts thinking in terms of limited autonomy—to view animals as actually having autonomy in some of these more limited forms. So if autonomy really is the basis of deontological rights, animals too should have them.

It is crucial to keep in mind the fact that I am only claiming that animals have autonomy to a limited degree. Unlike animals, normal adult humans are *highly* autonomous. We make plans about our lives as a whole, making decisions with an eye toward how we want our entire future to go. Our preferences here can extend quite far into the future: from the present to tomorrow, to next year, the next decade, and on and on to life's very end. What's more, our desires are not merely *temporally* extended, in this way, we also have preferences concerning a huge and unlimited range of different *aspects* of our lives: we have desires concerning who, if anyone, we should spend the rest of our lives with, what career or careers, if any, we should spend the rest of our lives occupying, where we want to live, how we want to dress, what kinds of food we want to eat, what sort of music we want to listen to, and so forth and so on, from the grand to the trivial. We make long term plans about how central aspects of our lives should go, and we make trivial decisions about what cereal to eat for breakfast in five minutes. We set goals for ourselves, large and small, and we deliberate about how best to accomplish those goals. And then, to the best of our abilities, we set about acting in such a way as to create for ourselves the lives that we have chosen. As I say, people are highly autonomous.

Clearly, animals are not autonomous to the extent that people are. But this is not to say that animals are not autonomous at all. Presumably, few animals have preferences about their lives as a whole, but for all that, I take it to be clear that they do have preferences about their lives. Animals still make choices, after all, even if less grand ones than some of the choices that we make. A dog, for example, may decide between chasing its tail and chasing after a squirrel. That may be a less impressive and far-reaching choice than your choice of career, but it is still a choice for all that. Nor should we think that autonomy is only involved when one is deliberating about one's life as a whole: your autonomy is also made manifest when you are doing nothing more important or significant than deciding whether to have the chocolate cake or the apple pie for dessert.

Animals have a significantly less developed ability to think about the distant future than we have, but for all that it would clearly be a mistake to think that they don't have preferences about the future at all: the bird catches the worm with the intention of bringing it back to the nest so as to feed its young; the squirrel hides the nuts with an eye toward eating them later. To be sure, animals presumably don't have preferences explicitly formulated using concepts like "the future," or "my life"; they don't ask themselves, "How do I want my life to go as a whole?" But that only shows that their autonomy is of a less advanced or less sophisticated form than our own. And the fact is, of course, that most of our own preferences about our lives are not formulated in such abstract terms either. For the most part, we simply have preferences—and the contents of those preferences simply concern larger or smaller aspects of our lives. Just as *your* "first-order preferences" (as we might put it) about what to eat, or where to walk, or what music to listen to, constitute much of what we would appropriately describe as your preferences about your own life, so too animals have first-order preferences about what to eat, or where to walk, or who to mate with, and these constitute *their* preferences about their lives. So in the relevant sense, animals do have preferences about how they want their lives to go, and of course they do try to act on those preferences, as best they can. So animals are autonomous, albeit to a lesser degree than people.

Presumably, animals also *vary* among themselves—that is, with regard to the *extent* of their autonomy. After all, desires about one's life can vary considerably along any number of dimensions. Desires can differ in terms of their temporal range (some involve a more distant future) or the breadth of subject matter (covering a wider range of aspects of the given individual's life); desires can be more or less logically complex (some, for example, may be conditional preferences, preferences about what to do *if* such and such occurs); some desires are self-conscious or explicitly involve notions of the self ("I want that"). Desires can also vary in terms of the extent to which they are the product of deliberation and reflection, and whether one has considered a wider or narrower range of alternatives (or none at all). It seems virtually inevitable that different types of animals will vary in their abilities here. Some animals, for example, will be able to think at least somewhat into the further future; others may be cognitively stuck in the present. Some can engage in rather sophisticated thinking about what will happen if they perform a given act; others will have much less deliberately chosen preferences.[4] In various ways, then, different types of animals will have more or less advanced forms of autonomy. Because of this, the strength of their deontological rights will vary as well.

One might object that even if it is conceded that in the relevant sense animals have preferences about their lives and how they want them to go, this does not yet show that animals are *autonomous*, not even in a limited way. For intuitively, at least, autonomy requires more than the having of preferences about the contents of one's life, it also requires that those preferences be more than instinctive. The preferences (and thus, the choices that follow from them), must be one's *own*. If every animal of a given kind has the very same sort of preferences—or would, if placed in similar circumstances—then we can hardly talk about the animal having their *own* view about how they want their life to go. It would be more appropriate to speak instead of a *generic* view, one that was "standard issue," as it were, for animals of the given kind.[5] And if one's preferences are generic in this way, then one can hardly be said to be *autonomous*.

The point is, I think, well taken. To say that animals have preferences about their lives, and that they then act on those preferences, as best they can, is only to note that animals have *agency* (in the sense of the term introduced in 1.3). But autonomy, we can now say, requires more than mere agency alone. It also requires that the given individual's preferences be truly *individual*, in the sense we have just been talking about, rather than generic. Putting the same point in slightly different language, autonomy requires the ability to set ends, in the sense that one must be able to set one's *own* ends, ends that differ at least somewhat from that of one's fellows.[6]

---

[4] For example, Singer describes an experiment in which scrub jays appear to reason appropriately about what steps to take *now* so as to fulfill specific desires that they realize they will have in the *future* (desires that are different from the ones they have now). *Practical Ethics*, p. 100.

[5] I take the distinction between "generic" and "individualized" preferences or points of view from Anderson, "Animal Rights and the Values of Nonhuman Life," pp. 292 and 295. However, Anderson's use of these locutions suggests that she may think of the distinction as a binary matter (one's preferences are either generic or individual), rather than being, as I will suggest, a matter of degree.

[6] It is sometimes suggested that deontological rights are based on the "separateness of persons" or the "distinction between persons" (e.g., Rawls, *A Theory of Justice*, pp. 27 and 29, or Nozick, *Anarchy, State, and Utopia*, pp. 32–3). But surely individual animals are also distinct (separate) beings, metaphysically speaking. Perhaps, then, some of this talk should be understood as giving voice to the thought that *individuality* matters.

Normal adult humans are clearly autonomous by this standard as well. It isn't merely that people have preferences about how their lives should go (in both large and small ways); those preferences vary tremendously from person to person, with no two people being quite identical. Each person's preferences are their own, each person's vision of how their life should go reflects *individual* choices that they have made, choices that would not necessarily have been made by others in similar circumstances. It is, for example, not instinct that drives one to study philosophy, since others readily neglect the topic. It is not instinct that makes you prefer the crème brulée to the banana cream pie. These are matters of individual choice. Our lives display individuality; they are not mere copies of a generic prototype.

Of course, that is not to deny that there are commonalities that run through normal human lives. We all want to eat, we all want to sleep; most of us want to have children and we dislike the absence of human companionship. Clearly our lives have generic elements or aspects. But for all that, they are highly individualized. We are, as I have remarked, highly autonomous beings.

But while it must be conceded that animals lead more generic lives than we do, and have more generic preferences, it would be an oversimplification to assert that the lives of animals are *simply* generic, full stop. It isn't as though lives must be either fully generic or else fully individualized. After all, as I just noted, even our *own* lives have some generic aspects. What we have, then, isn't so much a dichotomy as a spectrum. Species vary as to where they fall on the spectrum, but most will leave at least some room for individuality. Like us, all animals want to eat, and no doubt for many species the range of foods consumed may be rather small. But for all that, there may still be room for some individual choice. This guinea pig may prefer carrots, for example, while that one prefers green beans; this garter snake may prefer earthworms, while that one prefers insects. Similarly, then, but turning to other areas of choice, this seagull may prefer to nest in cliffs, while that one prefers trees. This shark may prefer being petted by someone she knows, while that one prefers to eat.[7] And this rabbit may like people, while that rabbit prefers the company of its own kind. Individuality also shows up in even smaller and more ephemeral ways. If we believe, as we should, that you display your individuality when, coming to a fork in the road, you go to the left while others might go to the right, then we should be prepared to say the very same thing about a dog.

---

[7] Balcombe, *What a Fish Knows*, p. 145. Referring to three tropical fish he had often observed in a restaurant aquarium, Balcombe says that they were "individuals with autonomous, independent lives."

For some animals, of course, it does seem as though little if anything nongeneric is in place. A fly no doubt makes choices, in some sense of that term, but they are arguably sufficiently instinctive that any other fly would make essentially the same choices in those circumstances. Here, then, it may make little sense to talk about the fly as having individual preferences, preferences of its *own*. But such a case is clearly at the far end of the spectrum, and it seems plausible to maintain that many animals have less generic, more individualized, lives than this. The level of individuality will vary from species to species, and it seems likely that no animal that falls short of being a person has anything like the degree of individuality that we have. But that is not to say that animals are lacking in individuality altogether.

So even if we agree, as I think we should, that autonomy requires individuality and not mere agency, we should not draw the conclusion that animals are simply lacking in autonomy. The right conclusion, rather, seems to be this: animals are less autonomous than people are, but nonetheless they are (or many of them are) autonomous to at least a limited degree. So if being autonomous is the basis of having deontological rights, then animals should be seen as having deontological rights as well. Animals will have *weaker* rights than people have, but restricted deontology errs in insisting that only people have rights at all.

Arguably, of course, there may be some animals that *are* completely lacking in autonomy. Perhaps that is true of houseflies, or other animals at the lower end of the evolutionary tree. I won't try to settle that question, since it would require specialized knowledge of a kind that I simply don't possess. Still, if there are such animals, then perhaps it is appropriate to deny them deontological rights; perhaps consequentialism really is the appropriate moral framework for animals like that. But even if so, this is a far cry from accepting restricted deontology. For restricted deontology, as we have defined that position, holds that it is people and *only* people that have rights. And that view, I have argued, cannot be maintained.

8.3 Resisting the Argument

Autonomy comes in degrees, or so I have argued, and while animals may not be as autonomous as we are, many are still autonomous to at least some extent.

Arguably, however, what I have just said may be somewhat inaccurate. Perhaps all I have really shown is that there is a *dimension* along which beings can be ranked, turning on the extent to which one has agency based on individualized preferences about one's life. But even if I am right that animals do have such preferences (and the resultant agency) to various degrees, it doesn't follow that they are *autonomous* to various degrees. Perhaps the concept of autonomy is restricted to beings that fall at the *high end* of the range defined by that dimension. That is to say, autonomy may be a bit like the concepts *tall* or *large*: despite the fact that all material objects have a greater or lesser height or size, it would be a mistake to claim that all objects are tall or large "to at least some extent," or "even if only to a lesser degree."

If the concept of autonomy is indeed restricted in this way (to individuals at the high end of the spectrum) then it may well turn out that animals aren't really autonomous after all, not even to a limited degree. In which case—one might object—it would turn out that animals don't really have rights at all, contrary to what I have argued.

Now as it happens, I doubt that this claim about the limits of the concept of autonomy is correct. I don't really think that the only time it is legitimate to call something autonomous at all is when it has (and acts on) a comparatively high degree of individualized preferences about its life. On the contrary, it seems to me in fact that we are perfectly comfortable (and appropriately so) saying of growing children, for example, that they display only a limited amount of autonomy, or that they have autonomous preferences only with regard to certain limited areas, or that they are somewhat autonomous, rather than being fully autonomous, and so on. Even very young children may have sharply defined individualized preferences about certain limited aspects of their lives (what they want to eat, what toys they want to play with, what music they enjoy, and so on), and it is natural to say that these preferences are the first manifestations of an ever growing level of autonomy. So to the extent that animals too have and act upon individualized preferences, even if only to a limited extent, then here too it seems appropriate to ascribe autonomy of a limited sort.

However, even if the more restrictive view about the nature of autonomy were correct, and it was only appropriate to call something autonomous if it had individualized preferences to a relatively high degree, that wouldn't really suffice to establish the validity of restricted deontology. For at this point the obvious question to ask would be why one would need to be *autonomous*— strictly speaking—in order to have rights. If autonomy is merely the label we give to cases where an individual has individualized preferences to a *high* degree, then presumably what grounds the possession of rights is actually the having of individualized preferences. And if that is the case then having (and acting on) such preferences should *suffice* for the possession of rights, whether or not one has *sufficient* individualized preferences (or has them in sufficiently advanced form) to count as "autonomous." Perhaps it wouldn't be accurate— strictly speaking—to say that those with only limited individualized preferences are "somewhat autonomous." But for all that, it does seem as though creatures like this should still have rights—albeit of a weaker sort.

In effect, I am saying even if it should turn out that the concept of autonomy really does function like the concept of large or tall, this won't really matter from the moral point of view. For if the notion of autonomy really does work like this then what is truly of moral significance is not autonomy per se, but the underlying dimension, agency based on individualized preferences about one's life. And since animals have that, to varying degrees, they too should have rights (of varying degrees).

So it shouldn't really matter, for our purposes, whether or not it really is legitimate to talk about the degree of autonomy of those who do have at least some individualized preferences but who fall at the lower end of the range. Either way, animals will have rights. Still, for simplicity of exposition I am going to assume that it *is* legitimate to talk this way. That is, I am going to assume that if you have (and act on) any individualized preferences at all, then it is legitimate to talk about *how* autonomous you are. Anyone drawn to the alternative idea—the idea that, strictly speaking, one can only be autonomous to any degree at all if one has a relatively *high* level of individualized preferences—is invited, in what follows, to replace my talk of autonomy with suitable language about individualized preferences.

My claim, then, is this: animals are autonomous, even if less autonomous than people are. So if, as we are assuming, autonomy is the basis for having deontological standing—that is, for possessing deontological rights—then animals too should be recognized as having deontological standing. At the same time, since animals are less autonomous than people are, their rights should be correspondingly weaker or more restricted.

I recognize, of course, that not everyone will accept the particular account of autonomy that I have offered here. And for that matter, not every deontologist will point to autonomy per se as the key property, the possession of which underwrites deontological standing. For our purposes, however, the crucial question is actually this: whatever exactly is the property that is thought to provide the basis of deontological standing (and whatever exactly is the precise analysis of that property), does that property come in degrees, and if so, do animals actually possess it to at least *some* extent, albeit to a smaller degree than that had by people? It seems overwhelmingly likely to me that the answer to this question will be yes. Or rather, that will be the case for the most plausible proposals concerning the feature that lies behind deontological standing.

For the sake of concreteness, I will continue to assume that the relevant property is indeed autonomy (and that autonomy should be understood at least roughly along the lines I have proposed). And in any event, an appeal to autonomy does seem to me the most common proposal concerning the basis of deontological standing. But whatever feature actually underlies such standing, as long as animals do possess it, even if they possess it to a lesser degree— and this does seem extremely likely to me—then animals too should have deontological standing. They too should have rights, though their rights will be weaker than the ones had by people.

In making this argument, I am of course appealing to an idea which seems to me both natural and plausible, namely, that if a given feature is the basis of deontological standing, then anyone who has any of the given feature should have at least some level of deontological standing as well, though a weaker deontological standing than that had by those who have more of the feature (or who have the feature to a greater degree). Thus, if autonomy really is the feature that underlies deontological standing, then anyone with any autonomy at all should have at least some of the protection afforded by deontological rights. It will simply be that those with lower levels of autonomy will have weaker or more restricted rights than those with higher levels.

Supposing this is right, can we conclude that animals with a higher moral *status* have stronger deontological rights than those with a lower moral status? In one sense, of course, this will follow trivially, since the possession of rights will be a central part of one's normative profile. Anyone with strong deontological rights would automatically qualify as having a (relatively) high moral status; and anyone said to have a high moral status would normally be expected to have such rights. But what I mean to be asking is this. We have already gone at least a little distance toward identifying the sorts of psychological capacities that provide the basis for having a higher moral status (see 5.3): these are the capacities that make for more developed forms of agency and open up the possibility of attaining higher and more valuable forms of welfare. How, then, does autonomy fit into this picture? Will those with relatively sophisticated capacities of the kind that we have already identified also tend to score well in terms of autonomy? Or might one's level of autonomy vary independently of the level of these other capacities?

A moment's reflection, however, makes the answer clear. It is indeed the possession of sophisticated capacities of the kind that we have already discussed that makes high levels of autonomy possible. One's ability to have highly individualized preferences about wider and more far-ranging aspects of one's life depends precisely on things like one's capacity for abstract and complex thought and emotion, including the ability to think further into the future; it depends on creativity, imagination, self-awareness, and self-knowledge.

Indeed, among the very capacities identified earlier as providing the basis for higher moral status were capacities for reflection and self-governance, and for individual, idiosyncratic, and autonomous choice. (Similar remarks would hold true for other plausible proposals concerning the basis of deontological standing. But I won't continue to belabor this more general point.)

Accordingly, we can safely conclude that autonomy will vary with the capacities that underwrite one's moral status more generally. So we can summarize the conclusion we have reached this way: people have a higher moral status than animals have, and so have stronger deontological rights as well. But animals do have such rights, and the higher the status of the given animal, the stronger the rights in question.

At least, that is the conclusion we will have reached if it really is right to suggest that any being with any degree of autonomy at all should have at least some deontological standing, and the higher the level of autonomy, the stronger the rights. That does seem to me to be the right position for the deontologist to take, and so I conclude, accordingly, that restricted deontology should be rejected.

However, a fan of restricted deontology might insist that I am wrong to think that one's deontological standing should vary continuously with the level of one's autonomy. On the contrary, they might insist, one will not possess any kind of deontological standing at all unless one is *sufficiently* autonomous. That is to say, unless one has a *high enough* level of autonomy, one will have no deontological rights at all.

To say this is not to return to the earlier suggestion that it is inappropriate to talk about animals as having autonomy but only to a limited degree. On the contrary, someone putting forward the current idea may actually be perfectly content to talk about animals as having real but limited autonomy. The claim, rather, is that it isn't good enough to have *some* autonomy, if one is to have deontological standing. One must have *enough*. In effect, there is a cutoff point, a minimum level required, below which one is not *sufficiently* autonomous to possess rights. And if we concede this point, then it becomes possible that the relevant minimum level of autonomy is actually set fairly high. Perhaps only *people* are sufficiently autonomous to meet the cutoff point. If so, then restricted deontology will turn out to be correct after all. Restricted deontologists can concede that animals are autonomous to some extent; they need only insist that they are not sufficiently autonomous to meet the cutoff point. So people will indeed have rights, but animals will simply lack them.

(Question: what should the restricted deontologist say about *marginal* cases—severely impaired humans who are not sufficiently autonomous to meet the cutoff point? Are they too to be denied deontological standing? I won't pursue that issue here, except to note that an appeal to the significance of modal personhood might conceivably be relevant, given that even the severely impaired generally *could* have been highly autonomous.)

It should be clear that to adopt a view like the one I have just described is to reject the principle I endorsed above: that whatever feature it is that underlies deontological standing, whoever has any of this feature at all will have at least some deontological standing, though the level of their standing will vary with the amount of the feature possessed. This principle rules out the very idea of there being a cutoff point of the relevant kind. So if autonomy really is the feature that underwrites deontological standing then any amount of autonomy should suffice to generate rights of at least a weak sort; there should be no further minimum level of autonomy required before one can have any kind of deontological rights at all.

Before pursuing this issue further, I first want to note a different problem that the variability of autonomy creates for the restricted deontologist. Even if we momentarily suppose that one must first reach a certain minimum level of autonomy before possessing deontological rights, we would still face what I previously called the problem of normal variation (in 6.4). For even if all animals fall below the cutoff, and all people fall above it, it still seems plausible to think that people will vary among themselves in terms of precisely *how* autonomous they are. Accordingly, even if there is a cutoff point for having deontological standing, it seems as though we are still left with the conclusion that those people with higher levels of autonomy than others should have a higher moral status, including stronger rights. And this is a conclusion, I imagine, that virtually no restricted deontologist will be willing to accept.[8]

Of course, it must be conceded that my own position also raises the problem of normal variation. After all, if the strength of your rights should vary with your level of autonomy—which is what I have been claiming—then it certainly seems to follow that some people will (by virtue of their greater autonomy) have stronger rights than others. So the problem of normal variation remains a live one for me too. Here, however, my point is just the more narrow one, that even if we were to embrace a cutoff point for deontological standing, this wouldn't make the problem of normal variation disappear. Even restricted deontologists must come to grips with it.

To be sure, if the restricted deontologist could claim that there simply are no differences in levels of autonomy *above* the cutoff point, then no problem of

---

[8] Cf. McMahan, *The Ethics of Killing*, pp. 248–51.

normal variation would arise here. But on the face of it, at least, this doesn't seem to be a plausible thing to claim. It is clear that people really do differ, for example, in terms of the extent to which they have long term plans concerning how they want their lives to go, or the extent to which they strive to put these individualized preferences into action. So if the relevant property really is *autonomy*, then there seems no easy way to escape the conclusion that rights really should vary, among people at least, one to the next. (Indeed, even if, somehow, there were an upper *limit* to the amount of autonomy one could have—that is, even if there were such a thing as perfect or complete autonomy—there is no good reason to think that all people are at, or anywhere near, this upper limit.)

Accordingly, if the deontologist is going to avoid granting rights to animals while denying variation in those rights among people, not only is she going to have to assert that there is a cutoff point (below which the possession of lesser amounts of autonomy is inadequate to ground rights), she is also going to have to claim—and this really is a further claim—that variation above this point is morally *inert*, doing nothing at all to make for larger or stronger rights. In short, her view must be this: too little autonomy does nothing at all to ground lesser deontological standing; but "too much" autonomy does nothing to give you *higher* deontological standing either. The "surplus," as it were, is simply wasted.[9] And what I want to say, by way of response, comes down to this: it is difficult to see why the significance of a continuously variable property like autonomy should be "flattened out" in this way.

8.4 Dichotomous Properties

The fundamental problem for restricted deontology is this. The restricted deontologist points to a particular property—autonomy—and says that this property is the basis of deontological standing. But that property is a variable one, it comes in greater or lesser quantities of varying amounts. As such, we would normally expect that property to yield variable results as well—rights of varying strength, corresponding to the degree or level of autonomy possessed. But that's at odds with the structure of restricted deontology. So the appeal to autonomy gets recast. Instead of asking *how* autonomous a given individual is, we are told to ask only whether the individual is *sufficiently* autonomous. Unfortunately, however, it is far from clear whether this shift can be adequately motivated.

---

[9] The term comes from Daniel Wikler, quoted in McMahan, *The Ethics of Killing*, p. 250.

Some such shift along these lines is unavoidable. Restricted deontologists need to identify a property that can be plausibly thought to underwrite deontological standing. But more than this, they need the property to be a *dichotomous* one, a property such that a given individual either simply has it, or else simply lacks it. The property cannot be one that someone can have to a greater or lesser degree, for that sort of property—a property which could be possessed in varying amounts—would immediately lead to the possibility of rights of varying strengths; it won't lend itself to the kind of flat, two-level view that the restricted deontologist believes in, where animals simply have no rights at all, and all people have rights of the very same strength. On the contrary, if the property that grounds deontological standing is variable, then what we will expect instead is that any individuals—including animals—with any amount of that property will have rights of at least some sort, and that the strength of the rights generated will vary with the amount of the property possessed.

So the restricted deontologist needs to appeal instead to a dichotomous property—one where questions of degree or extent don't even arise. They need a property that is "all or none," as we might put it—one which animals are simply lacking, and which all people have to the same degree. And what I have been arguing, of course, is that autonomy doesn't meet the bill; it comes in degrees, rather than being all or none. That's why the most straightforward appeal to autonomy won't do. It simply has the wrong logical form to provide the underpinnings for restricted deontology.

Of course, that's not to say that it is especially difficult to *construct* a dichotomous property out of autonomy. We can easily do that, once we stipulate the relevant cutoff point. We need only insist that, strictly speaking, the property relevant for deontological standing isn't really autonomy per se at all, since that is a variable property. Rather, the relevant property is the *dichotomous* one of having *enough* autonomy. For although individuals can vary widely in terms of *how* autonomous they are, there are still only two possible answers to the question of whether they are *sufficiently* autonomous, relative to the specified cutoff point: either they are, or they aren't. Accordingly, if the cutoff point is set at a suitably high level, then animals will simply fail to have the relevant property, full stop, and so will lack rights altogether; while people will have the relevant property, but to the very same degree, so will all have rights of the very same strength.

Here's an example that is sometimes used to illustrate the ideas at work here.[10] A circle can be thought of as dividing the plane into two parts, those points on

---

[10] Rawls, *A Theory of Justice*, p. 508.

the plane that fall on or in the interior of the circle, and those points that are outside the circle. Here, then, we have a dichotomous property: a point is either "within" the circle (taking this notion to include those points on the circle itself) or it is outside the circle. Equivalently, a given point is either *close enough* to the center, or it is not.

Note, however, that although this property is defined in terms of *distance* (that is, distance from the center), and although *that* property is clearly a variable one (points can be closer or farther away from the center, by varying amounts), nonetheless that fact is simply irrelevant, if the significant property is not distance per se, but rather the dichotomous property of falling within the circle (or being outside it). All points within the circle are *equally* within it; all points outside it are equally outside it. In particular, then, even when one point in the interior is closer to the center than another, that doesn't mean that it is within the circle "to a greater degree." Both points are *equally* within it. Similarly, even if a point falls just short of being within the circle, that doesn't mean that it is within the circle "to a limited degree" or "to some extent." On the contrary, if it falls short then it falls short, and it simply lies *outside* the circle, full stop.

Analogously, then, the restricted deontologist should say that autonomy is not, strictly speaking, the morally relevant property when it comes to deontological standing. We only use that property to construct the one that is genuinely relevant. What matters instead is the property of being *sufficiently* autonomous, of having a high enough level of autonomy. And *that* property really is dichotomous; either one has it or one does not. Indeed, even if one individual has more autonomy than another, if both have enough then it is *equally* true of each that they have enough: it is not more true of one than of the other that they do. So if having *enough* autonomy is what grounds deontological standing, then we need not worry about giving rights, albeit weaker ones, to animals that fail to have enough. Nor need we worry about giving stronger rights to those people that have *more* than enough. Any given individual will either have enough autonomy to have rights or they won't; and since it is equally true of all those that do have enough that they have enough, all those with sufficient autonomy will have equally strong rights.

That, at least, is the thought. But to be clear about what the restricted deontologist must claim is not yet to render those claims particularly plausible. To successfully defend restricted deontology it isn't enough to *name* the purportedly relevant property, it must also be intelligible how a property like that could matter in the specified way. But that, I think, is exactly what gets lost, when the restricted deontologist shifts from autonomy to *sufficient* autonomy.

It is, of course, easy enough to see how *autonomy* might matter for generating rights. Rights protect you (at least somewhat) from losing control over how your life goes; they give you space in which to act on your individual preferences. So an account of rights based on autonomy seems at least initially promising; we can see at least the outlines of how the underlying account might go. But when the restricted deontologist shifts from autonomy to sufficient autonomy that same account is no longer available to us. For that account would support the idea of rights for anyone with any level of autonomy at all; and that is precisely what the restricted deontologist denies.

If what matters is not autonomy per se, but having *enough* autonomy, then we are saying that there is a *particular* level of autonomy that has a unique moral significance. And it is hard to see what could make that so. What could it be about any particular amount of autonomy that could suddenly make rights come into existence, when smaller amounts of autonomy failed to do anything remotely like that? What is it about that particular level of autonomy that could make it the case that even higher levels of autonomy did no further normative work? Why wouldn't even more autonomy generate even stronger rights? It is questions like these that the restricted deontologist cannot answer.[11]

This is not to say that the claim that one must have a certain level of autonomy before one has any rights is incoherent. Rather, it seems philosophically unmotivated. In saying this, I don't mean to claim that it is arbitrary where one *places* the cutoff point. I mean, rather, that the very *idea* of this sort of sharp cutoff point seems arbitrary and unjustified. What could possibly explain why it would take having a certain *amount* of autonomy before one has any kind of rights at all? Why wouldn't we expect instead that *any* amount of autonomy will suffice to ground *some* sort of right?

In raising this objection, I certainly don't mean to suggest that all thresholds of any sort whatsoever are unmotivated and implausible. To escape the gravitational force of the earth, for example, one must attain a certain minimum velocity: anything less will simply be inadequate. To overcome the chemical bonds holding water molecules together as ice, the water must attain a certain minimum level of average kinetic energy: otherwise the ice just won't melt. So it isn't as though the very idea of a threshold is unacceptable.

Nor are thresholds necessarily problematic in the *moral* domain. Indeed, as we have already seen, most people are moderate deontologists and so believe in thresholds for rights. When there is *enough* good at stake, the moral force of the right not to be harmed is outweighed, making it permissible to impose a

---

[11] Cf. Arneson, "What, if Anything, Renders All Humans Morally Equal?"

harm of the relevant size even on an innocent person. But if there is too *little* good at stake the right simply won't be overcome. To justify infringing a right, one must meet the threshold.

We can turn this same example the other way around. Suppose there is a certain amount of good that can be achieved if we perform a certain act. Other things being equal, that provides some reason to perform the act in question. Imagine, however, that this act will involve infringing a right of some sort or the other. Does that render the act impermissible? Not necessarily. If the right is too *weak*, it won't be able to overcome or outweigh the reason to perform the act grounded in the good that can be accomplished. It is only if the right is *strong* enough that the justificatory force of the chance to produce the good will be outweighed. So here too we face a threshold: the right must be *sufficiently* strong—otherwise infringing the right in those circumstances will be permissible.

All of this is perfectly straightforward and not at all mysterious. We have thresholds when *one* feature or factor needs to be strong enough to overcome or outweigh another such factor. But nothing like this is in place with the suggestion that there must be *enough* autonomy before any rights at all are generated (no matter how weak). For what exactly is it that is supposed to be standing in the way of generating a very weak right? What is the moral force that must be *overcome*, before there can be any kind of right at all?

I cannot imagine what kind of answer might be provided to this question. Of course, a weak right might be too weak to overcome any particular countervailing moral consideration. It might not be strong enough, for example, to overcome the chance to produce a given amount of good. But what normative force stands in the way of generating the weak right in the first place? I can't think of any. So it seems to me that it is indeed arbitrary to insist that one must have a certain amount of autonomy before one can have any rights at all. On the contrary, it seems far more plausible to suggest—as I have been suggesting—that *any* amount of autonomy will suffice to ground a right of *some* sort or the other, though the smaller the degree of autonomy, the weaker the right will be.

Again, my complaint isn't that we can't construct dichotomous properties out of variable ones, or that we can't baldly assert that it is the dichotomous offspring that matters morally rather than the variable parent. Obviously, we can draw a cutoff point anywhere we want, and thus create the *logical* distinction between having more than this or less than this amount. We can then simply insist that unless you have that much of the relevant property—autonomy, as we are supposing—then you don't have any rights at all, but provided you have that much or more, you have rights, and the very same rights no matter how much more autonomy you have. Yes, we can *assert* all of that. But why would we think that morality actually *works* like that? Why should certain negligible differences in the amount of autonomy make all the difference in the world (when one individual falls just below the cutoff point while another falls just above it), while other quite large differences make no difference at all (when both individuals fall short of the cutoff point, or both exceed it)? It simply doesn't seem plausible.

As far as I can see, the only remotely promising line for the restricted deontologist to take is this. Imagine that there were some *other* property that actually mattered morally, a property distinct from both autonomy per se and from sufficient autonomy. Imagine that this other property was also a dichotomous property. But more than this, suppose that it was dichotomous by its very nature, as it were, rather than by constructive fiat. Finally, suppose that this naturally dichotomous property was somehow correlated with the proposed cutoff point for autonomy, so that if one had less than the sufficient level of autonomy it turned out that you were lacking in this other property as well, but that if you had enough or more than enough autonomy to meet the cutoff point, then you would *have* the other property.

If something like this were the case, then we could see why it might be rather tempting to think that what mattered was whether you were sufficiently autonomous or not. Really, however, what would actually matter was whether or not you had this *other* property. And since that other property was itself dichotomous, it really would follow that all those who were insufficiently autonomous would lack rights (since they would simply lack the genuinely relevant property), while all those who had sufficient autonomy would possess rights, and to the same degree (since they would all have the genuinely relevant property, a property that could not vary in degree or intensity). On such an account, being sufficiently autonomous wouldn't really do any moral work; but it would correspond to having (as opposed to lacking) the genuinely relevant dichotomous property.

That's all rather abstract, but we can easily illustrate the basic idea by returning to the example of the circle. If someone were to baldly insist that it *matters* whether one is inside a given circle or outside it, we might well wonder what could possibly make it so. Given that distance from the center is a variable property, what could possibly make it be the case that there was a particular cutoff in distance, such that it made all the difference in the world whether one was on one side or the other of that cutoff? Questions like these are analogous to the ones that I have been pressing against the restricted deontologist.

But for all that, of course, there *could* be a proper explanation. Suppose that the circle represents the perimeter of a pavilion. Obviously enough, then, if you are close enough to the center, then you will be under the roof of the pavilion, and if you are not, you won't be. Suppose, next, that it is raining. This means that if you are too far from the center you will get wet, but if you are *close enough*, you will remain dry. *All* that will matter is whether you are close enough to the center of the pavilion or not. It won't help at all if you are *almost* close enough: you will still get wet. And it won't matter either that one location under the roof is closer to the center of the pavilion than the other: either one will keep you dry, and both will keep you equally dry. Here then, despite the fact that distance is a variable property, all that matters is whether you are close enough to the center. Strictly, however, the reason being close enough matters is because it correlates with a different property, the one that is really doing the work here: whether you are *under the roof* or not. Being under the roof is a dichotomous property, and it is *this* property (along with the fact that it is raining) that explains why it matters how close to the center you are.

So once restricted deontologists concede, as I think they must, that autonomy comes in degrees, then if they are going to insist that what matters for having rights is being *sufficiently* autonomous, I think that what they need to do is to identify some *other* property, distinct from autonomy—a property which is naturally dichotomous and which is correlated with having sufficient autonomy. They then need to claim that it is actually this *other* property that is doing the moral work here, this other property that really explains why individuals either have or lack deontological rights. If the property was a naturally dichotomous one, rather than being artificially constructed out of an underlying variable property, then the worry about appealing to an arbitrary and unmotivated cutoff point would be eliminated, since the view wouldn't really appeal to any kind of cutoff point at all. All that would matter is whether or not one had the relevant dichotomous property.

If restricted deontologists could identify such a property perhaps their view could be preserved after all. But I have to confess that I cannot think of what that other property might be. Merely noting the possibility of there being a further property like this isn't at all the same thing as actually identifying it. A suitable candidate would have to be such that it was plausible to think that it might provide the basis of deontological rights. It would need to be a dichotomous property (so that those who lacked it would have no rights at all, and those who had it would all have rights of the same strength). It would need to be a naturally dichotomous property (to avoid the appeal to an unmotivated cutoff point). And of course, it would also have to be a property for which it was plausible to suggest that people *have* the property in question, while animals lack it. Finding such a property would be no small feat.[12]

If they *could* find one, restricted deontologists could even throw away the claim of correlation with autonomy, if they'd like. They need only insist that there is a property which can plausibly be claimed to underwrite deontological standing, a property that is naturally dichotomous, such that people have it and animals lack it. They could then argue for restricted deontology by appealing to this property directly, and stop talking about autonomy in this connection altogether. In any event, the crucial challenge for the defense of restricted deontology is to find a naturally dichotomous property—possessed by people but lacking in animals—that can be plausibly thought to provide the basis of deontological standing.

I do not myself see a way to prove that there is no property that will meet all these conditions. So I do not take myself to have *proven* that restricted deontology is a position that must be abandoned. But it does seem to me that the burden of proof should fall on those who claim that there is such a property, since it is far from obvious what the property in question might be. Speaking personally, I believe that this burden cannot be successfully discharged. Accordingly, I believe that, despite its intuitive appeal, restricted deontology should be rejected.

Instead, deontologists should stick to the common thought that deontological standing really does depend on autonomy (or on some other property similar to autonomy). Of course, as I have also argued, autonomy is variable rather than dichotomous. So the right conclusion for deontologists to reach, as far as I can see, is that rights come in varying strengths. Animals may be less autonomous than people are, but they are not lacking in autonomy altogether. So they too have rights, albeit weaker ones.

---

[12] What about the following proposal? Might deontological standing depend on *moral agency*, the capacity to act with an eye toward whether one's action would be morally right or wrong? Admittedly, moral agency isn't a *dichotomous* property; people (including children) clearly have it to varying degrees. So an appeal to this property won't establish the restricted deontologist's claim that all people have rights of the *same* strength. But isn't it at least true that *only* people are moral agents? (If so, then an appeal to moral agency might at least establish the restricted deontologist's claim that only people have rights.) This suggestion deserves fuller discussion than I can provide here; but arguably, even though animals are not moral *agents*—are not subject to moral requirements—they can perhaps display a more limited form of moral *agency*. To be sure, a person might do an action because she explicitly thinks of it as the morally right thing to do. Animals can't do that. But it is also true that, when acting, people often simply respond directly to the relevant moral reasons, without *thinking* of it in those terms. I suspect that even animals can have moral agency in this latter, more limited, sense.

9

Hierarchical Deontology

9.1 Weaker Rights

The most plausible form of deontology is one that grants deontological standing to animals and not only to people, where the strength of the rights accorded to any given individual varies with their moral status. This is, of course, a hierarchical view. Unlike restricted deontology, however, which is also a hierarchical view, this alternative does not display a hierarchical structure through excluding animals from deontology. Rather, it recognizes differences in status *within* deontology—holding that animals have weaker rights than people, and some animals weaker rights than other animals, by virtue of having less sophisticated or more limited forms of the relevant capacities. Let us call a view of this new sort *hierarchical deontology*.[1]

Now, as I have already noted, deontologists typically think that the property that provides the basis of deontological standing is autonomy (or some property closely related to autonomy). But we can use the term "hierarchical deontology" broadly enough to cover views that appeal to properties other than autonomy as well, provided that the property in question is a variable one which animals have, though only to a limited extent (so that the theory accords animals deontological rights, though of a weaker sort than those accorded to people). For our purposes going forward, then, the crucial issue is not what particular property is thought to provide the basis of deontological standing, but only that the theory recognizes that animals have rights, but weaker ones than people have.

Some people have argued, however, that the very idea of rights varying in strength in this way—so that, for example, a deer's right not to be harmed might be weaker than a person's, while a snake's might be weaker still—is something that should be rejected. The concern here is not so much with the various particular claims that might be made about whose rights are weaker

---

[1] This is, I believe, the sort of view that Kazez is proposing in *Animalkind*, though she doesn't use the terms "hierarchy" or "deontology."

than whose, but rather with the very idea that rights might vary in strength. That idea, it is sometimes suggested, is confused: one can have a given right or lack it, but no two instances of the very same right can vary in strength.

Here, for example, is a claim of this sort being made about the impossibility of rights varying in strength from person to person:

> Since rights are limits on how others may treat us, it makes little sense to say that one person is less of a right-bearer, or has weaker or less meaningful rights, than another.[2]

Of course, this particular claim is only being made with regard to the rights had by people. Note, however, that the reason given for denying the meaningfulness of talk of weaker rights—that rights are limits on how individuals may be treated—would presumably apply as well to any rights had by animals. So I take it that if the conclusion really did follow, it should be a more general one, covering animals as well: that it simply makes no sense to say that any one individual has weaker rights than another.

In any event, here's an example of the same claim being made *without* the restriction to people (the author intends to be speaking of animal rights as well):

> Possession of moral rights does not come in degrees. All who possess them possess them equally...[3]

But is it really true that a given right cannot come in a weaker or stronger version? Is the very idea of two individuals possessing the same right, except that one has a weaker version of the right than the other, something that should be dismissed out of hand as confused or incoherent or simply impossible?

It is difficult for me to see why we should think that. At the very least there is a straightforward way that the idea can be understood by those who are moderate deontologists. After all, moderates believe that rights can be outweighed, so that in the right circumstances it becomes permissible to perform an act infringing a given right, even though normally such an act would be forbidden. Moderates believe that rights have *thresholds*, such that if enough good is at stake the moral force of the right is overcome and it is permissible to infringe the right. In particular, of course, moderates hold that the right not to be harmed has a threshold, though the precise level of that threshold depends on the size of the harm being imposed.

---

[2] Sher, *Desert*, p. 147.   [3] Regan, *The Case for Animal Rights*, p. 268.

Suppose, then, that we have two individuals, both with a right not to be harmed. And suppose that we are considering imposing a harm of a particular size so as to achieve some good. How much good will it take to justifiably impose that harm? What is the level of the threshold, given a harm of that particular size?

It certainly seems conceivable that the answer might vary from one individual to the next. That is, it certainly seems *coherent* to suggest that the threshold—the amount of good that must be achievable before infringing the right becomes permissible—is greater for one individual than it is for another, even though the size of the harm to be imposed is the very same. It might take more good to justify imposing the given harm on the one individual than on the other. If thresholds could vary like this, then it would be natural and straightforward to say that the one individual's right not to be harmed is stronger in those circumstances than the other individual's right. The second individual could reasonably be said to have a weaker right in that situation, precisely by virtue of the fact that the threshold for the right was lower in the given case. And of course if something like this were true across the board—if the threshold was lower for *each* size harm that might be imposed—then it would be extremely natural to describe the second individual as having a weaker right not to be harmed. After all, by hypothesis it would take less good to outweigh the right, in any given circumstance.

None of this is yet to say that some rights *are* weaker than others, when possessed by one individual rather than another. It is simply to note that the idea of a given right being weaker for some than for others makes perfect sense. But of course we have already seen reason to believe that the most plausible version of deontology will be a *hierarchical* one, committed to precisely this kind of variation in the strength of rights. Animals will have rights, and people will have rights, but the strength of those rights will vary with differences in moral status. And clearly, as we now see, one way that they can vary is if the threshold for the given right varies. If animals have a weaker right not to be *harmed*, for example, we can understand this as saying (at least in part) that the threshold for an animal's right not to be harmed is *lower* than the threshold for a person's right not to be harmed. Similarly, if one animal—say, a snake—has a weaker right not to be harmed than another animal—say, a deer—then one thing we might anticipate is that both will have a right not to be harmed, but the threshold for the snake's right will be lower than the threshold for the deer's right (for any given harm).

No doubt, there are still other ways in which one right might be said to be weaker than another. Some of these will be considered later. But this first way—where the level of the threshold varies though the circumstances are the same—is clearly an important one, and it will be the focus of our discussion.

At first glance, of course, it looks like absolutist deontologists cannot avail themselves of this particular account of how a right might vary in strength. Since absolutists reject the very idea of finite thresholds for rights, they can hardly embrace the version of that idea in which one individual's thresholds are set lower than those of another. (Perhaps, then, the two authors quoted above are both absolutists.)

But we already know that there is reason to reject absolutist deontology. At least, there is reason to reject it if one is going to both extend deontological standing to animals and yet insist—as one should—that it is permissible for Tom, in our earlier example, to catch and eat fish or to hunt a deer, when this is the only way to keep himself alive. If the right not to be harmed simply has no threshold, then once we extend deontological standing to animals it follows immediately that one cannot kill a fish or a deer no matter how much good this would do. We could not even kill a single mouse, say, even if this were the only way to save hundreds, thousands, or millions of human lives.

I think that any conclusion like this is unacceptable, and I imagine that most or all deontologists will agree. Perhaps what all of this shows us is that anyone committed to absolutist deontology can be at best a *restricted* deontologist, according deontological standing to people but not to animals. But of course I have already argued that the position of the restricted deontologist cannot be justified. So if, as I believe, deontological standing should be extended to animals as well, one should reject the claim that rights can never have thresholds. Indeed, we had better place the thresholds for animal rights sufficiently low so that it is plausible to maintain that the threshold has been met in cases like the one described, where Tom will starve unless he kills and eats a deer.

Conceivably, however, a view like this might yet be acceptable to certain *types* of absolutist deontologists. I introduced the idea of the absolutist (in 7.2) as someone who thought that a person's right not to be killed could not be justifiably infringed no matter how many lives might thus be saved. Strictly, however, this didn't commit the absolutist one way or the other with regard to whether an *animal's* right to life—if such there be—would also be something that could never be outweighed, no matter how much good was at stake. Thus, it would be consistent for someone to hold that while a *person's* right to life has no threshold, the same isn't true for an animal's right to life. Perhaps then animals really do have a right to life (or, more generally, a right not to be harmed), and yet that right does have a (finite) threshold, one low enough to permit Tom to kill a fish, say, so as to keep himself alive.

Should a view like this—absolutist for the rights of persons, but moderate for the rights of animals—be called an "absolutist" one, or not? Nothing substantive turns on our answer to this question. The only important point is that a view like this seems coherent and that it too is an instance of hierarchical deontology: it too grants animals deontological rights, but it insists, appropriately, that those rights are weaker than the corresponding rights had by people. (Obviously enough, if an animal's right has a threshold while a person's does not, the animal's right is weaker—since the former, but not the latter, can be outweighed.)

So the idea of animals having weaker rights than people is a perfectly coherent one, and—more than that—one that deontologists have reason to accept. More particularly, they should accept the idea that one way that animal rights are weaker is by virtue of having lower thresholds.

Of course, the mere embrace of lower thresholds will not suffice, all by itself, to avoid the unacceptable claim that Tom cannot kill a fish. As we have already seen, the threshold for a *person's* right not to be harmed is normally thought to be extremely high—*so* high, in fact, that if the threshold for the fish's right not to be harmed is anywhere near that level it will still be forbidden for Tom to kill the fish. Thus, if the threshold is only "somewhat" lower for animals than it is for people that will still leave it at too high a level to make it permissible for Tom to proceed. Instead, the threshold must be *significantly* lower.

That's what the hierarchical deontologist will have to claim, then: not only are the thresholds of animal rights lower, they are significantly lower. But how is this to be accomplished? What would the requisite account of thresholds look like? We can turn to these questions next.

9.2 Thresholds

Intuitively, as we have noted, if there is going to be a threshold for the right not to be harmed, the level of that threshold will vary with the size of the harm. It takes considerably less good to justify pricking someone with a pin, for example, than it would take to justify punching them in the nose. In mathematical terms, we can say that the level of the threshold is an increasing function of the size of the harm.

According to those who accept hierarchical deontology, however, the level of the threshold is *also* a function of moral status, so that those with a higher moral status will have a higher threshold—other things being equal—than those with a lower status. It will take considerably more good to justify imposing a harm of a certain size on a person, say, than on a cow.

As a first approximation, then, if we put these two ideas together the result looks something like Figure 1.

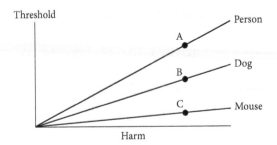

Figure 1. Thresholds with Variable Slope

In Figure 1, the X axis represents the amount of harm to be imposed. The Y axis represents the level of the threshold (the amount of good that must be at stake if imposing the relevant harm is to be permissible). I've drawn three lines, representing possible threshold functions for people, dogs, and mice.

(I am here adopting the stance of the moderate deontologist and assuming that there are thresholds even when it comes to harming a person. Anyone who prefers instead a position that accepts thresholds only for animals should relabel the top line, perhaps substituting some primate, or imagine it erased.)

Each of the lines slopes up and to the right, expressing the thought that as harm increases, so does the threshold. But the lines don't have the same slope. Rather, the line for the dog falls "under" the line for the person, just as the line for the mouse falls under the other two. This of course represents our idea that for any given harm, the threshold will vary with status, so that the lower one's moral status, the lower the value of the threshold.

Points A, B, and C illustrate this idea at work. Each of these points has the same X coordinate, so each point indicates the relevant threshold with regard to imposing a harm of the very same specific size. But the points differ in their Y coordinates, telling us that the threshold for imposing a harm of that size varies, depending on whether the harm is to be imposed on a person, on a dog, or on a mouse. In particular, of course, the threshold is higher if the harm is to be imposed on a dog rather than on a mouse, and higher still if it is to be imposed on a person.

As I say, that's the rough idea of what we are looking for. But the details remain obscure. We know we want the values of the Y coordinates of the various lines to be lower (yielding "lower" lines), as we move to beings with lower and lower status. But how *exactly* is this to be accomplished? As I say, the answer is a bit obscure because, or so it seems to me, we don't yet have a very precise notion of what individual threshold functions should look like.

Figure 1 displays one particular type of answer. The individual threshold functions are straight lines, going through the origin. The equation for a line like this is, of course, T = mh, where T stands for the level of the threshold, h stands for the size of the harm being imposed, and m is some suitable multiplier.

You will recall that this is the same equation we used previously (in 7.3), when we were examining the position of the unitarian moderate deontologist. Since unitarians believe that animals have the very same moral status as people do, it was appropriate to use the very same equation when calculating how much good would need to be done to justify, for example, Tom's killing a deer or a fish. We took into account, of course, the fact that if Tom killed a fish, say, this would be doing a great deal less harm than would be done if he were to kill a *person*. Accordingly, the relevant value of h was significantly smaller, and that resulted in a significantly smaller value for T as well. But the crucial point was that unitarians believed the underlying *equation* was precisely the same— whether dealing with animals or with people—so that, in particular, the relevant value of *m* had to be the same as well. In graphic terms this means that one single line would have sufficed to represent the threshold functions for both people and animals, since the threshold function would be exactly the same for everyone.

Currently, however, we are exploring what a *hierarchical* deontological view might look like, a view according to which the rights of animals have *lower* thresholds than the rights of people. And this raises the possibility that the value of m may not be fixed, but rather will vary, depending on the status of the individual being harmed. That of course is precisely the idea represented in Figure 1. Here we have *multiple* lines, one for each moral status. (Of course, only a very few such lines are actually drawn in the diagram.) All three of the lines drawn there are instances of the same *type* of equation—straight lines passing through the origin. But the values of m differ from one line to the next, so the *slopes* of the three lines differ from one to the other. Figure 1 thus represents a straightforward and natural proposal about how threshold functions might vary with status: as we consider individuals with lower and lower status, the value of m decreases as well. Since animals have a lower moral status than people, the appropriate values for m will be lower, resulting in lower thresholds for animals (for any particular size harm).

So that's at least one way that lower thresholds for animals could be generated. But there are other possibilities that should also be considered. Consider the fact that each of the lines shown in Figure 1 is a straight line. This means not only that as the amount of harm to be imposed increases, the level of the corresponding threshold increases as well, but also that it does so in a linear fashion: within any given line, each additional unit of harm to be imposed raises the threshold by the *same* amount. I suspect, however, that many people will think that this doesn't do justice to the way in which the threshold increases with the amount of harm to be done. Rather, as we increase the amount of harm the threshold should increase *disproportionately*, with each additional unit of harm raising the threshold by an ever increasing amount. If that's right, then the threshold functions shouldn't be drawn as straight lines, but rather as curves. That's what we have in Figure 2.

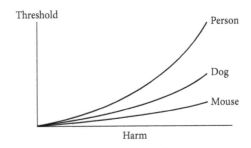

Figure 2. Thresholds with Variable Exponential Growth

There are various equations that would yield curves with roughly this feature, but the simplest, I suppose, is this: $T = h^n$. Here, instead of the threshold growing linearly with the size of h, it grows exponentially, where n stands for a suitable exponent. Thus, to calculate T we must raise h to the nth power. This will capture the thought that for larger and larger harms it will take disproportionately more good (exponentially more good) to justify imposing the harm.[4] (Note, incidentally, that if the threshold function is to display this kind of exponential growth as h increases, n must have a value greater than 1.)

Clearly, a view like this is also readily adaptable to the purposes of hierarchical deontology. While a unitarian sympathetic to this sort of threshold function would need to calculate T using the very same exponent regardless of

---

[4] Any view along these lines requires that there be a nonarbitrary way of individuating harms and harmful acts, so that there is an independent fact of the matter as to whether one has imposed a single harm of X units as opposed to, say, *two* harms of ½ X units each. Otherwise, the value of T will be an artifact of how we happen to describe the case. (For example, if n = 2, then if we describe the case as a single act of imposing X units of harm, then T will equal X^2. But if, instead, this is described as two distinct acts each imposing ½ X units of harm, then T will equal $(½ X)^2 = ¼ X^2$ for each of the two individual acts, for a total T of only ½ X^2—a combined threshold only half as high as under the first description!) However, since it is not my intent to defend any particular view with regard to thresholds here, I won't take the time to examine and evaluate the different proposals that might be made concerning this matter.

whether we were dealing with people or with animals, a hierarchical deontologist could simply insist instead that the value of n varies with the status of the individual being harmed. Indeed, I've already displayed this idea at work in Figure 2.[5] A dog will have a lower threshold than a person (even given the same value of h), thanks to the exponent taking on a lower value, and a mouse will have a lower threshold still, given an even lower value for the exponent.[6]

Here's a third way that thresholds might vary with status. Consider the fact that in both Figure 1 and Figure 2 the lines all pass through the origin. At first glance, of course, this particular feature may seem uncontroversial. We are talking about the threshold function for the right not to be harmed, after all, so if a given act doesn't actually involve imposing any *harm* on the "victim" (and that is, of course, what a zero value along the X axis represents), then that right hasn't actually been infringed in any way, and so questions of a threshold shouldn't even arise. There is no need to specify a minimum amount of good required in order to justify infringing the right, if there really isn't any infringement!

Nonetheless, the decision to have the lines pass through the origin does involve a substantive claim that many may want to reject. For it implies that as we reduce the size of the harm being imposed, the size of the threshold *approaches* zero. And that may not be what we believe. It might be, instead, that as the harm imposed gets ever smaller, although the level of the threshold shrinks in absolute terms, it doesn't quite approach the zero level. Perhaps there is a kind of "residual" badness or objectionableness about imposing even trivial harms on those with deontological standing, so that even for vanishingly small harms, the threshold remains at a nonnegligible level. This would

---

[5] For technical reasons, a more plausible equation than $T = h^n$ is the slightly more complex one, $T = (h + 1)^n - 1$. That's the sort of equation I've actually used in drawing Figure 2. (We are assuming that n has a value greater than 1. But this means that for very small values of h, where h is less than 1, $h^n < h$. So if $T = h^n$, this has the implausible implication that T has a value smaller than h. The more complex equation appropriately avoids this result. Furthermore, if $T = h^n$, then once we assign higher values for n to individuals with higher statuses, this will also have the unacceptable implication that when h is less than 1, the higher the given individual's status, the *lower* the value of T. The more complex equation avoids this implication as well.) Nonetheless, in my discussion of the threshold function I will continue to disregard this complication, so as to simplify the presentation of the basic ideas.

[6] At first glance it might seem that the idea of a nonlinear threshold function could also be put to work as part of a defense of the *unitarian* deontologist. For if the threshold grows exponentially as harm increases, then for smaller and smaller harms it will also *decrease* exponentially. Conceivably, then, if the value of the exponent were *great* enough, this could have the implication that killing an animal would have a *substantially* lower threshold than killing a person would have—since this generally involves the loss of significantly less welfare. Perhaps, then, a unitarian deontologist could justify Tom's killing a fish or even a deer after all, contrary to my earlier claims (which were, after all, based on the simpler equation $T = mh$). Unfortunately for the unitarian deontologist, however, any single value for n large enough to generate intuitively acceptable answers when it comes to killing a deer, say, will also generate intuitively *unacceptable* answers when it comes to imposing smaller harms on *humans*.

mean that there is always a certain baseline amount of extra good that must be achieved before any harms can be imposed at all, even trivial harms. In graphic terms, then, the threshold functions won't approach the origin as we move to the left, but rather they will approach suitable positive values along the Y axis. That's what we see in Figure 3.

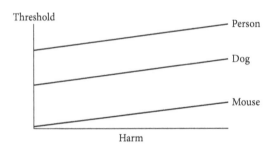

Figure 3. Thresholds with Variable Y Intercept

Here too I have drawn the diagram in such a way as to make it apparent how the hierarchical deontologist might take advantage of this new idea. Each line intercepts the Y axis at a positive coordinate, representing the idea that there is an ineliminable residual moral objection to harming someone with deontological standing, even if only in a trivial way. But unlike the unitarian, who would have to insist that the Y intercept is the very same for everyone, whether a person or an animal, the hierarchical deontologist can claim instead that the value of the Y intercept varies, depending on the particular moral status of the individual in question. For any creature at all with deontological standing, there is something ineliminably troubling about harming that creature, but the baseline size of the objection depends on its status. For those with only minimal deontological standing, the baseline objection might be very slight indeed.

In Figure 3, I've once again drawn the threshold functions as straight lines, indeed lines with the very same slope. They differ solely in terms of where they intercept the Y axis. Thus the corresponding equations all take this form: $T = mh + b$, where m is exactly the same for all three lines. It is only the new term, b, that shows any variation, since it is this term that tells us the baseline value for the threshold—the minimum amount of good that must be done before it becomes permissible to impose any sort of harm at all. Intuitively, that value will be smaller for a mouse than for a dog, and for a dog than for a person, and so the values of b are adjusted accordingly.

We have now seen three different ways that a hierarchical deontologist might lower the threshold while varying it with status. Figures 1, 2, and 3 represent the three different options, each option taken on its own. Thus, Figure 1 varies only the slope, m, Figure 2 varies only the exponent, n, and Figure 3 varies only the Y intercept, b.

But in principle, at least, a hierarchical deontologist might want to take advantage of all three of these methods. It could be that the relevant general formula for the threshold function looks something more like this: $T = mh^n + b$. Here we have three coefficients, three different values that affect the level of T (for a given value of h): m, n, and b. And in principle, at least, the hierarchical deontologist might claim that all three of these vary with status. That's the view shown in Figure 4.

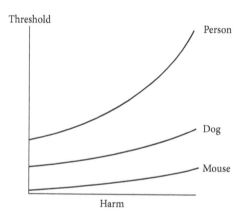

Figure 4. Thresholds with Variable Slope, Exponential Growth, and Y Intercept

The simplest view according to which all three of these coefficients vary with status would be one in which they vary in lockstep, each going down as the given individual's moral status goes down. That's certainly what we might expect, in any event, if status is indeed appropriately represented as a single number. But as have previously noted (in 5.1), it is possible that a more accurate representation of status would be in terms of a suitable n-tuple, where different capacities are relevant for grounding different dimensions of one's normative profile. On a more complicated view of this sort it could conceivably turn out that each coefficient is sensitive to a different (perhaps overlapping) set of capacities. Thus, for all we know at this point, it might turn out that squirrels, say, have a lower slope coefficient than bats have, but a higher Y intercept. If so, then the threshold function would turn out to be lower in one way (as compared to that of bats), while at the same time being higher in a different way. (In turn, this might mean that for a certain range of harms the threshold would be higher for squirrels than for bats, but for a different range of harms the reverse would hold.) Clearly, a comprehensive discussion of these matters would need to consider this possibility more carefully. But in keeping with our standard practice I am going to put this possibility aside and continue to assume that a single number suffices for representing status overall. Accordingly, we can assume as well that if all three coefficients really do vary with status, they do so at the same time and in the same direction.

Of course, even if we agree with all of this, there would still remain the unresolved task of determining *how*, exactly, each coefficient varies with status. This too is a complicated question, too complicated for us to examine here with any care. But I do want to offer a few quick remarks.

First of all, if the values of the coefficients go down with lower status, then one natural conjecture is that they approach their lowest possible values with statuses that are close to zero. In particular, then, we might conjecture that for animals with status close to zero the slope m will approach 1, the exponent n will approach 1, and the Y intercept b will approach 0.[7] This would mean that as status approaches zero, the equation for the threshold function, $T = mh^n + b$, will approach this: $T = h$. That is to say, for creatures with a status very close to zero, all it takes to justify imposing a given harm is that one produce as much good as the harm one is imposing. It would be permissible to impose a harm in any situation where there was some net benefit (in terms of the *overall* good) from doing so.

In effect, this is saying that as status approaches zero, the strength of the deontological aspect of the right approaches zero as well, so that, at the limit, it becomes permissible to treat the given animal in keeping with consequentialism rather than deontology. So this idea is very much in the spirit of the earlier suggestion (from 8.2), that deontological standing might be appropriate for all those animals with any kind of autonomy at all, while consequentialism might be the right approach for those animals (with standing) that are altogether lacking in autonomy. Initially, no doubt, a view like that may have sounded like it inevitably involved a kind of radical discontinuity between those animals with deontological standing and those animals lacking it. But if the thresholds for rights can be reduced in the way being described, then there need be no discontinuity at all: it is simply that as status approaches zero, the strength of the *deontological* aspect of the generated right approaches zero as well, effectively being eliminated. Conceivably, in fact, some might want to go even further, holding that deontological standing applies to all animals with any kind of moral status whatsoever, so that, strictly speaking, consequentialism never applies to anyone at all. It would just turn out that for all practical purposes we

---

[7] Of course, these aren't the lowest *logically possible* values for these coefficients; mathematically speaking, nothing rules out the possibility of slopes or exponents less than 1, or Y intercepts less than 0. However, these are the lowest values that are *morally* plausible.

won't be far off the mark if we say that consequentialism is the right approach for animals with very *little* moral status.

Second, if we suppose that the coefficients really do vary in this way with status, then this means that if we are given the amount of harm to be imposed on an individual, and the status of that individual, that should suffice to fix the threshold for imposing that harm. That is to say, the threshold can be viewed as a function of both harm and status—a *single* function, valid for everyone, people and animals alike. So there is a sense in which part of what the unitarian deontologist was saying was correct: the very same formula really can be used to establish the threshold for both animals and people. But of course the unitarian also believed that this formula was *indifferent* to the status of the individual in question, and it is precisely this further claim that is mistaken.

Third, returning to a point made at the very end of the last section, if the hierarchical deontologist hopes to accommodate the intuition that it is permissible for Tom to kill a deer or a fish to keep himself from starvation, then it won't suffice if the lower status of these animals reduces thresholds (compared to what they are for people) but only by a little, or only "somewhat." On the contrary, the reductions will need to be *significant*. Of course, recognizing the possibility of reducing one or more coefficients opens the door to finding a satisfactory solution to this problem; but it doesn't yet provide the details. Nonetheless, I won't attempt to evaluate more concrete proposals here. Until moral philosophers establish more about the actual shape of the threshold function (and the underlying equation), it is impossible to know exactly which coefficients we have to work with, and how modifying those coefficients would ultimately affect the resulting thresholds. So for the time being we must be content with the knowledge that in principle, at least, a suitable version of hierarchical deontology can accord deontological standing to animals while still insisting that the rights granted to those animals may be justifiably infringed when this is necessary to keep oneself alive.

Of course, it is also crucial to bear in mind the fact that in the example to which I keep returning—where Tom must kill and eat an animal to avoid starvation—harming some animal is indeed *necessary* if Tom is to stay alive. By hypothesis there is simply no other way for him to find adequate nutrition. It is only because of this stipulation that the hierarchical deontologist can point to the preservation of Tom's *life* (for the relevant period of time) as a good the achievement of which can be used to justify his infringing the animal's right not to be harmed. For we are only justified in infringing a right when doing this is *necessary* to achieve the relevant good—when there is no other way. (More carefully: when there is no other morally preferable way.) That's true in Tom's case, but—and this is the final point I want to make—it isn't true in our own. No one reading this book is required to eat animals in order to stay alive. So when doing the relevant calculations with regard to our own eating of animals, the relevant good to be compared to the threshold isn't the saving of our *lives*, but only the slight marginal increase in pleasure we may get from eating animal flesh rather than some vegetarian alternative. Obviously enough, this will make meat-eating tremendously more difficult to justify—typically, perhaps, impossible.

Let's turn now to a rather different possibility for what the threshold function might look like (Figure 5).

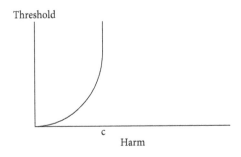

Figure 5. Threshold that "Goes to Infinity"

The key difference here from the earlier diagrams, besides only displaying a single line, is this: there is no longer a finite threshold for each level of harm. Rather, while there is a threshold for harms that are *small* enough, at a certain point—as we consider larger and larger harms—that ceases to be the case. For harms that are too large—equal to or larger than the point marked by c on the X axis—the threshold "goes to infinity," meaning that no amount of good can justify imposing a harm of *that* size.

A view like this may be attractive to certain deontologists with absolutist sympathies. The most extreme version of absolutism holds that it is never permissible to impose a harm on an innocent, no matter *how* much good is at stake, and no matter *how* small the harm. But some absolutists may be more modest in their rejection of thresholds, holding only that *certain* harms are such that no amount of good can justify imposing them, while other harms—ones that are small enough—can in fact be justified if enough is at stake. Thus, for example, it might be that *killing* an innocent person is never permissible, no matter how much good is at stake. The same thing may be true as well for various other large but nonfatal harms, such as loss of a limb, or paralysis.

But for harms that are *small* enough—harms smaller than the point marked by c—there *will* be a (finite) threshold. Punching someone in the nose, say, may well be permissible, if this is indeed the only way to attain a suitably large amount of good.

Should a view like this be called absolutist, or not? From the standpoint of the complete absolutist, perhaps not, since it would be absolutist only with regard to large enough harms, while more closely resembling moderate deontology for harms that are smaller. But once again, nothing substantive turns on what we call a position like this. The crucial point is that it seems to represent a coherent possibility for thinking about the nature of the threshold function, one that many will find attractive. In any event, I suspect that many people who were initially inclined to call themselves absolutists will find a view like this congenial. (Although I have known one or two people who were absolutist across the board, insisting that we cannot permissibly impose so much as a pinprick of pain on an innocent person even if this were the only way to save billions of other human lives, most self-styled "absolutists," I find, are perfectly prepared to endorse thresholds when it comes to imposing rela-tively *trivial* harms.)

If we let c represent the level of harm at which finite thresholds disappear, then the simplest equation yielding a curve like this is $T = h/(c-h)$, for values of h less than c (and undefined otherwise). And for current purposes the key point to recognize is that an approach like this can also be made use of by a hierarchical deontologist, since the value of c can be allowed to vary with status. More particularly, it might be suggested that c varies *inversely* with status, so that the higher one's status, the sooner one reaches the relevant cutoff point, beyond which harms cannot be justifiably outweighed. Equivalently, the lower one's status, the further to the east along the X axis one must go before reaching the appropriate cutoff point.

This would mean, for example, that a given size harm may well lack a finite threshold when the harm is to be imposed upon a person, say, and yet none-theless have a threshold if it is to be imposed, instead, on an animal with a sufficiently low moral status. Indeed, an animal with a low enough moral status may have a cutoff point set at a sufficiently high level of harm so that for all practical purposes any harm that we can actually impose may have a finite threshold. The threshold would still eventually go to infinity, as a theoret-ical matter, but only at a level of harm so great that we can never actually be in a position to impose it. (Suppose, for example, that there is an upper limit to the extent to which we can harm any given animal; then it would be an open question whether it is actually possible to impose a harm on any particular animal that is large enough to go beyond the level of harm marked by the relevant c.)

Furthermore, it seems that in principle at least we could combine this new feature—where the coefficient c varies inversely with status—with the other features we have already surveyed: variable slope, variable exponential growth, and variable Y intercept. Perhaps then the threshold function would be based on an equation something more like this: $T = m[h/(c-h)]^n + b$ (for values of h less than c, and undefined otherwise), where each of the coefficients, m, n, b, and c, vary appropriately with status. That might produce a set of threshold lines that look something like the ones shown in Figure 6.

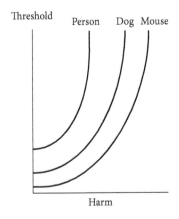

Figure 6. Thresholds with Variable Slope, Exponential Growth, Y Intercept, and "Going to Infinity"

There are, of course, even more exotic possibilities than the ones we have considered here,[8] more elaborate forms that the threshold function might take. But for our purposes these few examples should suffice to make good on the thought that hierarchical deontology can embrace a range of more particular views concerning the nature of the threshold function, all the while insisting that animals have rights with *lower* thresholds. Deontologists can accept the claim that animals really do have rights, but weaker ones.

---

[8] For example, I have been exploring a few ways in which thresholds might vary as a function of the status of the individual whose right is being infringed. But what about the possibility that the level of the threshold also depends upon the status of the *agent*? Could it be, that is, that if A is considering imposing a harm upon B, the level of the threshold (including the possibility of infinite thresholds) depends not only on B's status—the status of the right holder—but also on A's status—the status of the individual who would be imposing the harm? Could it be, for example, that as A's status increases, the relevant threshold gets lower, so that it is easier to permissibly impose a given harm upon a given individual? We are not used to contemplating such questions, and I won't tackle them here, but they will become pressing and acute if we ever encounter moral agents with a moral status significantly higher than our own.

9.3 Meeting the Threshold

Consider a case where the right not to be harmed has a finite threshold. This means that it would be permissible to impose a harm of the relevant size if this was the only way to bring about a good enough outcome, where the amount of good at stake has to be large enough to meet or surpass the threshold in question.

Now normally, in cases like this, when infringing the right brings about a great enough amount of good it does so by raising the welfare (or preventing the loss of welfare) of one or more beneficiaries. That is, one or more individuals have some of their own welfare on the line, and we reach the relevant threshold by virtue of adding together these various individual benefits. Thus, to return to one of our earliest examples of thresholds at work, if it is permissible to kill an innocent person when this is necessary to save 1,000 other people, then in a case where this many lives really are at stake, the reason the threshold has been met is because we take into account the value of saving the life of the first such beneficiary, as well as the value of saving the life of the second such beneficiary, and the third, and fourth, and so on, adding together in this way the value of each of the thousand (or more) lives saved. Or if, as we might suppose, punching someone in the nose is permissible if this is the only way to save 5 people from being tortured for an hour each, then in a case where this threshold has been met, what makes it the case that the threshold has been met is the fact that the total amount of welfare at stake is great enough (5 people each being saved from an hour of torture). So it is natural to describe a threshold in terms of the amount of welfare that must be at stake if the threshold is to be met.

Strictly speaking, however, thresholds should not be understood as being spelled out in terms of welfare, but rather in terms of the amount of *good* at stake. For in principle, at least, there can be other factors, besides the possibility of increasing well-being (or avoiding its loss) that may play a role in determining whether the threshold has been met. For example, anyone sympathetic to one of our distributive principles should be open to the possibility that among the good consequences that might justify infringing a right, not just the total amount of welfare but also the *distribution* of that welfare might be relevant. If the threshold has been met, this might be in part because infringing the right also helps reduce inequality, for example, or improves the extent to which people are getting what they deserve. What matters, in meeting the threshold, is not the amount of welfare per se, but rather the amount of good at stake.

I emphasize this point because it suggests a further way in which the hierarchical deontologist may want to take status into account. In calculating whether a given threshold has been met, we may not want to give equal weight to everyone's welfare, regardless of their status. It might be, instead, that a unit of welfare goes further toward meeting the relevant threshold when the welfare in question is that of an individual with a higher rather than a lower status. When an animal has a certain amount of welfare at stake, this may simply count less (toward meeting the threshold) than when a person does.

In raising this possibility, I do not mean to be simply recalling the fact that an animal's life will normally contain less welfare than a person's. That is certainly true, and because of it, we will indeed normally go further toward meeting any given threshold if a *person's* life is at stake, rather than, say, a cow's. But the possibility that I am entertaining here is a more radical one: that even if the cow has the very *same* amount of well-being at stake as a person does, the chance of benefiting the person by that amount simply counts *more* toward meeting the threshold than does the chance of benefiting the cow. More generally, the lower one's status, the less one's welfare counts—unit for unit—toward meeting the relevant threshold.

A cow's welfare counts less than a person's; a snake or bird's, even less.

A moment's further reflection, however, reveals that this is not, in fact, a new suggestion. It is simply an implication of the earlier proposal (made in 4.3) that an animal's welfare is less *valuable*—unit for unit—than a person's welfare, that the contribution made by increases in welfare to the goodness of an outcome are smaller, other things being equal, when the status of the relevant individual is lower. All we are doing now is taking that earlier idea and applying it in a new context. Thresholds are fixed in terms of the amount of good that must be done to justify infringing a given right. So if—as I have argued—the value of welfare depends on the status of the individual whose welfare it is, then it will take a larger amount of animal welfare to meet a given threshold than it would take if the welfare at stake belonged, instead, to people. We cannot simply attend to the total amount of welfare at stake, we must instead make use of a measure of well-being that is adjusted for status.

So in thinking about whether a given right can be permissibly infringed, it will be important to keep status in mind in at least two different ways. Not only will the status of the *right holder* be relevant for fixing the precise level of the threshold, the status of the various *beneficiaries* will be relevant as well, in determining whether the threshold in question has actually been met or not. The lower the status of any given beneficiary, the less their potential benefit counts toward meeting the threshold.

There is, in fact, a second way that status may come into play in determining whether or not a threshold has been met. When we add up the various (status adjusted) benefits, to see if they reach the relevant threshold, does every single benefit get added in (toward reaching the total), or must they be sufficiently large to be counted at all? Consider again the possibility of killing an innocent person, and suppose, for the sake of illustrating the worry, that the chance to save 10,000 human lives would be a great enough amount of good to justify doing this. Each such life saved constitutes a significant good, and the saving of 10,000 such lives would clearly add up to a very large good indeed. But what if, instead of saving all those lives, what we would achieve by killing the one were simply this: we could send a vast number of people to the movies, where they would enjoy themselves for two hours. Suppose there were no other way to gain *those* benefits. Do they count as well? Presumably, the boost in welfare from seeing a movie is genuine, though modest. But this seems to imply that if the number of people we could benefit in this modest way were *large* enough, we would still eventually have *enough* good at stake to meet the total set by the threshold.

Yet even those who think it permissible to kill one to save 10,000 may well resist the suggestion that it may be permissible to kill one to send ten billion people, say, *to the movies*. The thought, I suppose, is this: the individual benefits being added together here are simply *too small* to count. Or rather, somewhat more precisely, they are too small to count when the harm that we are contemplating imposing upon the one is something as significant as the loss of life.

I add this qualification because presumably the thought isn't that a small good (like the pleasure of seeing a movie) is too small in some absolute sense, too small to ever count toward meeting any kind of threshold at all. On the contrary, if the harm being imposed on the one were itself a relatively small one (such as being prevented from going to the park) presumably it would be morally legitimate to take into account modest benefits like moviegoing when determining whether the threshold had been met. So it isn't that there is some fixed, minimum size that a benefit must reach before it can *ever* be counted. Rather, the idea seems to be more like this: for a benefit to be counted toward meeting a threshold, it must be large enough—but the relevant *minimum* is itself a function of the size of the harm being imposed. When someone's life is at stake, movies are too trivial to count; but when something smaller is at stake, they may not be.

Not everyone shares this intuition, of course (and even those who do share it may not be prepared to endorse it), but many deontologists do. Accordingly, anyone sympathetic to this idea will need to introduce a suitable restriction on which goods can be counted toward meeting the threshold, a restriction that is itself appropriately relativized to the size of the harm involved.[9]

---

[9] See Brennan, "Thresholds for Rights," for further discussion of this idea.

The simplest approach along these lines would take the cutoff (below which a benefit or good cannot count) to be some fixed fraction of the given harm. Thus it might be, for example, that in order to count, a good must be at least 1/100th of the size of the harm being imposed, or 1/10th, or—more conservatively still—1/2 as large. The higher the fraction we settle upon, the fewer the goods that can be taken into account in deciding whether the threshold has been met.

For our present purposes we need not try to settle what the relevant fraction, f, comes to. (Plausibly, however, it will be less than 1: sending someone to the movies may be irrelevant when we are talking about taking someone's life, but arguably saving someone from paralysis or from losing all four limbs would not be.) The idea, then, is that a good can only count toward meeting the threshold when it is at least f times the size of the harm being imposed. This will give us the kind of variable cutoff point we were looking for, since even if we keep the fraction f fixed, as we vary the size of the harm the level of the cutoff will vary as well.

If we do adopt a restriction like this, then this points to yet another way in which the hierarchical deontologist may want to take status into account. Perhaps the precise value of f isn't fixed at all, but actually *varies*: not as a function of the size of the harm involved, but rather as a function of the *status* of the individual being harmed. In particular, it seems possible that the value of f is greater for those with a higher status, and lower for those with a lower status. As we consider individuals with higher and higher status, fewer and fewer benefits to others will make the cut.

This means that even if we keep the size of the harm constant, whether a given benefit is large enough to count will depend in part on the status of the individual being harmed. Certain benefits might be too small to count if it is a matter of imposing a given harm upon a *person*, for example, yet the very same benefits might be large enough to count if the harm is to be imposed instead on a rabbit, say, or a snake. The lower status of the animals would generate a lower value for f, so that benefits that might otherwise be too small to count (when the right holder is a person) would now be large enough.

I won't take the time to evaluate whether this kind of variable restriction on the minimum size of relevant benefits is one that accords sufficiently well with our intuitions. But I do want to point out that accepting a view like this might have an intriguing implication. For reasons we have previously discussed (see 4.2), creatures with a very low status may have a relatively restricted range with regard to the quality of their lives: even under the best of circumstances they may not be able to attain all that much welfare; even under the worst, they may not be able to lose that much. Conceivably, then, for beings with a relatively *high* status (and so, with a correspondingly high value for f), it could turn out that many harms are such that *no* benefit to creatures of sufficiently low status could be great enough to pass the status-relativized cutoff point. This might mean, for example, that when it comes to infringing the rights of those with a rather high status, no benefits to the very low status creatures would count at all—except perhaps for cases that involve imposing utterly trivial harms. If something like this were true, then for all practical purposes benefits to the low status creatures could be safely disregarded when deciding whether imposing a (nontrivial) harm on a high status being was justified: the potential benefits to the low status creatures would simply be too small to count. Even if shrimp are sentient, for example, it might be the case that their welfare is nonetheless irrelevant when it comes to imposing (nontrivial) harms on people.

As it happens, it isn't clear to me whether or not deontologists should *accept* this sort of status-relativized restriction on what is to count toward meeting a threshold (as opposed to having only a single, fixed value for f). Ultimately, perhaps, this may not be an idea that should be embraced by the hierarchical deontologist at all. I mention it, however, because the view is not without some intuitive appeal, and because if nothing else it offers a further illustration of how new and unfamiliar questions quickly present themselves, once we begin to incorporate status into our moral theory.

(There are, of course, even more extreme views of this same basic sort. Consider, for example, a position according to which benefits to individuals with a status that is too low compared to the status of the right holder simply don't count *at all*. That is, even if the benefits are technically large enough to pass the status-relativized cutoff, they are *still* irrelevant; if the status of the beneficiary is *too low* compared to that of the right holder—if the difference in status is simply too great—then the beneficiary's interests are simply not to be counted, no matter how much they may have at stake. As it happens, I find that this particular view has no appeal for me at all. But less extreme versions of the idea may still be legitimate.)

Let me mention one further condition on meeting the threshold that deontologists sometimes impose.[10] Suppose, as before, that we are justified in killing one person if this is the only way to save 10,000 others. Suppose as well that we agree that when the case at hand involves taking the life of a person, the chance of saving someone from losing a *limb* is in fact large enough to *count* (toward meeting the threshold). Of course, the possibility of saving merely one person

---

[10] See Brennan, "Thresholds for Rights," for this further condition as well.

from losing a limb won't provide nearly enough good to meet the relevant total in a case like this, but here I am just asking us to assume (plausibly) that even if certain benefits are too small to count toward meeting the threshold, avoiding the loss of a limb is not one of these: it is a large enough benefit to count. If so, then presumably this means that there is *some* number of limbs, whatever it might be, such that if killing someone were the only way to avoid *that* many people from each losing a limb then this would add up to a great enough total to meet the threshold. (That is to say, saving this many limbs does as much good as saving 10,000 lives.) Nonetheless, for all that, many of those who accept the threshold will have the intuition that it is still not permissible to kill in this case.

Why not? Because although the *total* amount of good at stake is large enough, *no one* among all that huge number of beneficiaries actually stands to gain as much as the victim will lose! True, losing a limb is no trivial matter, even in comparison to losing one's life, but still, for all that, losing one's life is a far worse harm than losing a limb. So if we do impose the loss of life, we are asking the victim to lose more than anyone else stands to lose. And at least some deontologists think this unacceptable. Perhaps, then, it isn't enough to demand that a large enough total amount of good be achieved when we impose a harm; perhaps it must also be the case that at least one of the beneficiaries would otherwise undergo a harm comparable to the one we are seeking to impose.

Note, after all, that if we were to kill one so as to save 10,000 *lives*, then each and every one of the beneficiaries has as much at stake as the potential victim does. Perhaps that is too much to demand, but—or so the thought goes—at the very least *someone* among the beneficiaries should have as much at stake as the right holder. Generalizing, we might insist that *whenever* we are considering imposing a harm of a given size, there must be at least one beneficiary who has the same amount at stake as our victim stands to lose.

Some might prefer to hold out for an even more demanding condition: that there be at least one beneficiary with *more* at stake than the right holder, perhaps a suitably large amount more. Alternatively, some may prefer a somewhat less demanding version of the condition: that there be at least one beneficiary with *almost* as much at stake—if not quite as much, at least some suitably large percentage of what the right holder has at stake. Without trying to settle on the precise requirement, then, what all of these proposals have in common is the idea that there is a second relevant fraction or proportion, p, such that imposing a harm is permissible only if at least one of the beneficiaries has at stake the relevant fraction of the harm being imposed. On more demanding versions of the view, p will be set at a number higher than 1, while on less demanding versions it will be somewhat lower than 1. And in our original statement of the idea, p is set at exactly 1.[11]

Again, not everyone wants to impose this further requirement, but I mention it because it suggests yet another way that the hierarchical deontologist might want to take status into account. Instead of thinking that there is a single proportion, p, relevant for all cases, perhaps this is another area where the relevant value varies as a function of status. In particular, perhaps the requisite proportion is higher when the right holder has a higher status. A view like this might express the thought that for creatures with low status it isn't particularly important that there be a beneficiary that comes especially close to having the same amount at stake as what we are considering imposing on the right holder. But as status increases this does become more important, and so the relevant proportion—*how* close at least one beneficiary must be—increases accordingly. When harm is to be imposed on an individual with relatively *high* status, it may simply seem inappropriate or unfair if none of the beneficiaries has at least as much at stake (or perhaps even more), but as we imagine creatures with lower and lower status, the demands of this requirement may be correspondingly reduced.

Here too, I won't try to evaluate whether this status-relativized version of the requirement should be embraced or not; that would require a more careful analysis than I can undertake here. But it does seem to me an idea that warrants further consideration.

Suppose we were to accept either this idea or the previous proposal (of a status-relativized approach to deciding which benefits are large enough to count) or both. Then these would constitute further ways in which the rights of animals are weaker than the rights of persons. Our main thought, of course,

---

[11] Some deontologists accept this requirement in a particularly extreme form. Instead of merely insisting that there be at least one beneficiary who has as *much* at stake as the right holder (or even somewhat more than that), they insist instead that there must be a beneficiary who can meet the *entire* threshold all by herself. Unlike typical moderates, then, who allow combining or aggregating benefits to different individuals in meeting the threshold, these *anti-aggregationists* insist that benefits may not be combined across individuals to reach the relevant total; if a given threshold is to be met at all, there must be at least one beneficiary whose benefit is large enough to meet the entire threshold single-handedly. Of course, if one accepts this version of the requirement then there will be many cases where for all practical purposes it is simply impossible to meet the relevant threshold—not because the threshold has "gone to infinity," but because in fact no *one* individual could possibly have enough at stake to meet the relevant total all by herself. Roughly speaking, then, only for relatively modest harms will the threshold be low enough that it can ever be met. Still, the lower the status of the individual being harmed the lower the threshold, so the greater the chance of meeting the threshold after all. (Note, incidentally, that if one does adopt this position, it may render moot the earlier, more modest requirement that all benefits must be "large enough" if they are to count toward meeting the threshold.)

has been that the comparative weakness of animal rights is revealed in the fact that those rights have lower *thresholds*. But if there are also relevant restrictions on *how* a given threshold can be met (where only large enough benefits count, or where at least one beneficiary must come suitably close to having as much at stake as the right holder), and if those restrictions are themselves weaker when the rights in question are the rights of creatures with lower status, then this provides a second (or perhaps a second and a third) way in which animals have weaker rights as well: by virtue of their lower status, animals have rights with less demanding restrictions on how those (already lower) thresholds can be met.

9.4 Other Principles

Hierarchical deontology extends deontological standing to animals, but does this in such a way as to take into account the differences in status that exist between people and animals (and between different types of animals). We have been focusing on the implications of this approach for our understanding of the right not to be harmed, but of course deontologists typically embrace a number of different moral principles, not just this one. Accordingly, a systematic exploration of hierarchical deontology would need to consider the effects of introducing consideration of status into these other principles as well.

Presumably, some of the results would be similar to those we have already considered. Moderate deontologists, at any rate, are not likely to think that it is only the right not to be harmed which can be permissibly infringed when there is enough good at stake. Many other rights (perhaps most, or even all) will have thresholds as well. So here too we might anticipate that animals will have the corresponding rights as well, but that the thresholds for these rights will vary with status, so that any given right can be more easily outweighed if the right holder is an animal rather than a person. Similarly, we might anticipate that if there are restrictions on how those thresholds can be met when the right holder is a person, then similar restrictions will be in place when the right in question is had by an animal instead—though the restrictions will be appropriately weaker in recognition of the animal's lower status.

Of course, there may be exceptions to these broad generalizations. Perhaps certain rights require more than merely possessing deontological standing if one is to actually have the particular right in question. That is, some rights may require further particular features or capacities (beyond being autonomous to some degree). If so, it might also turn out that some or all animals just don't have the relevant further features. In such cases, obviously, the relevant animals will simply *lack* the given right, rather than having it in a weaker form.

For example, if—as might well be the case—a right not to be lied to requires the ability to *understand* the given false assertion, then animals that cannot understand our language would presumably have no right not to be lied to by us. (Indeed, it isn't clear whether it even makes sense to say that one has *lied* to an uncomprehending animal.)

But even with regard to this very example, it is important not to overgeneralize in the opposite direction. On the one hand, it seems likely that some animals do understand at least some of our assertions, and in those cases, at least, there is no obvious reason why we should not extend to such animals a right not to be lied to. And on the other hand, whether or not it is possible to tell a lie to any given animal, it is clear that it is frequently possible to *deceive* an animal. Accordingly, to the extent that deontologists think it impermissible to deceive a person, hierarchical deontologists should similarly think it wrong to deceive animals. It is just that the right not to be deceived will be weaker for animals than it is for people, and weaker for some animals than it is for others.

Or perhaps in some cases we will find that we have reason to believe that differences in status make no difference to the level of the threshold (or to the restrictions on how the threshold can be met), so that animals have the same particular rights as people have, in just as strong a form. A hierarchical deontologist certainly needn't claim that in every single case an animal's rights are weaker than those of a person, only that this is typically the case. Still, absent an argument to the contrary, we will normally expect an animal's rights to be weaker, given that they generally have less developed or less sophisticated forms of the various capacities that underwrite rights.

In short, differences in status are likely to have a significance for still other rights, beyond those we have explicitly considered here. Indeed, going beyond this point, it is likely that differences in status will play a role in all sorts of other moral principles as well, regardless of whether those principles are best understood in terms of rights or not.

Consider, for example, the duty—accepted by most deontologists—to aid others. (Of course, some deontologists are indeed prepared to say that people have a *right* to be aided; but others deny the existence of any such right, and prefer to talk instead of a *duty* of beneficence, or a duty to aid. For our purposes we needn't take a stand on this issue.) There are, of course, debates about the strength of this duty—how much exactly one must be prepared to sacrifice to improve the well-being of others—but most deontologists do believe that there is at least some sort of duty along these lines.

Now, once we acknowledge that animals have moral standing, it seems that we should also recognize that the duty to aid requires aiding animals and not merely aiding people. That is, just as we must promote the welfare of other people (perhaps subject to the proviso that the cost to ourselves of providing such aid must not be unreasonably great), so too we must promote the welfare of animals (subject to the same proviso). Conceivably, of course, a *restricted* deontologist might try to resist this conclusion, insisting perhaps that the duty to aid only requires aiding those individuals with deontological standing, and insisting as well that animals lack standing of this deontological sort. But we have already seen reason to reject restricted deontology.

So we have reason to promote the welfare of animals, to come to their aid. Indeed, we have a *duty* to do so, just as we have a duty to come to the aid of other people. But for all that, most of us will find it plausible to hold that this duty is weaker when it comes to aiding animals than when it comes to aiding people.

Of course, to a certain extent this judgment may simply reflect the now familiar thought that people will frequently have more welfare at stake than animals do. To return to a point we first explored quite some time ago (in 2.2), if we have to choose between saving the life of a person and saving the life of, say, a kangaroo, then in all but the most extraordinary circumstances the person will have much more welfare at risk than the kangaroo. So if we save the person rather than the kangaroo we are simply doing more good, all things considered. All the more so if it is a matter of saving the life of a person rather than, say, a frog, or an iguana. Since a person will generally have more welfare on the line than an animal does (when other things are equal), it is hardly surprising that the duty to aid animals is generally weaker than, and loses out to, the duty to aid people.

But this observation, important as it is, may not capture the full extent of the thought that the duty to aid is weaker when it is a matter of aiding animals rather than people. I suspect that even when the *same* amount of welfare is at stake, most will think it morally more pressing to aid a person rather than a kangaroo, let alone an animal with an even lower status. It isn't merely that we can usually do more to aid a person than an animal, it is also true that unit for unit (of welfare) it is more important to aid the person. Indeed, the lower the status of the animal being aided, the weaker the moral reason to provide the aid.

This is, I think, an important point, but it may not be a new one. I have already argued (in 4.3) for the claim that the moral significance of a unit of well-being varies with the moral status of the individual whose welfare it is: the value of an outcome is increased by a greater amount—more good is done— when the increase in well-being goes to someone with a higher rather than a lower moral status. Suppose, then, that the duty to aid others is actually more accurately thought of as a duty to do *good* (or is, perhaps, derived from it). Then if it really is true that the value of welfare varies with status, the higher the status of the individual being aided the greater the amount of good being done (other things being equal). So the duty to aid will be stronger when it is a matter of aiding someone with a higher rather than a lower status, precisely because such aid does more good. Thus, if the duty to aid is weaker when it comes to aiding animals rather than people, this may simply be an implication of the earlier claim that we need to adjust welfare for status if we are to properly measure its moral significance.

Sometimes, however, the duty to aid takes a particularly demanding form. Deontologists sometimes talk about a duty to *rescue*, where the idea is that in situations where we are in the presence of individuals with an especially immediate and pressing need—where disaster looms unless we take immediate action—we have a particularly strong duty to come to the aid of those in need. In such cases, it is said, we have a duty to rescue, and the thought is that such a duty is considerably stronger (it asks more of us, and is less easily outweighed) than the more generic, everyday duty to aid (or to promote the good). Thus, for example, if a child were drowning in front of us we would normally think that a tremendous effort must be undertaken to rescue her—potentially involving far greater cost and inconvenience to ourselves than we would normally feel obligated to undertake so as contribute to, say, a mere charity. Similarly, when miners are trapped after a mining accident, people normally feel an especially strong duty to do all that can be done in the attempt to rescue them.

Interestingly, it is far less clear whether such a duty to rescue can also be subsumed under a more general requirement to promote the good. For sometimes it seems that the duty to rescue actually stands in the way of, and can morally outweigh, the possibility of bringing about an even better outcome overall. In the mining case, for example, many would think that we are required to expend resources here and now so as to save the endangered miners, even if those funds would otherwise be spent on making improvements to mine safety which might, in the long run, save an even larger number of lives. Thus, as with many other elements of deontological normative theories, the duty to rescue may sometimes demand that we act in a way that fails to bring about the best *outcome* overall. The thought is that it is more important to rescue a smaller number of known individuals, here and now, than it is to merely aid a somewhat larger number of currently unidentified ("merely statistical") people in the long run.

If there is indeed a deontological duty to rescue of this kind, then given the deontological standing of animals they too will be covered by such a duty. That is, we will have a duty to rescue not only people but animals as well. But for all that, a hierarchical deontologist can plausibly suggest that the duty to rescue is *weaker* when it is a matter of rescuing animals. Even if the very same amount of welfare is at risk, there may simply be a stronger duty to rescue a person—a duty that asks more of us, and is less easily outweighed—than there is to rescue, say, a deer. The idea, of course, would be that this duty, too, varies in strength with status, so that the lower the status of the individual in need, the weaker the duty to rescue them.

A view like this is certainly very much in the spirit of the other expressions of hierarchy that we have considered so far, but note that it is, for all that, logically distinct from the suggestion that the value of welfare varies with status. For as I have just observed, the duty to rescue does not readily lend itself to being reduced to a more general duty to promote the good (it can, indeed, oppose and outweigh it), so if—as I suspect—the strength of the duty to rescue also varies with status, this cannot simply be another relatively straightforward implication of the proposal that status affects the value of welfare. Rather, this will be a further, distinct, expression of the significance of status: not only does status affect the value of one's well-being (its contribution to the goodness of outcomes), it also affects the strength of one's claim to be rescued from disaster.

Next, consider the fact that neither the duty to aid, nor the more general duty to promote the good, nor the more particular duty to rescue, is unlimited. That, at least, is the view of most deontologists. If the cost to the individual agent of helping others (or otherwise promoting the good) is too great—it is said—then the agent is not, in fact, morally required to make the sacrifice in question. Thus, for example, while giving away most of one's savings to a suitable charity might well save a large number of lives—and thus do more good, overall, than spending the money on oneself or one's family—most of us do not think such sacrifices are obligatory.

This is a second main way in which deontologists differ from consequentialists, since consequentialists hold that if the overall results really would be better if one were to make a given sacrifice then one is indeed morally required to do so. In contrast, most deontologists believe that although you are indeed sometimes required to help others, you are not required to do this when the sacrifice involved becomes too large. At that point, rather, aiding others becomes morally *optional*: you are morally *permitted* to make the sacrifice, and this may in fact be morally commendable or praiseworthy, but you are not actually required to do this; you also have the option of saving your money instead, or spending it in some other, less optimal way. Indeed, even if we are dealing with a case of rescue, where the underlying duty is especially stringent, that duty is typically thought to give out if the cost to the agent of rescuing others becomes too high.

In short, most deontologists believe in the existence of moral *options*, which permit you to refrain from aiding others or from promoting the overall good, if the cost to you of helping would be too great. Of course, it isn't as though these options are themselves unlimited, so that one need never do anything for others at all. Partly, then, the question turns on how much it will *cost* you to benefit others. Furthermore, intuitively at least, the amount that you are required to do for others also depends at least in part on how much *good* you can do. Options permit you to favor your various interests—whether your own welfare, or that of your family or friends, or other personal causes—giving them more weight than they might merit from an impartial point of view, but there is a limit to how much greater weight we can give them. Sacrifices that might be optional if one could do only somewhat greater good for others might become obligatory nonetheless, if *enough* good is at stake.

Spelling out all these ideas precisely—what exactly does it take for the cost to be too great? how much extra weight can one give to one's own interests?—is a matter of some controversy, but an initial approximation of the underlying view might look like this: in deciding whether a given sacrifice is too large to be obligatory relative to the good that it could bring about, one is permitted to count that cost disproportionately when comparing it to the good that one could do. In doing your moral calculus, perhaps you are permitted to give those costs up to z times their objective (impartial) weight, for some suitable value of z. Thus, even if a given sacrifice would do more good for others than it would cost you, you are nonetheless permitted to refrain from making that sacrifice if the cost to you is greater than the gain for others when that cost is *multiplied by z*. (That is, if C represents the cost to you, and G the gain to others, then even when C is less than G, if C *times z* is greater than G, you are permitted to refrain from making the sacrifice.)

Options give you permission to act in ways that are less than morally optimal. But the extent of that permission depends on the size of the option, and so, in the approach we have just sketched, it will depend on the value we assign to z. If z has a value only slightly larger than 1, then agents are permitted to give their individual interests only slightly more than their objective weight, so the resulting options—the permissions to act in a less than morally ideal manner—will be slight. In contrast, if z has a significantly larger value, then options will be proportionately larger, and the agent will have considerably more space in which to pursue their own personal interests, rather than, say, aiding others.

(If one thinks about the size of options from the point of view of commonsense morality, then z seems to have a quite large value indeed.)

If we do think of options in these terms then it is easy to see yet another place where consideration of status might be introduced by the hierarchical deontologist. Instead of thinking of z as having a fixed value for all agents, perhaps the value of z is something that varies with status. In particular, perhaps z takes on a greater value for moral agents with *higher* moral status. This would have the effect of generating *larger* options for moral agents with a higher status, while moral agents with lower status would have more limited options.

Of course, most or all animals are not moral agents at all, in the sense that we do not take them to be subject to moral duties or obligations in the first place. (They lack sufficient capacity for normative reflection and self-governance to be subject to moral requirements.) A lion, for example, is under no moral obligation to aid others; it has no moral duty to rescue drowning gazelles. Accordingly, questions about the size of options are simply out of place when it comes to animals. If animals have no moral obligations at all, then there is no place for options to limit the *extent* of those obligations.

Because of this, it might seem that the idea just entertained—that the size of options might vary with status—has no purchase. To be sure, animals have a lower status than people, but since they are under no moral obligations they have no options either, so we are hardly going to want to say that their options are *smaller*, on account of that lower status.[12]

But even if it is true that no individual who fails to be a person is a moral agent, so that it makes little sense to talk about options having a smaller size for individuals with a *lower* status than that had by people, we should not overlook the possibility that there are, or could be, individuals with a *higher* status than ours. Recall the possibility of superior beings—individuals who are people but with a significantly more advanced or sophisticated set of capacities than our own. Presumably such beings would themselves be moral agents, and as such subject to positive moral obligations, such as the duty to aid or to rescue. For beings of this sort the question would indeed arise as to whether these duties were unlimited, or whether, instead, there were options putting limits on the extent of those duties. And if superior beings would also have options, then we might well wonder how the size of those options would compare to the ones that we have. The idea being entertained, of course, is that precisely by virtue of their higher status, z might take on a larger value for them than it does for us,

---

[12] What about the possibility of moral agents who are *minimal people* (in the sense described in 6.4)? Wouldn't more limited options at least make sense in this case? Perhaps, though it is unclear whether truly minimal persons could really be moral agents in the first place.

generating larger options, with greater permission to pursue their own interests, rather than coming to the aid of others.

Is such a view plausible? That will depend, of course, on the underlying basis or rationale of morality's including options in the first place. This is a controversial matter, too complicated to enter into properly here. But let me quickly mention two rather different possibilities. Conceivably, on the one hand, options are a kind of compromise that morality makes with human nature, a begrudging accommodation to the fact that normal adult human beings find it difficult or impossible to systematically adopt and act from a completely impartial point of view. But it might well turn out that superior beings would actually find it easier, rather than more difficult, to be motivated by a morally impartial perspective. If so, then if this somewhat negative account of options is correct (if options represent a compromise with human nature), superior beings might actually have smaller options, or none at all, rather than larger ones.

On the other hand, it could be that options are a reflection of the value and significance of our autonomy—our capacity to have and to act upon our own individualized preferences about how we want our lives to go. That is, perhaps options should be viewed more positively, as morality's recognition of the importance of giving each of us space in which to shape our own lives, forging our own special projects and relationships, rather than forever subjecting us to the demands of the greater good. If this more positive account of options is correct, then it might well turn out that superior beings would indeed have even *larger* options than our own. This could easily be the case if superior beings were even more autonomous than we are, and as such even more deserving of morally protected space in which to shape their own individual lives.

I won't pursue any of these questions further here. My goal is not to establish whether options really do vary with the status of the agent, nor, for that matter, whether the strength of the duty to aid or of the duty to rescue really does vary—as I have suggested each might—with the status of the individual in need of aid. I only wanted to illustrate the point that if one embraces hierarchical deontology, the potential significance of status is not at all limited to its role in a proper understanding of the right not to be harmed. On the contrary, status is likely to have systematic relevance, touching many or perhaps even most of the principles recognized within our overall normative theory. I suspect that if we ever become serious about acknowledging the moral standing of animals, we will find that we need to rethink a great many of our moral principles, modifying them or reinterpreting them—sometimes substantially—so as to properly take into account the pervasive moral significance of differences in status.

Let me close, however, on a slightly different point. As the mention of superior beings a moment ago should remind us, the possibility of such beings is one that even deontologists should acknowledge. There is, at any rate, certainly nothing about the turn from consequentialism to deontology (for those who chose to make it) that should render the possibility of superior beings any less likely. On the contrary, as I have already suggested, a hierarchical deontologist should be open to the possibility of beings with greater psychological capacities than our own, including an even higher degree of autonomy. As such, the natural position for the hierarchical deontologist to adopt is that such beings would have even stronger rights than our own (with higher thresholds, and more stringent restrictions on how those thresholds can be met). Similarly, it might well turn out that superior beings would have a stronger claim to be aided (other things being equal), or a stronger claim to be rescued.

Is this a troubling prospect? Some, no doubt, will find it so, but I do not. As I have already explained (in 6.2), to grant to some a higher moral status than our own is not to say that they are permitted to abuse us or to disregard our rights. This may be a common enough philosophical nightmare, but it is difficult to see what would justify it. Our rights would not disappear, our interests would still matter, even if there were other beings whose rights and interests counted even more significantly than our own. Admittedly, for reasons that we have just discussed, it could turn out that superior beings would have larger options than we have, and so would not be required to do quite as much as we are by way of helping others. But as I have also noted, it could equally well turn out that the opposite is the case instead: perhaps by virtue of their greater cognitive and emotional capacities—including greater capacities for normative reflection and self-governance—they might actually turn out to have *smaller* options than we have. Perhaps superior beings would turn out to have even *greater* obligations than we humans do, to come to the aid of those in need.

I might also note, in passing, that hierarchical deontologists also face the problem of what to say about marginal cases (see 6.3). If rights vary with status, for example, then it is difficult to see how the hierarchical deontologist can avoid concluding that humans who are sufficiently cognitively impaired will have weaker rights than the rest of us. Admittedly, the force of this conclusion can be moderated somewhat if we bear in mind the fact that modal personhood gives one a higher status than one would otherwise have (based on one's actual psychological capacities alone). But unless we are prepared to hold—implausibly, to my mind—that modal personhood gives one the very same status as that had by actual persons (or something rather close to it), it will be difficult to avoid the view that the rights of at least the most severely impaired are simply not as strong as the rights of normal adult humans.

To be sure, a *restricted* deontologist can avoid saying this, provided, of course, that they are prepared to grant deontological standing even to the severely impaired. Imagine that the restricted deontologist insists that all those with deontological standing of any sort have rights of the very same strength. Then if it really is true that the severely impaired do have deontological standing it will follow that the rights of the impaired are every bit as strong as our own. But the problem with saying all of this, obviously enough, is that there is no plausible ground for including the severely impaired among those with deontological standing while excluding animals. (And we have already considered at length the unacceptable implications of extending deontological standing to animals as well, if this is done within a *unitarian*, rather than a hierarchical, framework.) Here too, an appeal to the significance of modal personhood may soften the force of this point a bit; but not enough, I think, to answer the worry. Given how utterly impoverished and stunted one's capacities can be, there will be a significant limit to how much mere modal personhood can raise one's status, if one is *sufficiently* impaired. So if impaired humans all have rights of the very same strength as those had by normal, adult humans, then the same must be true of many or most animals as well—and *that* position, as we have seen, is an untenable one. As far as I can see, the only acceptable deontological position is a hierarchical one; and on any plausible version of that view the severely impaired will have weaker rights than the rest of us have.

Finally, it should be noted that even if we embrace hierarchical deontology, we still do not have an answer to the problem of *normal* variation that will satisfy everyone (see 6.4). I suspect that what is most deeply troubling about hierarchical views, at least for many, is the worry that the ordinary differences in capacities that we find as we move from normal adult to normal adult might generate small but real differences in our statuses. If this really is so, and if the hierarchical deontologist is right to claim that the strengths of rights vary with status, then nothing yet helps us avoid the unsettling conclusion that some normal adult humans will have stronger rights than others. That thought remains troubling—or, at least, many will find it so—but nothing in the basic idea of hierarchical deontology brings us any closer to finding a further response.

10

Defense

10.1 The Right to Self-Defense

Normally it is morally unjustified for one person to harm or kill another. That's because each of us has a right not to be harmed. We have of course already considered at length one important exception to this generalization, the exception that arises in cases where the *threshold* of the right has been met, so that the second person's right not to be harmed has been outweighed or overridden. But there is a second major exception, one that we've not yet examined, and it is this exception that will be our primary focus in the current chapter. This further exception arises in cases where one person is harming another as a means of *defending* herself against the second person's unprovoked attack.

What most of us believe, of course, is that each of us has a *right* to defend ourselves, even if this involves harming the attacker, perhaps even killing him. Thus, if Arnold will kill Brenda unless Brenda harms or kills Arnold first, we believe it is permissible for Brenda to do precisely that—to harm or even kill Arnold—even though normally it is forbidden to harm or kill another. As we typically put it, Brenda is permitted to kill Arnold by virtue of her right to self-defense.

Admittedly, not everyone accepts this common belief. Pacifists hold that there is no such right. It is wrong to harm another, they say, and it doesn't become permissible simply because the other person is trying to harm *you*. But this is a minority view, one that very few are attracted to. In what follows I am simply going to assume that this minority view is mistaken, though I won't attempt to defend that claim here. As with the other basic moral principles that we have discussed (such as the various distributive principles, or, indeed, the right not to be harmed) my goal here isn't to justify this principle, but only to consider its implications for our treatment of animals.

For similar reasons, then, I also won't survey the different accounts of the ultimate basis of the right to self-defense, nor will I take a stand on whether—when the aggressor attacks and it becomes permissible to harm in self-defense—it is better to say that the aggressor has lost or forfeited or waived his right not to be harmed, whether it is nullified, or overridden, or whether (as some might prefer to say) the right not to be harmed never actually ruled out such *defensive* harm in the first place. For our purposes it will suffice to say simply that there *is* a right to self-defense, and so it is permissible for you to harm or even kill another as part of defending yourself from their attack.

(As with the original right not to be harmed, consequentialists and deontologists differ as to whether this further right has intrinsic moral significance, or whether talk of such a right is instead merely a useful guide to decision making. But for simplicity of exposition, I will continue to cast the discussion straightforwardly, in the language of the deontologist.)

Of course, things are never *quite* this simple: it isn't as though anything goes when it comes to defending oneself. So let me next note a few relevant qualifications. First of all, and most relevant for the discussion that follows, there is a limit to how much harm one is permitted to impose on one's attacker, even when it is undeniably the case that one is indeed permitted to impose some harm. This point is easy to overlook if we focus exclusively on cases where the attacker is trying to *kill* you, since it is clear that you are indeed permitted to kill your attacker in cases like that. But imagine that the aggressor is not going to kill you, but only harm you in some significantly lesser way. Suppose, for example, that the aggressor is going to slap you, painfully, on your face. This too, we can imagine, is an unprovoked attack, and you are permitted to use force to defend yourself, harming your attacker, if there is no other way to stop him. But you are not permitted to *kill* him to stop him from slapping you! If you were to do that your response would be disproportionate. Rather, there is an upper limit to how much harm you are permitted to impose on your attacker, where this limit is a function of the amount of harm that he is trying to impose on you.

That's not to say that you are limited to imposing *no more* harm on the attacker than he would impose on you. It isn't as though you may only impose the *same* amount of harm or less. Intuitively, after all, even if the aggressor would only cut off my *arm*, rather than killing me, I am still permitted to kill him so as to prevent this from happening. So when it is a matter of defending myself against an unprovoked attack I can impose *more* harm—perhaps even considerably more harm—on the aggressor than the amount he is trying to impose on me. But still, as the example of killing to prevent a slap makes clear, there is a limit of *some* sort here: the amount of harm I am permitted to impose in defending myself depends on the amount of harm my attacker is trying to impose.

If we let H represent the amount of harm I am permitted to impose on the aggressor, while h represents the amount of harm that the aggressor is trying to impose on me, then what we are saying is that H > h but that nonetheless H is limited, depending on the size of h. As a first approximation, perhaps H is some simple multiple of h. Maybe I am permitted to impose twice as much harm, or ten times as much harm, or some such. If we let d stand for the relevant multiplier, then perhaps H = dh.

As it happens, I imagine that the relevant formula is rather more complicated than this. But for the time being, it isn't pressing to try to work out that more complicated function, nor is it important to try to settle the value of d. What is important is simply recognizing that there is a *proportionality* condition on permissible defensive harm, so that although it is permissible to harm your attacker there is a limit of some sort to the amount of harm you are permitted to impose.

Second, the right to self-defense also involves a *necessity* condition. Even if the amount of harm you are imposing on the aggressor falls within the limit set by the proportionality condition, it is still only permissible to harm the aggressor when this is *necessary* to defend yourself from the attack. Suppose, once again, that Arnold is attacking Brenda and aims to kill her. But imagine that there is no need for Brenda to kill Arnold to defend herself. Suppose that if she were to shout "Boo!" in a loud and fierce voice, Arnold would drop his weapon and run away in fear, leaving Brenda completely safe. If, despite knowing this, Brenda chooses to shoot and kill Arnold anyway, then this is not actually permissible, despite falling within the limit set by proportionality. Killing in self-defense is only permitted if it is necessary, not otherwise. Similarly, if shooting Arnold in the hand would suffice to render him harmless, then Brenda is hardly permitted to shoot him in the heart—killing him!— nonetheless. Intuitively, even when defending yourself against an unprovoked attack, you are required to limit yourself to the smallest amount of harm needed to successfully defend yourself.

No doubt, an adequate statement of this condition would be a complicated affair as well. For a complete statement of the necessity condition would need to take into account the fact that alternative methods of defending oneself may be less effective in one way or another. Perhaps they would be less likely to succeed, or would prevent only some, but not all, of the threatened harm. In defending yourself you are hardly required to settle for the least harmful method that has any chance of success whatsoever! But for our purposes we can set this point aside. Let's stipulate that in the cases we will be discussing, the necessity condition—whatever exactly it comes to—has been met: there is no sufficiently effective alternative to the course of action that the agent is contemplating taking as a means of defending herself.

Finally, let me note one way in which the right to self-defense is *less* restrictive than it might initially appear. What I have in mind is the fact that the right to self-defense does more than merely permit you to defend *yourself*. On the contrary, *others* are permitted to come to your defense as well. If Arnold is attacking Brenda, then not only is Brenda herself permitted to use force to stop Arnold, others may do this on her behalf. Strictly speaking, we might say, the right to self-defense isn't limited to *self*-defense; it is actually a right to *defense*. If you cannot defend yourself, others may do this for you. Indeed, even if you can do it yourself, others are still permitted to come to your aid. Of course, even when the defense is being mounted by someone else, the first two conditions are still in place: proportionality still limits the amount of harm that others may impose in the course of defending you, and necessity still requires that there be no less harmful (sufficiently effective) alternative. But the crucial point is that, special circumstances aside, *third parties* are permitted to come to the defense of someone being attacked. It isn't only the potential victim that has the right to use force.

This last point will be of particular significance for us, as we turn to a discussion of self-defense and animals. I want to examine cases in which animals are being attacked, and I want to examine cases in which animals are doing the attacking. To be sure, in some of the cases that we will be discussing there are other people involved, either as aggressors or as potential victims. But for the most part the questions I want to focus upon concern what we are permitted to do as *third parties*. That is, the question will be what you or I would be permitted to do in cases involving defense and animals, given that we are neither the ones launching the attacks nor the ones being attacked. Accordingly, in the examples that follow, think of yourself as a third party, considering the possibility of coming to the defense of the individual being attacked. I want to explore the permissibility of your doing this.

I must confess that the discussion that follows will not contribute much to the defense of the main claim of this book, that an adequate treatment of animal ethics will be a hierarchical one. I have already given reasons for thinking that we need to introduce a hierarchical approach into our value theory; and I have also argued that if we are deontologists then we will need to incorporate hierarchy into our deontological principles as well. At this point, therefore, the suggestion that hierarchy may also play a role in a proper understanding of the right to self-defense will hardly come as much of a surprise. But throughout our discussion of animal ethics I have also repeatedly claimed that extending our normative theory so as to explicitly cover animals turns out to be a surprisingly complicated and difficult undertaking; and the discussion of self-defense and animals can serve as an extended illustration of this point. No doubt, even when we restrict our attention to cases of one *person* attacking another, the issues surrounding the right to self-defense can be complex and sometimes puzzling. But as we will soon see, matters grow even more murky if one of the relevant parties is an animal.

10.2 Defending Animals

I have just described some of the more important features of the right to self-defense, where one person attacks another and the second then permissibly harms the aggressor so as to prevent the intended harm. As I pointed out, however, we believe it permissible for a third person to come to the aid of the potential victim as well, whether or not the victim is capable of defending herself. (It isn't as though we can only defend those who are utterly helpless or otherwise incapable of defending themselves successfully on their own.)

Is there in fact a moral *requirement* to come to the defense of the person being attacked? Our answer to that question will no doubt depend on our position with regard to some of the principles we touched upon earlier (in 9.4), such as, for example, the duty to aid, or the duty to rescue. Arguably, if the cost (or risk) to a third party is small enough then they may well be morally required to help the potential victim. Most of us would probably agree that in at least some circumstances coming to the defense of another is something that morality does in fact demand of us.

But let us put the question of moral obligation aside and focus instead on what may be a somewhat easier question. Are we at least *permitted* to come to the defense of the potential victim? The answer to that question really does seem obvious: special circumstances aside, one is certainly permitted to defend the potential victim, whether or not there is any kind of obligation to do so. Indeed, even if the cost of defending her is considerable—so that most would think there is no *duty* to come to the victim's aid—for all that, one is still normally *permitted* to help. If one person attacks another, third parties are normally permitted to use force to prevent or frustrate the attack: they can harm the aggressor in the course of defending the potential victim.

That's the situation, at least, if one person is attacking another person. But if we now introduce animals into the picture there are three new types of case to consider, since animals can fill either or both of the two roles, attacker or victim. First, then, there are cases where an animal is being attacked by a person, and we are considering the possibility of defending the animal.

Second, there are cases where a person is being attacked by an animal, and so we are considering defending the *person* against the animal. Finally, there will be cases where both the aggressor and the potential victim are animals, and so we must consider the permissibility of defending one animal from another. Let's consider each type of case in turn.

In the first sort of case an animal is being attacked by a person. The attack, we can suppose, is unprovoked. That is to say, it isn't that the animal "started it," by threatening or attacking the person first. (We will consider such cases later.) Rather, the person has simply chosen to harm the animal. Perhaps, for example, we have a case of hunting for sport, where one person has chosen to kill some animal—possibly a lion—for the sheer pleasure of it.

On the face of it, at least, the lion has a right to defend itself. Admittedly, we are not used to thinking in these terms; but of course, we are not used to thinking all that hard about the moral standing of animals in the first place. But if the lion has a right to defend itself, then it seems to follow that third parties can come to its defense as well. Which is to say, we are permitted to use force to stop the hunter; indeed, we are permitted to *harm* him if this is the only way to protect the lion. Suppose you have a rifle, and the only way to stop the hunter from killing the lion is to shoot the hunter first, injuring him. It seems that this would be a morally permissible thing to do.

This is a surprising conclusion. Few of us would normally think it morally permissible to injure a human hunter to prevent his killing his prey. But this certainly does seem to be the implication of taking seriously the thought that animals have a right to self-defense. If animals have such a right, then it really does seem permissible for third parties to come to their defense, even when this involves imposing harm, perhaps considerable harm, on the people who are attacking them.

Should we, perhaps, deny this claim? That is, should we deny that animals have a right to self-defense? Certainly some theorists would want to do that. It is easy to imagine a restricted deontologist arguing, first, that one has a right to self-defense only if one has deontological standing, and then insisting, second, that animals lack deontological standing.

I have, of course, already argued at length against the claim that animals lack deontological standing. As I have explained, animals may be less autonomous than people are, but it is a mistake to claim that they lack autonomy altogether, and it seems arbitrary and unmotivated to insist that one must have some particular threshold level of autonomy before having any kind of deontological standing at all. It seems much more plausible to suggest that animals do have deontological standing, and so have the various rights that go with that—including, of course, a right to self-defense. It is just that this right, like the others, will vary in strength, depending on one's status.

Furthermore, think how implausible it would be to insist that one is never permitted to harm a person who is trying to unjustifiably harm an animal. Picture a teenage boy who has doused a cat with gasoline, and is about to set it on fire. Imagine that we could save the cat by slapping the boy across the face. Do we really want to claim that this is forbidden? That one must never harm a person at all, in any way, even if this is the only means of defending an otherwise utterly defenseless animal? That seems to me an incredible claim to make. It is far more plausible to suggest that animals really do have a right to self-defense after all. As far as I can see, the only truly open question here is just how *much* harm we are in fact permitted to impose, when we are defending a threatened animal.

Return, then, to the case of the hunter and the lion. Presumably we are permitted to impose some harm here as well, to save the lion's life. But just how much harm are we permitted to impose? May we *kill* the hunter, for example, if this is indeed necessary to prevent him from killing the lion? That is less straightforward. Here we need to remember the proportionality condition. One is permitted to harm an attacker to defend their potential victim, but there is a limit to the amount of harm that one is permitted to impose. Recall the formula $H = dh$. This tells us that the upper limit on the harm that one can permissibly impose, H, depends both on the value of the multiplier, d, and on the amount of harm, h, that the attacker would otherwise impose on his victim.

Of course, we haven't tried to fix the value of d, but we do know that it is large enough to permit us to kill a person to stop them from killing someone else. So can't we conclude, accordingly, that it is permissible to kill the hunter too, if this is necessary to stop their lethal attack on the lion? Not quite, since we also know (see 2.3) that the harm imposed on a lion when its life is taken is smaller in size than the harm normally imposed on a person when *his* life is taken. Since the value of h is smaller when the victim is a lion rather than a person, the value of H will be smaller as well. So we cannot immediately infer that it is permissible to kill the hunter to save the lion's life. Perhaps the limit set by the proportionality condition is lower than this.

On the other hand, we don't yet know that it is *forbidden* to kill the hunter either. To be sure, we have just acknowledged that killing the hunter will typically impose a larger harm on him than the harm that he would otherwise impose on the lion. So if proportionality required that one impose no more harm on the attacker than they would impose on the potential victim then it would indeed normally follow that killing the hunter is wrong. But we also know that the proportionality condition is less restrictive than this; it permits you to do *more* harm, in the course of defending a potential victim, than the aggressor would impose. That is to say, d has a value greater than 1, perhaps considerably greater than 1, so that it really is permissible to impose a greater harm on an aggressor than they were going to impose. So perhaps it is permissible to kill the hunter after all, despite the fact that the lion would suffer a smaller harm were it to die instead.

I know that many people would prefer to dismiss this possibility out of hand. I take it that a more typical reaction to our example would be something like this:

> even when the killing of a certain animal would be wrong, and would wrong the animal itself, it would still be impermissible for a third party to kill the culpable human attacker, even if that were the only way to save the animal's life.[1]

Nonetheless, it seems to me that the permissibility of killing the hunter to defend the lion is a possibility to which we must remain open. In the absence of an attempt to pin down the value of d (not to mention a more precise estimate of the harm involved when a lion loses its life), I think we simply are not yet in a position to know whether killing the hunter is permissible or not.

There is, however, a further complication which we should consider as well. Is it really true that the value of d—whatever that comes to—remains constant, as we move from a case where the victim is a person to a case where the victim is an animal? Or might this be yet another place where hierarchy enters into our moral theory? Just as with several of the other moral variables that we have already discussed, perhaps the multiplier used to fix proportionality is itself something that varies with status.

As I have repeatedly suggested, the lower status of animals partly expresses itself in the possession of rights that are weaker in various relevant ways. It seems natural to wonder then whether this might be true with regard to the right to self-defense as well. After all, the right to self-defense serves to further protect the interests and well-being of those whose right not to be harmed in the first place is being threatened or violated. But if—as I have already argued—the latter right, the right not to be harmed, is weaker for those with lower status, then it seems reasonable to think that the former right, the right to self-defense, might be weaker as well. In particular, then, it might be that as

---

[1] McMahan, *The Ethics of Killing*, p. 420; the word "attacker" is capitalized in the original.

we move to individuals with a lower status than that had by a person, the proportionality condition becomes less permissive. In each case, presumably, the victim (or those coming to the victim's aid) will be allowed to impose more harm on the aggressor than the aggressor himself would otherwise impose on the victim. But for all that, it might be that the *extent* to which the victim (or those aiding her) can impose proportionately greater harm decreases, as the status of the victim decreases. That is, the multiplier, d, which sets the limit on proportionate response, may grow smaller, with the decreasing status of the victim.

If something like this is right, then it obviously introduces even further uncertainty into the question of how much harm we can impose on the hunter to prevent him from killing the lion. Even if we were confident of the value of d in cases where we are defending a person, it will turn out that the relevant value for d is lower when it is a matter of defending a lion rather than a person, given the lion's lower moral status. So there will be two ways, rather than just one, in which the limit set by the proportionality condition will be lower when the victim is a lion. On the one hand, as we have already remarked, the harm being imposed on the victim is smaller. And on the other hand, the size of the relevant multiplier may be smaller as well. Given that the limit to the harm that can be imposed on the hunter is generated by *multiplying* these two reduced values together (since $H = dh$), it follows that the reduction in the limit may be rather large.

Does this mean, then, that killing the hunter is forbidden? I think it remains the case that we just don't know enough, right now, to answer this question one way or the other. What we do know is this: nothing in our moral theory as it stands can rule this out.

Of course, it does seem reasonable to insist that even if it is true that we are permitted to kill the hunter to save a *lion*, the same will not be true regardless of what the animal is that the hunter is trying to kill. A bird, for example, will have a lower status than a lion, and a fish may have a lower status still. So the upper limit on permissible harm, set by the proportionality condition, will be significantly lower in both of these cases. On the one hand, the value for d will be correspondingly lower, and on the other hand, the harm being imposed on the animals (when their lives are taken) will be smaller as well. It seems virtually inevitable then—whatever we conclude about the case of lion hunting—that for many animals, animals with a sufficiently low status, killing the hunter to prevent the death of the animal in question will be morally forbidden, a disproportionate response.

Even if this point is conceded, however, that should not be taken to show that it is wrong to *injure* the hunter in cases involving, for example, birds or fish (or, for that matter, a lion, if killing should turn out to be disproportionate there as well). At best what these remarks about the possibility of a status sensitive proportionality condition show is that there is a *limit* to the amount of harm that can be imposed on the hunter—a limit that gets smaller as the status of the hunted animal gets lower. But they do nothing at all to suggest that we are not permitted to impose any kind of harm at all. It remains the case that if we choose to come to the aid of a hunted animal, there will be *some* amount of harm that we are in principle permitted to impose on the hunter in the animal's defense.

Of course, pragmatic considerations may be relevant here as well. It might be objected that if we do use force to protect animals from unprovoked attacks, in the long run this will almost inevitably be counterproductive. In any given case, to be sure, we may succeed in saving some particular animal from being harmed, but there is a serious danger that if we go about injuring those who are trying to harm animals not only may we fail to win over others to the cause of protecting animals, it may lead even larger numbers to write off a concern for animal ethics altogether (as a "dangerous" and "extremist" view that obviously does not deserve to be taken seriously). In the long run such an approach may harm more animals than it helps. Arguably, then, although in principle it may be permissible to harm (or even kill) people when this is necessary to defend animals, there may be compelling moral reason to refrain from regularly doing this.

I do think this argument should be taken seriously. But at the same time, it is worth noting that deontologists, at least, should be rather hesitant about offering it. For as we have also noted, deontologists typically believe in a duty to rescue—and like other deontological duties, the duty to rescue cannot typically be disregarded simply because the results might be better overall if one did. (Recall the common thought that one must spend significant resources rescuing those in need here and now, even if the money could do more good overall in the long run were it spent in some other way.) If animals have deontological standing then it seems that they too should be covered by the duty to rescue, and this seems to mean that one cannot justify failing to rescue any given animal under attack on the mere grounds that doing this may be better for a larger number of other animals in the long run. That sort of consequentialist consideration may simply be outweighed—from the deontological perspective—by a duty to come to the aid of the animals that are being threatened here and now.

(Of course, I have also suggested that the duty to rescue may be weaker when it comes to aiding animals rather than people. And in any event, we are only asking here whether it is *permissible* to harm those attacking animals, not whether it is required. Still, the deontologist's attitude toward rescue suggests that they should at least be troubled by any such appeal to consequentialist considerations when deciding whether to refrain from saving an animal from attack.)

One final point. In thinking about what we are permitted to do in defending an animal from a hunter's attack, I have been assuming that the hunter has no compelling justification for hunting and killing the animal. I certainly don't think, for example, that the pleasure one might get from hunting for sport will suffice to justify killing a lion (nor, for that matter, will it justify catching a fish). But things would of course be rather different if the person were hunting out of necessity, having no other way to feed himself or his family. Indeed, I have insisted upon this very point, arguing that on any plausible moral view it must be permissible for a person to hunt a deer, for example, or to catch a fish, if this is the only way to avoid starvation. But it is one thing to think it permissible to hunt an animal when there is no other way to keep yourself alive; it is quite another thing to think it permissible to hunt for sport (even if you will go on to eat the animal you have killed).[2]

10.3 Defending Against Animals

Turning now to a different sort of case, suppose that instead of having a person attacking an animal, we have an animal attacking a person. Imagine, for example, that a lion has wandered into an African village, and is now attacking a person who has done nothing to provoke it. Suppose that if we do nothing, the lion will kill her. What is it permissible for third parties to do in a case like this? May we kill the lion to defend its potential victim?

Admittedly, cases of unprovoked lethal attacks by animals against humans are relatively rare (though they do, of course, occur). In contrast, humans attack animals billions of times every year, killing them for food (although there is no need to do this, since virtually no one actually needs to eat animal flesh to stay alive). But regardless of their frequency, it will be

---

[2] Suppose we have a case where the person killing the animal really does have an adequate moral justification for doing this. Would it follow that we are no longer permitted to come to the animal's defense? Not necessarily. On certain views concerning the right to self-defense, a victim is sometimes still permitted to defend himself even though the attacker's action is *justified*. Conceivably, then, in at least some cases third parties might still be permitted to come to an *animal's* defense as well, even though the person attacking the animal is permitted or even morally required to mount the attack. But the relevant issues are complicated, and I won't explore them further here.

helpful to examine cases where it is indeed an animal attacking a human, rather than the reverse, since such cases raise some interesting philosophical issues.

This may seem a surprising thing to say, since initially at least this new type of case seems much more straightforward than the previous one. For example, while it is controversial to claim (as I have) that animals have a right to self-defense, no one denies that *people* have such a right. (Or rather, no one denies it other than pacifists; but I continue to put this position aside.) So that concern, at any rate, doesn't even arise in the present scenario: the victim here—the person being attacked by the lion—certainly has a right to defend herself, and it seems clear that third parties may come to her defense as well.

Similarly, consider a question I raised in the previous section: whether the multiplier d—used to fix the limit set by the proportionality condition—might be lower in cases where the victim has a lower status. That question doesn't arise here either. Since the victim in the current case is a *person*, her status is the same as that of the victim in our original examples (where one person attacks another). So there is no worry here that a lower status on the part of the victim might result in a lower value for d.

Furthermore, since the attacker in the present case is an animal, rather than a person, while the victim is a person, rather than an animal, it seems particularly likely that the harm being imposed on the lion—if we kill it—will actually be less than the harm that the lion will otherwise impose on its human victim. Normally, after all, a lion loses considerably less when it loses its life than a person does (when she loses *her* life). This seems to make it all the more obvious that killing the lion falls within the limits of the proportionality condition. One is ordinarily permitted to impose considerably more harm on the attacker than they would impose on the victim. Since in the present case *less* harm is being imposed, killing the lion seems to fall safely within the relevant limits.

For all these reasons, then, it may seem obvious both that killing the lion is permissible, and that there is little of interest to say about this case. And since I take it that pretty much everyone would agree that killing the lion is indeed permissible, here at least we have a case where hierarchical deontology accords well with the pronouncements of common sense.

But for all that, there are complications that arise in connection with this sort of case that do still need to be examined. We can start by reconsidering what the proportionality condition has to say about our example.

I have, of course, just pointed out that since the victim in our example is a person, there is no reason to think that her status somehow alters the value of the multiplier. While it does seem plausible to think that d may take on a lower value when the victim has a lower status, nothing like that is going on in the present case. Accordingly, there is no reason to think that d may have a lower value here than it normally would (that is, in cases where one person attacks another).

But we might well wonder, instead, whether the value of d is even *higher* than it would be when a person attacks another person. For it seems conceivable that the value of d might also be affected by the fact that the attacker is an *animal* rather than a person. In such cases, after all, defensive force is being directed against an individual with a lower status (as compared to that of a person). Perhaps this lower status results in a higher value for d.

Think about it this way. As we know, a victim and those aiding her are permitted to impose a greater amount of harm on an attacker than the attacker would have imposed on the victim. Still, as we also know, there is a limit to the amount of permissible harm that can be imposed in defending oneself or others. This limit reflects the fact that the despite the unjustified nature of the attack, the attacker is nonetheless a being with moral standing in their own right. (There would, after all, be no limit at all to what one could permissibly do to a falling boulder.) Perhaps, then, in those cases where the attacker has a lower rather than a higher moral status, the limit on defensive harm is less restrictive as well. Perhaps, that is, it is permissible to impose even greater harm on an attacker with a lower status. If so, then the value of d increases—more defensive harm can be imposed—as the status of the attacker goes down.

If all of this is right, then the proportionality condition may actually be sensitive to status in two different ways. On the one hand, as I argued in the previous section, it might be that the value of d goes down—so that less defensive harm can be imposed—when the status of the victim is lower. But on the other hand, as I have just pointed out, it might also be the case that the value of d goes *up*—so that *more* harm can be imposed—when the status of the *attacker* is lower. In short, the proportionality condition may actually be sensitive both to the status of the victim *and* to the status of the attacker.

(Similar ideas lie behind both proposals. Just as the limit on defensive force reflects the moral standing of the attacker, the very permissibility of defensive force presumably reflects—at least in part—the moral standing of the potential *victim*. So just as the proportionality condition becomes more restrictive as we imagine victims with lower status, it may grow *less* restrictive as we imagine *attackers* with lower status.)

That's certainly an intriguing possibility, one that we would easily overlook if we focused exclusively on cases where the attackers are people. But even if it's right, it only reinforces the conclusion we had already reached, that it is permissible to kill the lion. For if the proportionality condition is indeed sensitive to status in this second way, with the value of d going up in response to the lower status of the attacker (since lions have a lower moral status than people do), this will only serve to raise the limit set by the proportionality constraint. And since we were already confident that this limit could be met, nothing in this new point gives us reason to worry that it may not be permissible to kill the lion after all.

There is, however, a further complication which we have not yet considered, one which does raise the question of whether it is truly permissible to kill the lion. We need to ask about the implications of the fact that a lion is not really an example of what we generally have in mind when we think about deliberate aggressors.

What do we normally have in mind when we imagine a typical case of one person attacking another? Here's a partial list: First of all, the agent is in control of what they are doing. Indeed, we generally imagine that the attacker is a fully responsible moral agent. Second, they are fully aware that their action is going to harm the other person and, indeed, they are aiming at precisely that. Third, they have an adequate grasp of the basic facts of the situation, and have decided to attack on the basis of that understanding. Fourth, while they may or may not think of their act as morally justified, at the very least they do recognize that what they are doing is the kind of act that appropriately comes under moral appraisal, the sort of act that would normally stand in need of moral justification. But fifth, either they believe (correctly or not) that their act is indeed justified, or else they just don't care.

(I should perhaps add one more element. Since our particular concern at the moment lies with acts of aggression that uncontroversially trigger the right to self-defense, let us suppose that the attack is not, in fact, one that is morally justified.)

This isn't intended as a full and complete description of what is in place in a typical case of deliberate aggression, but it should suffice to make it obvious that there are many situations where one individual poses a threat to another without that first individual being a deliberate aggressor of this sort. Philosophers sometimes talk about *innocent threats* to cover cases like this.

Here are two familiar examples from the philosophical literature. First, imagine that the wind has lifted someone off the ground and has now thrown them down a pit where they will soon land on and thus kill a second person (who is at the bottom of the pit and cannot move out of the way). Here, the human projectile may well recognize the threat that they pose to the person at the bottom, but they have no control over what they are doing (it isn't as though they are deliberately throwing themselves) and they certainly do not aim to harm that other person. Second, imagine that a young child picks up a loaded gun, thinking it a mere toy: they have aimed the gun at someone else's heart, and they are about to pull the trigger. Here, the child is in control of what they are doing, but they have no idea that they are about to do something that is genuinely harmful.[3]

In both of these cases the person posing the threat to someone else falls short of being a full-blown deliberate aggressor. Something important that is present in the standard case is missing (different things, in the two cases). Still, it is undeniable that both of these people pose a threat to someone else, and unless they are somehow stopped another party will end up dead. Thus both the human projectile and the child with the gun are *innocent* threats: each is about to harm someone, but neither is an ordinary, deliberate aggressor.

Now a moment's reflection makes it clear that even an attacking animal is at best an innocent threat of some sort. To be sure, some of the standard elements of full-blown deliberate aggression are present here. When the lion charges the villager, for example, it presumably has control over what it is doing (like a normal aggressor, but unlike the human projectile), and presumably it also realizes that what it is doing will be harmful. Indeed, we can even imagine that the lion *intends* to harm its victim (again, like a normal aggressor, but unlike the child with the gun). But for all that, lions are not capable of the sort of moral reflection that would allow them to wonder whether their act is morally justified or not, or allow them to realize that attacking a person is an act that is potentially morally problematic. Indeed, it is precisely because we think that animals cannot engage in this sort of moral reflection (let alone self-governance based on that reflection) that we deny that they fall under moral obligations at all. So part of what makes the attacking lion an *innocent* threat is the fact that it is not a morally responsible agent, the sort of being who could and should be reflecting about the morality of what it is up to.

The question, then, is this: does the right to self-defense only cover defensive action taken against normal deliberate aggressors? Or does it also cover action taken against *innocent* threats? If you could defend yourself (or someone else) against the human projectile or the child with the gun by shooting and killing them first, would the right to self-defense make this a permissible thing to do?

Perhaps unsurprisingly, there is no consensus about the answer to this question. Some people are primarily impressed by the fact that innocent threats are *innocent*. Moved by this thought, they maintain that the right to self-defense

---

[3] See Nozick, *Anarchy, State, and Utopia*, p. 34, for a version of the first case, and Regan, *The Case for Animal Rights*, p. 293, for a version of the second.

does not go so far as to make it permissible to deliberately harm someone who falls short of being a deliberate aggressor. Others, however, are more impressed by the fact that innocent threats remain *threats*. They maintain, instead, that the right to defend oneself or others should not disappear simply because the risk of harm that one faces was not put in place deliberately.

A third possible position, of course, is that different answers apply to different *types* of innocent threats. As we have already observed, threats can fall short of being deliberate threats in a number of different ways. The human projectile, for example, has no control over what he is doing (strictly speaking, he isn't even acting). In contrast, the child with the gun does have control. On the other hand, the human projectile realizes that he is about to harm someone; in contrast, the child does not. Conceivably, differences like these may make a moral difference with regard to what one may permissibly do to the threat.[4]

A theory of this third sort would need to take cognizance of the fact that the lion does seem to be in control of its action and does seem to be aiming at harming its victim, but it does not have the capacity for moral reflection and so is not acting immorally in attacking its victim (although, for all that, it has no objective justification for the attack). Armed with a more fine-grained analysis of the various types of innocent threats, the theory might then tell us whether or not attacks by animals are the *kind* of threat against which defensive harm is permitted. Presumably, even advocates of this third approach may disagree with one another about the best answer to this last question.

I won't try to settle this dispute here. Instead, let's consider the implications of each of the two alternative bottom lines: (1) that defensive harm against innocent threats (either all of them, or at least those posed by animals) is permissible, or (2) that defensive harm against such threats (either all of them, or at least those posed by animals) is impermissible. As it happens, my sympathies lie with the first alternative. But either way, we need to complicate our discussion of defending against animals.

Suppose, first, that defensive harm against innocent threats is indeed permissible. Can we conclude, accordingly, that we can kill the attacking lion after all? Admittedly, the lion will only be an innocent threat, not a typical

---

[4] For example, one important argument for the impermissibility of harming innocent threats turns on the attempt to make us see such threats as morally analogous to mere bystanders, where the thought of course is that the right to self-defense does *not* make it permissible to deliberately harm a bystander. (See McMahan, *The Ethics of Killing*, pp. 405–9, and Otsuka, "Killing the Innocent in Self-Defense.") But whatever the merits of this argument for certain subclasses of innocent threats, it won't trivially extend to the case of animals, since I take it that the lion, for example—*unlike* a normal bystander—is consciously trying to harm its prey. Hence the possible need for a more fine-grained theory of innocent threats. Those hoping to construct such a theory will find a number of helpful distinctions in McMahan, *The Ethics of Killing*, pp. 400–1.

aggressor. But if even innocent threats provide suitable targets for defensive harm, won't it follow that it really is permissible to harm the lion to defend its human victim?

Not necessarily. For even if we agree that it can be permissible to defend against innocent threats, we might still want to insist that the very innocence of such threats has an effect on the *amount* of defensive harm that it is permissible to impose. Intuitively, after all, deliberate aggressors seem to open themselves up to a greater amount of defensive harm than seems appropriate when it is a matter of defending against a threat that falls short of deliberate aggression in one or more ways. Thus we might want to maintain that the proportionality condition is more restrictive—setting a lower limit on defensive harm—when one is dealing with an innocent threat rather than a standard, deliberate aggressor. The value of d may be smaller.

If that's right, then the permissibility of killing the lion remains unsettled. We may be confident that were the lion a *deliberate* aggressor the value of d would be high enough to make it permissible to kill the attacking lion. But if the innocence of the lion reduces the value of d then the upper limit on permissible defensive harm will go down accordingly. And if it goes down *sufficiently* far, then it might conceivably turn out to be forbidden to kill the lion after all. (It would, of course, still be permissible to harm the lion some-what, to defend its victim; but the amount of permissible harm might be too small to be effective.)

Speaking personally, I doubt that the value of d does go down quite that far. My own intuition is that it is permissible to kill the child who is about to pull the trigger on what they mistakenly think is a toy gun. And if the limit on defensive harm set by the proportionality condition remains sufficiently high to justify killing in that case, then I see no reason to think it won't do the same when it comes to killing the lion as well. Still, in the absence of a developed theory here (a theory of how the value of d varies with the innocence of the threat), I think it must be conceded that this conclusion could still be contested.[5] (Note, in particular, that a fine-grained theory of innocent threats might hold that the value of d depends on the particular *kind* of innocent threat we are dealing with; so generalizations here must be made with caution.)

---

[5] There is a further, related issue that should be noted here as well. Even if we suppose that it is permissible to defend *oneself* against the attack of an innocent threat, some would still deny that it is permissible for *third parties* to come to one's defense against innocent threats. Given the innocence of both the victim and the threat, might there be a kind of moral symmetry which makes it impermissible for third parties to take sides? (See Davis, "Abortion and Self-Defense.") I am not myself drawn to this view, though here too it might be important to distinguish between different *types* of innocent threats.

Turning now to the second alternative, let us suppose instead that defensive harm against innocent threats is *impermissible*. Then the argument sketched at the beginning of this section—the argument for the permissibility of defending against the lion—is altogether misguided. For that argument assumed that the attacking lion was a suitable target of defensive harm (since it was, after all, initiating an unprovoked attack). But if it really is the case that defensive harm aimed against innocent threats is forbidden, then given that the lion is an innocent threat an appeal to self-defense cannot here get off the ground. Thus, far from it being obvious that it would be permissible to kill the lion to defend its human victim, it would seem that we are justified in reaching instead the opposite conclusion: since the lion is only an *innocent* threat, we cannot actually kill it at all.

Actually, however, this new argument is itself a bit hasty. Despite what it initially sounds like, saying that defensive harm against innocent threats is impermissible is not the same thing as saying one can never be justified in harming an innocent threat. It is simply a way of asserting that the mere fact that the innocent threat is indeed a threat provides no *special* justification for harming it. Rather, harming an innocent threat will be morally on all fours with harming someone who poses no threat at all.

Now normally, of course, it is forbidden to harm someone who isn't threatening you (or threatening someone you are aiding). But as we have already noted, moderate deontologists believe that there is an important exception to this generalization: it is permissible to harm someone—even someone posing no threat to you—if enough *good* is at stake, that is, if the relevant threshold for their right not to be harmed has been met. Thus, even though the attacking lion is an innocent threat, and even if the right to self-defense does not extend to cover defensive harm against such threats, for all that, it might still be the case that it is permissible to kill the lion anyway—provided, of course, that saving the victim's life is a great enough good to meet the relevant threshold for the lion's right not to be harmed.

Is it plausible to think that the threshold has indeed been met? I think so (although nothing in hierarchical deontology per se requires one to say this). After all, I have already argued that it is permissible for Tom to kill a deer, given that this is the only way for Tom to keep himself alive. But the discussion of that case involved no appeal to self-defense at all (the deer obviously poses no *threat* to Tom). Rather, it simply seemed to me plausible to hold that saving Tom's life (even if only for a year) does *enough* good to outweigh the deer's right not to be harmed. Unsurprisingly, then, it also seems plausible to me to suggest that saving the life of the *lion's* human victim will do enough good to outweigh the *lion's* right not to be harmed as well. (The thresholds in the two cases are probably roughly comparable, and presumably saving the life of the lion's victim will normally do as much good—or more—as what Tom achieves when he kills his deer.)

So even if we were to agree that being an innocent threat does not make one liable to defensive harm, we might still conclude that killing the lion is permissible nonetheless, simply because its right not to be harmed has been *outweighed*. To be sure, that would be quite an implausible thing to suggest if the lion had the same moral status as a person (for then the lion's threshold would be far too high). But a position like this becomes available to us once we recognize that animals have a lower moral status than people have.

Suppose I am right in claiming that it is permissible to kill the lion even if the right to self-defense does not justify defensive harm against innocent threats. Then it will also turn out, trivially, that it is permissible to kill the lion even if the right *does* justify such defensive harm. After all, the right to self-defense merely permits (a limited amount of) harm in certain cases where it might not otherwise be justified; it doesn't do anything at all to *rule out* imposing harm in those cases where such harm would already have been justified *independently* of that right. So even if it should turn out that the innocence of an innocent threat lowers d significantly over what it would have been had the attacker been a deliberate aggressor, it will still be the case that one is permitted to kill the lion, by virtue of the simple fact that the lion's right not to be harmed has been outweighed by the good of saving its victim's life.

Let me note one final complication. In discussing the permissibility of defending against animals I have assumed throughout that the animal's attack is unprovoked. But things would look rather different if this weren't the case.

Return to the situation where one person, Arnold, is attacking another, Brenda. Ordinarily, of course, Brenda may defend herself, and others may permissibly come to her aid as well. But suppose that the reason Brenda is now being attacked by Arnold is because Brenda herself had unjustifiably "started it." Perhaps Brenda attacked Arnold first, or attacked someone else (who Arnold is now trying to defend). In such a case, Arnold's attack on Brenda is justified (as long as it meets the proportionality and necessity conditions), and Brenda cannot appeal to her right to self-defense to justify the use of force against Arnold. You can hardly plead self-defense if it is your fault that you now need to defend yourself in the first place. Nor can others ordinarily come to your defense, if it is your *fault* that you now need to be defended.

So suppose that the reason the lion is attacking a human is because the human attacked it first. Instead of imagining a lion wandering into a village, suppose that a hunter has started shooting at the lion and the lion is now charging the hunter in an attempt to defend itself. In a case like this the hunter can hardly claim that he is permitted to continue shooting on the ground that he is now *defending* himself against the lion's attack! You cannot initiate an attack on others and then argue self-defense when they—or others coming to their aid—resist that very attack.

One might wonder, however, whether the following is the case. Even if an appeal to the hunter's right to self-defense has been blocked thanks to his having initiated the hostilities, can he nonetheless claim that he is still permitted to defend himself, given that the good that will thus be achieved (saving his life) outweighs the lion's right not to be harmed? Of course, no such argument would be persuasive if he were hunting a *person* instead, someone who was now using lethal force to defend herself. Saving the hunter's life won't be a great enough good to meet the relevant threshold when it is a matter of killing another *person*. But precisely because a *lion's* right not to be harmed will have a lower threshold than a person's would, we might wonder whether killing the lion might be justified after all, even though the hunter is at fault for creating the problem in the first place.

I believe, however, that an adequate account of what it takes to meet the threshold of a right will block this line of argument as well. Moderate deontologists believe that it is permissible to harm another when enough good is at stake. But if the reason that your welfare is now at risk (unless another is harmed) is precisely because of your own earlier unjustified behavior, you cannot now count that good (your welfare) toward meeting the right's threshold. Had you not acted immorally in the first place, there would be no need now to harm another. Accordingly, when the lion defends itself against the hunter's unprovoked attack, it seems to follow that the hunter is not now permitted to defend himself.

(Here's a less clear case. Suppose that a hiker knowingly and recklessly enters a bear's den, and the mother bear mistakenly believes that the hiker poses a threat to her cubs. Has the hiker provoked the ensuing attack from the bear in a manner sufficiently egregious to nullify his right to self-defense? Can he here justifiably appeal to his own well-being and argue that the bear's right not to be harmed has been outweighed?)

10.4 Defending Animals Against Animals

We can now turn to the remaining basic type of case involving animals, that is, situations where one animal is attacking another. Suppose, for example, that a lion is attacking (without provocation) a zebra. Given our assumption that animals have deontological standing, and thus have a right to self-defense, are we permitted to come to the zebra's defense? If the only way to save the zebra is to kill the lion first, are we permitted to do this?

As usual, I am not here asking whether we are *required* to help the zebra. Doubtless, our views about the extent of our duty to aid or of our duty to rescue will affect the answer we give to that question.[6] But let us put those issues aside and focus instead on what we are *permitted* to do. Are we *permitted* to kill the lion? Unsurprisingly, the complications that we have examined in earlier stages of our discussion come into play here as well. Let's consider a few of them.[7]

The first point to notice, then, is that, as before, the lion is only an innocent threat, not a deliberate aggressor (since the lion is not a responsible moral agent). So we once again face the question of whether the right to self-defense permits defensive harm against innocent threats (or perhaps: against innocent threats of this *sort*). Our answer to this question may well affect the permissibility of harming the lion to protect the zebra.

It might be suggested, however, that there is no real need for us to consider this question. After all, when discussing the case where the lion's victim was *human*, I argued that even if one may *not* harm innocent threats—that is, even if there is no special liability to defensive harm arising from the fact that they are threats—it is nonetheless plausible to hold that the lion's right not to be harmed can be *outweighed*. And if it really is true that the threshold for the lion's right has been met (thanks to the life that can be saved), then there is no pressing need to settle the question of whether any *additional* justification for imposing harm can be found in the fact that the lion is posing a threat to its potential victim. Similarly, then, for the present case: can't we just insist that the relevant threshold has been met here as well, so it is permissible to kill the

---

[6] It is odd, however, that such a duty to save animals from animal predators is rejected by Regan (*The Case for Animal Rights*, pp. xxxvi–xxxviii) given that he grants animals what I am calling deontological standing. His argument turns on the fact that on the whole it must be true that prey species don't normally need our help to survive (since if they did, the species would have long since gone extinct). But it is hard for me to see what relevance that fact has, since there clearly can be cases where particular *members* of such species *do* need our help.

[7] Similarly, we might wonder: if it were possible to intervene on a *wide* scale, killing off predator animals so as to protect their prey, would *that* be permissible? Of course, given our current ignorance of the long term ecological effects, one might well worry that doing so systematically would prove disastrous. On the other hand, those attracted to a deontological duty to rescue should probably hesitate before appealing to this possibility as a way of avoiding the question. (Compare the similar remark in 10.2.) At any rate, for present purposes we can sidestep these worries by thinking about isolated cases of saving individual animals from attack. (But see McMahan, "The Meat Eaters," for a thoughtful discussion of some of the moral issues involved in systematically defending prey from predators.)

lion simply by virtue of the *good* that this will do, and in this way sidestep the question of whether it is permissible to harm innocent threats?

Unfortunately, however, it is far from clear that the threshold really has been met in the present case as well, given that we have moved from a situation where the victim was a person to one where the victim is a mere animal. For now, if we do kill the lion, the good we bring about is not the saving of a person's life but only the saving of a *zebra's* life. At a minimum, that will normally involve a great deal less welfare saved. What's more, by virtue of the lower status of the zebra (as compared to a person), that welfare will itself count less, unit for unit, than it would have had it been the welfare of a person. Together these two points imply that considerably less good is done by saving the zebra than by saving a person. So even if we are confident—as I believe we should be—that *enough* good is done to meet the threshold of the lion's right when it is a matter of saving the life of a *person*, we have no compelling reason to believe that enough good will be done to meet the threshold in the case where we will only be saving a zebra, rather than a person.

Indeed, there is reason to believe that there *won't* be enough good at stake, if it is only a matter of saving one zebra. Admittedly, zebras in the wild may be able to live a few years longer than lions do, and conceivably that may make for a bit more well-being gained (from saving the zebra) than is lost (from killing the lion). But even if we supposed that *twice* as much good would be done as the harm being imposed on the lion, presumably that wouldn't come close to meeting the threshold of the lion's right not to be harmed. It would take far more good than this before we could plausibly say that the lion's right not to be harmed has been outweighed.

(To be sure, I haven't attempted to establish even approximate thresholds for the rights of different animals—and I have, of course, argued at length that animals will have rights with much *lower* thresholds than the rights that people have. But those thresholds would have to be reduced to almost nothing if it really were the case that one could meet them even when there was only a *bit* more good to be gained overall. If it takes 1,000 human lives saved to justify killing an innocent person (and recall that this was on the low end of common opinion), and if animals really do have deontological standing, could it really take only *one* zebra life saved to justify killing an innocent lion?)

It would seem, then, that the threshold of the lion's right not to be harmed has not been met. (Or rather, it won't be met if only one zebra's life is at stake. Things might look rather different if a large enough number of zebras were endangered.) And this means, of course, that we cannot justify killing the lion by claiming that its right has simply been outweighed.

Suppose, then, that we *also* hold the view that it is impermissible to harm innocent threats. Then we cannot justify killing the lion by means of an appeal to the right to self-defense either. For if the fact that the lion is posing a threat to the zebra does not render the lion a suitable target for defensive harm, this line of justification is blocked as well. So if it is impermissible to harm innocent threats it will turn out that we are morally forbidden to kill the lion—not even if there is no other way to save the zebra.

Of course, it is compatible with this conclusion to insist, nonetheless, that it could still be permissible to *harm* the lion, provided that the harm imposed is sufficiently small. For as we imagine smaller and smaller harms, the threshold of the lion's right will grow progressively smaller as well, making it easier and easier to meet the shrinking threshold. If a *small* enough harm—perhaps wounding the lion in some small way—would nonetheless suffice to save the zebra's life (scaring the lion away), the threshold might well be met. In such a case, then, even those who think it impermissible to harm innocent threats can judge it permissible to help the zebra by injuring the lion (in this small way).

How small a harm would be sufficiently small? That's a question, I think, we are not yet in a position to answer. Not only would we need a more developed account of animal welfare (how much is the lion losing? how much is the zebra gaining?), we would also need a more adequate understanding of the threshold function, and conceivably a more settled view regarding the relative status of zebra and lion as well.

What we can say, however, is this: the case of a lion attacking a zebra is, of course, only one among countless cases where one type of animal attacks another. There is no reason to believe that *all* of these cases will be similarly difficult to settle. Much of the obscurity here follows from the fact that the zebra and the lion have more or less the same moral status (and more or less the same amount of welfare at stake). So if we imagine cases with more extreme differences between attacker and attacked we may get clearer and more sweeping verdicts.

For example, if we imagine that the attacking animal is one with a relatively high status while the animal being attacked is one with a very low one (perhaps an anteater eating an ant, or a wolf catching a fish), harming the attacker may be virtually never justified. Here, not only will the benefit to the animal being attacked not be great enough to justify *killing* the attacking animal, for all practical purposes there may be no harm at all that we can impose on the attacking animal that is small enough that it can be outweighed by the chance of saving the prey.

On the other hand, if we suppose that the attacking animal is one with a very low moral status while the animal being attacked is one with a relatively high one, it may be easy to reach the opposite judgment. Imagine, for example, that a black widow spider is about to bite and kill a kangaroo. Here we may assert with confidence that even if the only way to protect the kangaroo is indeed to *kill* the spider, the harm to the spider is small enough and the spider's status low enough that the threshold for the spider's right not to be harmed will be very easily met. The good done by saving the kangaroo's life will clearly outweigh the spider's right not to be harmed. (If you think that spiders lack moral standing altogether, substitute a suitable alternative—some poisonous creature that does have standing, but with a very low status.)

So in some cases, I think, it will be relatively easy to tell whether or not the threshold has been met. In others, it will be more difficult. But either way, if it is impermissible to kill innocent threats, then the fact that the attacking animal is indeed the one posing a threat to its potential victim simply plays no role in justifying the use of force against it. It will be permissible to harm a potential predator to save its victim only in those cases where it would *also* be permissible to harm some utterly uninvolved animal of the same type, an animal that was a mere bystander (if this too would save the original victim).

In contrast, if it is actually permissible to harm innocent threats, then the attacking animal is a suitable target for defensive harm. So even if the *threshold* for the right not to be harmed has not been met, it might yet be the case that one is permitted to harm or kill the attacker. This might make a difference if we return to our original case, where a lion attacks a zebra. I claimed that isn't plausible to think the threshold of the lion's right not to be killed has been met; at best only smaller harms can be outweighed. But if it really is true that it is permissible to harm innocent threats as a means of defending their victims then it may well turn out that killing the lion is permissible after all, if this is the only way to save the zebra.

Of course, even here it may seem difficult to say much with confidence, until we learn more about how the limit on defensive force is affected by the fact that the lion is indeed an *innocent* threat. As I have previously noted, even those who think it permissible to harm innocent threats typically believe that the proportionality condition is more restrictive when it is a matter of harming or killing an innocent threat rather than a deliberate aggressor. So until we learn more about how the value of d varies with the innocence of the threat it may seem impossible to be sure that we can justify *killing* the lion to save the zebra.

On the other hand, unless the value of d comes very close to 1 in such cases—which would effectively wipe out the right to impose more harm on an attacker than the attacker would otherwise impose on the victim—it looks as though proportionality would be satisfied here after all. For if I am right that the zebra has as much welfare at stake as the lion does (or perhaps even a bit more), then so long as one is permitted to impose *as much* harm on the attacker as the attacker would impose on its victim, proportionality will be satisfied.

Could the value of d reach 1, or even less? We wouldn't normally think so. (Or rather, those who think it permissible to harm innocent threats wouldn't normally think so.) I take it, for example, that those who think it permissible to harm innocent threats would normally agree that it is permissible to kill the child who is about to shoot what they mistakenly believe to be a toy gun, even if this will only save the life of *one* other person. In a case like this, at least, we assume that the value of d is indeed greater than 1 (perhaps significantly so). So perhaps we really are justified in thinking it permissible to kill the lion to save the zebra.

But even this last argument may be too quick, for it fails to take into account the fact that we are here dealing not with one *person* threatening another (as we have in the case of the child and the gun) but with one *animal* threatening another. Recalling the suggestion that the value of d may vary with the status of the attacker as well as with the status of the victim, we need to ask how this affects the permissibility of acting when the innocent threat is a lion and the victim is a zebra.

On the one hand, the fact that the attacker is only a lion—rather than a person—should serve to *raise* the value of d. This should make it even easier to justify killing the lion to save the zebra. But on the other hand, the fact that the victim is only a zebra—rather than a person—should serve to *lower* the value of d. This, in turn, should make it more *difficult* to justify killing the lion to save the zebra. Thus, when we move from a case where both the innocent threat and the victim are people to one where both are animals, there are two forces at work, pulling the value of d in opposite directions.

What is the net effect of combining these two opposing forces? Are the two influences on d equally strong (though opposed), or is one stronger than the other? I think we don't yet have a theory adequate to answer this question.

Suppose, for simplicity, that zebras and lions have exactly the same moral status. Can we safely conclude, given this assumption, that the reduction in d due to the fact that the victim is a zebra will exactly equal and cancel out the increase in d due to the fact that the attacker is a lion? If their two statuses are the same, won't their effects on d be the same as well? Not necessarily. For it could be that the rate at which d varies *differs*, depending on whether we are altering the status of the victim or the status of the attacker. If so, then it is possible that the two changes won't actually cancel each other out after all. Absent a more developed theory, it seems to me, we really don't yet know.

Where does all of this leave us? Often, I think, in the dark. That will be especially so if we move to cases where there are significant differences in status between the attacking animal and its prey. Imagine a wolf catching a salmon. May we harm the wolf to protect the fish? On the one hand, the lower status of the wolf (as compared to a person) would tend to raise the value of d; but on the other hand, the lower status of the salmon (as compared to a person) would tend to lower it. I find it reasonable to believe (though difficult to be sure) that the net effect here is to *lower* the value of d, given that a salmon's status is *considerably* lower than a wolf's. So even if we are permitted to harm innocent threats, we can do less here (if we are to meet proportionality) than if it were a matter of defending one person from another. Combine this with the fact that the salmon doesn't actually have a great deal of well-being at stake and it becomes quite difficult to say just how much harm we are permitted to impose on the wolf. It seems unlikely that we can kill it—while still meeting the limits set by the proportionality condition—even if harming innocent threats is permissible. But are there any harms at all that we can permissibly impose, if doing this would save the salmon? Presumably there are, though I find it impossible to say how much.

Nor, I think, is the situation all that much clearer if we take into account the fact that the wolf is catching and eating the fish out of necessity, so as to stay alive. I have argued, of course, that when a *person's* life is at stake there is enough good on the table to justify killing a fish. Even if we agree that the fish has a right not to be harmed, the threshold of that right, I claim, is met when it is a matter of saving a person's life. But is the same thing true when the life being saved is that of a wolf rather than a person? To my mind, at least, the wolf has sufficiently less well-being at stake (and that well-being counts for less, unit for unit) that I find the answer far from clear.

Suppose we stipulate, if only for the sake of argument, that the extra welfare gained by the wolf *is* great enough to outweigh the fish's right not to be harmed. Would this then mean that we are not permitted to impose any sort of harm on the wolf at all (if such harm would suffice to save the fish)? Even that claim is less than straightforward. Arguably, in certain cases one is permitted to defend oneself even against an objectively justified attack. Conceivably, then, in some such cases others might be permitted to come to one's defense as well. So even if the fish's right not to be harmed has been outweighed by the wolf's need, it might still be permissible for us to impose at least some limited harm on the wolf as a way of defending the fish. Given the current state of moral theory, I think we just don't know the answer.[8]

10.5 More on Proportionality

It may be of interest to say a bit more about the proportionality condition.

Our working assumption has been that the limit to defensive harm is set by the formula $H = dh$. That is, we are permitted to impose up to d times the amount of harm that would otherwise be imposed by the attacker, for some suitably large value of d.

Of course, I have suggested that the precise value of d may vary with status, going down when the individual defending herself (or being defended) has a lower status, or when the attacker has a *higher* status. But for the moment, let us put this point aside. Initially, at least, let's restrict ourselves to cases where both parties are people, that is, cases where one person is attacking another.

Even so, as I have also suggested, it may be that the value of d also depends on whether the attacker is a deliberate aggressor or an innocent threat. Even those who think it is permissible to harm an innocent threat typically think that the *amount* of harm one is permitted to impose is less than when one is defending against a deliberate aggressor.

To be sure, some of those who believe in the permissibility of harming innocent threats might insist that the value of d does not vary in this way. Perhaps the value of d remains the same even when the threat is an innocent one. But most, I think, would prefer to claim instead that although it is *permissible* to harm an innocent threat, the proportionality condition is more restrictive in such cases. That is to say, the value of d is reduced.

How *much* is it reduced? On some views the reduction is minimal, so that d takes on a value close to its original one. On other views the reduction is more severe, so that the value of d is reduced considerably. Instead of being permitted to impose 2 or 3 or even 10 times as much harm, one can only impose *slightly* more harm than the attacker would otherwise impose. Conceivably, in fact, some might place the value of d at something close to 1. (On such a view,

---

[8] Of course, as I pointed out in note 5, there are those who think that given the innocence of both the wolf and the fish it is impermissible for us to take sides and intervene at all. My own view is that the fact that the wolf is attacking the fish, while the fish poses no similar threat to the wolf, suffices to break the symmetry. What's less clear, however, is whether this justification for taking the fish's side remains in place if the fish's right has been legitimately outweighed.

one can impose only slightly more harm on an innocent threat than he would otherwise impose on his victim.)

Thinking of the debate in these terms assumes that there is indeed a single appropriate value for d when dealing with innocent threats. But as I have pointed out, one might prefer instead a more fine-grained account of innocent threats, according to which different *types* of innocent threats are assigned different values for d. On this alternative view it might be that for certain types of innocent threats d has a value close to (or even equal to) the one it has for deliberate aggressors, while for other types of innocent threats the value is lower, perhaps considerably lower. Perhaps for some innocent threats the value of d approaches 1.

Imagine an even more extreme view of this kind, one which allows d in certain cases to *reach* 1. That would mean that one can impose as *much* harm on the threat as the threat would otherwise impose, but no more than that. Of course, even here, this would still differ significantly from the situation where one is harming a mere *bystander*. After all, I cannot normally harm a bystander even if it's true that I am imposing no more harm on them than what I myself (or those I am defending) would otherwise undergo. On the contrary, when I *am* permitted to harm an innocent bystander this is only because imposing this harm is necessary to prevent a much *larger* harm to myself or to others.

But this, in effect, is very close to saying that when the person being harmed is a mere bystander—not merely an innocent threat, but rather not a threat at all—the value of d is *less* than 1. Instead of being permitted to impose *more* harm on the other person than would otherwise befall you (as you are permitted to do with deliberate threats and innocent threats), you are only permitted to impose *less* harm on the other person than what would otherwise befall you. That is, you must be preventing far *more* harm to yourself (or to others) than you are imposing on the bystander.

Viewed in these terms, we can think of the threshold for the right not to be harmed as simply being a special case of a much more general proportionality principle, one which sets appropriate limits across the board on how much harm one can impose on others. In some cases the one to be harmed will be a deliberate aggressor, in other cases one sort or another of innocent threat, while in still other cases the one to be harmed will be a mere bystander. But the same general rule will be in effect. It is just that as we move from the first type of case through the middle cases to the last type of case the value of d goes steadily down, eventually becoming less than 1.

On this proposal, then, thresholds are simply a special case of what proportionality requires if one is to permissibly harm another—one where the value of d is now sufficiently small (close enough to zero) so that the harm being prevented to yourself (or to others) must be much *greater* than the harm being imposed on others. When it is a matter of harming an innocent bystander, we might say, the value of the threshold T is so very large precisely because the value of d is itself so very small.

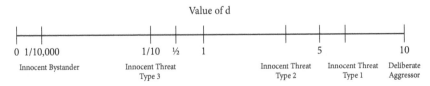

Value of d

| 0 1/10,000 | 1/10 ½ 1 | 5 | 10 |
| Innocent Bystander | Innocent Threat
Type 3 | Innocent Threat
Type 2 | Innocent Threat   Deliberate
Type 1   Aggressor |

Figure 7. Variable Values for Proportionality Multiplier d

The basic idea is displayed in Figure 7. (Note that the axis is not drawn to scale.) When it is a matter of harming a deliberate aggressor, or certain types of innocent threats, you are permitted to impose more harm on the other than would befall you (or those you are aiding). But when it is a matter of harming an innocent bystander—or, conceivably, certain other types of innocent threats— you are only permitted to impose *less* harm on the other than would otherwise befall you (or those you are aiding). The relevant ratios vary, and indeed invert, but perhaps these can all be viewed as instances of a more general moral phenomenon, one that is governed by a single underlying principle.[9]

If something like this is correct, then it is not at all surprising that we found it plausible to think that both the size of thresholds and the limits on self-defense arising from the proportionality condition are sensitive to differences in moral status. Despite initial appearances, perhaps these are not two distinct parts of our moral theory, governed by two distinct principles, but rather two different aspects of the very same underlying subject matter. So given status sensitivity in the one case, it won't be surprising to find it in the other one as well.

What's more, thinking of these issues along these lines suggests a form of status sensitivity that we have not yet explicitly embraced. Recall the sugges- tion that the limits set by proportionality on defensive harm may be sensitive not only to the status of the victim but also to the status of the attacker. Both have an effect on the value of d, although they pull in opposite directions (with d going *up* as the status of the victim increases, and going *down* as the

[9] The same general proportionality principle might also cover cases involving innocent *shields* of threats. (Imagine the attacker is deliberately using someone else as a human shield.) Although not everyone agrees, most feel it permissible to harm such shields when this is necessary to stop an unjustified attack. Here too, though, it seems as though a suitable proportionality principle will set appropriate *limits* on how much harm can be imposed on such shields.

status of the *attacker* increases). Shouldn't we then expect that a similar *double* form of sensitivity to status will hold when it comes to thresholds for rights as well?

We have, of course, long since embraced the thought that thresholds will be lower (other things being equal) when the right holder has a lower status. But what about the remaining form of sensitivity? What about the possibility that the level of the threshold also depends in part on the status of those being *benefited* by the doing of harm? Might the very level of the threshold be lower if the ones being benefited have a higher status?

We have already considered a possibility in the same neighborhood. I suggested previously (in 9.3) that it might be easier to meet a given threshold, even when the same amounts of welfare are at stake, if the well-being is going to individuals with higher rather than lower status. (This seemed particularly plausible given the thought that welfare has greater value when it accrues to those with higher status.) But that was a view about how to *meet* a given threshold, not a claim about how the *level* of that threshold was fixed.

So should we perhaps take the further step and conclude as well that the very level of a given threshold depends in part on the status of those who are being benefited by imposing the harm? (Or should we perhaps say, instead, that this is merely a different way of describing the very idea we have *already* endorsed?) That's an intriguing question, but one that I won't try to answer here.

Instead, I want to note one final point. In discussing the proportionality condition I have made use of a simple account according to which the limit on permissible defensive harm is set by the formula $H = dh$. As we have now seen, of course, it is plausible to think that there are several features that may affect the *value* of d. But we have not yet questioned the assumption that the limit is indeed set, straightforwardly, by simply multiplying the harm that the attacker would impose on his victim by the appropriate value for d.

In fact, however, it is likely that the relevant formula is rather more complicated than this. For as I have just been suggesting, thresholds and proportional harm may be two sides of the very same coin. And we have already seen reason to believe that the threshold function is more complicated than this simple approach to proportionality would entail.

In effect, if the threshold function really were just a special case of a more general proportionality principle, and if the relevant limit for defensive harm were set by the formula $H = dh$, then we should similarly expect that the threshold for the right not to be harmed would be set by an analogous formula: $T = mh$. (If thresholds are just a special case of proportionality, where proportionality is set by multiplying the harm to be imposed on the other by a suitable multiplier, then the level of the threshold should *also* be set by multiplying the harm to be imposed—in this case, on the right holder—by a suitable multiplier.[10])

But as we saw when discussing the threshold function (in 9.2), many deontologists think the relevant formula is more complicated than this. Instead of holding that $T = mh$, many would prefer something similar to $T = mh^n$ or $T = mh^n + b$, or perhaps even $T = m[h/(c - h)]^n + b$.

If one of these more complicated formulas is correct when it comes to setting the level of the threshold, then there is reason to believe that a comparably more complicated formula is correct as well when it comes to setting the limits of proportional defensive harm. And just as it seemed plausible to suggest that each of the relevant coefficients—m, n, b, and c—may vary with status, it seems reasonable to expect that the complete formula for proportional harm may similarly involve sensitivity to status at any number of distinct points.

I won't attempt to work out any of this here. But incomplete as it is, the current discussion should at least suffice to reinforce a point to which I have repeatedly returned: extending our normative theory so that it covers animals in a plausible and defensible manner will require complicating those theories in countless ways—ways that we have only just begun to explore.[11]

---

[10] More particularly, the multiplier m would have to equal 1/d. Here's why. If $H = dh$, this means that I am permitted to impose a harm on another provided that this harm is less than or equal to the harm to myself that I am trying to prevent, when that latter harm is multiplied by d. Equivalently, I may impose the harm provided that the harm to myself, multiplied by d, is *greater* than or equal to the harm being imposed on the other. Dividing both sides by d, this means I may impose the harm on the other provided that the harm I am preventing to myself is greater than or equal to the harm being imposed on the other *divided* by d, or, equivalently, multiplied by 1/d. But this is the same as saying that the threshold for infringing a right is equal to the harm I am imposing multiplied by 1/d. Thus the formula for the threshold would be $T = mh$, where h was the harm being imposed on the *other*, and m was set at 1/d.

[11] I can't resist mentioning one more example. Throughout this chapter I have assumed that the necessity condition on justified defense has been met. I've done this by assuming that it is simply impossible to successfully defend oneself (or others) without harming the attacker by the given amount. But it is obvious that a more adequate statement of this condition would actually need to take probabilities into account: just how *likely* is it that a given amount of harm will suffice (or fail) to disarm the attacker? I won't try to state a suitable version of this condition here, but I do want to note the intriguing possibility that the *degree* of necessity required may *also* vary with status—so that the lower the status of the attacker, or the higher the status of the victim, the *less restrictive* the necessity condition becomes.

11

Limited Hierarchy

11.1 A Suitable Step Function

A hierarchical approach to normative ethics emerges rather naturally from two plausible thoughts. First, the various features that underlie moral standing come in degrees, so that some individuals have these features to a greater extent than others do (or in more developed or more sophisticated forms). Second, absent some special explanation for why things should be otherwise, we would expect that those who do have those features to a greater extent would, accordingly, count *more* from the moral point of view. When we put these two thoughts together they constitute what is to my mind a rather compelling (if abstract) argument for hierarchy.

Some of the implications of this line of thought seem to me completely congenial. On the one hand, many animals clearly do have some of the features that ground moral standing, so these animals *count*, morally speaking. Indeed, it is plausible to think that they count for far more than we ordinarily recognize. (Certainly they count for far, far more than one would think, given the appalling ways we normally treat them.) But at the same time, I think it is also clear that animals have *fewer* of the relevant features than people have (or they have them to a lesser degree), so that animals count for *less* than people. All of which is just to say: there are different degrees of moral status, and people have a higher status than that had by animals. What's more, and this is a third plausible implication of this basic line of thought, since animals themselves vary, one to the next, in terms of their possession of the relevant features, some animals have a higher moral status than others.

Now it sometimes happens in philosophy that an abstract argument that seems otherwise persuasive has implications that are hard to accept. One then faces the difficult question of whether to accept the argument and its troubling implications or instead somehow resist the argument (and thus avoid the implications), by abandoning some initially plausible premise. Happily, we don't face this dilemma with regard to the abstract argument for hierarchy that I just rehearsed. For as I have been at pains to argue, these implications are plausible in their own right. Indeed, the hierarchical approach allows us to avoid various unattractive or absurd conclusions with which we might otherwise be saddled. Overall, then, the hierarchical approach is rendered even more plausible by virtue of its implications.

But that's not to say that there are no cases at all where hierarchy leads to results that may be surprising or even intuitively difficult to accept. On the contrary, I suspect that *no* position that we could adopt on the issues surrounding animal ethics will be a completely comfortable one for us to embrace. Accordingly, our aim should be to think through the comparative strengths and weaknesses of the various alternative views and tentatively accept the view that seems to offer the most attractive position overall—all the while recognizing that even the view that does best in terms of this comparative assessment will have at least some implications that may trouble us.

In an earlier chapter I identified three such implications of hierarchy, ones that might reasonably give us pause. First, just as ordinary adult human persons have a higher moral status than animals do, anyone who accepts hierarchy must be open to the possibility of superior beings, beings with a status even higher than our own. I know that this is a possibility that some would like to disallow, but speaking personally I think it shouldn't really bother us. The possibility of such beings may be a humbling one; but it's not, I think, unacceptable.

More worrisome, second, is the existence of marginal cases, humans with such severe cognitive impairments that they simply fail to count as persons at all. Given their restricted and diminished psychological capacities, it seems inevitable that their moral status will be lower than our own. I argued, of course, that an appeal to modal personhood can reduce the bite of this implication somewhat (giving marginal humans a higher status than animals that are their psychological peers), but I would not want to deny that most of us would find it difficult—initially, at least—to accept the thought that the severely impaired count for less. Nonetheless, since the alternatives (such as unitarianism) seem to me even less plausible, this does seem to me to be the view that we should, upon reflection, accept as well.

But that still leaves the third troubling implication, the problem of normal variation. It is one thing to accept that those with capacities far beyond ours (superior beings) or far below ours (marginal cases) would have a status different from our own. It is quite another thing to accept the claim that even ordinary adult human persons differ, one to the next, in terms of their moral status, with some of us having (slightly) lower status than others.

Even this last implication will not seem unacceptable to everyone. Viewed against the tremendous range of relevant capacities that we find among creatures with moral standing (think of the minimal agency and—perhaps—sentience of a fly, as compared to the incomparably rich cognitive and emotional lives of persons), the differences found among ordinary adult humans will be relatively trivial. For all practical purposes, then, these differences may be ones that are sufficiently limited that we are quite justified in simply disregarding them. On such a view, there may indeed be minor differences in moral status from one person to the next, but these differences will justifiably play no role in our moral deliberations.

As I say, some may find this last response sufficiently plausible and reassuring to put the concern to rest. Indeed, for the most part, that's true in my own case as well. But I know that many others will remain uncomfortable (to say the least) at the thought that there may be genuine, even if small, differences in our moral statuses. These people will understandably wonder whether there is a more robust answer to the problem of normal variation.

A response capable of giving all of us (that is, all normal adult humans) the very *same* moral status would need to somehow overcome the presumption stated above that variations in the features underlying moral standing should result in corresponding variations in moral status. The claim would have to be, rather, that certain minor variations in psychological capacities (the kinds of differences we see displayed among ordinary persons) actually make no difference to status at all. Instead of status increasing steadily with increases in the relevant capacities, status would have to grow less smoothly than this, remaining flat or constant over the range of variation we find among normal humans.

Of course, if there were only *one* moral status—if unitarianism were true—we would have this result automatically. For if there is only one status, not only does the normal variation in the relevant capacities that we find among ordinary persons make no difference to status, *no* variations in those capacities make any difference at all. Under unitarianism, after all, as long as one has moral standing of any sort, one's status is exactly the same as everyone else's, no matter how much it might be the case that other individuals have the relevant capacities to a greater or to a lesser extent. In effect, under unitarianism status would remain flat or constant across the board—for *all* beings with moral standing whatsoever—not just for ordinary adult persons.

But we have already seen ample reason to reject unitarianism. So a plausible view here is going to have to be a more complicated one than that. Another alternative, I suppose, would be a view according to which moral status can indeed vary and does indeed increase with greater capacities (as we move up the animal kingdom)—*until* we reach the range of capacities found among normal adult humans, at which point status stops increasing. (Conceivably, it might start up again once we get *past* the normal range of human capacities, so that superior beings might still have a status higher than our own.) The problem with a view like this, of course, is that it is difficult to see what could be so special about the particular range of capacities that normal humans happen to display, such that here and here alone small variations in capacity make no difference to status, while at other levels they do.

More plausible, I suspect, would be a view according to which this sort of feature—where certain variations in capacities make no difference to status— is found repeatedly, not just when it comes to normal human capacities. Perhaps status is *regularly* flat or constant over a given range of variation in capacities. But instead of imagining that all levels of capacity elicit the very same status (which is, after all, the unitarian position), we can suppose that there are a number of such ranges, where each such range elicits a different (constant) status.

Suppose we try to graph these different positions, letting the X axis represent increasing levels of the relevant psychological capacities and letting the Y axis represent the level of the corresponding moral status. Then the four views we have just discussed are displayed in Figure 8.

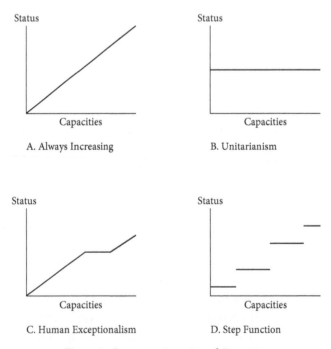

Figure 8. Status as a Function of Capacities

Figure 8A displays what we can think of as the default position, according to which status increases constantly with increases in the relevant capacities. Figure 8B shows the unitarian view, where all levels of the relevant capacities result in the very same single status. Figure 8C represents the human exceptionalism discussed a moment ago, where increased capacities normally result in higher status, but not when it comes to the range of capacities found among ordinary adult humans. Finally, Figure 8D shows the kind of view just imagined, one where the relevant capacities are divided into a number of distinct ranges, and each such range has its own corresponding status, with a higher status for a higher range. Within each range, instead of having status increase as capacities increase, the status is constant, so that the relevant part of the graph is flat, rather than moving up and to the right.

Figure 8D is a step function, and precisely because the entire graph is composed of a series of such steps, rather than having only a single such horizontal section (as in Figure 8C), it seems less ad hoc. Of course, the mere use of a step function doesn't *guarantee* that the problem of normal variation is avoided, because it is compatible with such an approach to have some people be at one step, while others (whose capacities fall in the next lower range) are at a lower one. But in principle, at least, a suitable step function could place all people at the very same step, thus avoiding the troubling claim that some people have a higher status than others.

Adopting a view like this could thus hold out the possibility of solving the problem of normal variation. It would also, obviously, have implications for what we should say about the status of *animals* as well. Instead of holding—as we have previously done—that whenever two animals differ in their capacities they differ in moral status as well, we will instead think of the animal kingdom as being divided into an appropriate number of broad categories, where each such category is assigned a single corresponding status. No doubt dogs will still have a higher status than fish, say, but minor variations in capacities among fish (for example) will not ground even minor differences in the resulting statuses.

For the time being, we can put aside the question of just how many such steps we should expect to find within the animal kingdom, and what the relevant groupings might look like. The crucial point for current purposes is simply that an appeal to a suitable step function would seem to be the most promising way to respond to the problem of normal variation, if one really does insist on a "robust" response (that is, if one isn't satisfied with the reply that the differences in status among people, though real, are too small to make a practical difference).

It may also be worth noting, if only in passing, that the sort of position I have just been describing needn't be seen as incompatible with the second premise of the abstract argument I sketched at the start of this section. As I intended that claim, at any rate, it wasn't an assertion that status *must* go up with increasing capacities. Rather, it was describing what we should expect to happen in the absence of some special mechanism capable of producing a *different* effect. That is, I meant only to suggest that status will increase with capacities *unless* there is some special mechanism or force that prevents this from happening. Those who embrace a step function can agree with this thought. They need only insist that there is such a mechanism, something that "overrides" the fact that there is a range of capacities that holds among normal adult humans (or, for that matter, among fish), blocking the effect—increasing status—that we would otherwise expect.

In principle, I suppose, an advocate of the step function needn't even posit any such mechanism. They could just insist that it is a simple brute fact about morality that status does vary with capacities, but as a *step* function rather than as a constantly increasing one. Perhaps there is nothing at all that we can say about why exactly this is so.

Nonetheless, while the possibility of such brute facts cannot be ruled out, it would of course be much more satisfying (and convincing) if a deeper explanation could be provided. So the question we need to ask is whether it is indeed possible to provide an independently plausible *explanation* of the step function, an account of a mechanism which might make it intelligible why status should often remain the same, even in the face of increasing capacities. Until we have that, it seems to me, the problem of normal variation has not been genuinely dissolved.

11.2 Practical Realism

What might such an account look like? Are there philosophical views to which we could appeal that would plausibly be thought to generate a step function? In what follows I want to lay out one possible proposal. There may be others worth considering as well, but this is the one that strikes me as most promising.

Ultimately, I will want to suggest that this particular proposal is available to a wide range of otherwise quite different views concerning the foundations of normative ethics.[1] But it will be easiest to start with a familiar example of the basic idea at work. We can isolate and then generalize the underlying idea later.

---

[1] For an introduction to some of the most important foundational theories, including the rule consequentialism I am about to discuss, see my *Normative Ethics*, part II.

According to *rule consequentialism*, a given act is permissible if and only if it conforms to the optimal set of moral rules or principles, where a set of rules is held to be optimal if the results of everyone obeying the rules would be better than what the results would be for any other set of rules. That is to say, roughly speaking, we first test rules to see what their results would be, and then, second, we declare the valid rules to be the ones with the best results.

Of course, it might be more accurate to think of rule consequentialism as a *family* of foundational theories, since we are not in a position to evaluate the various results (of the different candidate sets of rules) until we supplement the basic rule consequentialist idea with a theory of the good (a theory of what makes an outcome good). Rule consequentialists differ among themselves as to what the best theory of the good might be. But for our purposes a more important point is this. Rule consequentialists also differ about what exactly we mean when we talk about evaluating the results of "everyone" obeying the rules.

On one approach, that of the *ideal* rule consequentialist, the idea is meant quite literally. We are to ask what the results would be if literally all moral agents were to conform to the relevant rules, perfectly and without mistake. We thus think of the rule consequentialist test (what would the results be if everyone acted on such and such rules?) in a highly idealized fashion. No set of rules is too complicated, no agent ever fails to grasp the content of the rules being tested, no one ever misunderstands the implications of the rules, or fails to apply them accurately. (Similarly, no one ever fails to be sufficiently *motivated* to perform the act required by the rules in question.) We simply ask what the results would be if the acts that conform to the rules were always performed, without regard to whether this is a realistic prospect or not.

But there is a second approach, that of the *realistic* rule consequentialist, where instead of thinking of the test in these idealized terms we do take into account the various cognitive and motivational limitations of moral agents. If a set of rules is too complicated to remember accurately, or if the requisite moral calculations are too complicated to work out, then we recognize that mistakes will be made, and we take these into account in thinking about what the results would be. (Similarly, we take into account the possibility that some rules might be too demanding, so that agents might not be motivated to perform the specified act, or at least might not be prepared to do all that is asked of them.) On this alternative approach, then, when we ask about what the results would be if "everyone" were to act on the proposed rules, what we really have in mind is a more realistic sense of what the results are actually going to be if people accept or adopt the rules and *try* to act on them (for the most part), but then succeed only to a greater or lesser extent.

I will not here enter into the debate about which version of rule consequentialism is more plausible. I simply want to trace the implications of adopting the realistic approach. As I have just suggested, if we do adopt realistic rule consequentialism, then in comparing rules and looking for the optimal set, it is important to keep in mind our epistemic (and motivational) limitations.

This point helps to explain why realistic rule consequentialists often conclude that the optimal set of rules will not be a set that simply tells us to bring about the best consequences, full stop. This kind of consequence-focused rule might well have the best "test results" if only we could assume (as an ideal rule consequentialist *would* assume) that everyone could perfectly identify the act with the best consequences (and would always be motivated to perform it). But given our more realistic approach to testing rules we have to recognize that such a rule might well do less well (in terms of its results) than some alternative that picked out acts in a more readily identifiable manner.

Because of this, realistic rule consequentialists often suggest that the *optimal* set of rules, when evaluated under these more realistic testing conditions, will actually be something more like the rules of commonsense morality, where certain familiar act types (such as lying, or breaking promises, or harming another) are simply forbidden, and other act types (such as keeping your promises, or rescuing others in emergency situations) are required.

Consider the familiar deontological prohibition against harming others. Why might a rule like this emerge from realistic rule consequentialism? An important part of the answer is that harming others typically brings about worse results overall. So as a rough and ready generalization, then, if one avoids doing harm the results will normally be better. Yet presumably there can be cases where harming someone else actually has *better* results. What then? Unsurprisingly, rule consequentialists try to identify the most important types of exceptions, and then build these exceptions into the basic rule, so as to end up with a rule whose results would be better still. That's why, for example, rule consequentialists will typically embrace a version of the rule that makes an exception in cases of *self-defense* (since defending oneself against unwarranted attacks will generally lead to better results overall), and why many rule consequentialists incorporate *thresholds* into the rule as well, so that one can harm an innocent if a sufficiently *large* amount of good will be lost otherwise.

Nonetheless, even with these exceptions built in, there will still be cases where the conformity to the prohibition against doing harm will lead to worse results overall, cases where doing harm (though the victim is a mere innocent bystander, and the threshold hasn't been met) would lead to a better outcome. How then can the rule consequentialist justify prohibiting such acts of harm doing, despite this fact? Wouldn't a rule that permitted doing harm whenever the results would be better be *superior* from the perspective of rule consequentialism?

The answer lies in the adoption of a *realistic* approach to evaluating rules. We need to bear in mind the fact that if the rules of morality permitted doing harm whenever the results would be good, people would all too frequently *misidentify* whether they had actually found themselves in one of the relevant exceptional cases. While there might be an occasional instance of someone correctly identifying that they could do a bit more good by harming someone, the worry is that there would be many more instances of people mistakenly thinking that they were in such a case when in fact they weren't. The claim, then, is that given our actual epistemic limitations, a rule that forbids doing harm will actually have better results than one that permits it. Hence the basic prohibition against doing harm. (At the same time, it is plausible to think that if the amount of good at stake is *large* enough, the risks of misidentifying the situation will be smaller, and more worth taking. That's why many rule consequentialists conclude that the optimal rule here will still incorporate *thresholds* of an appropriate sort.)

There is, of course, more to say about all of this, but for our purposes the crucial point is this: despite the fact that rule consequentialism evaluates candidate rules in terms of their consequences, the *content* of the rules that emerge from this approach need not themselves be *stated* in terms of consequences (or, at least, need not be stated *exclusively* in terms of consequences). On the contrary, the optimal rules may appeal to rather different concepts (besides consequences), and draw distinctions that do not correspond precisely to the underlying facts about consequences. Because of our epistemic limitations, rules that carve up the moral topography in a manner rather different from ones that more directly reflect the underlying facts about consequences may still end up being optimal.

A closely related point is this: given those same epistemic limitations there will be a limit to the *complexity* of the optimal set of rules. If there are too many rules, or if those rules involve too many categories, governed by too many factors, the results of such rules might well turn out to be worse than the results we would attain with a simpler set. To be sure, a consideration like this would be irrelevant for the *ideal* rule consequentialist—since ideal rule consequentialists test candidate rules against the background assumption of perfect conformity. But for the *realistic* rule consequentialist, in contrast, attention must always be paid to the possibility that a more complex set of rules might be too difficult for realistically envisioned agents to apply accurately. Simplification may yield better outcomes. But if so, then here too we open the door to the possibility that the optimal rules, despite ultimately being grounded in a concern for consequences, may correspond only *imperfectly* to the consequences themselves.

Thus, given a realistic approach to rule consequentialism, the contents of the optimal rules may not correspond perfectly to the underlying facts about consequences. Obviously, that's not to say that they won't correspond to facts about consequences at all. After all, the optimal rules could hardly be *optimal* on a rule consequentialist account if they didn't correspond to the underlying facts about consequences to at least a significant degree. But as I have emphasized, the correspondence needn't be perfect; indeed, it is extremely unlikely that it will be. Instead, the optimal rules are likely to diverge in any number of ways, simplifying here, drawing new distinctions there, and smoothing things out in various ways so as to provide a realistically suitable set of moral rules.

Suppose we ask, then, what a realistic rule consequentialism might generate with regard to hierarchy and moral status. For reasons I have just been rehearsing, it is rather unlikely that the optimal set of rules will be ones that allow for moral status to vary continuously, where slight differences in psychological capacities always result in slight differences in moral status. On the contrary, any system like that is likely to be too complicated for us to use reliably, too open to our misidentifying where a given individual belongs. A simpler system is likely to do better from the perspective of realistic rule consequentialism.

Admittedly, the *underlying* facts may well be that psychological capacities can vary in trivial and almost indistinguishable ways. But precisely because of our epistemic limitations, any rule that asks us to identify individual capacities with that kind of precision is unlikely to be optimal. So we shouldn't really expect the optimal moral rules to involve an open-ended or unlimited number of possible levels of moral status, as we move from the bottom of the animal kingdom up to persons. What we should expect, rather, is something more coarse grained, something with a reasonably small number of potential levels, where for the most part it is relatively easy to assign a given individual their appropriate moral status, and where minor differences in psychological capacities normally make no difference in moral status at all.

In short, even though the underlying facts about the relevant capacities allow for an unlimited range of variation, the optimal *rules* won't reflect that fact as straightforwardly as we might initially have thought. On the contrary, a realistic approach to rule consequentialism should lead us to expect that although the optimal rules will indeed involve a hierarchical approach, with several different levels of moral status, these levels will be limited in number, and they will correspond only imperfectly to the underlying facts about the capacities themselves.

All of which is just to say, realistic rule consequentialism may well generate a set of rules that can be thought of in terms of a step function of the kind shown in Figure 8D. Instead of status increasing constantly with increases in the relevant capacities, many differences in capacity will make no difference to status at all, for there will only be a small number of possible levels at which any given individual can be placed. Of course, large enough differences in capacities between individuals (say, those found between a dog and a fish, or between a dog and a person) will still result in differences in moral status. But the hierarchical view that emerges from realistic rule consequentialism will be one that corresponds only imperfectly to the underlying facts about capacities.

If something like this is right, it holds out the promise of a robust solution to the problem of normal variation. If the number of steps is sufficiently small— and we have reason to expect this to be the case, given a realistic appraisal of our epistemic limitations—then it might well turn out that the kinds of variation in psychological capacities that we find as we move from one normal adult human to the next are simply too small to generate differences in status. All ordinary persons will be on the same step, with the very same moral status.

Admittedly, I would not want to claim that realistic rule consequentialism is *guaranteed* to generate a step function, nor, if it does, that it is guaranteed to place all normal adult humans on the very same step. But this does seem to me to be a very reasonable possibility, one that has a significant chance of being realized. So it might well be that the problem of normal variation can be resolved after all. Realistic rule consequentialism seems to show us at least one way that it might be done.

Suppose, then, that I am correct about all of this, and a realistic version of rule consequentialism can generate the kind of hierarchical step function that would constitute a solution to the problem of normal variation. Would that mean that those who prefer alternative accounts of the foundations of normative ethics (such as contractarianism, or the ideal observer theory) are out of luck? Must anyone troubled by the potential implications of normal variation either embrace rule consequentialism or go without a robust solution to the problem?

Not at all. For it seems to me likely that even those who prefer foundational theories other than rule consequentialism can avail themselves of the very same solution. That's because, as far as I can see, the ability of realistic rule consequentialism to generate a suitable step function isn't really due to the consequentialist strand in the theory at all. Rather, it is due to the *realism* in the theory, the fact that candidate rules are tested under realistic assumptions rather than idealized ones. And other foundational theories can be presented in similarly realistic versions as well.

That is to say, other foundational theories can similarly test or evaluate rules in such a way as to keep in mind our various epistemic and motivational limitations. The details will differ of course; they will depend on the specifics of the given foundational theory. But the same basic idea can be applied whatever one's foundational theory: one can always adopt a version of the theory which is sensitive to what we are *actually* like, one which uses realistic assumptions about our cognitive and motivational limitations when evaluating potential moral rules.

I won't undertake the long and detailed discussion that would be required to fully justify this thought, but let me quickly mention a few prominent foundational theories, saying just enough so that one can begin to see why a claim like this might be thought plausible.

Contractarians hold that the valid moral rules are those that would be agreed upon by suitably specified rational bargainers. And in principle, no doubt, those bargainers could take a wide variety of considerations into account in deciding whether to support or reject a given proposed rule. Which considerations will actually figure most prominently in their deliberations will depend, of course, on the details of the given version of contractarianism. But presumably one thing that they might well take into account is how easy or difficult it would be for actual moral agents to understand, apply, and act upon the rules in question. More precisely, a *realistic* version of contractarianism would allow the bargainers to do this. (In contrast, under an idealized version of contractarianism such considerations might be ruled out as disallowed during the bargainers' deliberations.) Here too, then, a set of rules that are too complicated might well be rejected; the bargainers might hold out for a simpler set of rules instead, where mistakes are less likely. Thus, when it comes to hierarchy in ethics a realistic version of contractarianism might produce a set of rules that rejects fine-grained distinctions in status, settling instead for a system that recognizes only a few different levels. In short, realistic contractarianism might generate a step function, instead of having status increase each time psychological capacities increase.

Ideal observer theorists have a different view. Rather than asking what rational bargainers would agree upon, they ask what rules would be favored by a suitably specified ideal observer. If we imagine someone perfectly rational, perfectly benevolent, impartial, fully informed, and so on, what moral rules would they give to us? On this account, the valid rules are those that would be favored by such an ideal observer (or ideal lawgiver). But here too, it is easy to imagine a version of this theory according to which when the ideal observer is comparing the relative merits of different rules, they take into account how likely *we* are—given our actual limitations—to be able to successfully *use* the rules in question. To be sure, the ideal observer may well be perfectly rational and omniscient, but *we* are not, and so on realistic versions of the ideal observer theory this fact figures prominently in the ideal observer's deliberations concerning which rules would be best for moral agents like us, creatures with significant epistemic (and motivational) limitations.

Or consider foundational theories involving universalizability tests, where the relevant question might be something more like this: what if everyone did that? Here too, of course, the precise form of the question differs in significant ways from one version of the test to the next, but the basic idea is to see whether a proposed rule is even suitable for being something that everyone is expected to accept and act upon. (Thus, for example, we might ask whether it would be rational to favor a given principle being universally valid—valid for everyone in all circumstances.) At first glance it might seem that views like this have no place for a realistic approach, since part of what we normally do in applying the universalizability test is to try to envision a world where everyone succeeds in acting on the given rule. But in fact, I think, there can be realistic versions of universalizability tests as well. For in deciding whether there can be such a world (a world where everyone acts on the rule) it might be relevant to consider whether the rule is too difficult for ordinary moral agents to correctly apply or to act upon. That is, in determining whether we can rationally favor a given rule being valid for everyone, we might be told to take into account whether normal moral agents can adequately understand the proposed rule, or whether, instead, they might find it too complicated, or might find themselves confused or mistaken about its implications. If so, then on a realistic version of universalizability, evaluating a given rule's suitability to be a valid rule will involve, in part, attending to our various actual cognitive (and motivational) limitations.[2]

There are, of course, still other foundational views, and even for the ones I have just discussed I have done no more than give some quick reasons to

---

[2] Some might think that Kant's own version of the universalizability test pays no attention to such considerations. But I think this would be a misinterpretation. After all, in determining whether certain maxims can pass the universal law formulation of the categorical imperative, Kant explicitly takes into account empirical facts about how people would react to having agents act on the proposed maxim. I see no reason for Kant or Kantians to rule out the thought that whether one can rationally will a given maxim to be a universal law similarly depends in part on empirical facts about how difficult it would be for people to determine what they are to do when they try to act on that maxim.

believe that there can be versions of the views in question that adopt a realistic approach to evaluating moral rules. But I hope I have said enough to render plausible the thought that there are or can be realistic versions of these different theories, and what's more, that the same is true for most (or perhaps even all) other foundational theories as well.

What all of these views have in common—at least, in the versions I have quickly gestured towards—is a realistic approach to evaluating moral rules. They differ, of course, as to the specifics of what it is that makes a moral rule valid (whether agreement by the bargainers, having been enjoined by an ideal observer, being universalizable, or—in our original example—having the best results). But they agree that when evaluating rules it is important to be realistic about what moral agents like us are capable of understanding and knowing (as well as what we are capable of being motivated to do). They all thus share a commitment to being realistic, in one sense of the term, in the practical domain. They share a commitment to something we might call *practical realism*.[3] And what I am suggesting is that if one accepts practical realism, then pretty much regardless of what particular foundational theory it is that one accepts, one is likely to end up with a normative theory that includes only a few different levels of moral status, since more complicated approaches to status will be poor choices for moral agents with the kinds of limitations that we actually have.

The bottom line, then, seems to be this. There is in fact a potential solution to the problem of normal variation, and it is one which may be available regardless of whatever else you accept about the foundations of normative ethics. Provided that you accept practical realism—the thought that moral rules are to be evaluated with an eye toward our actual epistemic and motivational limitations—then it may be that the hierarchical view that emerges will involve a step function, rather than having status change with each change in capacities. Arguably, then, despite the differences in psychological capacities that we really do find among people, all of us may nonetheless have the very same moral status.

11.3 The View that Emerges

I have suggested that theories that incorporate practical realism may end up with a coarse-grained approach to hierarchy, one where instead of having a

---

[3] It should be noted that practical realism in this sense has no particular connection, one way or the other, to certain metaethical or metanormative debates that get also discussed under the rubric of "realism." Those latter debates turn on whether there really are moral or practical facts that are (in the relevant way) independent of our attitudes. But practical realism in my sense of the term is simply a claim that when evaluating moral rules we should attend to what moral agents are actually like.

continuum of possible levels for moral status there will only be a fixed number of such levels (so that even individuals who differ in terms of their psychological capacities may have the same status). Is there more that we can say about this? More that we can predict about the hierarchical theory that will emerge?

I do want to offer a few conjectures, but it is worth emphasizing the point that they are indeed only conjectures. Precisely because practical realism attends to empirical facts about the kinds of rules that we are well suited or ill suited to try to act upon, it is to a significant extent an empirical question what rules will emerge as optimal from any given foundational theory. So any conjectures I offer here remain just that—mere conjectures—until the relevant empirical work is done.

Similarly, it is important to bear in mind that the precise rules that emerge will also depend on the particular foundational theory that one embraces (whether rule consequentialism, contractarianism, universalizability, or what have you). Since it is not my intent to develop any of those theories here, at best all I can point to are a few broad features that, I suspect, will be common to those accounts.

Nonetheless, it does seem possible to make a few predictions. The most important of these is of course the very claim I have already made, that theories that embrace practical realism will generate only a few different levels of status. I'm not prepared to offer an exact number, but it seems likely that there won't be more than a half dozen or so. (Perhaps, if we ever do encounter superior beings, we may need to add a few more.) My thought here is that much more than this would already involve us in a larger number of levels than we can readily call to mind.

It isn't so much that we cannot readily think to ourselves that there are ten or twenty—or even more—levels of status. It is, after all, easy enough to think that some creatures have a status represented by the value 1, others by 0.9, others still by 0.8, and so on, down to 0.1. (Or, for that matter, 1, 0.99, 0.98, 0.97, and so on.) The worry, rather, is that the more categories there are, the more difficult it becomes to identify who goes where, and this difficulty radically increases the chances of making a mistake.

Perhaps, then, we will have only a handful of categories: one for persons, and another few dividing up the animal kingdom into large groups with roughly similar capacities. Perhaps those covering animals will simply include one level for extremely intelligent animals (that is, animals with fairly developed psychological capacities), one for moderately intelligent animals, and one final level for minimally intelligent animals. Or perhaps the divisions will be a bit narrower than that, with one or two more levels than this.

I hesitate to actually attempt to demarcate the relevant divisions, since I know too little about the actual capacities of different animals, but if only for the sake of illustrating the *kind* of approach I have in mind, let me just suggest that there might be one level for the most intelligent animals, those closest to being full-blown persons (like dolphins, whales, squid, or great apes), another for highly intelligent animals (like dogs, pigs, parrots), another for "midlevel" animals (rabbits, cows, squirrels), still another for "lower" animals (other birds, fish, reptiles), and one last level for the very lowest animals, with the least developed psychological capacities (such as insects and spiders). Again, the point here is not to claim that these *are* the relevant divisions, but only to suggest that the actual divisions will be comparably broad and inclusive, with relatively clear indicators of which types of animals fall into which groups.

The idea here would be to have not only a relatively small number of groupings, but also a relatively easy way to assign a given animal to its relevant group. After all, it would hardly be feasible to expect us to undertake a detailed investigation of a given animal's specific psychological capacities each time we were going to interact with one. This makes it almost inevitable that in normal circumstances we will assign a given animal on the basis of its species (or, more likely still, on the basis of even larger, more general biological categories).

An approach like this would be similar to what we saw when the rule consequentialist favored a rule prohibiting doing harm. Although harming an innocent isn't *always* the act with the worst consequences, there is nonetheless a broad correlation in place, so that normally we do better to simply avoid such acts rather than trying to directly calculate the possible consequences of our actions. Because of this, despite its imperfections, a coarse-grained rule like "don't harm the innocent" still earns its place as part of the optimal set of moral rules. Similarly, then, even though assigning status on the basis of species (or family, order, or even class) will not always correctly identify a given animal's overall level of psychological capacities, there should nonetheless be broad correlations, so that ordinarily we will do better to assign on the basis of broad biological groupings, rather than trying to directly determine the given animal's capacities. (Indeed, given the near universal ignorance and underestimation of the cognitive and emotional capacities of animals, left to our own devices most of us would routinely place animals at far too low a level if we had to estimate capacities directly.)

Does this mean that the view that emerges will have abandoned the individualistic approach to status that I endorsed earlier? To some extent, perhaps, but not completely. For despite our rather limited ability to size up the psychological capacities of individual animals, it would be silly to suggest that we are altogether incapable of doing this, under any circumstances whatsoever. Recall the fanciful example (from 5.2) of the golden retriever who has been given a supervitamin and has now miraculously been turned into a person (while still remaining, nonetheless, a dog). We might well be able to recognize that this particular dog has psychological capacities far exceeding that of ordinary dogs—that this dog, unlike ordinary dogs, is a person. (Imagine, for example, that the dog begins to discuss with us its plans for next summer, or that we translate the poetry it has been writing!) In such extraordinary cases it will presumably be appropriate to give the dog the very same status as we ourselves have, despite the fact that it remains canine. Similarly (if a bit less extreme), if a snake, say, were to display psychological capacities at the level of, for example, a cat, then once we recognized that fact it would be appropriate to give it a correspondingly higher status.

Cases like this would be somewhat similar to the rule consequentialist's recognition that despite the suitability of a general prohibition against harming the innocent, the right not to be harmed should have a threshold. For even though we are not normally very good at identifying cases where *slightly* more good would be done by doing harm, when the amount of good at stake is *great* enough our judgment to the effect that we are now in an exceptional case becomes much more reliable. Accordingly, a rule that permits doing harm in such extraordinary cases is actually optimal. Similarly, then, while the optimal rule for assigning status (given practical realism) is likely to tell us that in *ordinary* circumstances we are to do this on the basis of biological classification, it is also likely to recognize *exceptions*, unusual cases where we should assign a given individual a higher status—or, for that matter, a lower status—than that to be given to its biological peers.

An especially important example where we would probably be justified in departing from the ordinary practice of assigning status on the basis of biological classification might be that of marginal cases, humans who are so severely impaired as to fall short of being a person. Just as it should be possible to recognize animals who tremendously *exceed* the psychological capacities typical of their kind, and just as optimal rules for assigning status should allow for more individualized assignments in such cases, it also seems clearly possible to recognize humans who fall tremendously *short* of the psychological capacities typical of normal adult humans and who should thus be assigned a lower status than the rest of us have. And tragically, as we also know, such cases—unlike our imaginary example of the golden retriever who is a person—are all too real.

Where then should we expect marginal cases to be placed? What status will they be given? To say that they will have a lower status on the step function is not yet to say on what step they will be placed. In this connection it is worth recalling one last time the role that modal personhood may play in raising one's status. Since we do seem capable of recognizing cases that involve a significant degree of modal personhood, there is no reason to assume that practical realism will direct us to simply disregard this feature altogether. Furthermore, although it hasn't played an important role in our discussion to date, it is also worth bearing in mind the fact if we adopt practical realism then it is important to attend not only to our epistemic limitations but also to our *motivational* ones. So if it should turn out—as might well be the case—that we are simply incapable of being motivated to conform to a set of rules that would direct us to treat impaired humans as no better than their psychological peers, then we should anticipate that the severely impaired will have a higher status than we might otherwise have expected (based on their actual capacities alone).

Suppose, then, that on the optimal classificatory scheme that emerges from practical realism there is a group for animals that fall just short of being persons, or that are persons but only in a more limited way than normal adult humans. It is conceivable that marginal cases may belong here as well (despite having less developed capacities than the various animals that are assigned to this level). Alternatively, it might turn out that practical realism will direct us to distinguish between more and less severe *instances* of marginal cases. (Perhaps those who fail to be persons but who nonetheless manifest a reasonable degree of agency will be assigned a higher status than those who are so impaired that they display little or no agency at all.) Indeed, given the likelihood that we are not particularly effective at identifying impaired humans who fall *just* short of being persons, it could easily turn out that the optimal rules will tell us to place even the significantly impaired at the same level as ordinary persons. Perhaps only the most extreme and unmistakable cases of severe cognitive impairment will be assigned a lower moral status at all.

I am not prepared to choose among these various alternatives; too much turns on empirical matters I don't feel at all confident about. (I am particularly uncertain as to what motivational limitations there might be concerning how we are able to treat impaired humans.) But the point remains that practical realism could play a significant role in determining the moral status of the severely impaired, and this might well result in assigning them a higher status than we might otherwise think warranted.

In broad outline, then, the kind of view that I think most likely to emerge if one accepts practical realism looks like this: there will be only a small number of levels of status, and in ordinary circumstances individuals will have their status assigned on the basis of species or other, broader, biological classifications, though in exceptional cases—where the individual clearly has significantly higher or lower capacities than is normal for creatures of their kind—appropriate adjustments (up or down) to status are to be made. Clearly, any number of details remain to be worked out, but it does seem to me that this kind of *limited hierarchy* (as we might call it), is the most likely implication of practical realism.

For reasons that I have suggested, I think it unlikely that there will be all that many different levels of status in such a system, probably no more than four, five, or six, or so. But in principle, of course, the number could be higher than that, if we, as moral agents, have rather higher epistemic abilities than I am currently inclined to give us credit for. Still, even if the number of levels were twice or three times what I am imagining (and I very much doubt it could be much higher than that), it is extremely unlikely that more than one of these levels applies to normal adult humans. So however the details get worked out, it does seem reasonable to expect that an appeal to practical realism will solve the problem of normal variation. In effect, a suitable form of limited hierarchy will have only one level "to spare" to cover the full range of ordinary human capacities.

It might be claimed, however, that I have actually been too *liberal* in describing the number of levels that will emerge from practical realism. I have suggested there may be as many as six or so, but conceivably, of course, the number might be even smaller than that. Since it is, after all, an empirical matter (at least in part) how many levels are optimal, anyone who embraces practical realism must be open to the possibility that given our actual epistemic limitations it is a mistake to generate a system with *any* distinctions in moral status at all. That is to say, it might be that the optimal set of rules, given practical realism, would involve only one single status, with the very same status being assigned to all creatures with any moral standing at all. This is, of course, the unitarian position. So in principle, at least, we can see how one possible argument for unitarianism might emerge out of an appeal to practical realism.

Less extreme, though still more limited than what I have suggested, would be a view according to which the optimal set of rules would recognize only *two* different levels of moral status, one for persons and another for animals. On such a view, all animals would have the very same moral status, though people would nonetheless have a higher one. Conceivably, a version of restricted deontology might be defended along lines like this, although it would also be possible to defend, instead, a view where animals were granted deontological standing but of a weaker sort than the deontological standing granted to persons.

As I say, views of these more extreme types do seem possible, and in principle, at least, someone who appeals to practical realism should be prepared to entertain their possibility. But that's not to say that it seems especially likely that views of these more extreme sorts will emerge. On the contrary, it seems to me that these views go too far in their pessimism about our epistemic abilities. At least, that's the case if they are defended (as I have just been considering the possibility of doing) by means of an appeal to practical realism.

To be sure, anyone who embraces practical realism must take full cognizance of our epistemic limitations. And I have of course been emphasizing the thought that if we do this we are led to a more limited form of hierarchy, one with at most a small number of levels of moral status. But practical realism requires not only that we be realistic about our limits, it also requires that we be realistic about our *abilities*. So should the suggestion be made that we are altogether incapable of successfully drawing any distinctions at all (not even one between persons and animals) or at most *one* such distinction (precisely that between persons and animals), then it seems to me that any such assessment of our epistemic abilities is unduly crimped. It would run afoul of practical realism to have too many levels of moral status. But it would also run afoul of that very same idea to have too few.

Of course, it must be conceded that if even a limited form of hierarchy is to be adequately defended one must eventually show just how and why one's favored foundational theory supports a hierarchical approach to status in the first place. Although I have been suggesting that practical realism—if one accepts it—puts pressure on hierarchical views to guarantee that there are neither too many nor too few levels, I haven't tried to argue at all for the claim that it is in fact a *hierarchical* view (of some sort) that will emerge from the most plausible foundational theories. Or rather, a bit more accurately, I haven't tried to do that directly. For I *have* argued in earlier chapters that only a hierarchical normative theory will yield intuitively acceptable answers on a number of different moral issues. So I presume that any *acceptable* foundational theory will, in fact, not only grant animals moral standing, it will also generate hierarchy of some sort. Still, I haven't tried to explore exactly how and why such hierarchy would emerge from any given foundational view. That is work for another occasion.[4] The only point I am trying to establish here is that *given*

---

[4] Nonetheless, there is at least one approach to the foundations of normative ethics that might find many of the requisite ideas already introduced here. I have in mind those accounts which centrally emphasize the thought that morality must appropriately reflect the *kinds* of beings it is intended to cover. (See *Normative Ethics*, pp. 280–94.) On the one hand, then, hierarchy might be thought to emerge naturally out of the attempt to suitably reflect the significant differences that exist between animals and people (in particular,

that an adequate foundational view will in fact generate hierarchy at the normative level, if we *also* embrace practical realism then the result will be a limited hierarchy of the sort I have been describing.

11.4 Pretense

There is, however, one further point that should be discussed. Suppose I am right and practical realism will lead us to moral rules that recognize only a limited number of levels, so that minor differences in psychological capacities will generally make no difference to one's status. Should we really conclude that this is indeed the *truth* about status—that it takes the form of a step function—or should we hold instead that this is merely a convenient fiction (the use of which is no doubt justified by the practical impossibility of our trying to work with a system of rules more finely attuned to the underlying truths)? If two eagles, say, differ from one another in their psychological capacities, is it really the case that they have the very *same* moral status, or is this merely a rough approximation of the truth, one that is good enough, for all practical purposes, so that we are to be excused for ordinarily thinking in these terms?

It is tempting to think that the only plausible answer here is that a step function approach is indeed nothing more than a convenient fiction. After all, it might be urged, how can it be that even relatively large differences in capacities ordinarily make no difference at all to status (when those differences fall *within* the range represented by a given step), and yet minor differences can sometimes make quite a *large* difference to status (when those differences *cross the boundary* between one step and the next)? Either differences in capacities make a difference to status or they don't. But while limited hierarchy attempts to have it both ways—the argument continues—the underlying moral truth about status cannot possibly work like that. At best it might be that we are justified in *acting* as though it did, if that is the closest that we can ordinarily come to the truth (given our epistemic limitations) in everyday deliberations.

Although tempting, I think this argument is misguided. For there certainly are cases where minor differences of the right sort can make a significant difference even though much larger differences often make none at all. Here's a familiar example, from outside the domain of morality. Suppose that on a particular stretch of highway the speed limit is 65 miles per hour. Then it makes

---

the differences in their psychological capacities); and on the other hand, practical realism—and its resultant limits on that hierarchy—might be thought to emerge naturally out of the attempt to suitably reflect the actual abilities and limitations of ordinary moral agents.

no legal difference whether you are going, say, 50 miles per hour or 64 miles per hour. This fourteen mile per hour difference in speed, though perfectly genuine and far from trivial, simply make no difference at all to whether you are breaking the law. Yet a difference of a mere two miles per hour can make a tremendous difference, if it is the difference between going 64 miles per hour and going 66: if you are going 64 miles per hour you are driving legally; if you are going 66, you are breaking the law.

The crucial point to notice about this case is that it would be an obvious mistake to claim that minor differences in speed must either make a difference (to the legality of your driving) everywhere or nowhere. On the contrary it is perfectly plain that there can be and are sharp boundaries that get drawn, and that they can turn on quite small differences, even though much larger differences elsewhere do not matter at all.

Similarly, it would be an obvious mistake to suggest that this view about the nature of speed limits is merely a convenient fiction—as though the real truth about traffic law must be something more complicated, where perhaps each additional increment in speed is slightly more illegal, and all our talk about a sharp line is nothing more than a mere pretense, justified by its practical convenience. On the contrary, although the underlying facts about speed and safety (which ultimately support the adoption of our various speed limits) may well be complex, the claim that it is legal to drive at 65, but illegal to drive at 66, is no mere fiction. It is the plain, unvarnished truth about the law.

Something similar then might well be the case with regard to morality. Consider, one more time, the example of rule consequentialism and its prohibition against doing harm. Imagine a situation where doing harm would in fact lead to better results overall, but for all that, the amount of good at stake is below the relevant threshold. According to rule consequentialism it is no mere convenient fiction to assert that doing harm in such a case is forbidden. On the contrary, rule consequentialism asserts that one is morally *required* to conform to the optimal rules. That is the plain, unvarnished truth about morality. So even though the underlying facts about the consequences of doing harm may be complex, and even though a rule against doing harm may only capture those facts about consequences imperfectly, if it really is the case that a rule against doing harm is one of the optimal rules (as it may well be, given practical realism), then acts that do harm to innocents without meeting the relevant threshold really are forbidden, full stop, even if the results might be better here if one broke the rule. This is no mere pretense. It is an account of what moral requirement *consists* in.

Suppose, then, that a realistic rule consequentialist account supports a system of rules according to which there are only a limited number of moral statuses, and minor differences in psychological capacities normally make no difference to one's status. According to the rule consequentialist's account of morality, this will be the literal truth about moral status, not a mere approximation of the truth. On such an account, when practical realism drives us toward a limited form of hierarchy this is not a mere convenient *fiction* about status. Rather, the divisions demarcated by that limited hierarchy will themselves constitute the very facts about status under discussion. Practical considerations here help *generate* moral truth, rather than merely leading us to approximate it.

A similar view is of course available to those who prefer alternative accounts of the foundations of normative ethics. According to rule contractarianism, for example, right and wrong is *constituted* by the rules that the bargainers would agree upon. These rules are no mere fiction, at best a better or worse approximation of the underlying truth about what is "really" required of us. Similarly, then, the designations of status that would be agreed upon by the bargainers would constitute the *facts* about status, not mere approximations of them. And if realistic rule contractarianism would generate limited hierarchy, then the claims about hierarchy laid out in that account would be the literal truth, no mere pretense.

I won't belabor this point with regard to other foundational theories. But each of them, I think, is similarly capable (mutatis mutandis) of resisting the suggestion that the views about status that would be generated by a realistic version of the theory are a mere fiction. On the contrary, each theory can be developed in such a way as to hold that limited hierarchy is the literal truth.

On the other hand, that is not to say that one *must* understand the significance of limited hierarchy in this way. It is *also* possible to develop versions of foundational theories that do view practical realism as generating nothing more than convenient methods of approximating a more complicated moral reality. This alternative approach is similar to the view of the *direct* or *act* consequentialist, who thinks of the rules of commonsense morality as helpful guides, nothing more, not constitutive of the facts about right and wrong. On this more "deflationary" stance, practical realism still reminds us to develop rules that take our epistemic (and motivational) limitations into account. And under normal circumstances there will be no better way to deliberate than to do our best to conform to those optimally designed rules. But for all that, even the optimal rules are mere approximations of the moral truth, and if we ordinarily go about thinking in terms of these rules and these rules alone, then although this attitude may be an incredibly useful fiction, it remains the case that those rules are indeed mere conveniences, not themselves perfectly accurate representations of the underlying moral facts. Similarly, then, while it might well be the case that, given our actual limitations, we can do no better than to guide ourselves by some suitable version of limited hierarchy, this may still be no more than an approximation of the underlying truth. It might well be that the *truth* about status is that it really does vary each time capacities change.

Strictly speaking, of course, even on this second account it isn't quite accurate to think of limited hierarchy as a mere *convenience*—as though at any moment we could justifiably decide to stop thinking in these terms and choose instead to undertake the more complicated process of ascertaining each individual's real moral status. For if it really is the case that limited hierarchy is the *optimal* approach to determining status (for moral agents with the particular epistemic limitations that we really do have), then to decide to forego deliberating in these terms is to make it overwhelmingly likely that we will get far more wrong than we get right. Thus, even if limited hierarchy is a fiction—a mere approximation of the underlying truth about status—it may well be a fiction that we cannot possibly improve upon, when we are engaged in actual deliberation (as opposed to abstract moral theorizing).

Which of these two positions is the correct one? Is limited hierarchy constitutive of the truth, or a mere approximation of it? That's not a question I am going to try to settle here (although, as it happens, my sympathies lie with the second, deflationary account). For as I have already intimated, the choice between these two accounts is part of a much larger, ongoing debate within normative ethics concerning the precise significance of the rules we appropriately use in everyday moral deliberation. Still, though the two sides disagree about the exact significance of the rules that emerge from this process, both sides agree that there is an important place for rules that have been crafted with an eye toward our actual abilities and limitations; and for our purposes that may be agreement enough. Either way, the essential point is this: in our everyday interactions with animals we should be guided by a hierarchical approach, but a limited one.[5]

11.5 How to Count Animals

In broad outlines, the view we have arrived at bears a striking resemblance to what may well be the commonsense view. For I imagine that most people

---

[5] What about experts in animal psychology? Could it be that *they* are justified in using a more fine-grained account of status rather than the much more limited one that the rest of us should be using? That's an intriguing possibility, but thinking about it properly would require taking a position on the advantages and risks involved in having different moral agents making use of different moral rules. And that is too complicated a question for us to try to address here.

would concede that animals count morally, and they would certainly also insist that animals count less than people do. Similarly, I take it to be something like the commonsense view that although animals count, they don't all count in the same way: some matter more, morally, than others do. Furthermore, I imagine that most people either accept or come close to accepting something very much like a *limited* hierarchy view, according to which there are at most only a small number of morally relevant divisions within the animal kingdom, with higher animals (for example, dogs, monkeys, and whales) counting for more than other animals (such as chickens, rabbits, and mice) who in turn count for still more than the rest (like fish, perhaps, or maybe insects).

But this very similarity brings us back to a concern I expressed at the outset, that my position will be misconstrued and taken to be a defense of something like current attitudes and practices toward animals. After all, people count more than animals do, right?

I hope it is clear that any such interpretation would be a gross misunderstanding of my actual view. Animals count for less than people do, but they count for far, far more than we ordinarily acknowledge.

The day may come when it will be common to look back on mankind's long history of abuse of animals and recognize it as the disgrace and horror that it is. But that day is not yet upon us. Conceivably, then, given the widespread mistreatment and disregard for animal interests that continues to this very day—indeed, given the innumerable ways in which abuse of animals runs almost unnoticed through countless aspects of human life—it may well be the case that the most *pressing* task for moral philosophy with regard to animals is to establish that they really do count morally, and that they count for a tremendously great deal more than we seem ready to acknowledge (given the horrific ways we actually treat them).

Crucial though it is, that is not the task I have undertaken here. For it seems to me that no such project can be successful unless it is undertaken in full acknowledgment of another essential fact about animals—the fact that although they do count morally, they count for *less* than people do. The moral theory with regard to animals that we need to be defending is indeed a hierarchical one; and until that fact is more widely recognized in the philosophical literature, I suspect that many of our efforts to secure decent and just treatment for animals will be doomed to failure.

Perhaps that is an overly pessimistic assessment. I hope so. But even if so, at the very least it seems obvious to me that our understanding of ethics—not just animal ethics, but all of ethics—will be confused and incomplete until such time as the significance of status is properly taken into account.

I trust it is also clear, however, that all I have done in this book is to scratch the surface in terms of working out such a theory. There are any number of moral principles that I haven't discussed at all, and even for those few areas where I have tried to take a closer look, for the most part all I have really done is to offer some rough, preliminary suggestions about what a suitable account might conceivably look like. The devil will be in the details, and the details are yet to come.

References

Anderson, Elizabeth. "Animal Rights and the Values of Nonhuman Life." In *Animal Rights*, edited by Cass Sunstein and Martha Nussbaum, 277–98. Oxford, 2004.

Arneson, Richard. "What, if Anything, Renders All Humans Morally Equal?" In *Singer and His Critics*, edited by Dale Jamieson, 103–28. Blackwell, 1999.

Balcombe, Jonathan. *What a Fish Knows*. Scientific American/Farrar, Straus & Giroux, 2016.

Barron, Andrew, and Colin Klein. "What Insects Can Tell Us about the Origins of Consciousness." *Proceedings of the National Academy of Sciences* 113 (2016): 4900–8.

Belshaw, Christopher. "Death, Pain, and Animal Life." In *The Ethics of Killing Animals*, edited by Tatjana Visak and Robert Garner, 32–50. Oxford, 2016.

Bramble, Ben. "The Case Against Meat." In *The Moral Complexities of Eating Meat*, edited by Ben Bramble and Bob Fischer, 135–50. Oxford, 2016.

Brennan, Samantha. "Thresholds for Rights." *The Southern Journal of Philosophy* 33 (1995): 143–68.

Crisp, Roger. "Equality, Priority, and Compassion." *Ethics* 113 (2003): 745–63.

Davis, Nancy. "Abortion and Self-Defense." *Philosophy & Public Affairs* 13 (1984): 175–207.

DeGrazia, David. "The Distinction Between Equality in Moral Status and Deserving Equal Consideration." *Between the Species* 7 (1991): 73–7.

——. "Response." *Between the Species* 7 (1991): 79–80.

——. *Taking Animals Seriously*. Cambridge, 1996.

Feldman, Fred. *Pleasure and the Good Life*. Oxford, 2004.

Frankfurt, Harry. "Equality as a Moral Ideal." In *The Importance of What We Care About*, 134–58. Cambridge, 1988. Originally published in *Ethics* 98 (1987): 21–43.

——. "The Moral Irrelevance of Equality." *Public Affairs Quarterly* 14 (2000): 87–103.

Frey, R. G. "Moral Standing, the Value of Lives, and Speciesism." In *The Ethical Life*, 4th ed., edited by Russ Shafer-Landau, 283–99. Oxford, 2018. Originally published in *Between the Species* 4 (1988): 191–201.

——. "Response: Autonomy, Animals, and Conceptions of the Good." *Between the Species* 12 (1996): 8–14.

Gruen, Lori. *Ethics and Animals*. Cambridge, 2011.

Harman, Elizabeth. "Creation Ethics: The Moral Status of Early Fetuses and the Ethics of Abortion." *Philosophy & Public Affairs* 28 (1999): 310–24.

——. "The Potentiality Problem." *Philosophical Studies* 114 (2003): 173–98.

Kagan, Shelly. "Equality and Desert." In *What Do We Deserve?* edited by Louis P. Pojman and Owen McLeod, 298–314. Oxford, 1999.

——. *The Geometry of Desert*. Oxford, 2012.

——. *Normative Ethics*. Westview, 1998.

——. "Rethinking Intrinsic Value." *The Journal of Ethics* 2 (1998): 277–97.

——. "Singer on Killing Animals." In *The Ethics of Killing Animals*, edited by Tatjana Visak and Robert Garner, 136–53. Oxford, 2016.

——. "What's Wrong with Speciesism?" *Journal of Applied Philosophy* 33 (2016): 1–21.

Kazez, Jean. *Animalkind*. Wiley-Blackwell, 2010.

Kitcher, Philip. "Experimental Animals." *Philosophy & Public Affairs* 43 (2015): 287–311.

McMahan, Jeff. "Cognitive Disability, Misfortune, and Justice." *Philosophy & Public Affairs* 25 (1996): 3–35.

——. *The Ethics of Killing*. Oxford, 2002.

——. "The Meat Eaters." In *The Stone Reader*, edited by Peter Catapano and Simon Critchley, 538–45. Norton/Liveright, 2015. Originally published online in The Stone, *New York Times*, September 19, 2010, opinionator.blogs.nytimes.com/2010/09/19/the-meat-eaters.

Mill, John Stuart. *Utilitarianism*. Originally published 1863.

Nagel, Thomas. "What is it like to be a Bat?" In *Mortal Questions*, 165–80. Cambridge, 1979. Originally published in *The Philosophical Review* 83 (1974): 435–50.

Nozick, Robert. *Anarchy, State, and Utopia*. Basic Books, 1974.

Nussbaum, Martha. "Beyond 'Compassion and Humanity.'" In *Animal Rights*, edited by Cass Sunstein and Martha Nussbaum, 299–320. Oxford, 2004.

Otsuka, Michael. "Killing the Innocent in Self-Defense." *Philosophy & Public Affairs* 23 (1994): 74–94.

Parfit, Derek. "Equality or Priority?" *Ratio* 10 (1997): 202–21.

——. *Reasons and Persons*. Oxford, 1984.

Persson, Ingmar. "A Basis for (Interspecies) Equality." In *The Great Ape Project*, edited by Paola Cavalieri and Peter Singer, 183–93. St. Martin's Griffin, 1993.

Rawls, John. *A Theory of Justice*. Harvard, 1971.

Regan, Tom. *The Case for Animal Rights*, 2nd ed. University of California, 2004.

Sher, George. *Desert*. Princeton, 1987.

Singer, Peter. *Animal Liberation*, updated ed. HarperCollins, 2009.

——. *Practical Ethics*, 3rd ed. Cambridge, 2011.

Temkin, Larry. *Inequality*. Oxford, 1993.

Thomson, Judith Jarvis. *The Realm of Rights*. Harvard, 1990.

Vallentyne, Peter. "Of Mice and Men: Equality and Animals." *The Journal of Ethics* 9 (2005): 403–33.

Warren, Mary Anne. "Difficulties with the Strong Animal Rights Position." *Between the Species* 2 (1986): 163–73.

Index